P9-CMM-330

PRENTICE HALL
HISTORY OF MUSIC SERIES

H. WILEY HITCHCOCK, editor

MUSIC IN MEDIEVAL EUROPE, *Jeremy Yudkin*
MUSIC IN THE RENAISSANCE, *Howard Mayer Brown*
BAROQUE MUSIC, *Claude V. Palisca*
MUSIC IN THE CLASSIC PERIOD, *Reinhard G. Pauly*
NINETEENTH-CENTURY ROMANTICISM IN MUSIC, *Rey M. Longyear*
TWENTIETH-CENTURY MUSIC: AN INTRODUCTION, *Eric Salzman*
MUSIC IN THE UNITED STATES: A HISTORICAL INTRODUCTION,
  H. Wiley Hitchcock
MUSIC IN LATIN AMERICA, *Gerard Béhague*
FOLK AND TRADITIONAL MUSIC OF THE WESTERN CONTINENTS, *Bruno Nettl*
MUSIC CULTURES OF THE PACIFIC, THE NEAR EAST, AND ASIA, *William P. Malm*

MUSIC
IN MEDIEVAL EUROPE

JEREMY YUDKIN
School of Music
School for the Arts
Boston University

PRENTICE HALL, ENGLEWOOD CLIFFS, NEW JERSEY 07632

Library of Congress Cataloging-in-Publication Data

Yudkin, Jeremy.
  Music in medieval Europe.

  (Prentice Hall history of music series)
  Bibliography: p.
  Includes index.
  1. Music--Europe--500-1400--History and criticism.
I. Title. II. Series.
ML171.Y8 1989   780'.902   88-32495
ISBN 0-13-608225-4
ISBN 0-13-608192-4 (pbk.)

Cover art:
From an early fourteenth-century manuscript of secular German songs,
Heidelberg Universitätsbibliothek, Cod. Pal. Germ. 848, "Manessische
Liederhandschrift," fol. 122r.

ISBN 0-13-608225-4 CASE
ISBN 0-13-608192-4 PAPER

Printed in the United States of America
20 19 18 17 16 15 14 13 12 11 10 9 8 7 6 5 4 3 2 1

PRENTICE-HALL INTERNATIONAL (UK) LIMITED, *London*
PRENTICE-HALL OF AUSTRALIA PTY. LIMITED, *Sydney*
PRENTICE-HALL CANADA INC., *Toronto*
PRENTICE-HALL HISPANOAMERICANA, S.A., *Mexico*
PRENTICE-HALL OF INDIA PRIVATE LIMITED, *New Delhi*
PRENTICE-HALL OF JAPAN, INC., *Tokyo*
SIMON & SCHUSTER ASIA PTE. LTD., *Singapore*
EDITORA PRENTICE-HALL DO BRASIL, LTDA., *Rio de Janeiro*

TO KATHRYN,
sine qua non

FOREWORD

Students and others interested in the history of music have always needed books of moderate length that are nevertheless comprehensive, authoritative, and engagingly written. The Prentice Hall History of Music Series was planned to fill these needs. It seems to have succeeded: revised and enlarged second editions of books in the series have been necessary, and now a new cycle of further revisions exists, as well as a completely new book on music in the Middle Ages.

Six books in the series present a panoramic view of the history of music in Western civilization, divided among the major historical periods—Medieval, Renaissance, Baroque, Classic, Romantic, and Twentieth-Century. The musical culture of the United States, viewed historically as an independent development within the larger Western tradition, is treated in another book; and one other deals with music in Latin America. In yet another pair of books, the rich folk and traditional musics of both hemispheres are considered. Taken together, these ten volumes are a distinctive and, we hope, distinguished contribution to the history of the music of the world's peoples. Each volume, moreover, may of course be read singly as a substantial account of the music of its period or area.

The authors of the books in the Prentice Hall History of Music Series are scholars of international repute—musicologists, critics, and teachers of exceptional stature in their respective fields of specialization. Their goal in contributing to the series has been to present works of solid up-to-date scholarship that are eminently readable, with significant insights into music as a part of the general intellectual and cultural life of man.

H. WILEY HITCHCOCK, *Editor*

PREFACE

This book is written with a single aim: to introduce to a wider audience the rich treasures of music from medieval Europe. Although today a greater variety of music is available both in print and in recorded form than ever before, our educational and performing institutions are still highly conservative in their training and programming. Students and professional musicians are mostly uninformed about the huge quantity of music that lies outside the narrow band of one hundred and fifty years designated as the "common practice" era. As a result, people are deprived of the largest part of their musical heritage. If music students occasionally rise to the challenge of programming a composition from the Middle Ages on their recitals, if educated amateurs occasionally enrich their leisure hours by listening to medieval music, the aim of this book will have been achieved.

It becomes clear in studying a musical era from the distant past that much is missing. Trends are established, consequences are drawn, and all on the basis of what has survived. Sometimes there are reasons for this survival: an important group of works is widely disseminated and discussed at the time of its composition. But sometimes it is a matter of chance: pieces are copied onto the back of a manuscript, or are pasted into the binding of a book, and their accidental discovery changes our entire view of the period.

One writes a history of music constantly aware of the many such pieces that have *not* survived and of how different the overall picture might look if they had. It has been estimated that between eighty and ninety per cent of all manuscripts produced during the medieval period are no longer extant.

A considerable amount of the musical legacy of medieval Europe has been deliberately omitted as being beyond the scope of this book. No detailed examination has been made of the music of the Eastern liturgy, although Byzantine and other Eastern chants certainly deserve serious study in their own right. Also the so-called "folk" music of Northern and Eastern peoples—Russian polyphony in parallel seconds, the winter epics of Romania, Slavic war-songs—some of which may represent a living survival of the Middle Ages, has been left to other experts. One day perhaps we shall be able to produce a fuller picture of music in medieval Europe, taking into account both East and West, North and South, both written and unwritten forms, both "folk" and art music. Perhaps then these distinctions will seem less meaningful than they do today.

This book contains a considerable amount of music—far more than the companion volumes in this series. Music from the Middle Ages is much less easily obtainable than that of other repertoires, and it seemed advisable to include as many representative examples as possible, rather than expecting readers (and teachers) to hunt down elusive editions and rare publications. In fact, much of the music presented here has been re-edited from the standard editions or newly transcribed directly from the manuscripts. Only rarely is a previous edition followed precisely.

The texts follow medieval orthography, irregular and inconsistent as that may be. This includes the omission of accent markings in Old French and the other vernaculars. The one exception is the superscript *e* (umlaut) in Middle High German, which is found in the manuscripts, but modernized here.

All texts, including sacred and secular, prose and verse, Latin and vernacular, have been newly translated. In the translations I have aimed at clarity and transparency, avoiding archaisms. I have also attempted to capture the *tone* of the originals—high-flown in some cases, thought-provoking in others, popular and slangy in still others.

The presentation and layout of the examples, both in their text and in their music, is designed to illustrate as clearly as possible the form and structure of the original compositions. Most pieces are given in their entirety. For a few of the longer ones, there was room only for an extract: in these cases a clear idea is given of the scope and dimensions of the piece, and a reference to a complete modern edition is provided.

Two 90-minute cassettes have been produced especially for this book.* They contain a considerable number of the most important musical

---

*For the contents of the cassettes and ordering information, please see pages 611–12.

examples in vivid, imaginative performances. Also, at the end of each chapter, a Discography is given. Both the cassettes and the discographies are tied directly to the examples printed in the book, so that students may *hear* as well as see the music they are studying. This is important for all music; with a repertory as unfamiliar as the one considered here, it becomes particularly vital. Performances in the discographies have been chosen for their artistry and their understanding of the music. In some cases, several recordings are listed, so that different interpretations of the same piece may be compared. It will of course be understood that at a time of great turmoil in the recording industry the availability (and even the numbering) of certain items cannot be guaranteed. Most libraries, however, carry a considerable number of the recordings listed here; many of the newer ones may be purchased at record stores. For some few pieces no recording could be found. The author hopes that this book will play enough of a role in stimulating informed performances of medieval music that by the time of the second edition these gaps can be filled.

In producing a book such as this, one is constantly aware of how much is owed to others. I mention first my Director of Studies at King's College, Cambridge—Robert Bolgar—whose extraordinary breadth of knowledge and deep, abiding humanity affected several generations of students. His death has left a rent in the fabric of world scholarship. It was William Peter Mahrt of Stanford University who first taught me how to *think* about music of the Middle Ages. His influence is everywhere in this book. Thomas Binkley has brought much of the medieval repertoire to life in the recordings he has made with the Studio der frühen Musik and other groups. Without his genius and imagination we would have a barer, far less informed view of the treasures of medieval music as sounding works of art. His generosity and commitment are illustrated by the two cassette tapes which he produced especially for this book. Both I and my readers are deeply in his debt.

Then there are the countless scholars in the United States and Europe whose work is slowly pushing forward the frontiers of our knowledge about the medieval era and about the role that music played in it. Many are friends and colleagues; nonetheless, for all of them I must content myself with a group acknowledgement. H. Wiley Hitchcock, the author of one of the books in this series, is also series editor. I am most grateful to him for his painstaking, sensitive, and insightful comments on everything from the overall structure of this book to its tiniest details. It was nothing but a pleasure to work with him.

My colleagues in SUMMA—David Hughes, Joseph Dyer, and Edward Nowacki—have provided constant encouragement and support for this and many other projects. Joe Dyer was especially generous with his time, answering the telephone at all hours of the day and night to field unusual questions about the liturgy—and almost everything else. He was also kind enough to read the first several chapters of this book while they were still in draft form and to offer constructive criticism.

David Stillman, an expert in languages, kindly advised me in regard to some of the idiosyncrasies of Gallego-Portuguese and Old French. He even came up with a complete linguistic analysis of the Cantiga de Santa Maria that appears as one of the examples in Chapter Seven.

Much of the extremely laborious task of copying out the musical examples, tracking down rare editions, ordering microfilms, and the like, was carried out by my research assistant, Teresa Neff. She was a patient and reliable collaborator, with many helpful suggestions that directly affected the way the whole project evolved. She has my sincere thanks.

My son, Daniel Alexander, is learning to push the keys of my computer. If there are any extra Ds in the text, it is his fault.

Finally, it is impossible to express here the extent to which I have relied upon my wife, Kathryn, during the preparation of this book. The dedication says what I mean.

CONTENTS

LIST OF MUSICAL EXAMPLES

xvii

THE MASS FOR PENTECOST (Chapter Four)

MATINS FOR THE NATIVITY (Chapter Five)

Many of these musical examples are recorded on two 90-minute cassette tapes that are available from the publisher. Information regarding these cassettes may be found on pp. 611–12.

MUSIC
IN MEDIEVAL EUROPE

ONE

THE MIDDLE AGES

When were the Middle Ages and what were they in the middle of? The term was invented by writers in the Renaissance, an era which prided itself on being a reincarnation or rebirth (*renaissance*) of Classical Antiquity. They thought of the centuries intervening between the end of the Classical period and the beginning of their own as an interim era—an age in the middle, or Middle Ages, in its plural form. The implicit scorn in the term is well captured by fifteenth- and sixteenth-century writers such as the music theorist, teacher, and polymath Heinrich Glarean, who describes those years as a time "when honorable study and fine scholarship were lying asleep."[1]

A similar view of the Middle Ages is still with us today. In the modern mind the word "medieval" is equated with the meanings "outmoded," "bad," or "cruel."[2] But this book aims to show that medieval music is as sophisticated, as demanding, and as deeply rewarding as any artistic achievement in the history of Western culture.

---

[1]*Dodecachordon* I, xvi, 43.
[2]Fred Robinson, "Medieval, The Middle Ages," *Speculum* LIX (1984): 745–756.

The dates for the beginning and end of the Middle Ages vary enormously depending upon the field under investigation and the country or countries involved. The beginning is sometimes given as the date of the conversion to Christianity of the Roman emperor Constantine (312), or the fall of Rome (410), or the end of the Roman Empire (476); and the end has been suggested as occurring in 1300 (the setting of Dante's *Divine Comedy*), 1453 (the fall of Constantinople and the invention of printing), or 1517 (the beginning of the Reformation).

Glarean and the other Renaissance writers were wrong, of course. The "revival" of learning so touted in the fifteenth and sixteenth centuries was in many ways a continuation of medieval scholarship. It was medieval scholarship and the medieval enthusiasm (ambivalent though it was) for Classical culture that made any embracing of Greek and Roman literature, art, and architecture possible in later years.

The Middle Ages, however, were different from the eras that preceded and followed them. That is why, imprecise as it is, we need a term to distinguish this period from others. But the plural form of the name gives some indication of how diverse the period was. It was several ages, not just one. It also lasted longer than any other period in our history. The Renaissance lasted two hundred years; the Romantic era, less than a century. In the shortest formulation of the boundaries given above, the Middle Ages encompassed eight hundred years; in the longest, twelve hundred years.

LIFE IN MEDIEVAL EUROPE

The medieval period was one of extraordinary contrasts. It was a time in which brutality and spectacular violence were rampant. In Cyprus in the thirteenth century, crusaders besieging Nicosia in the name of Christ catapulted the heads of their captured prisoners like stones over the city walls. In England in that same century, a burglar was flayed and his skin nailed to the door of the palace whose treasury he had been caught rifling. In France in the fourteenth century, a highwayman was cut into four pieces, which were then displayed over the gates to the city of Paris. Death was everywhere: in simple diseases, in accidents of nature, in short journeys. It swept wholesale through the land in periodic wars, in natural disasters, or in recurring waves of the relentless plague. Deformity, mental disease, and missing limbs were common. Medicine was not far advanced, and medieval weapons of war maimed at least as often as they killed.

Life was often very short indeed, for the rate of infant mortality was extraordinarily high. Beyond infancy, average life expectancy was in the forties (less for women, who frequently died in childbirth), and people of

Toads and worms feed on the corpse of François de la Sarraz, as depicted on his tomb, Château de la Sarraz, Vaud.

fifty or sixty were considered old. The physicality of death was a constant preoccupation: paintings, stained-glass windows, and even sculptures contain gruesome depictions of decomposing corpses providing meals for worms. Life after death could be endless torment or heavenly peace; a great deal of money and effort was expended to avoid the former and ensure the latter.

And yet, however much one tried to control one's fate, a great deal lay in the hands of chance. Medieval men and women would have used the word "fortune." In medieval Italian *fortuna* meant a storm; in those days people could avoid a storm no more effectively than they could avoid the vicissitudes of medieval life. Fortune is depicted in hundreds of medieval illustrations as a woman manipulating a wheel. Four human figures are displayed as the wheel turns—one ascending, one triumphant at the top, one falling, and one crushed at the bottom. The wheel is constantly in motion. Our modern notion that we may control our destinies was entirely foreign to the Middle Ages.

Within this constant turmoil, life was highly stratified. The majority of people were peasants and worked the land. They were poor and uneducated, and most remained so from generation to generation. Many were hardly more than slaves; some were literally slaves and could be bought and sold. A highly systematized chain of allegiances led from peasant to vassal to local lord to king. Outside the secular hierarchy but intimately connected with it was the equally stratified hierarchy of the Church. Local bishops might be as powerful as secular rulers; often they were more so. Violence was instigated as frequently by the Church as by greedy overlords.

The boundary between rich and poor was by no means always fully accepted. The aristocrats built their castles for protection from each other, but there were threats also from another quarter, for there were peasant revolts in England, France, Spain, and Germany. Despite the gorgeous clothing, pomp, and pageantry of the nobles, life was cold and uncomfortable even for them. Warfare was their work, hunting almost their only pastime. Malnourishment was chronic.

Religion played a constant role in everyday life, from the harvest to the hunt. Priests were called in to bless everything from animals to duels to children. Local superstitions, magic, and elements of old pagan customs mingled with Christian beliefs to add color and vivacity to religious fervor. Christianity actually took many of its practices and much of its calendar from the ancient Romans. Many feasts were not established until well after the fact: Christmas, for example, did not become widely observed until the fourth century.

Many of the monasteries in the countryside were established by local noblemen just so that the monks might pray for them and their families. In the towns the clergy were heavily involved in urban politics. In either case, everyone had a stake in the honesty and piety of the churchmen. Yet there was widespread corruption. Clergy could be uneducated, ambitious, and uncouth: some were married in violation of their vows; many took bribes. The separation between ordinary life and religious life in the Middle Ages was not so marked as it is today.

To us the dividing line is clear. We feel that we may either choose religion or ignore it. In the Middle Ages life was more unified: church and state were often the same; wars, weather, harvest, knighthood, and marriage were directed by God. Dawn was God's promise of a new day and a sign for illicit lovers to part. Poets dreamed of sitting down to fabulous feasts and heady wines with St. John the Baptist in heaven. The names of

A narrow street in the city of Troyes, hardly changed from the thirteenth century. From Joseph and Frances Gies, *Life in a Medieval City* (New York: Harper and Row, 1969).

David and Saul were mixed with those of ghosts and goblins. The summer sun arising marked both Christ's resurrection and the birth of Venus, goddess of love.

In the towns of the later Middle Ages, the streets were narrow and usually unpaved; garbage and waste often mingled with the mud. Different sections of the town housed the various trades, and the smell from the butchers' section, where animals were slaughtered, overpowered even the pervasive odor of horse manure. Houses were often overcrowded, with whole families sharing a room. Even in the houses of wealthy merchants only one of the rooms had a fire; ceilings were low; and there was little light, since the windows were made of parchment. The toilet was outside in the yard. Mattresses were made of straw, and fleas were a constant problem.

Throughout the medieval period, famine was an ever-present and deadly danger. Diet was heavily based upon grain, and small changes in climate or rainfall, along with a high incidence of crop disease, often led to widespread starvation. Between the mid-ninth and mid-tenth centuries there were at least twenty recorded famines; mortality was so high that the entire population of Europe declined severely. Chroniclers reported incidences of cannibalism; during a particularly severe famine of the eleventh century a wide variety of grades and cuts of human flesh was available at one market in Burgundy.

Diseases now rare, such as scarlet fever, tuberculosis, and measles, claimed countless lives, and pestilence periodically ravaged the population. The bubonic plague, known as the Black Death, spread like wildfire throughout Europe in various outbreaks. People died in such numbers that there was no time for proper burial; bodies were piled into communal graves. Two particularly massive outbreaks, in the sixth and fourteenth centuries, actually wiped out more than one-third of the population of Europe.

War, too, took its toll. From local raids for provisions to the great organized rampages called crusades, the Middle Ages were constantly rent by violence. Towns could be laid under siege for years until the population surrendered or died of starvation. Village and country people were defenseless against marauding bands of footloose soldiers or knights returning from a crusade. Armies were mostly made up of men who owed military service to a lord or king. Little philosophical or idealistic fervor drove them; their motive was pillage, their reward booty along the way.

Fire and flood were also common disasters. In one medieval flood in the Netherlands, fifty thousand people died. In 1188 a huge portion of the city of Troyes was destroyed by fire, including the cathedral and hundreds of houses. At a time when most houses were made of wood, city streets were narrow, and heating and cooking were done by open fire, a few sparks could easily produce an inferno.

Cripples and lepers were commonly seen in the streets. They announced their passage by bells or rattles—the cripples to encourage charity, the lepers to warn people away. In the late Middle Ages thousands of leper colonies were scattered all over Europe. A suspected sufferer was made to attend his own funeral service and then banished for life. The mentally ill were sometimes tied to the wooden choir partition in church for their own edification. Along with disease, doctors were everywhere. Their main remedies (for almost everything) were potions made of herbs and constant bloodletting. The local barber was dentist and surgeon as well, and most operations were performed without any anesthesia. Trepan-

A leper and a cripple make their way down a city street, Bibliothèque de l'Arsenal, Paris. Giraudon/Art Resource, New York. Used by permission.

ning—cutting out segments of the skull—was another resource. Its survival rate was not very high.

The life of a ruler was no safer than that of his subjects. In the last few centuries of the Middle Ages, one Emperor, two Scottish kings, and three English kings were murdered; and two English kings, two French kings, and five Scottish kings were captured or killed in battle.

Travel was slow and uncomfortable. Poor roads, unsanitary lodgings, and fraudulent innkeepers took their toll, and highwaymen were a constant menace. Most people traveled by foot; only the rich could afford horses.

A trepanning procedure in progress, Hierony-
mus Braunschweig, *Handywarke of Surgeri,*
1525. From Anders Piltz, *The World of Medieval Learning,* tr. David Jones (Totowa, NJ:
Barnes and Noble Books, 1981). Used by permission.

Trial by combat and trial by ordeal were still practiced until late in
the medieval period. The former involved the simple expedient of a fight or
duel between the disputants. In the latter, a person could try to prove his
innocence by grasping a hot bar of metal or by being tied to a chair and
thrown into a pond. God's intervention would determine guilt or innocence.

To save time, confessions could be extracted by torture. Punish-
ments were severe and ranged from fines to public floggings to death by
strangulation. They also included, for particular crimes, the loss of a hand,
being smeared with honey and exposed to flies, and (for murder within
one's own family) being put into a leather sack together with a dog, a
rooster, a snake, and a monkey and being thrown into the nearest river.

Women were often regarded with suspicion for their supposed gifts
of magic and weaving of spells. Many were burned alive as witches. Since
the exercise of political rights depended upon the bearing of arms, women

had no power in local politics. All universities, the professions, and the vast majority of positions within the Church hierarchy were closed to them. Females were denounced by the clergy for their sin, which was inherited from Eve. A woman was an "evil temptress," a "stinking rose," a "perilous object." Less vicious, but more dismissive, was the view of the great thirteenth-century philosopher Thomas Aquinas: "Woman should be made use of as a necessary object that is needed to preserve the species and to provide food and drink."

Jews, too, were easy targets. Despite the enormous debt owed by Christianity to Judaism—including the very concept of a single God, the centrality of books, and an advanced code of morality and ethics—or perhaps because of it, the Christian world treated its Jewish inhabitants with hatred and violence. Since the establishment of Christianity, the Jews of Europe had lived in fear. Subject to pervasive discriminatory laws, Jews were exploited for their learning and industry. They were harassed, murdered by mobs, or expelled *en masse* from their homes. The crusades in the eleventh and twelfth centuries created an excuse for widespread massacres. In the thirteenth century a council of the Church in Rome ordered all Jews to wear distinctive dress, including a peaked hat and a yellow patch on their clothing. Jews were blamed for military defeats, for natural disasters, and for outbreaks of plague. Many Jewish communities were annihilated after the outbreak of the Black Death in the fourteenth century. Virulent anti-Semitic statements and prayers were included in the official liturgy. (Only very recently have some of these been removed.) A German medieval historian has written: "Measured in terms of duration, magnitude, and conscious suffering, there is nothing in the history of Europe, or even of the world, to compare with the martyrdom of the Jews of medieval Europe."[3]

THE MEDIEVAL HERITAGE

Against this background of turbulence, disaster, discrimination, and death must be put the extraordinary achievements of medieval Europe in intellectual and cultural life, in technology, and in the establishment of social institutions. The Middle Ages have bequeathed to the Western world a rich legacy of thought, literary and philosophical accomplishments, art treasures, and architectural wonders.

Some of the writings of this period are monuments of Western civilization: Augustine's *Confessions, Beowulf,* Dante's *Divine Comedy,* and Chaucer's *Canterbury Tales.* A highly developed system of textual analysis

[3]Friedrich Heer, *The Medieval World,* p. 312.

was developed during the Middle Ages in which at least four levels of interpretation were involved. Those who were educated were highly educated indeed and were often knowledgeable in every known field of human endeavor. Many people spent their lives in the pursuit and preservation of learning. Books and manuscripts were highly prized, for parchment was expensive, all copies were made by hand, and a whole day might be needed to produce two or three pages. Some manuscripts, made especially for rich patrons or ceremonial occasions, were lavishly illustrated with exquisite miniature paintings and were enriched with bright colors and gold leaf, which glow with fervor and intensity even today.

We marvel still at the breathtaking beauty of the medieval cathedrals, with their soaring vaults, their stained-glass windows, and their stirring sculptures. They were built by thousands of dedicated craftsmen in an age of anonymous skills. The architects, designers, engineers, masons, sculptors, painters, bricklayers, and carpenters who spent their lives on these extraordinary buildings have left no names for us to venerate. They knew their work would outlive them.

Some of our most precious modern institutions were established in medieval times. Among these are the university itself, the parliamentary system, constitutional monarchy, and trial by jury.

Less well-known are the technological innovations of the Middle Ages. These provided the impulse for widespread social change and laid the foundations for many of the social and economic systems of the modern world.

In the sixth and seventh centuries the invention of a heavy wheeled plough facilitated the cultivation of large areas of Europe which had previously been left unexploited because of their dense, clay soil. This in turn led to increased food production and a significant growth in population. Further impetus was provided by the adoption of the padded horse collar, in place of a light harness, and the invention of the horseshoe.

In the eighth century the development of safer oceangoing ships encouraged raids of Vikings from Scandinavia and changed the racial, linguistic, and cultural makeup of Europe.

From the ninth to the eleventh centuries several more naval innovations increased sailing safety and efficiency. These included the lateen sail, which facilitated sailing into the wind, the double pulley for rigging, and the astrolabe, which measured distances and calculated positions by sighting on stars. The result was the establishment of new trade routes and a shift in the balance of economic power towards the Mediterranean. In this period the utilization of water power for mills to grind grain or, later, to drive presses and hammers for the iron industry increased rapidly. By 1086 there were six thousand mills operating in England alone.

The stirrup changed the way medieval warfare was waged and led to the superiority of mounted, heavily armed cavalry over footsoldiers; this in turn increased the prestige of the warrior classes—knights—who came from the ranks of the rich landowners.

The rate of technological innovation increased during the last part of the Middle Ages. In the twelfth century came the spinning-wheel, the mechanical clock, and the immensely efficient wheelbarrow. In the thirteenth century the broad-beamed, high-sided cargo ship known as the cog revolutionized transportation. Charts and compasses were spectacularly improved; windmills increased mechanization; and eyeglasses became widely available. In the fourteenth century the steel crossbow, plate armor, and gunpowder led to radical changes in the art of warfare, while the gentler arts were altered forever by the adoption of paper and of printing from blocks and fixed metal type.

Perhaps as remarkable as these inventions were those that did not actually come to fruition during the medieval period. Inventors and dreamers invented and dreamed in the Middle Ages just as they do today. Among the devices of their fantasy were diving bells, invisible handcuffs, ships that moved without sails or oarsmen, and flying machines.

THE YEARS 400–1000

The Middle Ages as a whole may be divided into two very broad periods: 400–1000 and 1000–1400. In the first of these periods there was constant tension between continuity and change. Administration, laws, and customs from the old Roman Empire persisted along with new patterns of Christian and feudal hierarchies, economic systems, and social and cultural life. Roman units of organization in the countryside, based on land ownership and slave labor, continued alongside the new medieval villages with their large, free, peasant populations. Gradually, the land-owning class came more and more to dominate those who cultivated the land, and a strictly stratified society developed. Old and new religions also co-existed: in the sixth century large areas of Europe were still pagan, and pagan and Christian communities lived side by side. By the eighth century Christianity had overtaken most of Europe, including previous holdouts such as the Italian countryside, southern Germany, and Britain as far north as Scotland.

Intellectual and cultural life underwent a series of swings between vigorous growth and marked decline. After the collapse of the Roman Empire, secular culture continued uneasily within the Christian world. Fortu-

nately, early Christian writers were able to justify the adoption of the sophisticated literary works of pagan Rome, though they did so with
ambivalence. Monasteries played a vital role in the preservation of ancient
learning and literature. In the artistic realm, almost nothing of the architecture of the early Middle Ages has survived; buildings were mostly wooden
and fell victim to fire. But jewels, sculpture, and metalwork from this period reveal a growing sense of artistic purpose.

Contrast and ambiguity marked the relationship of the hereditary
European kings with the Church. In the seventh and eighth centuries the
Carolingian dynasty forged a new and powerful alliance with the Church,
which gave divine authority to kingship—an advantage other medieval
kings were not slow to appropriate.

Further variety was lent to the central Middle Ages by the Arab conquest of the Iberian peninsula. By the ninth century there was a large Muslim presence in the region, which gained considerable intellectual, architectural, and commercial diversity as a result. It was only very much later
that Christian monarchs, through treaty, political marriage, and warfare,
were able to recapture the area.

By the early ninth century the primarily agricultural economy of Europe had become diversified by industrial products such as metalware and
glass and by natural products such as cloth, furs, and timber.

Education was limited to a very few, and in this area change came
gradually. In the ninth century the great ruler Charlemagne could hardly
read or write. Partly as a result of his impetus, however, education spread
slowly from the palace school to the clergy. Charlemagne's aim was to edu-
cate the entire population, and monastic schools extended their influence
in the countryside, while cathedral schools dispensed learning in the towns.
It was the cathedral school of Paris that eventually grew into the first university in medieval Europe. In this period, too, a new art and architecture
emerged from an amalgam of Roman, Eastern, Celtic, and local traditions.

The ninth and tenth centuries in Europe were the age of invasions
from the north. Viking seamen attacked the western shores, plundered the
coastal villages, reduced the newly settled states and kingdoms to disorder,
disrupted the economy, and spread death and destruction. But they had
other effects too: new elements were added to some of the emerging European languages, especially English; and castles and fortifications were built
in England, northern and western France, and northern Italy. These increased the power of local landowners and led to further militarization of
the upper classes and oppression of the peasants.

Political entities were established, diverse but relatively stable, as
opposed to the tribal communities of the past. They were unified—apart
from important minority groups such as the Jews or the Muslims in the Iberian peninsula—by a single Christian culture. Governments began to be

centralized and controlled all aspects of the economy, such as taxation and the minting of money.

By the year 1000 a Europe recognizable to the modern world had taken shape. The clash between pagan and Christian, between barbarian and Roman, between tribal and settled, had ended. Great trading routes tied the various regions together, and a new middle class of merchants arose. The towns, where people gathered for trade and where governments were established, began to grow in importance. More and more of the forested or marshy regions of central Europe were converted to productive agricultural land. The upper-class landowners, increasingly powerful, turned into the aristocratic knights of mythical fame. Schools flourished, regional styles of architecture arose, and literary accomplishments in biography and history were many.

THE YEARS 1000–1400

The period from 1000 to 1400 was marked by even more striking contradictions and ambiguities. In the year 1003, Leif Ericsson discovered America, nearly five hundred years before Christopher Columbus. But this was an isolated event, for Europe was still a closed society, a world unto itself.

In the early part of this period, however, one phenomenon captured the European imagination. Between 1096 and 1217 there were five organized crusades. Their announced aim was the conquering of the Holy Land. In fact, they were political excuses for unifying the restless European nobility, who were involved in constant rivalrous wars, and for plundering the fabulous wealth of the East. Italian coastal cities, which provided ships and arms, made fortunes from the crusades. Indulgences were offered by the popes, who promised forgiveness from sin and a perfect afterlife for those killed in battle. Thus the crusades were at once spiritual quests, lengthy travel junkets (many knights took their wives and entire households with them), and amongst the most shameful episodes in the history of Christianity. In the first crusade, at the capture of Jerusalem, as many as one hundred thousand Muslims—men, women, and children—were massacred. In the third crusade three thousand prisoners were murdered and disemboweled in the search for gold. In 1204 the crusaders captured Constantinople, and centuries of artworks, artifacts, and precious manuscripts were pillaged and destroyed.

These high-minded assaults against the outside "enemies" of Europe turned quickly to religious repression and civil war, as crusades were launched against internal dissenters of the Church, especially against those

A miniature from a fifteenth-century manuscript displays a mixture of new and older weapons (cannons, longbows, crossbows, swords and lances): a town is besieged, while pitched battles rage across the countryside, Bibliothèque Nationale, Paris.

who espoused a different view of Christianity. The Albigensian crusade against heretics in the south of France destroyed a flourishing civilization, and what began as public, open warfare soon turned to the hidden, ruthless evils of the Inquisition.

　　The period was also marked by constant conflict between the two great ruling institutions of the age—the papacy and the empire. This conflict had become endemic to the Middle Ages since the founding of a new line of emperors by Charlemagne. The popes had a powerful weapon, however. They could order the closing of the churches throughout a realm; services would cease, and the people would be deprived of all comfort, all means of intercession with God.

On the other hand, the twelfth century was a time of great intellectual and physical daring. New ideas flowed into Europe; teachers attracted throngs of young people; and the Gothic style, that dizzying architecture reaching heavenward in defiance of common sense and gravity, took France, and then England and Germany, by storm. Triumphs of inspiration and mechanical engineering, the Gothic cathedrals were dependent upon some technical features, such as the pointed arch, and directly engendered others, such as the flying buttress.

A struggle attended the birth of the new universities in the thirteenth century. Who was to control them? The papal court at Rome? The local bishop of the town? In the end it was the universities themselves that won the struggle. The guilds of masters and students were to govern themselves. This battle was fought in Paris, where the bishop was strong and his contacts with Rome close. A splinter group from Paris founded Oxford University, and a splinter group from Oxford founded Cambridge—both deep in the countryside, far from the reach of the nearest bishops. In the universities the semester system was instituted, with the academic year beginning in the autumn. Education was based upon the liberal arts, the humanistic foundation of learning since ancient times (see pp. 27–29).

The new universities of the thirteenth century instigated another great intellectual conflict—that between faith and reason. Did faith require the abdication of reason, or could reason be used to bolster and justify faith? The answer was not straightforward, and the intellectual investigations and wranglings of the time engaged some of the greatest and most profound thinkers of the Western tradition. In the meantime science made slow advances. Magnetism was beginning to be understood for the first time. Medicine became a legitimate subject of study, overcoming the resistance inherent in the view that the human body was made in the image of God and should therefore not be tampered with.

In England the first steps towards political representation were taken. Henry II curbed the corruption of the barons, extended the coverage of the law, protected farmers against illegal seizure of their land, and instituted the practice of trial by jury. These enlightened moves set the stage for further advances. It was from Henry's son, the morally bankrupt King John, that the great medieval statement of political freedom was wrested in 1215—the Magna Carta, a document which ensured that even the monarch was subject to the law of the land. The next hundred and fifty years saw the establishment of Parliament and its division into two houses, with representatives from both the upper and the middle classes from each region of the country.

At the end of the thirteenth century, a large number of Europeans got their first impressions of a world outside their own through the travels of the Venetian Marco Polo to and from the East, including the great civilization of China.

The fourteenth century was a time of superb achievements in all forms of painting—murals, panels, and manuscript illuminations. Some of the most exquisite works of art of the entire Middle Ages date from this time. Knighthood had become increasingly a social convention, and the joust a public spectacle. Norms of etiquette, deportment, and details of dress occupied the minds of the rich. Luxurious banquets were laid on by noblemen for weddings and other celebrations. Poetry flourished. But in the midst of it all the Black Death swept through Europe like the medieval pictures of Death with a scythe; the Church was rent by schism; and the Hundred Years' War dragged relentlessly on.

THE ROLE OF MUSIC

Music played a vital role in the medieval world. The lengthy and complex evolution of the Christian liturgy in both monastic and urban communities was accompanied by a parallel evolution in its music. Music was initially designed for carrying prayer to God, but it soon came to function as a means of organizing, articulating, and dramatizing the liturgy itself. Medieval writers devoted considerable attention to music. Soon the notes came to be regarded as sacred, just like the words they set. A constant ambivalence existed between attitudes toward the beauty of music and those toward its liturgical function. Augustine, for example, took so much pleasure in music that he thought it suspect.

Outside the Church, too, music enjoyed a healthy vitality, as it fused the new cult of love with the cult of the Virgin. The secular poems of the Middle Ages were set to melodies that could emphasize the texts' structural variety and unity. Drama brought people out of the street into the church to witness the enactment of the great stories of their Christian heritage. Drama also left the church to instruct the people with moral tales or present the worthy lives of saints for imitation. Unfortunately, the music of the streets and taverns and country villages, since it was rarely written down, is almost completely lost to us, though the glimpses we have are tantalizing evidence of a rich and lively tradition.

Later, music became the artistic pursuit of intellectuals and sophisticates, who combined the melodies of the Church with secular interests and concerns, or abandoned their ties with sacred music to find ever more interesting ways to set their poetry. Secular songs became the province of rich and noble courts, and subtle polyphonic versions of these songs were woven in aristocratic chambers for the delight of educated patrons.

Today music is almost inescapable. This was not true in the Middle Ages. Music was of rare occurrence, and each sound had import. Bells marked the passing of the hours or the celebration of festivals; drums and wind instruments were heard in battles or processions; noble families would be entertained after a banquet with the sound of a single singer telling heroic tales or weaving stories of love; and the chanting of a choir in unison signified a sacred service.

The contrasts and contradictions of the whole of medieval life are reflected in its music. It ranges from the most explicit love songs to savage satires to the highest realms of spirituality. It reflects the homesickness of a crusader, political intrigues, loss and mourning, delight and joy. There are rich and elaborate repertories designed for performance by talented groups of professionals and simple, repetitive melodies for reciting stories. The clergy were the patrons of complex motets and scathing dramas which criticized . . . the clergy. The composers included kings and princes, monks and minstrels. Music was designed for celebrating a new cathedral, for accompanying a dance, for insulting a rival.

But the unity of secular and religious life in the Middle Ages is there too. In the eleventh century the Bishop of Rennes was the author of love lyrics. In the twelfth century a monk could be equally at home writing songs to the Virgin and songs to local virgins. Combining a popular song with the sacred chant did not seem strange. Composing a setting of a text for the Mass in the latest secular style was only to be expected. Life and religion were one, and music reflected them both. Music enlivened the monasteries and the churches, the town halls and the banquet halls of the Middle Ages. It was sung under ladies' windows, at funeral services, and in processions. It rang across battlefields; it echoed in castle courtyards; it lent dignity to coronations and joy and sanctity to weddings. It gave color to the age. In experiencing it today, we can learn about the inner life of medieval Europe as in no other way.

BIBLIOGRAPHICAL NOTES

The bibliography of the medieval era is immense. A useful and highly readable reference work is *Dictionary of the Middle Ages,* ed. Joseph R. Strayer, 13 vols. (New York: Charles Scribner's Sons, 1982–).

For the early period, Archibald R. Lewis, *Emerging Medieval Europe, A.D. 400–1000* (New York: Alfred A. Knopf, Inc., 1967) is clear and short. The richness and depth of the later period are brilliantly captured in Friedrich Heer, *The Medieval World: Europe 1100–1350,* trans. Janet Sondheimer (New York: The New American Library, 1962) and Johan Huizinga, *The*

Waning of the Middle Ages: A Study of the Forms of Life, Thought, and Art in France and the Netherlands in the XIVth and XVth Centuries (London: E. Arnold and Co., 1924; reprinted 1952).

The best overall historical survey is C. W. Previté-Orton, *The Shorter Cambridge Medieval History,* 2 vols., (Cambridge: Cambridge University Press, 1971). Colin McEvedy, *The Penguin Atlas of Medieval History* (London: Penguin Books, 1961) has illuminating maps and brief accompanying historical summaries.

Daily life is portrayed in Joseph and Frances Gies, *Life in a Medieval City* (New York: Harper and Row, Inc., 1981) and Christopher Brooke, *The Structure of Medieval Society* (London: Thames and Hudson, Ltd., 1971).

The developments in medieval technology are surveyed in Lynn T. White, *Medieval Technology and Social Change* (Oxford: The Clarendon Press, 1962) and J. D. Bernal, *The Emergence of Science,* the first volume of the four-volume study *Science in History* (Cambridge, Massachusetts: M.I.T. Press, 1971).

Two books approach medieval philosophy and institutions from different viewpoints: William R. Cook and Ronald B. Herzman, *The Medieval World View: An Introduction* (New York: Oxford University Press, 1983) and David Knowles, *The Evolution of Medieval Thought* (New York: Random House, 1962).

Of the many illustrated volumes, those accompanied by the most informative texts include *The Flowering of the Middle Ages,* ed. Joan Evans (London: Thames and Hudson, Ltd., 1966) and Colin Platt, *The Atlas of Medieval Man* (New York: St. Martin's Press, Inc., 1980).

Anthologies of medieval music are W. Thomas Marrocco and Nicholas Sandon (eds.), *Medieval Music: The Oxford Anthology of Music* (London: Oxford University Press, 1977) and Richard H. Hoppin (ed.), *Anthology of Medieval Music* (New York: W. W. Norton and Co., Inc., 1978). The latter volume is accompanied by a detailed survey of the repertoire by the same author: Richard H. Hoppin, *Medieval Music* (New York: W. W. Norton and Co., Inc., 1978). Other books on medieval music include Gustave Reese, *Music in the Middle Ages* (New York: W. W. Norton and Co., Inc., 1940); John Caldwell, *Medieval Music* (Bloomington: Indiana University Press, 1978); and Giulio Cattin, *Music of the Middle Ages I,* trans. Steven Botterill (Cambridge: Cambridge University Press, 1984) and F. Alberto Gallo, *Music of the Middle Ages II,* trans. Karen Eales (Cambridge: Cambridge University Press, 1985).

An analysis of modern attitudes towards the Middle Ages is presented by Fred Robinson, "Medieval, The Middle Ages," *Speculum* LIX (1984): 745–756.

TWO

THE THEORETICAL TRADITION
OF ANTIQUITY

THE ANCIENT WORLD

Medieval Europe received a major portion of its cultural heritage from Antiquity—from Greek civilization and the Roman Republic and Empire that succeeded it. The group of rival city-states of southeastern Europe that was formed in the eighth to the sixth centuries B.C. gradually became more unified with the help of religious festivals and athletic contests such as the Olympic games. Athens emerged as the foremost of these states and in the fifth century B.C. was the seat of a thriving cultural and intellectual life which left its mark on the entire course of Western civilization. Drama, music, poetry, sculpture, architecture, philosophy, statecraft, and literature all came to maturity in this century and the next.

Greek culture was carried to the furthest corners of the known world by Alexander the Great (356–323 B.C.). After Alexander's death, renewed warfare broke out and weakened the structure of the Greek states. Meanwhile, Rome was increasing its power and ambitions, and in 146 B.C., after the Fourth Macedonian War, the Greeks became subjects of the Roman Republic. Greek culture was taken over wholesale by the Romans, and much of Latin literature was modeled on that of the Greeks.

With the rule of Julius Caesar (c. 100–44 B.C.), the nobly-born leader of the people, the Republic came to an end. After Caesar's death Augustus was proclaimed the first Roman emperor, and with his benevolent dictatorship as a starting point the Roman Empire flourished for the next two hundred years. It extended from Scotland to North Africa and from the Caspian Sea to the Iberian peninsula. Literature and the arts were encouraged, though they still tended mainly to imitation of Greek models. Ambivalence towards the new religion of Christianity was demonstrated by alternating persecution and acceptance, but with the conversion of the emperor Constantine (c. 288–337) and his issuance in 313 of the Edict of Milan, requiring tolerance of the new religion, Christianity became firmly established in the Empire.

That Empire was now declining. It was divided into two sections, and the capital was moved from Rome to Byzantium (later known as Constantinople after the emperor Constantine; now called Istanbul). Eventually this division became permanent, and there were two empires, the Eastern and the Western, with Constantinople as the capital in the East, and Rome giving way first to Ravenna and then to Milan or Trier as the capital in the West. In the fifth century, invaders from Germany and the north made ravaging sorties into Italy, and the city of Rome itself was conquered more than once. The last Roman emperor, Romulus Augustulus, was removed from power in 476 by the Germanic tribe known as the Goths.

But the cultural and imperial tradition of ancient Rome did not disappear. It was carried on by later, foreign, rulers who mimicked Roman styles and called themselves emperors. It continued unbroken in many ways in the Eastern Empire; and it found renewed life in the kingdom of Charlemagne and the Holy Roman Empire of later centuries. The very language of the Roman Empire, Latin, formed the basis of the Romance languages such as French, Italian, and Spanish, which developed in Europe, and was used in the liturgy of the Church and as the international language of scholarship throughout the Middle Ages.

MUSIC IN ANTIQUITY

Much of the medieval attitude towards music was derived from Classical Antiquity. Medieval treatises constantly quote or depend upon ideas that may be traced directly to Greek or Roman writers. In order to understand medieval views on music, therefore, it is important to examine the main strands of ancient musical thought and theory that passed through to later times. It is an unfortunate fact that very little actual music has survived from the Classical era—enough to give some hint as to what it must have been like, but not enough to provide a repertoire for conclusive study. This

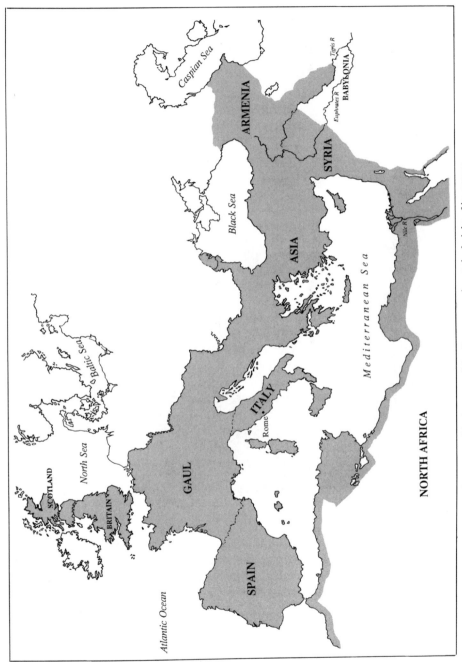

The geographical extent of the Roman empire at the height of its power.

Lyre player taking part in a music contest. Greek vase of c. 500 B.C., Staatliche Kunstsammlungen, Kassel.

chapter, therefore, will confine itself to tracing the main elements of ancient theories of music, both speculative and practical, touching, however, only upon those that directly influenced medieval thought and practice.

In the ancient world, music had special importance. The Greek word for music (*mousiké*) was derived directly from the word for the Muses, the nine daughters of Zeus who were responsible for the arts. In ancient Greece, music was believed to have sacred as well as moral, therapeutic, and educative power. It was used as an inherent part of sacred rites and in the performance of the great tragedies of Greek religious drama. The theory developed that music on earth was a reflection of the greater "music of the spheres"—a harmony created by the relative distances and rates of motion of the planets, a harmony that was constantly present, if only people were sufficiently sensitive to hear it. This was a higher order of music, one with which humanity should strive to be in tune.

These ideas found expression in the work of Pythagoras (c. 580–507 B.C.), who taught that numbers provided the means for understanding the universe. His philosophy encompassed not only the distant planets but also the actual facts of human experience. He discovered through empirical observation that musical intervals could be expressed through numerical ratios. The importance of this discovery cannot be over-emphasized. It has provided musicians and theorists ever since with the ability to work in a rational manner with sounds and their relationships.

There are two versions of the story of Pythagoras' discovery. One involves the sound of hammers of different weights:

> Pythagoras was curious for a long time and tried to find a way to establish in his mind the principles of consonance by the solid and consistent use of reason. One day, when by divine will he happened to be passing a blacksmith's workshop, he heard that the hammers, as they were beating, were somehow producing a consonance, although they made different sounds. Realizing that he was in the presence of the answer to his problem, he was amazed, and approached the shop. He discovered that there were four hammers which were in consonance. One, which weighed twice as much as the second (2:1), formed an octave with it. The other two hammers produced a fourth and a fifth, and were in the ratios of 4:3 and 3:2.[1]

The other story describes Pythagoras making his discovery from the proportions of a stretched string.

The results are the same. The interval of an octave can be expressed in the mathematical ratio 2:1, a fifth in the ratio 3:2, and a fourth in the ratio 4:3. All the other intervals also can be expressed as ratios, and thus there is a rational and calculable basis for the whole of music.

These two primary elements of the work of Pythagoras—the philosophical belief in the universal significance of music and the practical discovery of its mathematical basis—were extensively developed by Plato (c. 429–347 B.C.). For Plato, music had such power that he believed it should be carefully controlled. The right music could ennoble the soul, provide proper training for future leaders, and restore equanimity to disturbed personalities. The wrong music could undermine social and personal peace.

Plato's view of what was right and wrong in music depended to a large extent upon technical features which were discussed by music theorists of his time and later. The most important of these was Aristoxenus (4th century B.C.), a student of Aristotle and a prolific author, who developed a comprehensive plan of classification for music. This plan involved

[1]Boethius, *De Institutione Musica* I, x (ed. Friedlein 197–8).

Pythagoras overhearing the blacksmiths, Bayerische Staatsbibliothek, Munich.

the organization of the elements of music in ways which we now take for granted, but which then were new. Aristoxenus described an overall system which included all the notes available (about two octaves) in a series; he arranged them in groups of four, each group being known as a tetrachord, and each tetrachord having the same order of intervals; and he gave all the notes names.

Aristoxenus also classified the elements of melody and rhythm into organized groups or "modes." The melodic modes were built from scales with differing patterns of intervals, while the rhythmic modes were based on patterns derived from poetry and dance. The melodic modes were given names which corresponded with the names of other Greek peoples, such as the Dorians, Lydians, and Phrygians, and each of them was associated with a particular affect or quality. The Dorian mode, for example, was thought to embody bravery, while the Phrygian mode was said to be warlike.

These systematic arrangements of the elements of music were profoundly important for the later history of musical theory and practice. Music now had a scale system, the concept of different intervals, and a method of rhythmic organization.

Two other aspects of the music and musical theory of Antiquity should be mentioned here, although the links from them to the Middle Ages seem to be indirect or to have been broken through time.

The first relates to instrumental music. We know that instrumental music played an important role in the ancient world, for it was extensively discussed by contemporary writers. Instruments were associated with both amateur and professional performance, and for the professional musicians there were contests at public festivals. In these contests the performer depended upon set melodies or melodic formulas (*nomoi*), which seem to have been quite extensive and which were associated with one or more of the melodic modes. The performer would improvise upon these melodies, while keeping closely to the format and atmosphere of the original. (The parallel between these formulas and the Japanese *honkyoku* or Indian *raga*, with their traditional melodies and emotional qualities, is clear.) The Greek *nomoi* may have formed the basis for the formulas by which the melodic modes in medieval music were later identified.

The second aspect is the early existence of musical notation. The Greeks had a sophisticated system of musical notation which differentiated between vocal and instrumental music and was capable of indicating rhythmic values. That this technique was lost to medieval musicians is indicated by the fact that we have no written music from the Middle Ages before the ninth century.

BOETHIUS

Greek musical theory was transmitted to the Middle Ages primarily through the work of one man who lived about eight hundred years after its initial formulation. Anitius Manlius Severinus Boethius (c. 475–525) was an influential Roman statesman and author. He was born into a noble family and became a consul and minister to the emperor Theodoric. Later in the emperor's reign, Boethius was falsely accused of treason, imprisoned, and finally executed without trial. While he was in prison, Boethius wrote his most famous work, *The Consolation of Philosophy,* a philosophical essay which adapted the principles of Plato and Aristotle to current thought and became a standard of spirituality for the Middle Ages.

Other books written by Boethius include theological essays, translations and commentaries on Classical works of logic (especially those of Aristotle), and didactic treatises. Among the latter was a book on music, *The Principles of Music (De Institutione Musica),* which became the stand-

Greek musical notation on a funeral column. The notation begins above the sixth line of the inscription. Nationalmuseet, Copenhagen.

ard textbook on the subject in European schools and universities for over a thousand years and was enormously influential on medieval attitudes towards the art of music.

Many aspects of Boethius' music treatise will sound familiar. He writes that music has a prominent place in education and philosophy, for it can have moral influence over people. Music can be divided into three types: music of the universe (*musica mundana*), music of human beings (*musica humana*), and instrumental music (*musica instrumentalis*). In order for people to comprehend and deal with music rationally, musical sounds must be represented as numbers, and the ratios between the numbers will allow proper judgment of consonance and dissonance. Boethius also describes in detail the Greek note system, tetrachords, intervals, and the melodic modes with their names.

A further aspect of Boethius' *De Institutione Musica* that became important in the later Middle Ages was his definition of a musician. A true musician, according to Boethius, is not the performer or the composer, but the educated and rational thinker who can judge performances and compositions.

> There are three types of person that are involved in music. The first type performs on instruments, the second composes songs, and the third judges the performances and the songs.
>
> The type that is completely consumed by instruments is separated from the understanding of musical knowledge. These people spend all their efforts showing off their skill on their instruments. So they are like slaves, for they use no reason and are without any thought.
>
> The second type is the composer. These people compose songs not by thought and reason but simply by a certain natural instinct. They are also separated from music.
>
> The third type has the ability to judge. They can ponder rhythms and melodies and songs in general. It is these people who are completely devoted to reason and thought and can therefore rightly be considered musicians.[2]

This view, clearly taken from the Greeks, was predominant in Western culture until quite recently. Throughout the Middle Ages and beyond, it was the educated listener, the one who had sufficient understanding of the structure and nature of music to judge what he was hearing, who was classed as the true musician.

THE SEVEN LIBERAL ARTS

How, then, were people educated in medieval times, and how did music fit into the curriculum? The fully developed system of education in the Middle Ages was based upon the seven liberal arts. These were divided into two groups—the *trivium* ("three ways") and the *quadrivium* ("four ways"). The trivium was made up of the verbal arts—grammar, rhetoric,

---

[2]Boethius, *De Institutione Musica* I, xxxiv (ed. Friedlein 224–5).

and logic—while the quadrivium involved the mathematical arts—arithmetic, geometry, music, and astronomy. The "liberal" arts (from the Latin word *liber,* meaning "free") were those which could be pursued by free people, as opposed to the mechanical arts, such as carpentry and building, which were performed by slaves.

The position of music as one of the subjects in the quadrivium reveals much about Classical and early medieval views on the subject. Number, ratio, and proportion were the central components of musical structure, and instruction in music concentrated heavily upon these aspects, often with no mention of practical elements.

The division of the educational curriculum, like much else in the medieval period, reached back to Classical times. Plato had already proposed a two-part educational system to prepare the way for the highest pursuit, the study of philosophy. After Rome had taken over much of Greek civilization, the standard Roman education was based on grammar, rhetoric, and literary history and criticism. By the fifth and sixth centuries the complete curriculum with its standard order and arrangement of subjects had spread widely. Mainly responsible for this were three writers whose works were copied and read constantly throughout the Middle Ages: Martianus Capella, Cassiodorus, and Isidore of Seville. The range of their knowledge has led to their being called the "encyclopedists."

Martianus Capella was the author of an unusual work entitled *The Marriage of Philology and Mercury,* written about 425, which, in an elaborate and allegorical setting, gives an account of the nature and content of the seven liberal arts. The section on music sets forth several definitions of music (which became a favorite device of later treatises) and transmits some aspects of Greek theory, especially regarding metrics (poetic meters) and rhythm and the moral qualities of music.

A more straightforward approach was taken by the Roman writer Cassiodorus (c. 485–585). Cassiodorus was a contemporary of Boethius and, like him, came from a noble Roman family. He became a senator and consul and actually succeeded Boethius to the post of minister to the emperor Theodoric. After the defeat of Rome by Byzantium, Cassiodorus retired from the world of public affairs to devote himself to a life of contemplation and religion. He founded a monastery, where he lived and wrote, and where the monks were occupied, in their hours away from religious duties, in copying and thus preserving for posterity many manuscripts of ancient works. It was for the monks of this monastery that Cassiodorus wrote his *Principles of Sacred and Secular Letters,* which is in two books, the first concerning sacred knowledge, the second summarizing the seven liberal arts. The chapter on music is a brief review of musical consonances and the melodic modes, with some definitions and etymological derivations of the term music. It ends with a list of other Greek and Latin writers on the subject.

The last of the encyclopedists was Isidore of Seville (c. 560–636). Isidore was born in Spain and became a voluminous writer and theologian. He was appointed bishop of Seville about the year 600 and was later designated a saint. The tendency to define terms and examine their meanings that we see in earlier works was carried to its logical conclusion in Isidore's *Etymologies or Origins,* an examination of technical terms and their meanings in all known fields of knowledge. The first three books of the *Etymologies* are devoted to the seven liberal arts. The section on music is partly based on Cassiodorus as well as on Greek tradition, and it contains an extended discussion of metrics.

Although the treatment of music by these three writers was very brief, especially compared to Boethius, their influence on the medieval educational system as a whole was immense. They helped to transmit Classical culture to later times, and to preserve it in times of social and political turbulence. Their works epitomized ancient learning and established the seven liberal arts as the basis for the educational curriculum of the Middle Ages. They wrote at a time when the old order was being dissolved and the Roman Empire divided into East and West. In retrospect it is possible to see that, but for the efforts of compilers and encyclopedists such as these, centuries of Classical culture might have been lost.

One further aspect of their work needs to be mentioned. As Christianity gained a hold in the West, a clash between pagan (Classical) culture and Christian doctrine was inevitable. Christian thinkers looked with ambivalence upon the achievements of a civilization that had not recognized the one God, and yet they were reluctant to jettison the primary cultural heritage of the Western world. Boethius and the three encyclopedists served to merge Classical and Christian ideals in education. Cassiodorus had advocated the interdependence of the two, with his parallel books on sacred and secular letters and with the work of the monks at his monastery in copying and preserving ancient texts. Isidore—saint, bishop, and scholar—lent the authority of his name to the entire tradition of Classical learning. The fact that Cassiodorus and Isidore were Christians, while Capella and Boethius were not, symbolizes the transition between the old world and the new.

AUGUSTINE

One final figure important in this context is the man known as Augustine (354–430). Aurelius Augustinus was born in a Roman province in North Africa. His father was pagan and his mother Christian. He was educated at Carthage, on the Mediterranean coast, and then traveled to Rome and soon thereafter to Milan, where he was appointed Professor of

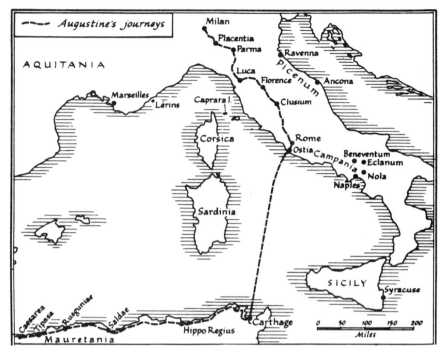

The journeys of Augustine in Italy and North Africa. From Peter Brown, *Augustine of Hippo* (Berkeley: University of California Press, 1967). Reprinted by permission of Faber and Faber Ltd.

Rhetoric for the city. This was an important position, as the imperial court was then in residence in Milan, and Augustine was responsible for official speeches. While in Milan, Augustine was profoundly moved by the learning and spirituality of Ambrose, the bishop. He decided formally to embrace Christianity and was baptized by Ambrose in 387. On his return to North Africa, Augustine founded a religious community with a group of friends, where he lived until he was called to assist the Bishop of Hippo, an important town nearby. Eventually Augustine succeeded to the bishopric himself, and he remained in this position for the next thirty-five years until his death. He was later declared a saint.

Augustine is regarded as one of the greatest figures in the history of the Church, and as the founder of theology. His many works reveal him as the possessor of an intellect of great clarity and profundity, a writer of eloquence, and a man committed to searching out the truth of his own humanity. He was a prolific author, and his *City of God* and *Confessions* are classics of Christian Latin literature. Amongst his writings survives part of a work on music, entitled *Concerning Music (De Musica)*. This was intended to take its place as one of a series of books on the seven liberal arts. Unfortunately the other books are not extant, and *De Musica* itself is incomplete. It consists of five sections on rhythm, analyzing in great detail all the possible combinations of poetic meter, and a sixth section concentrating on the universal significance of musical numbers, derived from Plato.

Augustine, however, was not content to discuss music only in the formal and educational context of the seven liberal arts. Music plays a considerable role in his other writings, and the conflict between his view of it as sacred medium and as the source of purely sensuous appeal sets the stage for some fascinating and profound reflections on the part of this man, who was given to the most rigorous self-examination. He questioned whether his delight in the beauty of music was not in itself sinful, but he was able to conclude that the power of music to convey the meaning of the sacred texts separated it from the mindless pleasures:

> The days were not long enough as I meditated upon and found delight in the depth of Your design for the salvation of the human race. I wept at the beauty of Your hymns and canticles, and was deeply moved at the sweet sound of the singing of Your church. The sounds poured into my ears, and the truth distilled in my heart, so that my sense of devotion overflowed, and the tears ran from my eyes. And I delighted in them.[3]

Music here is not the mathematical calculation of intervals and proportions but the vehicle of profound expression and the inspiration to spiritual devotion. If profound and influential thinkers such as Augustine had not been able to accept music into their worship, the fast-growing liturgy of the new Church would have been very different indeed.

SUMMARY

Music, as a highly developed art, played a central role in the life of ancient Greece. Its power to purify or corrupt derived from its connection with the mystical order of the universe. At religious gatherings Greek music was an integral part of sung drama and the focal point of virtuoso instrumental performance. Philosophers and theorists investigated its components and devised systematic methods for analyzing intervals, scales, rhythms, and melodies. A notational system, which distinguished between vocal and instrumental music, was also in use.

Out of the ruins of the Roman Empire, which had absorbed the culture of the Greeks, some of these aspects of musical thought survived by means of an educational system that included music as one of the seven liberal arts. The encyclopedic writers summarized some of the theory and

[3]*Confessions* IX, vi, 14.

practice of the Greeks, while Boethius transmitted in great detail the mathematical and proportional nature of musical intervals and the scale and melody systems of Greek theory, together with the ancient view of the ethical and universal nature of music in the world of humanity. Augustine, Roman intellectual and diplomat, later bishop, and ultimately saint, was torn between the seductive power of music and its role as bearer of the words of worship. Fortunately for the history of music, it was the latter notion that triumphed.

DISCOGRAPHY

An interpretation in sound of several of the surviving musical fragments from Antiquity may be heard on Atrium Musicae de Madrid, *Musique de la Grèce Antique,* Harmonia Mundi HM 1015. Some also appear on *History of Music in Sound, vol. 1: Ancient and Oriental Music,* RCA Victor LM–6057; and *2,000 Years of Music,* Folkways Records FT 3700.

BIBLIOGRAPHICAL NOTES

The richest study of the influence of Classical Antiquity on the educational, literary, and cultural history of the West is R. R. Bolgar, *The Classical Heritage and Its Beneficiaries* (Cambridge: Cambridge University Press, 1954; reprint 1977).

Ancient Greek attitudes towards music may be perused in Andrew Barker (ed.), *Greek Musical Writings Volume I: The Musician and his Art,* Cambridge Readings in the Literature of Music (Cambridge: Cambridge University Press, 1984). An essay which surveys the period is Isobel Henderson, "Ancient Greek Music," in *The New Oxford History of Music, Volume I: Ancient and Oriental Music* (Oxford: Oxford University Press, 1957).

The music treatise of Boethius is presented in translation, with an introduction and notes, by Calvin M. Bower in the *Yale Music Theory in Translation* series.

For discussions of the seven liberal arts see *The Seven Liberal Arts in the Middle Ages,* ed. David L. Wagner (Bloomington: Indiana University Press, 1983) and William Harris Stahl, *Martianus Capella and the Seven Liberal Arts* (New York: Columbia University Press, 1971).

Peter Brown, *Augustine of Hippo* (Berkeley: University of California Press, 1967) is a fascinating and humane revelation of the life and times of Augustine.

THREE
CHANT AND LITURGY

Most of the extant music from the Middle Ages is liturgical music of the Catholic church. In order to understand this music, therefore, it is important to learn something about the formation of the Catholic liturgy and the role that music plays in it.

Liturgical music is practical music. It is designed to form an integral part of formal religious observances which vary greatly in their length, content, and design. Primarily, therefore, the nature of the music is tied directly to its function in the service. Inherent in the development of liturgical music, however, is a tension between its functionality and the aural pleasure that it gives. Some aspects of liturgical music go beyond the plain necessity of religious function and tend towards the flourishing of artistic aims. This has been regarded by some as the celebration of the divine in humanity and by others as the triumph of the human over religious restriction. Here it is important only to recognize that throughout the history of music and liturgy a conflict has existed—between the necessary and the superfluous, the plain and the elaborate.

THE DEVELOPMENT OF THE CHRISTIAN CHURCH

Christianity was a direct descendant of Judaism, for Jesus and his followers were Jews, and their practices and beliefs were part of the ancient Jewish tradition. Christian morality was derived from Jewish ethical teachings and behavior, and the Jewish Bible was regarded as sacred scripture. In liturgical practice, therefore, we should expect the early Church to have been based on the religious observances of the Jews. In many ways this was true, and elements of Jewish practice remain in the official Catholic liturgy to this day. These include beginning the celebration of a feast at sundown on the previous day, retention of the word Sabbath for Saturdays, and the centrality of large parts of the Jewish Bible in the liturgy. Most of these texts were translated from the Hebrew into Greek or Latin, but some Hebrew words remain—such as *Amen* ("In truth"), *Sabaoth* ("Hosts"), and *Halleluyah* ("Praise God").

Clearly, however, the early Christians wanted to distinguish themselves from the mainstream of Judaism, but exactly when distinctly identifiable forms of Christian worship were first established is not known.

Christianity was from the very beginning intent on missionary activity, and its early adherents like St. Paul soon managed to spread the new religion from the province of Palestine to Greece, Rome, and Alexandria. For the first two and a half centuries of its growth the Church lived uneasily within the confines of the Roman Empire and was subject to frequent disturbance from imperial intolerance without and sectarian division within. Some pagan Roman customs even found their way into the liturgy. After the adoption of Christianity by the Roman emperor Constantine and the division of the Empire into two parts, the Eastern church was ruled separately from Constantinople. Its leader became the undisputed head of the Byzantine Empire. In the West, power was divided between the emperors and the popes. The popes, as bishops of Rome, successors to the first bishop, St. Peter (?–c. 65), claimed authority from the beginning over all the churches in the West. As the number and extent of these churches grew, so did the power of the popes. And as imperial control weakened, the popes gained more of the prestige and reverence that had once belonged to the emperors.

LITERATURE AND LANGUAGE OF THE EARLY CHURCH

The three hundred years or so following the conversion of Constantine (roughly from the fourth through the sixth centuries) were marked by the activity of a number of brilliant and influential Christian writers and scholars. These men are known as the Fathers of the Church, and the work they produced is called patristic literature. Many of them wrote in Greek, which was the language of the early Church and its Eastern adherents. But as Christianity spread throughout the empire and new converts in the West became more numerous, Latin succeeded Greek as the language of scholarship, theology, and liturgy. A reminder of the Greek period of the liturgy is given in the words *Kyrie eleison* ("Lord, have mercy") and *Christe eleison* ("Christ, have mercy"), which were retained in a central Christian service (the Mass) in their Greek form.

Among the Greek Fathers were Clement of Alexandria, Origen, St. Basil, and St. John Chrysostom. The principal Latin Fathers were St. Ambrose, St. Augustine, and St. Jerome. All of these writers carried the highly developed Jewish tradition of biblical exegesis and commentary into the Christian context. Origen and St. Jerome worked particularly to determine the canonical texts of the Bible. St. Jerome (c. 347–420), who, like Augustine, was highly educated in Classical scholarship, is best known today for his translation into Latin of the Hebrew Bible and the Greek New Testament. For his work on the Jewish texts he learned Hebrew and consulted several rabbis. The resulting Latin Bible with all of these texts is known as the *Vulgate* (meaning common or popular edition); it was the standard Christian version for the entire medieval period (and, incidentally, until modern times).

The attitude of the Church Fathers towards music was an ambivalent one. We have already seen how Augustine struggled to justify his enjoyment of it, and there are echoes in some of the patristic literature of distinctly Platonic views and the necessity for control over musical endeavors. Many of the Fathers draw a strict line between the everyday music of the streets and theaters in the late Empire and the music of worship. Clement of Alexandria deplores the injury to souls caused by the decadent and impure music of banquets. St. John Chrysostom calls for a ban on the songs of actors and desires that only music leading to the glory of God and the propagation of the divine word be cultivated.

Instruments and dancing may once have played a role in the worship of the Church, as they did in older Jewish ceremonies, for statements abound condemning their use. Careful commentary was contrived to explain passages in scripture calling for instruments: what was meant by the "instrument" of worship was prayer, and the ten-stringed psaltery was said to be only a symbol for the Ten Commandments.

DEVELOPMENT OF THE LITURGY

The exact form of the liturgy in the early days of the Church is difficult to determine. There was continual growth and change in the first few centuries of the Church's history, and moreover several different forms were developing, some of which are still extant as individual variants of Eastern Orthodox Christianity (Coptic, Armenian, Syrian, etc.).

During the first three hundred years of the existence of the Church, two basic types of liturgical observance developed. They were quite distinct from one another. One involved the ritual celebration of the Last Supper and later became known as the Mass; the other centered on prayers, readings from scripture, and the singing of psalms and was later called the Office. In all the developing forms of Christianity these two types of service, the Mass and the Office, became standard. (In the Eastern churches the Mass is usually known as the Divine Liturgy or Offering.)

From the fourth century on, the increased tolerance of Christianity contributed to an enormous expansion in the Church. In the same way that different forms of liturgy developed between East and West, in the West alone different liturgical styles crystallized. These fall into two main groups: the Roman, which developed in the city that was the ancient center of the Empire, and the non-Roman, including such liturgies as the Celtic, Mozarabic, Ambrosian, and Gallican. However, whereas the Eastern liturgies were differentiated by language as well as by different ritual practices, the Western liturgies were all unified by a common language: Latin. In this sense, then, the different liturgies in the West may be said to have been regional varieties of a single practice.

These regional varieties almost all fell into disuse in the later Middle Ages as the Roman rite was adopted throughout Europe, but their diversity contributed certain elements to the history of the Church's liturgical music, which should be mentioned in this context.

The Celtic liturgy grew up in Ireland and Scotland and parts of southeastern England. Irish monasticism flourished in the sixth and seventh centuries, and not only did it contribute many treasures to the history of art—such as the *Lindisfarne Gospels* and the *Book of Kells*—it was also responsible for the founding of the monastery of St. Gall in central Europe, where a large number of early manuscripts of notated music were written.

The Mozarabic liturgy developed in Spain and Portugal, and although it was suppressed in favor of the Roman rite in the eleventh century, it is still in use to this day in one chapel in the Cathedral of Toledo. Elements it has in common with the Roman liturgy include melodic formulas for the singing of psalms, a mixture of Latin and Greek texts, and a distinction between simple and more elaborate melodies depending upon the function of the music within the liturgy itself.

St. Ambrose of Milan gave his name to the Ambrosian liturgy, though the actual music that survives from this rite dates from as late as the twelfth century. We hear from Augustine and other sources, however, that Ambrose introduced the practice of singing psalms in antiphonal manner

Illuminated page from the Lindisfarne Gospels, British Library, London.

(two groups singing in regular alternation) and the Eastern custom of singing hymns (non-Biblical strophic songs) in the service. These hymns were newly written and marked an important stage in the expansion of the liturgy.

The Gallican rite was the liturgy in use in the Roman province of Gaul, a province which covered an area corresponding to most of modern France, Belgium, Switzerland, and part of Germany. This area became the kingdom of the Franks, the largest unified realm in medieval Europe. The Gallican rite included some elaborate melodies and ceremonies, some of which found their way into the Roman rite when it was adopted in the Frankish kingdom. The resulting synthesis is even believed to have influenced the liturgy back at Rome, after the Frankish kingdom reached its zenith under Charlemagne at the end of the eighth century.

Other forms of the Christian liturgy have been identified from this period, each with its own type of music and ritual. These include the Ravenna rite, the Benevantan rite from southern Italy, and music of the so-

Map showing the extent of the Frankish Kingdom in early ninth-century Europe.

called Old Roman repertory, whose relationship to the Roman rite is still very much a subject for debate. In general it must be remembered that in the Middle Ages, when travel was slow and difficult, and contact between different regions was infrequent, many different forms of religious worship could become established simultaneously. From one town to another, even from one church to another, the rituals and practices of liturgical observance could vary to a considerable extent. Especially at a time when music was not yet written down, the form of even a single melody could develop in different ways in different places. Even after the general establishment of the Roman rite throughout the West, slightly different local versions of the liturgy could be identified in places such as Salisbury and York in England, or Lyons in France. These local versions are known as "uses." Some became quite influential, such as the Sarum Use (called thus from a corruption of *Sarisburia*—Latin for Salisbury), which spread throughout England in the thirteenth and fourteenth centuries. And there were many others. In fact, complex though this discussion of liturgies may seem, it represents a much simplified version of the actual state of affairs in the varied history of the early liturgy of the Christian Church.

CHARLEMAGNE

One of the most important elements in the stabilization and regularization of these disparate liturgies was the rise to power of Charlemagne and the flourishing of his empire. The name Charlemagne is an Old French version of the Latin *Carolus Magnus,* meaning Charles the Great. Although the empire he forged (called "Carolingian") soon dissolved, it marked a high point in the revitalization of cultural and intellectual activity in Europe. Charlemagne spent much of his long reign (768–814) waging expansionist (and successful) wars, but he was also a brilliant diplomatist and legislator, a social reformer who wore simple clothes and led a frugal life, and even something of a theologian. If he was not himself very well educated, he believed passionately in the liberating power of study and he imported one of the most learned men of his time from England to take charge of education throughout his realm.

Alcuin had been head of the important cathedral school at York, and was both flattered and challenged by the task of reforming an entire culture in a kingdom where books were scarce and learning had become enfeebled. Charlemagne, the king and warrior, treated Alcuin with deference and respect, and Alcuin admired the lofty aims and passionate desire for learning in his charismatic king. "I loved so much in you," wrote Alcuin, "what you were seeking in me."

In 800 Charlemagne was crowned emperor in the ancient Roman tradition. This consolidated his claim to the largest realm in western Eu-

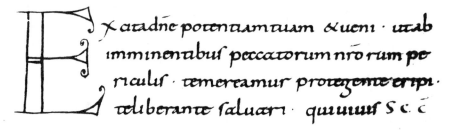

Example from the ninth century of the clear and elegant script known as "Caroline minuscule," which evolved during the reign of Charlemagne, Landes- und Stadtbibliothek, Düsseldorf.

rope, and made permanent the division between the Byzantine empire in the East and the one later known as the Holy Roman Empire in the West. Henceforth, emperors, claiming succession to the ancient Roman empire, considered themselves the secular rulers of Christendom, as the popes were the spiritual rulers.

Charlemagne's great unified realm did not last long after his death. Divided into separate kingdoms, it once again became disputed territory, ultimately evolving into the two countries we know now as France and Germany. Charlemagne's great task, however, had been unification, and an important part of this task involved the chant and liturgy of the Church. Roman and Frankish chants were consolidated and spread throughout the empire, disparate elements were resolved, and a systematic method of classification was developed. During his reign musical notation also evolved, which encouraged stable preservation and transmission of a repertoire which until that time had depended upon memorization and repetition. The music that has come down to us, therefore, from the first eight hundred years of the history of the Church is the result of centuries of development in fluid form, amalgamated for political reasons into a more or less unified whole, and crystallized at one point in its evolution.

MUSIC IN THE LITURGY

The central role of music in the liturgy of the early Church was that of a vehicle for words: music was to carry the words of worship to the people and also to God. For the recitation of a text among a group, the natural form of expression is that of a voice raised in pitch. From there it is a logical step to the creation of melodic variants which will delineate, for clarity and comprehension, the sentence structure of the text. This technique was already highly developed in Jewish synagogue worship, which may have begun to replace Temple worship after the destruction of the First Temple (586 B.C.) and received special impetus after the Romans destroyed the Second Temple in the year 70.

In the synagogues, which were houses of education and study as well as houses of worship, the central form of religious observance was the recitation of sacred texts. This was performed by members of the congregation rather than by a rabbi or priest, and involved readings from the five Books of Moses and the Prophets, in a standard order and through a fixed cycle. Actual melodies or recitation formulas have not survived from this period, but sixth-century notational signs show that this musical declamation closely reflected the sentence and phrase structure of the text.

The singing of a small number of psalms, especially the group Nos. 113–118, known as *Hallel* (psalms of praise), was also a part of synagogue worship. Although the way these were rendered in music at the time is not known, the structure of the poetry, with each verse divided into two parallel halves (a device common to all ancient Hebrew poetry), suggests that they might have been sung responsorially—the congregation responding to a cantor—or antiphonally—two groups alternating at each verse. The beginning of Psalm 96 illustrates well the division of verses into parallel halves and the resulting possibilities for responsorial or antiphonal singing:

Psalm 96

> O sing unto the Lord a new song;
> > sing unto the Lord all the earth.
> Sing unto the Lord, bless his name;
> > show forth his salvation from day to day.
> Declare his glory among the heathen,
> > his wonders among all people. . . .

In all of the variants of the liturgy in the early centuries of the church, and in the Roman rite which came to be the standard Christian liturgy of the West, music was a factor that was inherent in the worship service. Music carried the words of scripture and ritual; it distinguished between the different functions of the texts; it delineated parts of the service; and it heightened and intensified the rhetorical quality of the words. Almost no sections of any service in the medieval liturgy were performed without music, and the few that were, such as prayers spoken in silence by the priest, were particularly distinguished by their non-musical form. Music did not accompany the liturgy; it was part of the liturgy.

In order to understand the wide range of styles in the liturgical music of the Middle Ages, one must understand the nature of the services—their intent, form, and structure. Before we turn to them, however, some discussion of terminology as it applies to the music of the liturgy will be helpful.

The huge quantity of monophonic, or single-line, melodies that make up the first and largest musical repertory of the Middle Ages is sometimes known collectively as Gregorian chant. It takes its name from the brilliant and charismatic pope St. Gregory I (c. 540–604; pope 590–604).

Like many of the distinguished figures already mentioned, Gregory was an educated Roman citizen and statesman. At the age of thirty, he was appointed Prefect of Rome. His spiritual dedication, however, encouraged him to convert his house into a monastery. He served in the important position of papal representative to Constantinople for seven years before returning to Rome, where he was elected pope. During his papacy, he greatly strengthened the power of his office, bringing the prestige of the pope in line with that of the emperor. He was an accomplished administrator and organizer, and was the author of many influential tracts. His *Dialogues,* which recount the lives of the saints, remained popular throughout the Middle Ages. Together with Ambrose, Augustine, and Jerome, he is known as one of the four Doctors of the Church.

Traditionally Gregory is supposed to have composed the entire body of liturgical chants at the bidding of the Holy Spirit, and he is often depicted in miniatures of the Middle Ages writing or dictating music. By the ninth century the church melodies were already known as "Gregorian," and the legends about Gregory were becoming established, including the claim that he had founded the *Schola Cantorum* or papal choir. Even if his activities were not so extensive, his name has served as a focal point of musical identification for over a thousand years.

The disadvantage of retaining the traditional term "Gregorian" for the entire corpus of Western chant is that it tends to distort the historical position of the enormous amount of music that was composed in later centuries. Liturgical chant continued to be composed in quantity throughout the Middle Ages and later, some melodies being written as late as the seventeenth and eighteenth centuries. Thus it seems less misleading to refer to this music simply as chant or plainchant (another term often used, although, as has been mentioned before, the music is anything but plain). It became known as plainchant from the fact that it is performed unaccompanied, in unison, and without clearly definable rhythm. But, as we shall see, within the confines of these limits plainchant can represent some of the most subtle and sophisticated music in our history.

PLAINCHANT

During the fifteen hundred years or so during which most of the plainchant repertory developed, tens of thousands of melodies were composed. The sheer size of the repertory has created difficulties for modern scholars attempting to gain an understanding of this music. Yet a great deal of work has been done. Although some questions remain unanswered, especially those having to do with the relationship between various versions and historical revisions of chant, an overall view of styles, functions, and qualities of the plainchant repertory is possible. It must be remembered, however, that with a body of music of this size, generated over such a long period of time, simplification of complex trends and broad generalizations are a necessity. The subject of Western chant alone has produced a modern bibliography of over nine hundred items: books, catalogues, indices, monographs, and scholarly articles. Here we can only touch upon the surface of the topic.

Text and Music

Chant melodies are vocal settings of texts. This must not be forgotten, for in the liturgy word and music are indissolubly connected. The music is composed to words, which form grammatical units of sense, and the music reflects this sense. This does not mean that the music is "emotive" in the modern usage of the term, nor does it mean that the music indulges in "word painting" as in the Renaissance and Baroque eras (although instances of both of these practices can be cited). It means rather that in the clearest possible way the music is tied to the *structure* of the text, illuminating and clarifying the grammatical sense.

Let us examine a chant for the reading of the Gospel in the Mass service, recalling that the simplest and most audible way of rendering a text to an assembled group is to sing the text upon a heightened pitch. The earliest chants must simply have been repetitions of a single pitch for every syllable of the text (Ex. 3-1a).

EXAMPLE 3-1 a–f Chant for the Gospel of the Mass.

(a)

Di - xit Je - sus di - sci - pu - lis su - is: vos es - tis sal ter - rae.

Dixit Jesus discipulis suis: vos estis sal   Jesus said to his disciples: You are the
    terrae.   salt of the earth.

From there it was not a difficult step to add small inflections to such a line to represent the end of a sentence (Ex. 3-1b), or to indicate the beginning of the whole reading (Ex. 3-1c), or the end (Ex. 3-1d), or even to represent in the music the form of a question (Ex. 3-1e).

Di - xit Je - sus di - sci - pu - lis su - is: vos es - tis sal ter - rae.

Dixit Jesus discipulis suis: vos estis sal terrae.

Jesus said to his disciples: You are the salt of the earth.

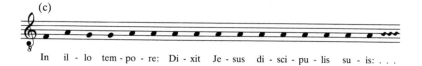

In il - lo tem - po - re: Di - xit Je - sus di - sci - pu - lis su - is: . . .

In illo tempore: Dixit Jesus discipulis suis . . .

At that time Jesus said to his disciples . . .

. . . i - ste ma - gnus vo - ca - bi - tur in re - gno cae - lo - rum.

. . . iste magnus vocabitur in regno caelorum.

. . . he will be considered great in the kingdom of heaven.

Quod si sal e - va - nu - e - rit, in quo sa - li - e - tur?

Quod si sal evanuerit, in quo salietur?

And if salt loses its saltiness, of what use is it?

For long sentences, the halfway point (at "commas") can also be indicated by the music, by ending those phrases on a different pitch and with a different formula than those used for the ends of sentences. The complete chant then reflects the entire grammatical structure of the text (Ex. 3-1f).[1]

---

[1]Throughout this book the presentation and layout of the musical examples has been designed to display as clearly as possible the form and structure of the originals.

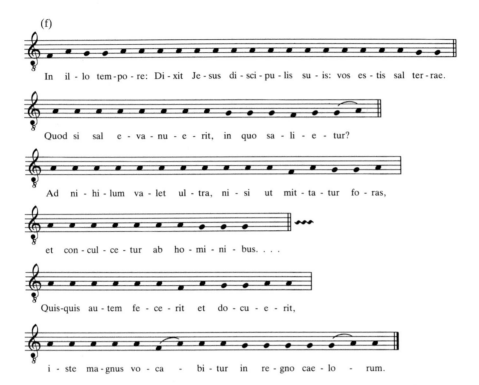

(f)

In il - lo tem - po - re: Di - xit Je - sus di - sci - pu - lis su - is: vos es - tis sal ter - rae.

Quod si sal e - va - nu - e - rit, in quo sa - li - e - tur?

Ad ni - hi - lum va - let ul - tra, ni - si ut mit - ta - tur fo - ras,

et con - cul - ce - tur ab ho - mi - ni - bus. . . .

Quis-quis au - tem fe - ce - rit et do - cu - e - rit,

i - ste ma - gnus vo - ca - bi - tur in re - gno cae - lo - rum.

In illo tempore: Dixit Jesus discipulis suis: vos estis sal terrae.	At that time: Jesus said to his disciples: You are the salt of the earth.
Quod si sal evanuerit, in quo salietur?	And if salt loses its saltiness, of what use is it?
Ad nihilum valet ultra, nisi ut mittatur foras,	It is worthless, except to be thrown outdoors,
et conculcetur ab hominibus. . . .	and trodden underfoot by men. . . .
Quisquis autem fecerit et docuerit,	But if anyone follows my precepts and teaches them to others,
iste magnus vocabitur in regno caelorum.	he will be considered great in the kingdom of heaven.

In another chant from the liturgy (Ex. 3-2), we notice that although the musical inflections are different, the same overall pattern of opening and closing formulas, half endings, full endings, and question formulas is used as in the previous one.

EXAMPLE 3-2   Chant for the Gospel of the Mass.

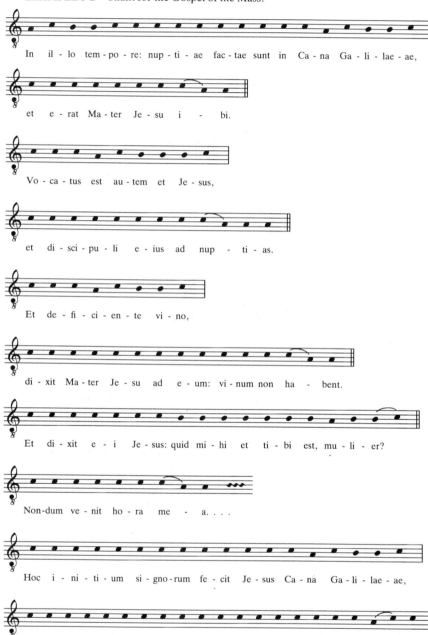

In il - lo tem - po - re: nup - ti - ae fac - tae sunt in Ca - na Ga - li - lae - ae,

et   e - rat Ma - ter Je - su i - bi.

Vo - ca - tus est au - tem et Je - sus,

et di - sci - pu - li e - ius ad nup - ti - as.

Et de - fi - ci - en - te vi - no,

di - xit Ma - ter Je - su ad e - um: vi - num non ha - bent.

Et di - xit e - i Je - sus: quid mi - hi et ti - bi est, mu - li - er?

Non-dum ve - nit ho - ra me - a. . . .

Hoc i - ni - ti - um si - gno-rum fe - cit Je - sus Ca - na Ga - li - lae - ae,

Et ma - ni - fe-stam fe - cit glo - ri - am su - am et cre - di - de-runt in e - um

di - sci - pu - li e - ius.

In illo tempore: nuptiae factae sunt in
    Cana Galilaeae,
et erat Mater Jesu ibi.
Vocatus est autem et Jesus,
et discipuli eius ad nuptias.

Et deficiente vino,
dixit Mater Jesu ad eum: vinum non
    habent.
Et dixit ei Jesus: quid mihi et tibi est,
    mulier?
Nondum venit hora mea. . . .
Hoc initium signorum fecit Jesus Cana
    Galilaeae,
et manifestam fecit gloriam suam et
    crediderunt in eum discipuli eius.

At that time there was a wedding at
    Cana in Galilee,
and the mother of Jesus was there.
Jesus was also invited
together with his disciples to the
    wedding.
And when the wine ran out,
Jesus' mother said to him: They have no
    more wine.
And Jesus said to her: Of what concern
    is that to you and me, woman?
My hour has not yet come. . . .
This sign at Cana in Galilee was the first
    of the signs that Jesus made,
and he made manifest his glory, and his
    disciples believed in him.

There are several such chants in the liturgy, in which most of the text is sung upon a single pitch. This pitch is known as the "reciting tone," and it serves to provide a stable anchor around which brief grammatical flourishes may move. This pitch is retained in the ear, with the result that the direction of the musical line may be judged against it. In the following chant (Ex. 3-3) the reciting tone is A. A feeling of incompletion is created at the ends of the half sentences by ending them on G, but the ends of the full sentences return to the reciting tone A.

EXAMPLE 3-3   Chant for the Oratio of the Mass.

Pre - ces po - pu - li tu - i, quae - su - mus Do - mi - ne, cle - men - ter e - xau - di,

et qui iu - ste pro pec - ca - tis no - stris af - fli - gi - mur, pro tu - i no - mi - nis glo - ri - a

mi - se - ri - cor - di - ter li - be - re - mur.

Per Do - mi - num no - strum Je - sum Chri - stum, Fi - li - um tu - um,

qui te-cum vi-vit et re-gnat in u-ni-ta-te Spi-ri-tus San-cti De-us.

Per om-ni-a sae-cu-la sae-cu-lo - rum. A-men.

Preces populi tui, quaesumus Domine, clementer exaudi,	Hear the prayers of your people magnanimously, we request O Lord,
et qui iuste pro pecatis nostris affligimur, pro tui nominis gloria misericorditer liberemur.	and may we, who are justly punished for our sins, be mercifully released for the glory of your name.
Per Dominum nostrum Jesum Christum, Filium tuum,	Through our Lord Jesus Christ, your Son,
qui tecum vivit et regnat in unitate Spiritus Sancti Deus.	who lives and rules with you as God in the unity of the Holy Spirit.
Per omnia saecula saeculorum. Amen.	For ever and ever. Amen.

In Example 3-4 a longer-range plan is in effect. Although the half sentences return to the reciting tone C, the whole sentences end on B, and the final C is not reached until the end of the entire chant. Example 3-4a is one sentence from this chant. The reciting tone is C and the formula for the half sentence returns to that pitch. But the end of the sentence has a melodic inflection that ends on B (Ex. 3-4b). The feeling of incompletion that this creates is not resolved until the conclusion of the entire chant, when the C is definitively reached (Ex. 3-4c). Example 3-4d is the chant in its entirety.

EXAMPLE 3-4 a–d   Chant for the Epistle of the Mass.

(a)

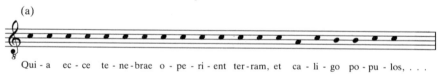

Qui-a ec-ce te-ne-brae o-pe-ri-ent ter-ram, et ca-li-go po-pu-los, . . .

Quia ecce tenebrae operient terram, et caligo populos, . . .	For behold, shadows will cover the earth, and darkness will cover the people, . . .

(b)

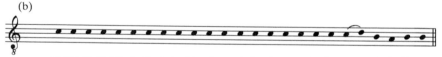

. . . su-per te au-tem o-ri-e-tur Do-mi-nus, et glo-ri-a e-ius in te   vi-de-bi-tur.

. . . super te autem orietur Dominus, et . . . but the Lord will rise above you,
gloria eius in te videbitur. and his glory will be seen on you.

(c)

Om - nes de Sa - ba ve - ni - ent, au - rum et tus de - fe - ren - tes,

et lau - dem Do - mi - no an - nun - ti - an - tes.

Omnes de Saba venient, aurum et tus Everyone will come from Sheba, bring-
deferentes, ing gold and incense,
et laudem Domino annuntiantes. and announcing praise to the Lord.

(d)

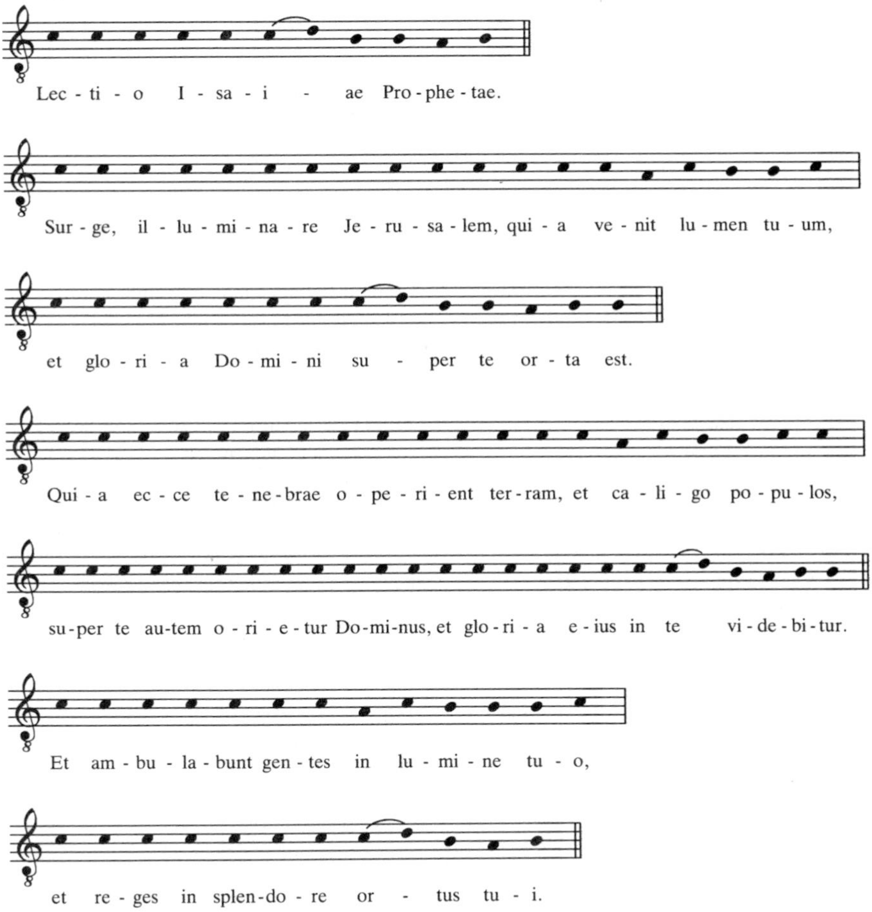

Lec - ti - o I - sa - i - ae Pro - phe - tae.

Sur - ge, il - lu - mi - na - re Je - ru - sa - lem, qui - a ve - nit lu - men tu - um,

et glo - ri - a Do - mi - ni su - per te or - ta est.

Qui - a ec - ce te - ne - brae o - pe - ri - ent ter - ram, et ca - li - go po - pu - los,

su - per te au - tem o - ri - e - tur Do - mi - nus, et glo - ri - a e - ius in te vi - de - bi - tur.

Et am - bu - la - bunt gen - tes in lu - mi - ne tu - o,

et re - ges in splen - do - re or - tus tu - i.

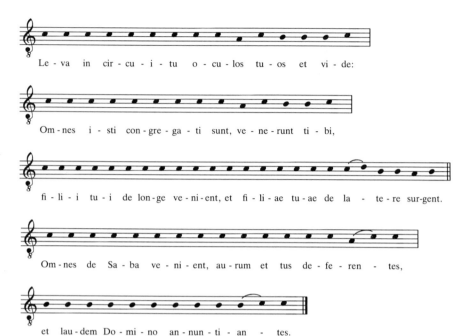

Le - va in cir - cu - i - tu o - cu - los tu - os et vi - de:

Om - nes i - sti con - gre - ga - ti sunt, ve - ne - runt ti - bi,

fi - li - i tu - i de lon - ge ve - ni - ent, et fi - li - ae tu - ae de la - te - re sur-gent.

Om - nes de Sa - ba ve - ni - ent, au - rum et tus de - fe - ren - tes,

et lau - dem Do - mi - no an - nun - ti - an - tes.

Lectio Isaiae Prophetae.	A reading from Isaiah the Prophet.
Surge, illuminare Jerusalem, quia venit lumen tuum,	Arise and shine, Jerusalem, for your light has come,
et gloria Domini super te orta est.	and the glory of the Lord has risen above you.
Quia ecce tenebrae operient terram, et caligo populos,	For behold, shadows will cover the earth, and darkness will cover the people,
super te autem orietur Dominus, et gloria eius in te videbitur.	but the Lord will rise above you, and his glory will be seen on you.
Et ambulabunt gentes in lumine tuo,	And nations will walk in your light,
et reges in splendore ortus tui.	and kings in the splendor of your rising.
Leva in circuitu oculos tuos et vide:	Lift your eyes up round about and see:
Omnes isti congregati sunt, venerunt tibi,	They have all gathered together and have come to you;
filii tui de longe venient, et filiae tuae de latere surgent.	your sons will come from far away, and your daughters will raise themselves up from your side.
Omnes de Saba venient, aurum et tus deferentes,	Everyone will come from Sheba bringing gold and incense,
et laudem Domino annuntiantes.	and announcing praise to the Lord.

These examples, simple though they may be, demonstrate two very important facets of plainchant. One is the unity of text and music in this repertory: the notes mirror the structure of the text. The other is the ability of the music to create pitch centers, even though it is monophonic. It is crucial to realize that chant, despite being constructed out of a single line of music, depends upon a highly developed, fluid system of pitch goals and expectations. Composers could exploit these for artistic purposes and manipulate them both in obvious and, sometimes, in extremely subtle ways. The pitch system of the Middle Ages was not the same as that of later music, but it was at least as logical, and in many ways more colorful, as we shall see.

The use of a reciting tone is evident in many chants in the Mass and Office services. One particularly noteworthy use is in the singing of psalms in the Office. Psalms are written, as we have seen, in verses that are divided into parallel halves. When most of the text is sung to a reciting tone, and the half verses and full verses are indicated by different melodic formulas, the structure of the poetry becomes very clear. Here some of the text of Psalm 113 is laid out with the half endings and the full endings indicated:

Psalm 113

> When Israel went out of Egypt, (*half ending*)
> > the house of Jacob from an alien people; (*full ending*)
> Judah was his sanctuary, (*half ending*)
> > and Israel his dominion. (*full ending*)
> The sea saw it and fled: (*half ending*)
> > Jordan was driven back. (*full ending*)
> The mountains skipped like rams, (*half ending*)
> > and the little hills like lambs. (*full ending*)

Example 3-5 shows how the music exactly parallels this structure.

EXAMPLE 3-5 Psalm 113, verses 1–4.

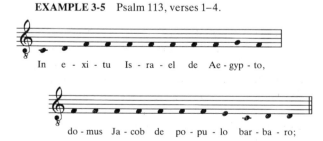

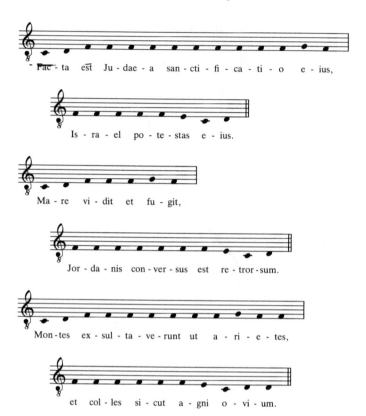

In exitu Israel de Aegypto,	When Israel went out of Egypt,
domus Jacob de populo barbaro;	the house of Jacob from an alien people;
Facta est Judaea sanctificatio eius,	Judah was his sanctuary,
Israel potestas eius.	and Israel his dominion.
Mare vidit et fugit,	The sea saw it and fled,
Jordanis conversus est retrorsum.	Jordan was driven back.
Montes exsultaverunt ut arietes,	The mountains skipped like rams,
et colles sicut agni ovium.	and the little hills like lambs.

This way of singing psalms became closely and traditionally associated with the psalms themselves, so that when certain verses of psalms appear in other parts of the liturgy (which they often do), the music is commonly in this format of reciting tone with closing formulas. For example, the first verse of Psalm 138 is used as a part of the Introit (the opening chant) of the Mass for Easter, and is sung there in such a format. Example 3-6a shows the original psalm verse with its formulaic music. A small inflection at the beginning of each half line leads into the reciting tone A; both the half verse and the full verse end with their distinguishing formulas. Example 3-6b shows the Introit chant from the Mass for Easter Sunday. The psalm verse (indicated by the abbreviation V. for "verse") that is part of this chant uses the same music as in Example 3-6a.

EXAMPLE 3-6 (a) Psalm verse; (b) Introit of the Mass for Easter Sunday.

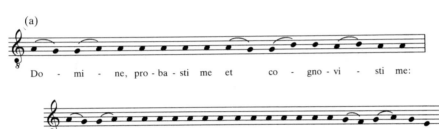

(a)

Do - mi - ne, pro - ba - sti me et co - gno - vi - sti me:

tu co - gno - vi - sti ses - si - o - nem me-am et re - sur - rec - ti - o - nem me-am.

| Domine, probasti me et cognovisti me: | O Lord, you have tested me and now you know me: |
| tu cognovisti sessionem meam et resurrectionem meam. | you know my sitting down and my rising up. |

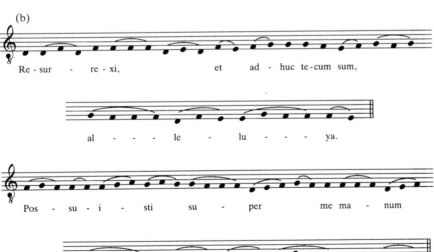

(b)

Re - sur - re - xi, et ad - huc te - cum sum,

al - le - lu - ya.

Pos - su - i - sti su - per me ma - num

tu - am, al - le - lu - ya.

Mi - ra - - - bi - lis fac - ta   est sci - en - ti - a

tu - a, al - le - lu - ya,   al - le - lu - ya.

℣. Do - mi - ne, pro - ba - sti me et   co - gno - vi - sti me:

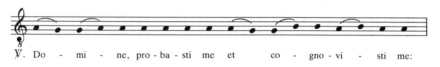

tu   co - gno - vi - sti ses - si - o - nem me - am et re - sur - rec - ti - o - nem   me - am.

Glo - ri - a Pa - tri, et Fi - li - o, et Spi - ri - tu - i San - cto,

si - cut   e - rat in prin - ci - pi - o, et   nunc,   et sem - per,

et   in   sae - cu - la sae - cu - lo - rum.   A - men.

Re - sur - - re - xi, . . .

Resurrexi, et adhuc tecum sum,
   alleluya.
Posuisti super me manum tuam,
   alleluya.
Mirabilis facta est scientia tua,
   alleluya, alleluya.

I have arisen, and I am still with you,
   alleluya.
You have placed your hand upon me,
   alleluya.
Your knowledge has become won-
   drous, alleluya, alleluya.

℣. Domine, probasti me et cognovisti me:
tu cognovisti sessionem meam et resurrectionem meam.
Gloria Patri, et Filio, et Spiritui Sancto,
sicut erat in principio, et nunc, et semper,
et in saecula saeculorum. Amen.

Resurrexi, . . .

℣. O Lord, you have tested me and now you know me:
you know my sitting down and my rising up.
Glory to the Father, and to the Son, and to the Holy Spirit,
as it was in the beginning, both now and always,
and for ever. Amen.

I have arisen, . . .

Another part of the Easter Introit is also sung to the same pattern as the psalm verse. This part, which begins "Gloria Patri . . .," is sung at the end of every psalm. It is sung to exactly the same formula as the psalm and acts in every respect as though it were part of the psalm; since it comes at the end it receives the concluding musical ending. This text is known either as the *Gloria Patri* or as the Lesser Doxology. Doxology means "the saying of glory," and there are several different Christian doxologies. The Lesser Doxology is, however, of the most frequent occurrence, as it is used at the end of every psalm and in the Introit of every Mass.

These kinds of chants, based mostly on a reciting tone and with small formulas for beginnings and endings, are obviously amongst the simplest chants musically. They may be called *recitational* in style. The next simplest style of chant is *syllabic*—in which there is a real melody, as opposed to the basic monotone of the recitational style, but in which almost every syllable receives only one note. Within this style of chant there is a considerable range of melodies from the simple to the elaborate. All share the characteristic of having mostly a single note for each syllable of text.

A simple syllabic chant is the *Pater Noster,* part of which is given as Example 3-7. Here the melody moves within a narrow range of a fourth (G–C) and is confined almost exclusively to conjunct motion. Notice that here too, as in the recitational chants, the sentence structure is reflected in the pitch endings of each phrase. The half phrases all end on G, an incomplete sound in the context of the chant, but the endings of whole sentences are on A, a sound of finality.

EXAMPLE 3-7 *Pater Noster,* beginning only.

Pa - ter no - ster, qui es in cae - lis,

san - cti - fi - ce - tur no - men tu - um.

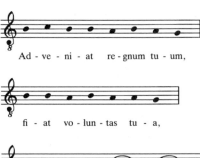

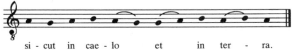

Pater noster, qui es in caelis,   Our Father, you who are in heaven,
sanctificetur nomen tuum.   may your name be made holy.
Adveniat regnum tuum,   May your kingdom come,
fiat voluntas tua,   and your will be done,
sicut in caelo et in terra.   on earth as it is in heaven.

A very large number of chants are written in syllabic style. A slightly more elaborate chant, covering the range of an octave within its short time span, but still primarily syllabic, is the hymn *Rerum Deus Tenax Vigor,* the first stanza of which is given as Example 3-8.

EXAMPLE 3-8   Hymn, *Rerum Deus Tenax Vigor,* first stanza.

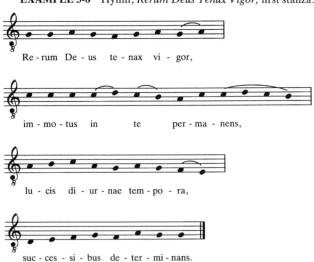

Rerum Deus tenax vigor,	O God, the conserving force of all things,
immotus in te permanens,	unmoveable and unchangeable,
lucis diurnae tempora,	who throughout the hours of every day,
successibus determinans.	does order life's procession.

Both the *Pater Noster* and the hymn contain a few syllables that are each given a small group of notes. This is quite common in chants that are otherwise mostly syllabic. These groups of notes are notated in the medieval manuscripts in symbols called *neumes*. Many of the more elaborate syllabic chants contain several neumes, such as the Gloria chant from which Example 3-9 is drawn.

EXAMPLE 3-9 Gloria, beginning only.

Glo - ri - a in ex - cel - sis De - o.

Et in ter - ra pax ho - mi - ni - bus bo - nae vo - lun - ta - tis.

Lau - da - mus te.

Be - ne - di - ci - mus te.

A - do - ra - mus te.

Glo - ri - fi - ca - mus te.

Gra-ti - as a - gi-mus ti - bi prop-ter ma-gnam glo - ri - am tu - am. . . .

Gloria in excelsis Deo.	Glory to God in the highest.
Et in terra pax hominibus bonae voluntatis.	And on earth peace to men of good will.
Laudamus te.	We praise you.
Benedicimus te.	We bless you.
Adoramus te.	We adore you.
Glorificamus te.	We glorify you.
Gratias agimus tibi propter magnam gloriam tuam. . . .	We give thanks to you on account of your great glory. . . .

When a chant contains mostly neumes for the syllables of its text it is known as *neumatic*. The Sanctus chant given as Example 3-10 has most syllables of its text set to neumes. Occasional words or parts of words are set syllabically ("Domini," for example), but the neumes far outnumber the single notes. As can be seen, neumes can contain different numbers of notes. In the Sanctus the smallest neume has two notes and the largest has ten.

EXAMPLE 3-10   Sanctus.

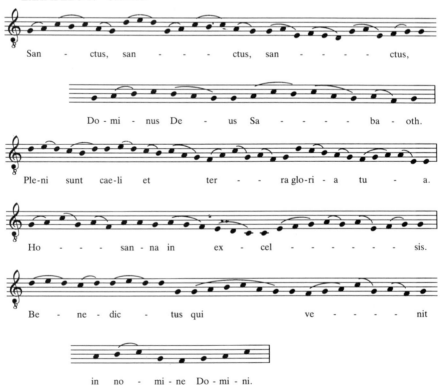

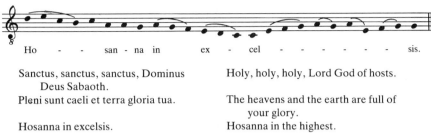

Ho - - san - na in ex - cel - - - - - - - sis.

Sanctus, sanctus, sanctus, Dominus Deus Sabaoth.	Holy, holy, holy, Lord God of hosts.
Pleni sunt caeli et terra gloria tua.	The heavens and the earth are full of your glory.
Hosanna in excelsis.	Hosanna in the highest.
Benedictus qui venit in nomine Domini.	Blessed is he who comes in the name of the Lord.
Hosanna in excelsis.	Hosanna in the highest.

The dividing line between a syllabic chant that has several neumes and a neumatic chant that has some syllabic writing is obviously not clear cut. Nevertheless, these categories are useful ways of classifying a large number of chants.

A fourth style of chant is known as *melismatic*. A *melisma* is a long, florid collection of notes given to a single syllable of text. Melismatic chant is usually basically neumatic but includes elaborate melismas, sometimes of twenty or thirty notes to a syllable. The Gradual for the Christmas Mass (Ex. 3-11) is highly melismatic. On the penultimate syllables of the words "meo" and "meis" the chant unwinds long melismas that cover thirty-seven and twenty-five notes respectively. That this is not "word painting" in the later sense of the term is made clear by the neutral force of both of these words in the text (the words are different forms of the possessive adjective meaning "my"). Melismas in chant are extraordinarily powerful, partly because they are usually *not* linked to the text. They are wordless, exuberant passages of pure music, which gain a special intensity from the inherent restraint of the chant in which they are contained.

EXAMPLE 3-11   Gradual of the Mass for Christmas.

Te - cum prin - ci - pi - - - - - - um in

di - - - - - - - - e

vir - tu - - - - - tis tu - - -

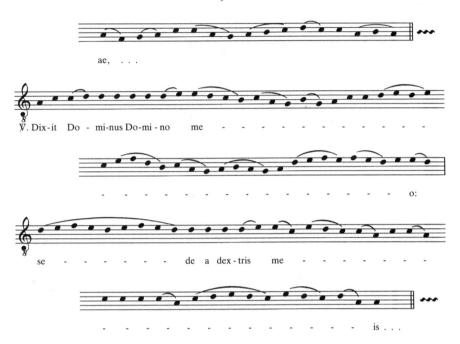

ae, . . .

℣. Dix-it Do - mi-nus Do-mi - no   me - - - - - - - - - - -

- - - - - - - - - - - - o:

se - - - - - - de a dex - tris   me - - - - - -

- - - - - - - - - - - - - is . . .

Tecum principium in die virtutis tuae . . .	With you is the beginning in the day of your virtue.
℣. Dixit Dominus Domino meo: sede a dextris meis . . .	℣. The Lord said to my Lord: sit at my right hand.

One particularly notable position for a melisma is at the final syllable "-ya" of the word "Alleluya" in the Alleluya chant of the Mass. Indeed, this melisma acquired a special name: the *jubilus* ("song of joy"). The word Alleluya is a transliteration of the Hebrew *Halleluyah* ("praise God"), and settings of this word were associated in the synagogue and early church with joyful expression.

EXAMPLE 3-12   Two Alleluyas, beginnings only, each with jubilus.

(a)

Al - le - lu - ya.

Alleluya.   Alleluya.

(b)

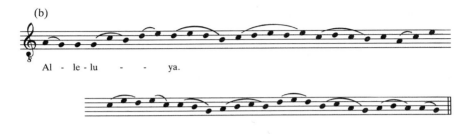

Al - le - lu - - ya.

Alleluya.   Alleluya.

Sometimes the jubilus is about twice as long as the first part of the Alleluya chant itself (Ex. 3-12a). Sometimes the jubilus can be several times longer and more elaborate than the opening of the chant (Ex. 3-12b).

The importance of this system of stylistic classification of chant according to the distribution of notes to text goes beyond its convenience as an analytical method. Some of these musical styles are associated with particular items in the liturgy, and are tied to the function of these items and their place in the service. In the Mass, for example, there is a place where there is a reading from one of the Gospels. This reading is always sung in recitational style. Hymns are almost invariably set to syllabic chant. The Introit (opening chant) of the Mass is usually neumatic. And the Gradual and Alleluia of the Mass are highly melismatic.

This distinction between different styles of chant is very important liturgically. As will be seen, each chant has its own particular place and function in the liturgy, and chants are classified by this liturgical function as well as by their music and text. In the Mass, for example, near the beginning of the service, a chant known as the Kyrie is always sung. In every Mass, at the same place in the Mass, a Kyrie is sung, and every Kyrie has the same words. However, there are a large number of Kyrie melodies, usually neumatic, and these different melodies may be sung on different occasions. As another example: near the middle of the Mass a chant known as the Gradual is sung. The Gradual always occurs at the same place in the Mass, and the music is usually melismatic, but the text and the actual musical setting change from day to day.

This points up a further facet of the relationship between text and music in the liturgy. Sometimes the text remains the same from service to service, and sometimes the text changes according to the day in the Church year. Sometimes there is music that is always associated with a particular text, and sometimes the music can change. It must be remembered that the Christian liturgy grew and developed over a period of many hundreds of years and in a very broad geographical area; its form is therefore quite complex. The matter of texts remaining the same or changing from day to day is a particularly important one in the history of the liturgy, and one that had considerable consequences on later musical developments. We shall deal with it by examining the two major forms of worship in the Christian liturgy—the Mass and the Office—in the next two chapters. First, however, we must discuss some further aspects of the nature of plainchant in general.

Shape and Melodic Style

In monophonic music, where the direction of the line is not obscured by other voices, the shape of a melody takes on particular importance. Also, when the range of the melody is relatively narrow, as it is in much of plainchant, the shape of the line impresses itself particularly clearly upon the senses.

Often chant melodies take the form of an arch. This may be a single arch, as in Example 3-13a, or a double or even a triple arch, as in Example 3-13b. A particularly frequent device is a steep ascent, often by leap, at the beginning of the melody, followed by a slowly descending line or series of waves (Ex. 3-13c). What is common, however, to all these shapes, and to the many complex combinations and variants of them that exist is an ending that is low in the range, giving a sense of completion and repose.

EXAMPLE 3-13   Arch forms in chant: (a) Benedicamus Domino, beginning only; (b) Kyrie, second phrase only; (c) Antiphon, beginning only.

(a)

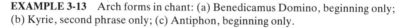

Be - ne - di - ca - mus Do - - - - - - - - - - - - - mi - no.

Benedicamus Domino.   Let us bless the Lord.

(b)

Chris - te,

e - le - - i - son.

Christe, eleison.   Christ, have mercy.

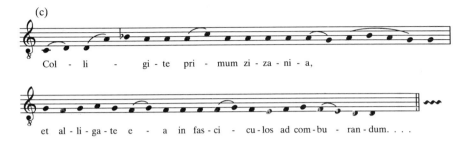

Colligite primum zizania,
et alligate ea in fasciculos ad com-
    burendum. . . .

First collect the weeds,
and put them into bundles for burn-
    ing. . . .

This distinction between intensity and repose is vital to the quality of plainchant. It is at a level of considerable subtlety and refinement, in which a shift of a few notes can make a dramatic difference. In some chants, as we shall see, there is a contrast in performance between music intended for a group of singers (the choir) and music for soloists. Frequently found in this type of chant is a subtle intensification of the solo lines by their being placed slightly higher in range than the surrounding choral music—set, as it were, in relief against a slightly darker background.

A further aspect of the shape of the chant is the intervallic construction of the melodies themselves. Chant melodies are predominantly composed of conjunct lines, with movement in seconds. Leaps are relatively rare; thus, when they do occur, they take on special import. Thirds are the most frequent, both ascending and descending. The most common melodic style in plainchant, therefore, is of conjunct motion varied by some intervals of a third. Fourths and fifths are not common, and they occur mostly ascending. Upward leaps of a fourth or fifth are often followed by a compensating line that is mostly conjunct, as we have seen in Example 3-13c. Larger leaps are rare indeed.

Another important element is the use of melodic motifs. Some chant melodies appear to have been composed from a small number of motifs, which are assembled, juxtaposed, combined, and recombined in a flexible and fluid manner. These motifs may be used as building blocks for a single melody. They may also often be found in several different melodies of the same type, for example in several Graduals. The use of similar motifs for chants of the same type extends even to the apparent existence of standard melody forms, which seem to have been used as frameworks for the creation of chant melodies and could be adapted to different texts.

Within a single melody, the motif may range from a simple cadential formula to larger units. In the Communion chant given as Example 3-14, both phrases end with the same cadential formula (marked x)—a neumatic ending on E ("[de]disti" and "mea"). A slight variant of this formula appears also at an earlier grammatical pause in the text, on the word "Domine" (x').

EXAMPLE 3-14   Communion.

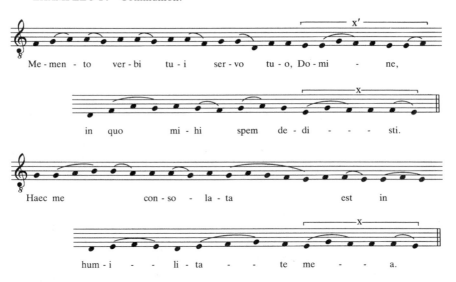

Memento verbi tui servo tuo, Domine,	Remember your word to your servant, O
in quo mihi spem dedisti.	Lord, which gave me hope.
Haec me consolata est in humilitate	It was this that gave me comfort in my
mea.	trouble.

In the Tract given as Example 3-15, three whole phrases, each in arch form (marked x, y, and z), are repeated in the course of the melody. This time the repetition is *across* the grammatical units of the text, even at one point dividing a word ("protector"), thus creating a tension between the two constructional elements. The large-scale phrase repetition provides an overall sense of unity to the music.

EXAMPLE 3-15 Tract, respond only.

Can - te - - mus Do - - mi - no,

x

glo - ri - o - se e - - - nim

y

ho - no - ri - fi - - ca - - tus est,

z

e - quum et ar - cen - - so - - rem

x

pro - ie - cit in ma - - re,

y

ad - iu - tor et pro - tec - tor fac - tus est mi - hi in

z

sa - - - lu - - tem. . . .

Cantemus Domino, gloriose enim
 honorificatus est,
equum et ascensorem proiecit in mare,

adiutor et protector factus est mihi in
 salutem. . . .

Let us sing to the Lord, for he has been
 gloriously honored,
the horse and the chariot he has thrown
 into the sea,
he has become my helper and protector
 for my safety. . . .

In the previous two examples, phrase repetition is used for formal and structural purposes. As we shall see later in our analysis of some of the chants of the Mass, a melodic motif may also be used to highlight certain words in the text.

The Melodic Modes

In the eighth and ninth centuries a new system of analyzing plainchant was developed. The adoption of this system coincided with the stabilization of the liturgy in the West and the deliberate standardization of plainchant under Charlemagne. It also coincided with the development of musical notation—a practice which likewise had the effect of regularizing the repertoire. The system was an amalgamation of several different ingredients, including Byzantine melody classifications and Greek music theory as transmitted to the Middle Ages by Boethius and the early encyclopedic educators.

The system involved the classification of all melodies into four basic types or *modes*. These types were simply numbered according to their Greek names: *protus* ("first"), *deuterus* ("second"), *tritus* ("third"), and *tetrardus* ("fourth"). Protus melodies were those which ended on D, deuterus on E, tritus on F, and tetrardus on G. All four of these types could be further subdivided into pairs, called *authentic* ("leading") and *plagal* ("subsidiary"), depending on the range of the chant.

Many theorists discussed the modal system, and different solutions to analytical questions were suggested. The chant repertoire, which had developed over centuries, was now required to fit into a rationally conceived but necessarily limited scheme. The problem was solved in two ways: by assignment and by adaptation. Theorists assigned chants to one or other of the modes. If slightly different criteria were used, or if the chant itself were modally ambiguous, different assignments could result; and they occasionally did. Chants were also adapted to conform to the modal system: if a note or two was out of place, other notes were substituted. If a chant ended on the wrong pitch, it was rewritten to end on the right pitch.

By the eleventh century general agreement as to theoretical criteria had been achieved, and new chants were written in conformity with the prevailing system. The modal doctrine was given its classic formulation by the Italian theorist Guido of Arezzo (c. 990–1040), whose treatise *Mikrologus* ("Little Discussion") became widely known and was extensively copied throughout the Middle Ages.

The system of the melodic modes is often used as the primary tool of melodic analysis for medieval music. It must be remembered, however, that for some of the compositions in the chant repertoire, especially those of earlier origin, it is of only partial usefulness. For later music, especially that composed after the fullest development of the system, it can be uniquely enlightening.

The modal system in its most complete manifestation was based on the fourfold ending scheme cited above, in which the protus, deuterus, tritus, and tetrardus ending schemes were subdivided into authentic and plagal versions. These were numbered from 1 to 8, the authentic modes being given Greek names derived from the names of the Greek cities and states in ancient theory. The names of the plagal modes simply followed those of the authentic, with the addition of the designation *hypo* ("below"). This initial system is outlined in the chart below.

Protus (D)	Authentic	Mode 1	Dorian
	Plagal	Mode 2	Hypodorian
Deuterus (E)	Authentic	Mode 3	Phrygian
	Plagal	Mode 4	Hypophrygian
Tritus (F)	Authentic	Mode 5	Lydian
	Plagal	Mode 6	Hypolydian
Tetrardus (G)	Authentic	Mode 7	Mixolydian
	Plagal	Mode 8	Hypomixolydian

Later the designations were restricted to the modal numbers and the "ethnic" names. Also the eight modes began to be regarded as diatonic octave patterns, which were analyzed into their different species of fourth and fifth. The determining element in each of the different fourths and fifths of the modal octaves is, of course, the placement of the half step. It is this which characterizes both the individual species of the fourths and fifths and gives particular and distinct color to every one of the modes. In the Dorian fifth, for example, the half step comes between the second and third notes, between E and F. In the Lydian fifth, the half step comes between the fourth and fifth notes, between B and C.

It is the overall placement of the fourths and fifths which determines whether a mode is authentic or plagal. In the authentic modes the fourth occurs above the fifth, in the plagal modes it occurs below the fifth.

Modes are further characterized by the designation within each of a "reciting tone." This is the pitch upon which the recitation of a chant centers. In the hierarchy of modal designation the reciting tone is second in importance only to the very last note of the chant, the "final." After considerable disagreement, medieval theorists ultimately decided that modal classification would be determined by the final. If a chant ends on D, whatever else it does before that, then the mode must be either Mode 1, Dorian, or Mode 2, Hypodorian. The decision as to which of the two it is, the authentic Dorian or the plagal Hypodorian, is determined by the range of the chant, the placement of the fourth and fifth, and the reciting tone.

Example 3-16 gives all the modes, with their fourths and fifths marked and their finals and reciting tones designated. Two general observations may make it easier to remember some of the details of the system:

1. Each authentic/plagal pair shares the same final.
2. Authentic modes have their reciting tones a fifth above the final; plagal modes have their reciting tones a third above the final; all reciting tones that would in this way occur on B, however, are moved to C. The one exception to this pattern, is Mode 4, whose reciting tone is A instead of G.

EXAMPLE 3-16   The melodic modes.

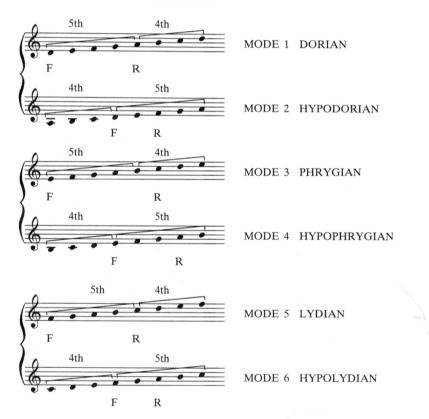

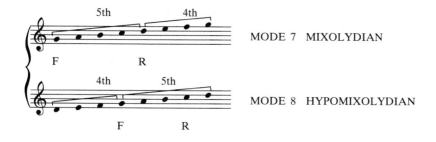

MODE 7 MIXOLYDIAN

MODE 8 HYPOMIXOLYDIAN

F = final   R = reciting tone

A brief discussion will exemplify some of these different elements. Let us examine Mode 1, Dorian, and Mode 2, Hypodorian. Mode 1 is authentic: it has the fourth above the fifth. The reciting tone is A. Mode 2, Hypodorian, is plagal: the fourth is below the fifth. Its reciting tone is F. The final of both modes is D.

Let us also examine a few short melodies in terms of this system of modal analysis. The melody in Example 3-17a opens with the fifth G–D and establishes the reciting tone D. It fills out the upper fourth of the mode, D–G, and its final is G. This melody therefore is clearly in Mode 7, Mixolydian.

EXAMPLES 3-17a–c Melodies exemplifying the melodic modes: (a) melody in Mode 7, Mixolydian; (b) melody in Mode 8, Hypomixolydian; (c) melody in Mode 3, Phrygian.

(a)

Example 3-17b, however, which also opens and cadences on G, has C as a reciting tone, and centers on the fourth D–G below the final. This melody would be classified as Mode 8, Hypomixolydian, the plagal version of the previous mode.

(b)

Because of the characteristic combination of final, reciting tone, range, and placement of half steps, each mode has its own special melodic quality. The Phrygian mode, Mode 3, is particularly distinctive because the final is approached from above by a half step. The melody of Example 3-17c is in Mode 3, Phrygian. Its final is E and its reciting tone is C.

(c)

Each of the eight modes has its own unique combination of characteristics. With such a broad palette, therefore, plainchant is immensely rich in colors. These colors are delicate, but distinct, and give the entire plainchant repertoire its unique character.

Another aspect of modal analysis must be considered here. A melody does not have to stay in a certain mode throughout its entire length. A chant may start out in one mode and cadence in another; or it may be primarily in one mode but move for one or more of its internal phrases to the realm of another. There may even be more than two modes represented. The modes within a certain melody may be closely related, such as the authentic and plagal versions on the same final, or they may be more distant. The transition from one mode to another can be extremely subtle if the modes share certain characteristics. Mode 1 and Mode 8, for example, have the same range: they both lie within the octave D–D. Their differences lie in their reciting tones, A and C respectively, and in their finals: the final of Mode 1 is D; the final of Mode 8 is G. A melody can move fairly easily, therefore, from Mode 1 to Mode 8. Other shifts are also possible. A transition between modes can be affected by means of a common note. Three of the modes, for example, share a reciting tone on C.

In analyzing the modal aspect of chant, it is important to note that the rigid schemes given above do not cover all the practical aspects of the melodies as they have come down to us. The modal system was developed after a large amount of the chant repertoire had already evolved. Although some of the melodies were adapted to fit the system, some remain ambiguous or unclassifiable. Even in melodies that do clearly fit into the modal scheme, there are two factors that are not reflected in the chart above. These are 1) melodic extensions to the octave and 2) use of B♭.

The modes theoretically span an octave. But in practice the range of a melody may exceed its modal octave by one or even two notes in either direction. This is important for a clearly understandable reason. In focusing upon a note as a point of reference or as a structural element, a melody often needs to approach that note both from above and below. In a Mode-1 cadence upon D, for example, we often find that the melody touches upon the C below the D somewhere before the end so that the D is, as it were, "fixed" by the melody. (See Ex. 3-18.) In the Mode-5 opening of Example 3-19, the reciting note C is firmly established by a single move to the note D above the "correct" Lydian fifth. The Mode-1 melody in Example 3-20 reaches two steps above the Dorian octave to F.

EXAMPLE 3-18 Antiphon in Mode 1, Dorian, final cadence.

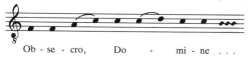

. . . vi - si - ta - ti - o - nis tu - ae, al - le - lu - ya.

. . . visitationis tuae, alleluya.   . . . of your visitation, alleluya.

EXAMPLE 3-19 Antiphon in Mode 5, Lydian, opening phrase.

Ob - se - cro, Do - mi - ne . . .

Obsecro, Domine . . .   I beseech you, O Lord . . .

EXAMPLE 3-20 Gradual in Mode 1, Dorian, portions only.

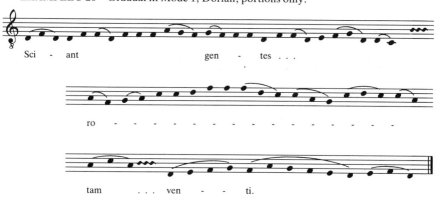

Sci - ant   gen - tes . . .

ro - - - - - - -

tam . . . ven - - ti.

Sciant gentes . . . rotam . . . venti.   Let the nations know . . . thistledown
                                                    . . . of the wind.

If some chant melodies extend beyond the modal octave, others often do not even fill out the octave, having an overall range of a fifth or sixth. In modal analysis, careful consideration must be given to all aspects of modal quality, especially the final, the reciting tone, and the fifths and fourths, not just to the anticipated octave designations.

The appearance of a B♭ in some chant melodies might also be expected to cause difficulties in modal analysis, as the change of position of the half step which the B♭ causes might be thought to cause a complete shift in modal assignation. This is not, however, the case. The B♭ seems to have occurred in chants without its having been regarded as causing a modal shift. It may be thought of as a melodic inflection rather than as a change of mode.

In some modes the appearance of the B♭ is quite common—Modes 1 and 4, for example. These modes often have internal cadences on F, thus perhaps encouraging a melodic inflection to avoid the tritone between B♮ and F. Modes 5 and 6, in which F is a very important pitch (the final of these modes), occur with the B♭ so frequently that it is possible to speak of "alternative" Lydian and Hypolydian modes (those with a constant B♭).

We should also recognize that chant melodies sometimes make use of standard melodic motifs (some have been discussed above) to reinforce their modal qualities. Each mode, in fact, tends towards certain structures and formations of melodic phrases. Some motifs are designed to announce or confirm a particular mode and are associated in the repertoire with that particular mode. A very common opening for Mode-1 melodies, for example, is a rather striking motif, which announces the Dorian fifth (see Ex. 3-21). Often this appears with the lower C as a focusing note (see Ex. 3-22).

EXAMPLE 3-21   Antiphon in Mode 1, Dorian, opening motif.

Hi   sunt qui cum mu-li - e - ri - bus   non sunt co-in - qui - na - ti. . . .

Hi sunt qui cum mulieribus non sunt   These are they who have not had inter-
    coinquinati. . . .   course with women. . . .

EXAMPLE 3-22   Introit in Mode 1, Dorian, opening motif.

Gau-de - a - mus om - nes   in   Do - mi - - - no . . .

Gaudeamus omnes in Domino . . .   Let us all rejoice in the Lord . . .

A frequent announcing motif for Mode 7, which presents the fifth G–D but has some of the intermediate steps filled in, is shown in Example 3-23.

EXAMPLE 3-23 Antiphon in Mode 7, Mixolydian, opening motif.

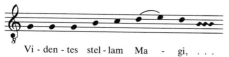

Vi - den - tes stel - lam Ma - gi, . . .

Videntes stellam Magi, . . .   When the Wise Men saw the star, . . .

And the approach to a Mode-3 cadence, with its characteristic descending half step to the final, is commonly found in the form given in Example 3-24.

EXAMPLE 3-24 Alleluya in Mode 3, Phrygian, cadence only.

[Al - le] - lu   -   -   -   -   -   ya.

[Alle]luya   [Alle]luya.

Finally, although most chant melodies appear on their designated modal pitches, some are transposed. This does not cause the modal designation to change, even though the names of the notes may be different, for the relationship of all of the notes to one another is retained. With the application of a consistent B♭, for example, the Phrygian mode, Mode 3, can be transposed from E to A, thus retaining all of its intervals intact. The melody in Example 3-25 ranges an octave from A, with the addition of a G below the final, but it has a B♭ throughout. The mode is therefore Mode 3, Phrygian, transposed to A. The quality of the Phrygian mode is retained, including the characteristic final cadence. Similarly, the Mode-1, Dorian, opening of the melody in Example 3-26 is perfectly clear, although the chant has been transposed to A.

The modal system is a useful method of understanding the melodic structure of plainchant and its subtle and often shifting pitch focus. This is especially true if it is combined with the other ways of looking at the melodies that have been discussed and if it is understood in its historical perspec-

EXAMPLE 3-25   Communion in Mode 3, Phrygian, transposed to A.

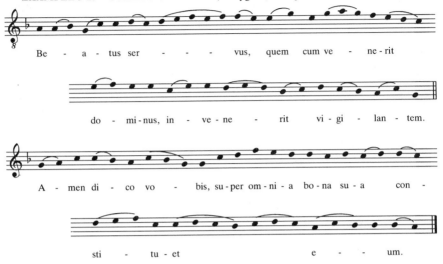

Be - a - tus ser - - - - vus, quem cum ve - ne - rit

do - mi-nus, in - ve - ne - rit vi - gi - lan - tem.

A - men di - co vo - bis, su-per om - ni - a bo-na su - a con -

sti - tu - et   e - - um.

Beatus servus, quem cum venerit dominus,   Happy is the servant whom the master finds
   invenerit vigilantem.   watchful when he comes.
Amen dico vobis, super omnia bona sua   Truly I say to you, he will appoint him in
   constituet eum.   charge of all his belongings.

EXAMPLE 3-26   Introit in Mode 1, Dorian, transposed to A.

Ex - au - di, Do - - - mi - ne, . . .

Exaudi, Domine, . . .   Hear, O Lord, . . .

tive. Comprehensive analysis of liturgical function, textual structure, note-to-syllable ratio, melodic shape, interval usage, pitch focus, and modal category provides some important insights into this flexible and subtly elusive repertoire that forms the basis of our entire Western musical tradition.

SUMMARY

The Christian religion, as an offshoot and modification of Judaism, took over many elements of Jewish practice: the cyclic reading of scripture, group prayer, and a scholarly approach to texts and commentary. Most importantly from the musical point of view, it also adopted the public recitation of sacred texts to musical formulas—a technique which clarified the meaning and structure of the texts while intensifying their presentation. By the late fourth century, Christianity was undergoing enormous expansion. Different forms of liturgy were established throughout Europe, including major distinctions between East and West and further regional uses. The form that ultimately prevailed in western Europe was the result of a synthesis between the liturgy in the Frankish kingdom and Roman practice. This synthesis was brought about by means of a deliberate attempt at unification under the powerful and charismatic leader Charlemagne.

A huge body of plainchant has survived from this period, a repertory ranging from the simplest of reciting formulas to the most elaborate and ornate melodies. Central to them all is the text; and the relationship between text and music remains one of the most distinctive and illuminating aspects of the repertory. Also helpful to an understanding of the sophisticated nature of plainchant are aspects of liturgical function, melodic shape and architecture, motivic usage, and the system of melodic modes, which, despite its limitations, provides a means of identifying the subtle colors and fluid shifts with which this music moves.

COMMENTS ON NOTATION AND PERFORMANCE

The development of musical notation was another of the many significant achievements of the Middle Ages. As we saw in Chapter Two, a sophisticated method of notation, distinguishing between instrumental and vocal music, had been invented by the Greeks but was lost to the early medieval world. It was not until the reign of Charlemagne that a new notational system was devised to preserve and transmit the growing repertory of liturgical chants.

This system seems to have developed with regional variants in different parts of Europe, but all had the same fundamental characteristics. Signs were drawn in the manuscripts above the words of the chant to indicate the relative pitches of the notes. Single notes were drawn either as a dot or a line. If several notes were to be sung to one syllable, they were drawn as a connected group (a neume). A long melisma was written as a number of neumes one after the other.

This notation was perfectly suited to its task, which was to *remind* singers of the relative pitches of the notes, the shape of each neume, and the number of notes in each neume or melisma of a melody they had learned earlier. It was not designed to inform people of melodies they had never heard before. For hundreds of years melodies had been preserved simply by memory; for now all that was needed was a notational aid to the memory.

An example of this notation may be seen in Example 3-27. This is a facsimile of a page from one of the earliest notated manuscripts, from the ninth century. It was made in St. Gall, a famous medieval monastery (see pp. 36 and 221) and shows the chants for two services—the second and third Sundays of Advent ("Dominica II" and "Dominica III"). The individual notes and the neumes and melismas are clearly drawn above each syllable, and the shape of each neume graphically indicates the direction of that portion of the melody. For the long melismas, space is left between syllables or words to make room for the notes. What is not shown by this notation is the absolute pitch of the notes (there is no clef) and the change of pitch from one neume to the next, since the neumes are all drawn more or less on a straight line. But for someone who had already heard the melody, the system was invaluable.

The next stage was the modification of the notational system to enable it to display in more detail the overall shape of the melody. The modification involved the use of "heighted" neumes—neumes whose pitch relationship to each other is represented on the page. An example of heighted neumes is given in Example 3-28, a manuscript from the tenth century.

Even more accurate representation of pitch came with the invention of the staff around the year 1000. At first only a single line was used, around which the notes were grouped. Then two lines were adopted, on the pitches C and F. It was important to keep the position of these particular pitches clear, since they involved the all-important half steps in the scale. Example 3-29 illustrates the two-line staff. In the original manuscript the two lines are drawn in different colors; the upper line indicates F, the lower line C. At the left-hand side of the page the small letters "e" and "a" indicate respectively the space below the F and a very faint additional line below the C. Gradually, more staff lines were employed, one or another of them being designated in pitch by a *clef* (a "key" to the pitch). By the twelfth century the four- or five-line staff, with a clef for C or F, was in common use.

The performance of plainchant is unfortunately an art whose secrets have been lost. In the eighth and ninth centuries, we can be sure, there were many vocal and rhythmic subtleties in chant performance, since the notation, as well as conveying pitches, also contains many directions about performance. These directions may be seen by a careful examination of Example 3-27. The tiny letters written above the neumes (c, t, etc.) indicate rhythm, speed, dynamics, and vocal quality. Also, the shape of the neumes was sometimes modified to indicate the stressing or accentuation of certain notes. The exact meaning of these signs and, indeed, the details of performance style must certainly have differed from place to place, as did the lit-

EXAMPLE 3-27 Facsimile from manuscript St. Gall 359, ninth century.

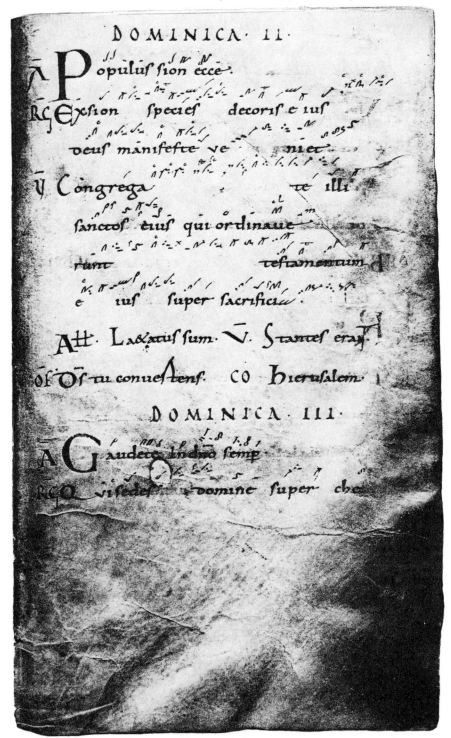

EXAMPLE 3-28   Facsimile from manuscript Laon 239, tenth century.

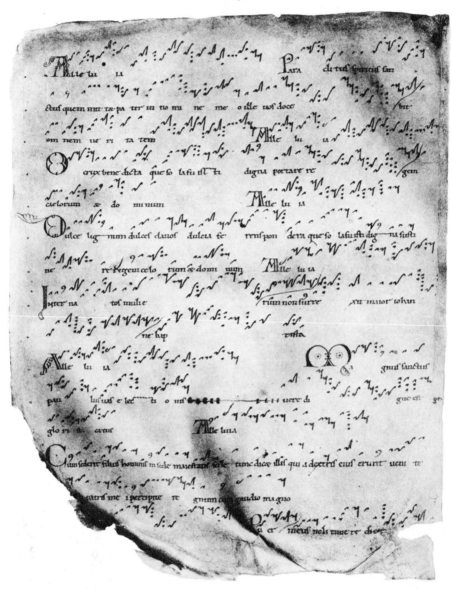

urgy itself. But the fact that there was a complex performing tradition cannot be doubted.

This subtle, detailed, and highly inflected performance of chant must have given way very early to a far more straightforward style, for already by the twelfth century the music was being described as *cantus*

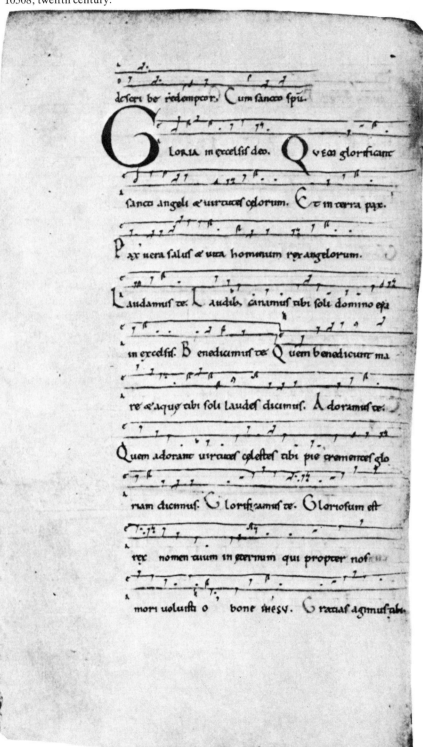

planus—plain chant—and the descriptive letters and modified neumes were no longer in use.

Many experiments have taken place in recent years in the modern performance of chant. The greatest controversy has been over its rhythm. Theories range from a strict metrical approach, to an "accentualist" interpretation, in which the accentuation of the text determines the rhythm, to a rhythm in more or less equal notes. It is this last method, with its smooth style, detached sound, and rounded contour, that has become the most widely used today. It has been championed, in scholarly articles, printed editions, and recordings, by the monks of Solesmes in western France, whose work is supported by the Vatican. It may or may not bear much resemblance to the performance of chant in the twelfth century and later. It is unlikely that it represents the sound of chant in its early notated history.

Issues of medieval vocal production, ornamentation, and pronunciation of Latin have yet to be adequately addressed. The first two of these may not be susceptible of solution, since descriptions are scarce or nonexistent. Much may be done in the way of correct pronunciation, however, as throughout the Middle Ages Latin was probably pronounced in the same way as the local languages. The uniform pronunciation of Latin heard in performances today is an anachronistic product of the Renaissance.

Various modern methods of notation are used for chant. The Vatican editions have adopted a regularized version of the square notation of the thirteenth century. Some books use modern note shapes, primarily the eighth note, beaming the notes together to indicate neumes. In this book, the musical examples of plainchant are transcribed in a non-committal form of notation, with black note heads and without stems. This conveys the pitches, their relationship to the text, and their original groupings (neumes are indicated by slurs) but avoids questions of rhythm, ornamentation, vocal style, and dynamics.

DISCOGRAPHY

Example 3-1   Chant for the Gospel of the Mass (music).
Choir of the Monks of the Benedictine Abbey of St. Martin, Beuron, *Liturgia Paschalis,* Archiv 3088/90 (Side VI).

Example 3-3   Chant for the Oratio of the Mass (music).
Choir of the Monks of the Benedictine Abbey of St. Martin, Beuron, *Liturgia Paschalis,* Archiv 3088/90 (Side V).

Example 3-4   Chant for the Epistle of the Mass (music).
Choir of the Monks of the Benedictine Abbey of St. Martin, Beuron, *Liturgia Paschalis,* Archiv 3088/90 (Side V).

Example 3-6b Introit for the Mass for Easter Sunday.
Benediktiner-Kloster, *Gregorianischer Choral,* Archiv 2533 131; also on
Choir of the Monks of the Benedictine Abbey of St. Martin, Beuron, *Liturgia Paschalis,* Archiv 3088/90 (Side V).

Example 3-7 *Pater Noster.*
Choir of the Monks of the Benedictine Abbey of St. Martin, Beuron, *Liturgia Paschalis,* Archiv 3088/90 (Side VI).

Example 3-9 Gloria.
Chor der Mönche der Benediktiner-Erzabtei St. Martin, Beuron, *Prima Missa in Nativitate Domini Nostri Jesu Christi,* Archiv 198 153.

Example 3-11 Gradual for the Mass for Christmas.
Chor der Mönche der Benediktiner-Erzabtei St. Martin, Beuron, *Prima Missa in Nativitate Domini Nostri Jesu Christi,* Archiv 198 153; also on Benediktinerabtei, Münsterschwarzach, *Gregorianischer Choral: Die grossen Feste des Kirchenjahres,* Archiv 2723 084 (Side I); and Benediktiner-Kloster, *Gregorianischer Choral,* Archiv 2533 131.

Some widely differing interpretations of chant performance may be heard on the following records: Schola Antiqua, *Tenth-Century Liturgical Chant,* Nonesuch H-71348; Schola Antiqua, *A Guide to Gregorian Chant,* Vanguard VSD 71217; Pro Cantione Antiqua, *Medieval Music: Sacred Monophony,* Peters International PLE 114 (Oxford University Press OUP 161). The latter two recordings clearly demonstrate several different approaches. The most pervasive modern style may be heard on any one of the many recordings by the monks of Solesmes (London records).

Iegor Reznikoff, *Alleluias and Offertories of the Gauls,* Harmonia Mundi HM 1044, attempts to present a reconstruction of the early Gallican chant style; and Ensemble Organum, *Chants de l'église de Rome,* Harmonia Mundi HMC 1218, interprets the chant of Rome as it might have been sung prior to the Carolingian synthesis.

BIBLIOGRAPHICAL NOTES

Works that discuss the difficult issue of the formation of the early Christian liturgy include Paul F. Bradshaw, *Daily Prayer in the Early Church: A Study of the Origin and Early Development of the Divine Office* (New York: Oxford University Press, 1982); Dom Jean de Puniet, *The Mass: Its Origin and History* (New York: Longmans, Green and Co., 1930); Clifford Dugmore, *The Influence of the Synagogue Upon the Divine Office* (London: Oxford University Press, 1944); Eric Werner, *The Sacred Bridge,* 2 vols. (London: D. Dobson, 1959–1984); and James W. McKinnon, "On the Question of Psalmody in the Ancient Synagogue," *Early Music History* VI (1986), pp. 159–191.

An illuminating volume of readings and commentary from the early Christian era is James McKinnon (ed.), *Music in Early Christian Literature* (Cambridge: Cambridge University Press, 1987).

Other books on liturgical history include: Theodor Klauser, *A Short History of the Western Liturgy: An Account and Some Reflections,* 2nd edition (Oxford: Oxford University Press, 1979); John H. Miller, *Fundamentals of the Liturgy* (South Bend, Indiana: Notre Dame Press, 1959); Gregory Dix, *The Shape of the Liturgy* (Westminster: Dacre Press, 1945); Thomas Talley, *The Origins of the Liturgical Year* (New York: Pueblo Publishing Co., 1986); *The Study of Liturgy,* ed. Cheslyn Jones, Geoffrey Wainwright, Edward Yarnold (New York: Oxford University Press, 1978). This last is a particularly useful collection of short essays on a wide range of topics.

A helpful discussion of the old regional rites is Archdale A. King, *Liturgies of the Past* (London: Longman, Green, 1959).

Gregory's contributions are presented in Jeffrey Richards, *Consul of God: The Life and Times of Gregory the Great* (London: Routledge & Kegan Paul, 1980).

Still the best study of plainchant in English is Willi Apel, *Gregorian Chant* (Bloomington: Indiana University Press, 1958). An important translation from the German is Peter Wagner, *Introduction to the Gregorian Melodies,* 2nd edition, trans. Agnes Orme and E. G. P. Wyatt (New York: Da Capo Press, 1986).

A wonderfully readable account of Charlemagne's life and times is Lewis Thorpe (trans.), *Einhard and Notker the Stammerer: Two Lives of Charlemagne* (Harmondsworth: Penguin Books, Ltd., 1969). Also fascinating and detailed is Pierre Riché, *Daily Life in the World of Charlemagne* ([Philadelphia:] University of Pennsylvania Press, 1978).

A clear and concise survey of questions relating to the performance of chant is Lance Brunner, "The Performance of Plainchant: Some Preliminary Observations of the New Era," *Early Music* X (1982): 317–328.

FOUR
THE MASS

During the first few centuries of Christian liturgical history, two main forms of worship developed: the Mass and the Office. Both of these types of service became established in different ways in different places and at different times. Any generalizations as to standard formats are bound to ignore certain specific practices and to misrepresent the variety and complexity of historical reality. As with all broad overviews, however, some gain may offset these losses. A general framework is established, against which the actuality of practice at a specific time and place may later be measured.

This chapter will consider the Mass, which developed as a symbolic re-enactment of the Last Supper and in which the central events are the consecration and partaking of bread and wine. The elaborate ceremony that grew up in the Middle Ages around this core is known as the Mass from the Latin word *missa*. The word may have come into usage as a Latin rendering of the Greek *leitourgia* ("service") or from the final words at the conclusion of the service, *Ite, missa est* ("Go you are dismissed").

STRUCTURE OF THE MASS

There are two main sections of a medieval Mass. The first concentrates on scriptural readings and has as its focal point a reading from one of the Gospels. It is known as the Fore-Mass. The second is known as the Eucharist (Greek for "the giving of thanks") and centers on the blessing and partaking of the bread and wine. There is no break between the two sections.

The form of the Mass changed over the centuries, both during and after the Middle Ages. The version that we shall discuss represents a form that became more or less standardized in the ninth and tenth centuries. At the same time, as we saw in Chapter 3, the music for the liturgy became more stable, partly as a result of this standardization of the liturgy and partly as a result of the spread of notation. (It should be understood, however, that styles and practices still varied considerably from place to place.)

The following table presents the main items in both parts of the Mass, together with an indication of the musical style of each item and a designation as to the nature of its text. "Proper" refers to texts that change from one service to another; "common" designates texts that always remain the same. Throughout the year, some texts change from one day or week to the next and from feast to feast; these texts therefore are "proper" or "appropriate" to the day or season. The chants that remain the same every day are "common" to every occasion. The interlacing of proper and common texts in both the Mass and the Office allows for stability in the liturgy, while it distinguishes one day from the next and marks the changes in the seasons. It also provides the opportunity in both Mass and Office for highlighting a particular feast day (Easter, for example, or Pentecost) with texts that are especially appropriate to that day.

THE MASS

Item	*Style*	*Text*
Fore-Mass		
1. Introit	Neumatic	Proper
2. **Kyrie**	Neumatic	Common
3. **Gloria**	Syllabic	Common
4. Oratio	Recitational	Proper
5. Epistle	Recitational	Proper
6. Gradual (Alleluya)	Melismatic	Proper
7. Alleluya (Tract)	Melismatic	Proper

8.	Sequence	Syllabic	Proper
9.	Gospel	Recitational	Proper
10.	**Credo**	Syllabic	Common

Eucharist

11.	Offertory	Melismatic	Proper
12.	Secret	Spoken in silence	Proper
13.	Preface	Recitational	Proper
14.	**Sanctus**	Neumatic	Common
15.	Canon	Spoken in silence	Common
16.	Pater Noster	Syllabic	Common
17.	**Agnus Dei**	Neumatic	Common
18.	Communion	Neumatic	Proper
19.	Post-Communion	Recitational	Proper
20.	Ite, Missa Est (Benedicamus Domino)	Neumatic	Common

The preceding table gives the major items of a medieval Mass, not of a modern one, for certain items have changed since the Middle Ages. It also omits the elaborate movements and rituals which grew up around the Mass, involving vessels and vestments, candles, books, and incense, all imparting to the service a dignity and established sense of order.

There are different ways of analyzing the structure of a medieval Mass. The climax of the Fore-Mass, for example, is the reading from the Gospel (Item 9), and that of the Eucharist is the partaking of the bread and wine during the Communion (Item 18). But from the musical point of view they take on a slightly different perspective. Although the Gospel and Communion are both high points of their respective parts of the Mass, they are very different musically. The Gospel is chanted to a recitational formula centering mostly upon a single pitch, while the Communion is sung to a quite elaborate neumatic melody. This has to do with the different functions of the items: the reading from the Gospel centers upon the actual words of the text, carefully chosen for their relevance to the day; while the Communion chant is sung during the act of communion itself.

During the Mass, then, there is a direct connection between musical style and liturgical function, and before we can concentrate upon the music alone, we should examine the function of each of the chants in the service.

Some chants are sung during the course of some action. These are primarily the Introit, the Offertory, and the Communion. The Introit is sung during the entrance of the clergy, including the priest who presides over the Mass (the "celebrant"), and the incensing of the altar. The Offer-

tory accompanies the preparation of the bread and wine, and a further incensing of the altar. The Communion is sung during the actual partaking of
the bread and wine. These chants may be shortened or extended to accommodate the time necessary for the actions involved.

The Gradual and the Alleluya are the most elaborate musical items
in the Mass. They are often highly melismatic and create a sense of intensity
preparatory to the reading from the Gospel.

Of the common chants the most important are the Kyrie, Gloria,
Credo, Sanctus, and Agnus Dei. The function of these chants is inherent in
the words, for they incorporate petition (Kyrie: "Have mercy;" Agnus
Dei: "Have mercy," "Give us peace"), praise (Gloria: "Glory to God;"
Sanctus: "Holy, holy, holy"), and profession of belief (Credo: "I believe"). They are linked also in another way, for their texts are the main
ones that are invariable, remaining the same at every Mass on every occasion. The importance of this fact has led to these common chants of the
Mass being named as a group: the Ordinary of the Mass. (*Ordinarius* in
Latin means "usual" or "customary.") The items that make up the Ordinary of the Mass are printed in bold in the preceding table.[1]

The celebration of a Mass in the Middle Ages was articulated and
dramatized in a variety of ways. First, there were hierarchical distinctions
among the different people designated to perform the different parts of the
liturgy. Texts and functions were divided between the celebrant and the
other members of the officiating clergy, and between the clergy and the
choir. Secondly, there was a visual distinction. The service was articulated
by movement and spatial positioning, from the opening procession to
movement around the altar to different points in relation to the altar for the
different readings. Finally, there was an articulation by means of the varying forms of the text: prayers, scriptural readings, exclamations of praise,
excerpts from the psalms, the profession of belief, and the blessing of the
sacrament.

In all of this music played a central role. Music differentiated the
participants, highlighted the motions, and distinguished the texts. There
was a clear aural distinction between the different people reading or singing, between the places from which the sound came, and between speech
and silence, reading and recitation, and solo and choral as well as simple
and elaborate singing.

Let us now look closely at one particular Mass as it might have been
celebrated in medieval times.

---

[1]For a discussion of the slightly ambiguous position of Item 20 of the Mass (Ite, Missa
Est/Benedicamus Domino) in relation to the main Ordinary items, see p. 133.

THE MASS FOR PENTECOST

One of the most important feasts of the year in the Catholic liturgy is the Feast of Pentecost. Pentecost is the equivalent of the Jewish feast of *Shavuot,* a feast that commemorates the giving of the Torah (Jewish law) to Moses on Mount Sinai. The Hebrew word Shavuot ("[seven] weeks") refers to the fact that the Jewish feast is celebrated on the fiftieth day (seven weeks) after Passover. The Christian feast (Pentecost means "fiftieth" in Greek) comes fifty days after Easter and celebrates the coming of the Holy Spirit and the beginning of the history of the Church. From the white clothes of the converts who were baptized on this day derives the English name Whitsun or Whitsunday. Pentecost is the final feast during the period of rejoicing that follows the Easter season, and as a result many of the Mass texts have the joyful exclamation "Alleluya" ("Praise God") added to them. In the following discussion we shall consider the general nature of each item and its music, as it might appear in any Mass, and then analyze the specific chant that occurs in the Mass for Pentecost.

Fore-Mass

The Mass opens with the singing of an Introit (Item 1 in the table on p. 84). Introits are characterized by the following form: a neumatic melody, sung both at the beginning and at the end of the Introit, frames the singing of a psalm verse and the Gloria Patri. This framing melody is called an "antiphon," from its association with the antiphonal singing of the psalm. The antiphon opens with a short introductory phrase, known as the "intonation," which is sung by a solo singer or a small group of solo singers from the choir, to set the pitch and the tempo. (This use of an intonation for solo singers at the opening of the Introit is common to all chants. Its conclusion is usually marked in the chant books by an asterisk.) The remainder of the choir joins in after the intonation and continues singing through to the end of the chant. The form of the entire Introit may be represented in the following way:

Antiphon	Psalm Verse and Gloria Patri	Antiphon
Soloist, Choir	Choir	Choir

Originally, a different number of psalm verses could be included in the Introit to accommodate the length of time necessary for the entry of the clergy at the opening of the Mass. The standard form of the Introit, however, became fixed with only one psalm verse and the Gloria Patri, framed by the singing of the antiphon. As we saw in the previous chapter (p. 55), the Gloria Patri is treated musically as though it were another psalm verse.

The text of the Pentecost Introit (Ex. 4-1) stresses the power of the Holy Spirit with an image of pervasive wisdom; the psalm verse reinforces this image by picturing the flight of God's enemies. The music is opened by an intonation (up to the asterisk) that outlines the fifth D–A, stresses the A, and cadences on F. This suggests Mode 1, Dorian. However, the antiphon continues with a quick ascent to C, the reciting tone of Mode 8, Hypomixolydian, and cadences on G at the first "alleluya." During the remainder of the antiphon, C continues to be the main reciting note, and, although the melody descends to F, the final cadence before the psalm verse is on G, the final of Mode 8.

The psalm verse (indicated by the abbreviation ℣. in the music) immediately leaps the fourth G–C, continues on the reciting tone, and cadences clearly on G, again the final of Mode 8. The Gloria Patri repeats the music of the psalm verse (with an additional ending for the "Amen"), and the whole antiphon is then immediately sung again. The final cadence is again on G. Despite the opening intonation with its coloring of Mode 1, the Introit is firmly in the Mixolydian mode.

The music of the antiphon is a moderate and balanced mixture of neumes of two or three notes, and the melody is formed as a gentle series of waves, while the psalm verse and the Gloria Patri stand out with their syllabic setting and reiterated reciting tone. The lowest note, the opening D, is not reached again until just before the end of the Gloria Patri. Apart from this pitch, the range of the chant is exactly one octave. The grammatical structure of the text is clearly underlined by the two cadences on G at the ends of the complete sentences in the antiphon. Both cadences employ the same musical phrase, which further clarifies the structure of the text. The half and full endings of the psalm verse and the Gloria Patri are articulated in a clear way, while the closing cadence of this section ("Amen") is marked by the drop to D and an approach to the final G from below.

The second item in the Mass is the Kyrie (Item 2 in the table), the first part of the Ordinary of the Mass. Its textual form is particularly noteworthy. It consists of three sentences, the third of which is a repetition of the first:

Kyrie, eleison.	Lord, have mercy.
Christe, eleison.	Christ, have mercy.
Kyrie, eleison.	Lord, have mercy.

Each of these three sentences is sung three times. The symbolic representation of the Trinity that this implies was noted often by medieval commentators.

EXAMPLE 4-1 Introit of the Mass for Pentecost.

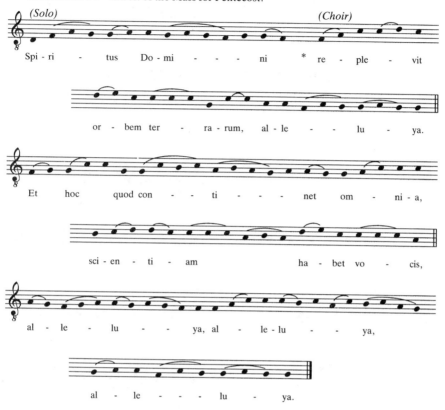

(Solo) (Choir)

Spi - ri - tus Do - mi - ni * re - ple - vit

or - bem ter - ra - rum, al - le - lu - ya.

Et hoc quod con - ti - net om - ni - a,

sci - en - ti - am ha - bet vo - cis,

al - le - lu - ya, al - le - lu - ya,

al - le - lu - ya.

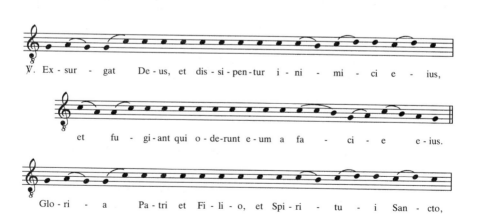

℣. Ex - sur - gat De - us, et dis - si - pen - tur i - ni - mi - ci e - ius,

et fu - gi - ant qui o - de - runt e - um a fa - ci - e e - ius.

Glo - ri - a Pa - tri et Fi - li - o, et Spi - ri - tu - i San - cto,

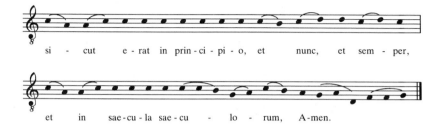

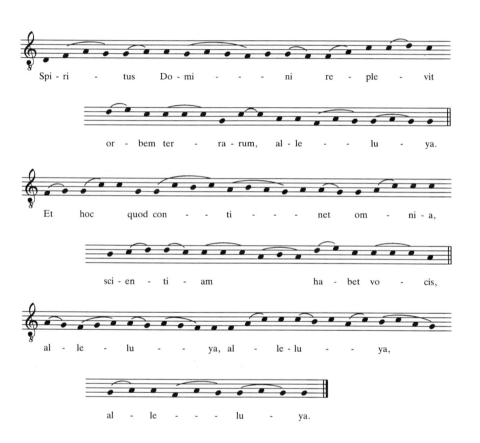

Spiritus Domini replevit orbem ter-
  rarum, alleluya.
Et hoc quod continet omnia, scien-
  tiam habet vocis,
alleluya, alleluya, alleluya.

The spirit of the Lord has filled the
  world, alleluya.
And that which contains all things
  has knowledge of his voice,
alleluya, alleluya, alleluya.

℣. Exsurgat Deus, et dissipentur inimici eius,
    et fugiant qui oderunt eum a facie eius.
Gloria Patri et filio, et Spiritui Sancto,
    sicut erat in principio, et nunc, et semper,
    et in saecula saeculorum. Amen.

Spiritus Domini replevit orbem ter-rarum, alleluya.
Et hoc quod continet omnia, scien-tiam habet vocis,
alleluya, alleluya, alleluya.

℣. Let God arise, and let his enemies be dispersed,
    and let those that hate him flee from his face.
Glory to the Father, and to the Son, and to the Holy Spirit,
    as it was in the beginning, both now and always,
    and for ever. Amen.

The spirit of the Lord has filled the world, alleluya.
And that which contains all things has knowledge of his voice,
alleluya, alleluya, alleluya.

Although the text for the Kyrie remains constant, many melodies were composed for it. They are generally neumatic with short melismas. A soloist or a small group of soloists from the choir sings the intonation on the first word and the full choir continues the chant to the end. The music for the third statement of the last sentence is usually deliberately altered, both as a musical summary of the preceding material, and as a practical signal to the choir that the statement is the final one.

The Kyrie of the Pentecost Mass (Ex. 4-2) is in Mode 1, the Dorian mode. The intonation begins and ends on the reciting tone, and the continuation of the first phrase makes the clear descent of the fifth A–D that defines the Dorian mode. This descent is made first by stepwise motion and then by skip. The phrase ends on the final of the mode. The second phrase ("Christe eleison") begins again on the reciting tone and makes a series of progressive descents to the final, ending with the same cadential formula as the first phrase. The third phrase explores a new range in the mode by moving above the reciting tone to C and stressing the area of the mode between A and C before cadencing on the reciting tone (instead of on the final). The final phrase (the third statement of the last "Kyrie, eleison") is distinguished by a double statement of the opening of the phrase, including the introductory upward skip and the higher music around C.

The tripartite nature of the text is underscored and its grammatical structure reinforced by the music. Each of the three sentences of the text either begins or ends on the final or the reciting tone of the mode. However, a deliberate contrast is established between the first two sentences and the third. The first two are set to music which descends in a series of curves from the reciting tone to the final. The music for the last sentence reverses this pattern. It begins on the final and rises to the reciting tone, finally delin-

EXAMPLE 4-2   Kyrie of the Mass for Pentecost.

Kyrie, eleison.	Lord, have mercy.
Kyrie, eleison.	Lord, have mercy.
Kyrie, eleison.	Lord, have mercy.
Christe, eleison.	Christ, have mercy.
Christe, eleison.	Christ, have mercy.
Christe, eleison.	Christ, have mercy.
Kyrie, eleison.	Lord, have mercy.
Kyrie, eleison.	Lord, have mercy.
Kyrie, eleison.	Lord, have mercy.

eating a reversed arch to reach the A once more. The conclusion of this chant away from the final is unusual and leaves an open-ended feeling.

The Gloria is always the second item in the Ordinary of the Mass (Item 3 in the table). It is characterized by a long text which opens with a quotation of the angels' acclamation to the shepherds on Christmas night ("Glory to God in the highest") and continues with statements of praise interspersed with petitions. The deliberately repetitive nature of the text ("Domine . . .," "Domine . . .," "Domine . . .;" "Qui . . .," "Qui . . .;" "Tu solus . . .," "Tu solus . . .") ties these various elements together and makes a powerful prose construction. Its length tended to preclude ornamental or elaborate settings, and the music of most Gloria melodies is syllabic with occasional very short neumatic passages. The sectional nature of the text seems to have encouraged internal phrase repetition in the music. The opening intonation is sung not by a soloist from the choir but by the celebrant (the presiding priest).

The Gloria of the Mass for Pentecost (Ex. 4-3) is in Mode 4, Hypophrygian. The setting is syllabic, but a neumatic motif stands out, which draws attention to the words "Pater" (in the eighth phrase), the two appearances of "Christe" (phrases 9 and 16), and the word "Spiritu" (phrase 17). The motif is introduced partially on the "te" of "Glorificamus te" in the sixth phrase and appears in final form on "Amen" at the end of the chant, by approaching E, the final of the mode, both from above and from below. The unification of the chant by this repeated motif has a liturgical and symbolic, as well as a musical, function, for it links the words that refer to the three manifestations of God: "Father," "Son," and "Holy Spirit." Further musical unity is achieved by having every phrase end on the final, E; by the use of parallel phrases on the three statements of the text that begin with the word "Domine"; and by parallel phrases on the two statements "Qui tollis." The chant ranges over a complete octave from the C below the final to C above, with most of the music lying in the fourth between the Hypophrygian final E and the reciting tone A.

EXAMPLE 4-3 Gloria of the Mass for Pentecost.

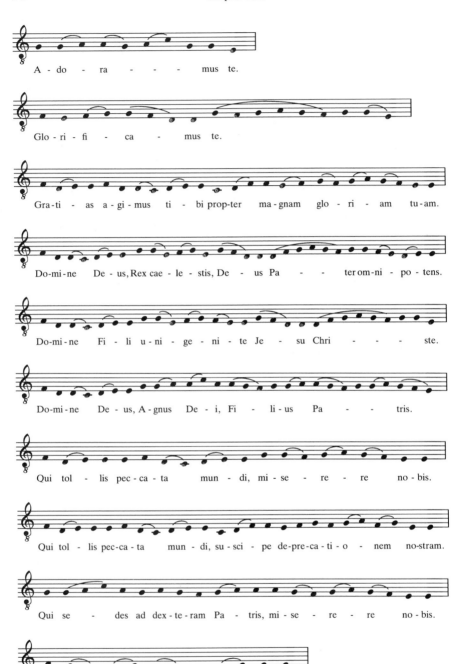

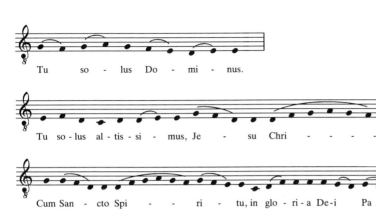

Tu so - lus Do - mi - nus.

Tu so - lus al - tis - si - mus, Je - su Chri - - - - - ste.

Cum San - cto Spi - - ri - tu, in glo - ri - a De - i Pa - tris.

A - - - - - - - - - - men.

Gloria in excelsis Deo.	Glory to God in the highest.
Et in terra pax hominibus bonae voluntatis.	And on earth peace to men of good will.
Laudamus te.	We praise you.
Benedicimus te.	We bless you.
Adoramus te.	We adore you.
Glorificamus te.	We glorify you.
Gratias agimus tibi propter magnam gloriam tuam.	We give thanks to you on account of your great glory.
Domine Deus, Rex caelestis, Deus Pater omnipotens.	O Lord God, heavenly King, God the omnipotent Father.
Domine Fili unigenite Jesu Christe.	O Lord the Son, only-begotten Jesus Christ.
Domine Deus, Agnus Dei, Filius Patris.	O Lord God, Lamb of God, Son of the Father.
Qui tollis peccata mundi, miserere nobis.	You who take away the sins of the world, have pity on us.
Qui tollis peccata mundi, suscipe deprecationem nostram.	You who take away the sins of the world, hear our plea.
Qui sedes ad dexteram Patris, miserere nobis.	You who sit at the right hand of the Father, have pity on us.
Quoniam tu solus sanctus.	Since you alone are holy.
Tu solus Dominus.	You alone are the Lord.
Tu solus altissimus, Jesu Christe.	You alone are the most-high, Jesus Christ.
Cum Sancto Spiritu, in gloria Dei Patris.	With the Holy Spirit, in the glory of God the Father.
Amen.	Amen.

   The Oratio ("Prayer") of a Mass (Item 4 in the table) is sometimes known as the Collect, since the priest offers a collective prayer for all those who are present. It is sung by the celebrant to a simple reciting formula. It opens with a standard interchange between priest and choir, and the recitation continues primarily on a single pitch but with different half endings and full endings. The choir sings the final "Amen." (The choral responses are marked R̷ in the score.)

   The text of the Oratio for Pentecost (Ex. 4-4) refers to the Holy Spirit, one of the central aspects of the celebration for the day, and the power of the Holy Spirit to spread the word of God. The text from "Per Dominum nostrum Jesum Christum" to the end is the standard ending for the Oratio and for other prayers in the Mass, just as the word "Oremus" ("Let us pray") is the standard opening. The reciting formula is simple, with a step upwards to the reciting tone at the beginning of phrases and a step down at the half close. The full close is indicated by the single step down for two syllables and a return to the reciting tone for the final two syllables.

EXAMPLE 4-4   Oratio of the Mass for Pentecost.

da no - bis in e - o - dem Spi - ri - tu rec - ta sa - pe - re,

et de e - ius sem - per con - so - la - ti - o - ne gau - de - re.

Per Do - mi - num no - strum Je - sum Chri - stum Fi - li - um tu - um,

qui te - cum vi - vit et re - gnat in u - ni - ta - te e - ius - dem Spi - ri - tus San - cti De - us.

Per om - ni - a sae - cu - la sae - cu - lo - rum.

(Choir)

℟. A - men.

Dominus vobiscum.	The Lord be with you.
℟. Et cum spiritu tuo.	℟. And with your spirit.
Oremus.	Let us pray.
Deus, qui hodierna die corda fidelium Sancti Spiritus illustratione docuisti.	O God, who on this day instructed the hearts of the faithful by the light of the Holy Spirit,
da nobis in eodem Spiritu recta sapere,	grant that we may know what is right in the same Spirit,
et de eius semper consolatione gaudere.	and always rejoice in its consolation.
Per Dominum nostrum Jesum Christum Filium tuum,	Through our Lord Jesus Christ, your Son,
qui tecum vivit et regnat in unitate eiusdem Spiritus Sancti Deus.	who lives and rules with you as God in the unity of the Holy Spirit.
Per omnia saecula saeculorum.	For ever and ever.
℟. Amen.	℟. Amen.

The Oratio in a Mass is followed by the Epistle (Item 5 in the table), a reading from the Epistles or Acts of the Apostles, sung to a formula that is usually quite simple. The Epistle was sung in the medieval Mass by the Subdeacon, who stood to the south side of the altar (medieval churches usually faced east, towards Jerusalem).

The text of the Epistle for the Mass for Pentecost (Ex. 4-5) is taken from the Acts of the Apostles and tells the scriptural story of the coming of the Holy Spirit. It is introduced by a statement of its source. The recitation formula centers on C and makes use of a downward skip of a third and a rising half step for the half close, and, for the full close, a two-note rising neume with an ending on the lower note of the half step. There is a special inflection for the questions and a more ornamental concluding formula for the final cadence, with strong emphasis on the rising half step to the final C. The miraculous narrative is thus reported in the clearest possible way, with

EXAMPLE 4-5   Epistle of the Mass for Pentecost.

Lec - ti - o   Ac - tu - um   A - po - sto - lo - rum.

In   di - e - bus   il - lis: Cum com-ple - ren - tur   di - es   Pen - te - cos - tes,   e - rant om - nes

di - sci - pu - li   pa - ri - ter   in   e - o - dem   lo - co.

Et   fac - tus   est   re - pen - te   de   cae - lo   so - nus   tam-quam ad - ve - ni - en - tis

spi - ri - tus   ve - he - men - tis,

et   re - ple - vit   to - tam   do - mum   u - bi   e - rant   se - den - tes.

Et ap - pa - ru - e - runt il - lis dis - per - ti - tae lin - guae tam - quam i - gnis se - dit - que

su - pra sin - gu - los e - o - rum.

Et re - ple - ti - sunt om - nes Spi - ri - tu San - cto,

et coe - pe - runt lo - qui va - ri - is lin - guis, prout Spi - ri - tus San - ctus da - bat e - lo - qui il - lis.

E - rant au - tem in Je - ru - sa - lem ha - bi - tan - tes Ju - dae - i, vi - ri re - li - gi - o - si

ex om - ni na - ti - o - ne, quae sub cae - lo est.

Fac - ta au - tem hac vo - ce, con - ve - nit mul - ti - tu - do,

et men - te con - fu - sa est, quo - ni - am au - di - e - bat un - us - quis - que lin - gua su - a

il - los lo - quen - tes.

Stu - pe - bant au - tem om - nes, et mi - ra - ban - tur, di - cen - tes: Non - ne ec - ce om - nes i - sti

qui   lo - quun-tur, Ga - li - lae - i   sunt?

Et quo-mo-do nos au - di - vi-mus un - us-quis-que lin-guam no-stram, in qua na - ti su - mus?

Par-thi, et Me-di, et Ae - la - mi-tae, et qui ha - bi-tant Me - so - po - ta - mi-am, Ju-dae-am,

et Cap-pa - do - ci - am, Pon-tum, et A - si - am, Phry-gi - am, et Pam-phy - li - am,

Ae - gyp-tum, et par - tes Li - by - ae, quae est cir - ca Cy - re - nen,

et ad - ve-nae Ro-ma - ni, Ju-dae - i quo-que, et Pro-se - ly - ti, Cre - tes,   et A - ra-bes.

Au - di - vi-mus e - os lo - quen - tes no-stris lin-guis ma-gna - li - a De - i.

Lectio Actuum Apostolorum.	A reading from the Acts of the Apostles.
In diebus illis: Cum complerentur dies Pentecostes, erant omnes discipuli pariter in eodem loco.	On that occasion: When the days of Pentecost were finished, all the disciples were together in the same place.
Et factus est repente de caelo sonus tamquam advenientis spiritus vehementis,	And suddenly there came a sound from heaven, as though a powerful wind were coming,
et replevit totam domum ubi erant sedentes.	and it filled the whole house where they were sitting.
Et apparuerunt illis dispertitae linguae tamquam ignis seditque supra singulos eorum.	And scattered tongues as though of fire appeared to them, and it sat upon every one of them.

Et repleti sunt omnes Spiritu Sancto,	And they were all filled with the Holy Spirit,
et coeperunt loqui variis linguis, prout Spiritus Sanctus dabat eloqui illis.	And began to speak in various languages, according as the Holy Spirit gave them voice.
Erant autem in Jerusalem habitantes Judaei, viri religiosi ex omni natione, quae sub caelo est.	And there were Jews living in Jerusalem, religious men from every nation under heaven.
Facta autem hac voce, convenit multitudo,	And when this was heard, a crowd gathered,
et mente confusa est, quoniam audiebat unusquisque lingua sua illos loquentes.	and they were amazed, because each one of them heard them speaking in his own language.
Stupebant autem omnes, et mirabantur, dicentes: Nonne ecce omnes isti qui loquuntur, Galilaei sunt?	They were all astounded, and in wonderment, and they said: Behold, are not all these men who are speaking Galileans?
Et quomodo nos audivimus unusquisque linguam nostram, in qua nati sumus?	How is it that we have each heard our own language, the one to which we were born?
Parthi, et Medi, et Aelamitae, et qui habitant Mesopotamiam, Judaeam, et Cappadociam, Pontum, et Asiam, Phrygiam, et Pamphyliam, Aegyptum, et partes Libyae, quae est circa Cyrenen,	Parthians, and Medes, and Elamites, and those who live in Mesopotamia, Judea, and Cappadocia, Pontus and Asia, Phrygia and Pamphylia, Egypt, and the parts of Libya that are around Cyrene,
et advenae Romani, Judaei quoque, et Proselyti, Cretes, et Arabes.	and strangers from Rome, Jews also, and Proselytes, Cretans, and Arabs:
Audivimus eos loquentes nostris linguis magnalia Dei.	We have heard them speaking of the great acts of God in our own languages.

the textual structure underlined and with the heightened emphasis of musical delivery.

As already mentioned, the Gradual and the Alleluya (Items 6 and 7), which follow the reading of the Epistle and precede the reading from the Gospel, present the most elaborate music of a Mass. Both are responsorial chants, which means that they contain music that is divided between a solo singer and the whole choir. (On special occasions and high feasts it was common to use several soloists for the solo sections to underline the importance of the day. For the sake of simplicity the ensuing discussion will refer only to one singer.)

The Gradual takes its name from the Latin word "gradus," meaning "step," since the solo singer used to stand on the step leading up to the pulpit from which the Gospel would be read. The responsorial form of the

Gradual is indicated below. The soloist sings the intonation, and the choir continues the introductory music, which is repeated later and is known as the refrain or "respond.") The soloist then sings the psalm verse, after which the entire music of the respond is repeated by the choir.[2] There is thus a dramatic alternation between solo and choral singing, which in the Gradual is emphasized by the physical position of the solo singer, and which makes it and other responsorial chants the musical highpoints of liturgical services.

Respond	Verse	Respond
Soloist, Choir	Soloist	Choir

The form of the Alleluya is very similar to that of the Gradual. It too is a responsorial chant. There are some slight differences from the method of singing the Gradual, however. The soloist begins by singing the intonation, and instead of simply continuing, the choir repeats the music of the intonation and then continues. (In the Alleluya the continuation is made up of the melismatic jubilus.) The soloist then sings the verse, and the choir joins in the final phrase. In the repetition of the respond ("Alleluya"), the intonation is again sung by the soloist, and the choir, without repeating the intonation, continues with the jubilus.[3]

This pattern may be represented as follows:

Alleluya	Verse	Alleluya
Soloist	Soloist	Soloist
Repeated by choir + jubilus	Ended by choir	Jubilus by choir

Graduals and Alleluyas are the most melismatic of all the chants in the Mass. They are dramatized further by the striking change in texture between choral and solo singing and by the fact that the solo music of the verse often lies in a high range.

As indicated in the table of the entire Mass, the Gradual and Alleluya were sometimes replaced by other items. The Gradual was sometimes replaced by an Alleluya; and the Alleluya was sometimes replaced by a Tract. These substitutions were dependent upon the liturgical calendar, which required changes in the standard format according to the season of

---

[2]By a process of abbreviation which seems to have begun in the early Middle Ages, sometimes only a portion of the respond was sung after the psalm verse. This process reached the point where the choir joined in on the last few words of the verse, without repeating the respond.

[3]As with the Gradual, the singing of the Alleluya also was abbreviated, until the whole of the final respond was omitted.

the year. This was a complex matter, but in the case of the Gradual and the Alleluya, the following facts are sufficient: (1) In the period following Easter the Gradual was replaced by an Alleluya; (2) during Lent and other penitential seasons the Alleluya was replaced by a Tract. The logic of this arrangement is clear enough. The Alleluya was regarded as a chant of great joy, and in the period of rejoicing after Easter two Alleluyas were sung. For the same reason the Alleluya was avoided completely at times of special solemnity.

Since Pentecost falls during the period of rejoicing after Easter (marking in fact the close of that period), the Mass for the feast contains two Alleluyas. The first Alleluya, *Alleluya, Spiritus Sanctus* (Ex. 4-6) is in the Hypodorian mode with a range of A–A and a final on D. The intonation outlines the lower fourth of the mode and touches on the reciting tone (F) before cadencing on the final. The jubilus lies mostly in the upper part of the octave with a move to the transposed alternate Lydian fifth, G down to C, before a return to the reciting tone F and a clear delineation of the upper fifth of the Hypodorian, A down to D, before the cadence on D. The solo verse ranges widely within the octave A–A and has a long melisma on the penultimate syllable of "perlustravit."

EXAMPLE 4-6   Alleluya, *Spiritus Sanctus,* of the Mass for Pentecost.

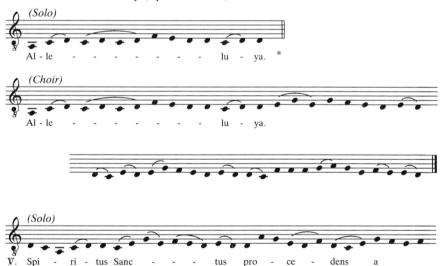

thro - no a - po - sto - lo - - - - rum   pec -

- - to - ra in - vi - si - bi - li ho - - - - -

- - di - e   per - lu - stra - - - - - - - -

(Choir)

- - - - - - - - - - - vit po - ten - - - - - -

ti - a.

(Solo)   *(Choir)*

Al - le - - - - - - - - - lu - ya   *

Alleluya.
Alleluya.

Alleluya.
Alleluya.

℣. Spiritus Sanctus procedens a throno
   apostolorum pectora invisibili
   hodie perlustravit potentia.

℣. The Holy Spirit proceeding from
   its throne has today purified the
   hearts of the apostles with invisible power.

Alleluya.

Alleluya.

The music of the end of the verse, for the word "potentia," exactly mirrors that for the opening word "Alleluya," a sort of repetition common to Alleluya compositions. It is at this point (on the word "potentia") that the choir recommences singing. The chant is then rounded off by the soloist and choir again singing the word "Alleluya."

There are two levels of musical contrast in this chant which serve to reinforce the structure of the text. The first level is found in the jubilus which lies mostly in the higher part of the modal octave and is thus set off from the opening intonation. The second level is found in the solo verse, with its single textual exclamation of wonder, which increases the intensity of the music by filling out the whole of the modal octave and containing several ornamental flourishes and an especially florid melisma just before the choir enters. The sense of the passage is not completed until the choir sings the final word of the sentence. This interaction between soloist and choir and the interdependency between them for the verbal sense of the text contributes to the dramatic intensity of the chant. The framing of the verse by the respond "Alleluya," the contrast between syllabic and highly melismatic singing, and between solo and choral texture, make this and other Alleluyas among the richest chants of the liturgy.

The texts of both Alleluyas express in few words the purifying power of the Holy Spirit. The second Alleluya for the Pentecost Mass, *Alleluya, Paraclitus* (Ex. 4-7), refers to the miraculous "teaching" mentioned in the Oratio and the Epistle.[4] Its text, however, is taken from the Gospel reading for the day (see Ex. 4-9, seventh line of the reading). The music begins with an intonation that leaves the mode ambiguous. It stresses D at the outset but ends on G. However the jubilus corrects this ambiguity by touching on the outer points of the Dorian fifth (A down to D) and cadences on D, although the pitch G remains prominent in the music. The solo verse ("Paraclitus . . .") continues to reaffirm the Dorian mode by concentrating on the D (the final of the mode) and the A above (the reciting tone), even containing two direct skips between those pitches. The florid melisma on the penultimate syllable of "docebit" is remarkable for its wide range and the thrice reiterated descent to the final. The last two words of the verse, those at which the choir re-enters, use the same music as the opening "Alleluya"

---

[4]A version of this chant, in its original tenth-century notation, may be seen at the top of Example 3-28 on p. 78.

setting, which creates a sense of closure. In this second Alleluya in the Mass there is no repetition of the respond after the verse, for the next item in the Mass, the Sequence, takes its place.

EXAMPLE 4-7   Alleluya, *Paraclitus,* of the Mass for Pentecost.

Alleluya.   Alleluya.
Alleluya.   Alleluya.

℣. Paraclitus Spiritus Sanctus, quem   ℣. The Protector, the Holy Spirit that
    mittet Pater in nomine meo, ille   the Father sends in my name, it
    vos docebit omnem veritatem.   will teach you all truth.

The Sequence (Item 8) developed rather late in the history of the liturgy and will be discussed in more detail in the next chapter. However it quickly became a standard feature of the medieval Mass and therefore deserves a place in our present overview of the "typical" Mass. Sequences were related to the Alleluya that preceded them, though the exact nature of the relationship and the reasons for the development of the Sequence are still matters of controversy among scholars. For our purposes it is sufficient to know that the Sequence is at least in some sense a part of the Alleluya that precedes it, because it takes the place of the final repetition of the respond at the end of that item:

Alleluya   **Verse**   **Sequence**

The texts of Sequences are proper, being specifically related to the season or feast. The most notable feature of Sequence texts is their verse format. They are written mostly in rhyming couplets, with both lines of each couplet having the same number of syllables. The couplets, however, can vary in length and number of syllables. Often the first and last lines stand alone. Sequence melodies are primarily syllabic, with only occasional, brief neumatic passages, and each couplet (or single line standing alone) receives a new phrase of the melody.

The Sequence for the Pentecost Mass (Ex. 4-8) is unusually short, consisting of only six lines, yet it conforms to this general pattern. There is an opening single line of 5 syllables, a couplet of 14 syllables per line, another couplet of 14 syllables per line, and a final single line of 7 syllables. The pattern may be illustrated as follows:

		Melody Phrase
Line one:	5 syllables.	A
{ Line two:	14 syllables.	B
{ Line three:	14 syllables.	B
{ Line four:	14 syllables	C
{ Line five:	14 syllables	C
Line six:	7 syllables	D

The Sequence ends with an "Amen" and the word "Alleluya." The text contemplates further qualities of the Holy Spirit, especially in its capacity as "Paraclitus" ("Protector")—a word reiterated from the verse of the second Alleluya.

Modally the Pentecost Sequence is ambiguous. Although the range of the chant is an octave from G, the music ends on D. The first line moves up from G to C in stepwise motion and returns in the same fashion, suggesting the lower fourth of the transposed (alternate) Lydian mode, but it then reaches higher and cadences on C. The remainder of the lines all begin and end on D and remain mostly in the upper fourth D–G, suggesting Mode 1 or 2. Unity is imparted to the melody by recurring phrases: the music for the end of the first couplet (lines 2 and 3) is used again for the ending of the second couplet (lines 3 and 4), and the music for the last line is taken from the beginning of the second couplet (lines 3 and 4).

The syllabic style of the music and repetition of each musical phrase for the second line of each couplet clearly stress the verse format of the text. The parallelism of the verse is reinforced by the parallelism of the music.

Immediately after the Sequence a reading from the Gospel (Item 9) takes place. This reading was chanted by the Deacon from the pulpit on the north side of the altar. Considerable ceremony was often involved in carrying the gospel book itself from the altar where it lay, through the choir, to the pulpit. The recitation formula for the Gospel is usually quite simple. The reading itself is always preceded by the standard interchange between

EXAMPLE 4-8   Sequence, *Fulgens Praeclara,* of the Mass for Pentecost.

1. Fulgens praeclara,
2. Paracliti sancti consolationem piam,
3. Expectamus sanctam repromissionem tuam,
4. Per acta ascensionis sacra sollemnia,
5. Qui es regressus in caelum nube tectus clara,
6. Pollens laude aeterna.
   Amen.
   Alleluya.

1. Shining splendor,
2. We await the pious consolation of the holy Protector,
3. Your holy promise of salvation,
4. Through the solemn act of the ascension,
5. You who returned to heaven covered by a cloud,
6. Esteemed with eternal praise.
   Amen.
   Alleluya.

the reader and the choir and the introductory statement of the source of the passage to be read (also concluded by the choir).

The Gospel reading for Pentecost (Ex. 4-9) comes from St. John. The chant uses a downward skip of a third and a rising whole step for the half close and a descending whole step for the full close. The concluding formula is an extended elaboration of the half close. The text, which recounts how Jesus prophesied the coming of the Holy Spirit, is thus clearly and simply projected. The importance of the reading is underscored by the ceremonial carrying of the book, the new location, and the designated reader. The music itself is a framework of unadorned clarity.

EXAMPLE 4-9   Gospel of the Mass for Pentecost.

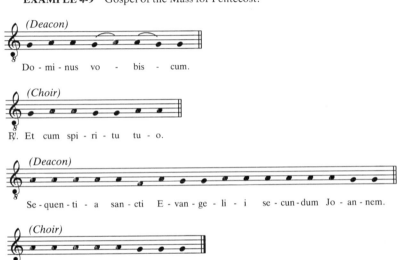

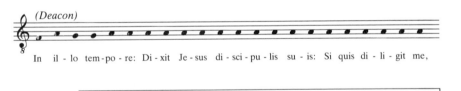

Qui non di - li - git me, ser - mo - nes me - os non ser - vat.

Et ser - mo - nem quem au - di - stis, non est me - us,

sed e - ius, qui mi - sit me, Pa - tris.

Haec lo - cu - tus sum vo - bis, a - pud vos ma - nens.

Pa - ra - cli - tus au - tem Spi - ri - tus San-ctus, quem mit - tet Pa - ter in no - mi - ne me - o,

il - le vos do - ce - bit om - ni - a,

et sug - ge - ret vo - bis om - ni - a, quae-cum - que di - xe - ro vo - bis.

Pa - cem re - lin - quo vo - bis.

Pa - cem me - am do vo - bis.

Non quo - mo - do mun-dus dat, e - go do vo - bis.

Non tur - be - tur cor ve - strum ne - que for - mi - det.

Au - di - stis qui - a e - go di - xi vo - bis: Va - do et ve - ni - o ad vos.

Si di - li - ge - re - tis me, gau - de - re - tis u - ti - que, qui - a va - do ad Pa - trem,

qui - a Pa - ter ma - ior me est.

Et nunc di - xi vo - bis pri - us - quam fi - at,

ut cum fac - tum fu - e - rit, cre - da - tis.

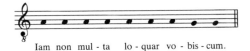

Iam non mul - ta lo - quar vo - bis - cum.

Ve - nit e - nim Prin - ceps mun - di hu - ius,

et in me non ha - bet quid - quam.

Sed ut co - gno - scat mun - dus, qui - a di - li - go Pa - trem,

et si - cut man - da - tum de - dit mi - hi Pa - ter, sic fa - ci - o.

Dominus vobiscum.

R̶⁷. Et cum spiritu tuo.

Sequentia sancti Evangelii secundum Joannem.

R̶⁷. Gloria tibi Domine.

In illo tempore: Dixit Jesus discipulis suis: Si quis diligit me, sermonem meum servabit, et Pater meus diliget eum,

et ad eum veniemus, et mansionem apud eum faciemus.

Qui non diligit me, sermones meos non servat.

Et sermonem quem audistis, non est meus,

sed eius, qui misit me, Patris.

Haec locutus sum vobis, apud vos manens.

Paraclitus autem Spiritus Sanctus, quem mittet Pater in nomine meo, ille vos docebit omnia,

et suggeret vobis omnia, quaecumque dixero vobis.

Pacem relinquo vobis.

Pacem meam do vobis.

Non quomodo mundus dat, ego do vobis.

Non turbetur cor vestrum neque formidet.

Audistis quia ego dixi vobis: Vado et venio ad vos.

Si diligeretis me, gauderetis utique, quia vado ad Patrem,

quia Pater maior me est.

Et nunc dixi vobis priusquam fiat,

ut cum factum fuerit, credatis.

Iam non multa loquar vobiscum.

Venit enim Princeps mundi huius,

The Lord be with you.

R̶⁷. And with your spirit.

Continuation of the holy Gospel according to John.

R̶⁷. Glory to you, O Lord.

At that time: Jesus said to his disciples: Anyone who loves me will follow my teachings, and my Father will love him,

and we will come to him and make our abode with him.

He who does not love me will not follow my teachings.

And the teachings you have heard are not mine,

but my Father's, who sent me.

I have said these things to you while I was with you.

But the Protector, the Holy Spirit, whom my Father will send in my name, it will teach you everything,

and it will remind you of everything that I have told you.

I leave peace to you.

I give you my peace.

And I give, not as the world gives.

Let not your heart be troubled or afraid.

You heard what I said to you: I go and I shall return to you.

If you loved me, you would rejoice, for I go to my Father,

for my Father is greater than I am.

And now I have told you before it happens,

so that when it does happen, you may believe.

Now I shall not say much to you.

For the Prince of this world is coming,

et in me non habet quidquam.	and he has nothing in me.
Sed ut cognoscat mundus, quia diligo Patrem,	But so that the world may know that I love my Father,
et sicut mandatum dedit mihi Pater, sic facio.	and that my Father has instructed me thus, thus do I do.

The Gospel was sometimes followed by a homily or sermon, which comprised a commentary upon the passage just heard, or by a reading from one of the Fathers of the Church on the significance of the day or feast. If there was no homily, the third item of the Ordinary of the Mass, the Credo (Item 10 in the table), was sung immediately after the Gospel. The Credo was a late addition to the Mass and retains its opening form in the singular ("I believe") from its ancient use in the ceremony of baptism. Its text presents a list of attributes of Christ, framed by the statements of belief. Compared to the large number of melodies for the other items in the Ordinary of the Mass, very few were composed for the Credo. This may have been because of the length of the text, the lateness of its introduction into the Mass, or its traditional association with one particular melody. It is the celebrant who sings the intonation of the Credo as he does for the Gloria.

The Credo for the Pentecost Mass (Ex. 4-10) is sung to the traditional Credo melody. The setting is almost completely syllabic, with occasional two-, three-, or four-note neumes which continually reappear. Indeed the whole chant is made up of a small number of melodic motifs combined and recombined in different patterns. Of these, only three will be mentioned, although careful analysis will reveal more. The opening intonation formula, with its two descending minor thirds (G–E and F–D) and two ascending whole steps to A, is found elsewhere in the melody in slightly varied form (marked x in the music); and the second phrase, on "Patrem omnipotentem," with its ornamental B♭ and cadence to G, also occurs frequently (marked y). This use of motivic technique, and the pattern of drawing attention to important words in the text ("unum Deum," "Jesum Christum," "Deum verum," "[consubstanti]alem Patri," "[Spi]ritu Sancto," "adoratur," etc.) by setting them to the same notes of the chant (marked z), bring the Credo close to the style of the Gloria, the only other long text out of the five Ordinary items, and the only other chant in the Mass for which the celebrant sings the intonation. Further unity is brought to the long string of short sentences in the Credo text by ending every one except for the first and the last two on the same pitch (G). Indeed, starting on the third phrase ("Et in unum Dominum"), the formation of each phrase is remarkably similar, giving the impression of a series of varied, but fundamentally similar, musical lines. Against this unity a tension exists, for the establishment of A as a cadential pitch (in the intonation) is not confirmed until the penultimate phrase of the chant ("Et vitam venturi saeculi"). The final "Amen," despite its smooth common-tone link, abruptly shifts the pitch focus back to E.

EXAMPLE 4-10 Credo of the Mass for Pentecost.

Credo in unum Deum,
Patrem omnipotentem, factorem caeli et
    terrae, visibilium omnium, et invisi-
    bilium.

I believe in one God,
the omnipotent Father, creator of the
    heaven and earth, of everything
    visible and invisible.

Et in unum Dominum Jesum Christum, Filium Dei unigenitum.
Et ex Patre natum ante omnia saecula.

Deum de Deo, lumen de lumine, Deum verum de Deo vero.
Genitum, non factum, consubstantialem Patri, per quem omnia facta sunt.

Qui propter nos homines, et propter nostram salutem, descendit de caelis.
Et incarnatus est de Spiritu Sancto ex Maria virgine.
Et homo factus est.
Crucifixus etiam pro nobis, sub Pontio Pilato passus et sepultus est.

Et resurrexit tertia die, secundum scripturas.
Et ascendit in caelum, sedet ad dexteram Patris.
Et iterum venturus est cum gloria, iudicare vivos et mortuos.
Cuius regni non erit finis.
Et in Spiritum Sanctum, Dominum, et vivificantem, qui ex Patre Filioque procedit.
Qui cum Patre et Filio simul adoratur et conglorificatur, qui locutus est per prophetas.
Et unam sanctam Catholicam et apostolicam ecclesiam.
Confiteor unum baptisma in remissionem peccatorum.
Et expecto resurrectionem mortuorum.

Et vitam venturi saeculi.
Amen.

And in one Lord Jesus Christ, the only-begotten Son of God.
And born from the Father before all time.

God of God, light of light, a true God of a true God.
Born, not made, of one substance with the Father, by whom all things are created.

Who descended from heaven on behalf of us men and our salvation.
And was made flesh by the Holy Spirit through the Virgin Mary.
And became a man.
Indeed he was crucified for us, and under Pontius Pilate suffered and was buried.

And he arose on the third day, in accordance with the Scriptures.
And he ascended into heaven, and sits at the right hand of the Father.
And he will come again in glory, to judge the living and the dead.
And there will be no end to his kingdom.
And in the Holy Spirit, the Lord and giver of life, which proceeds from the Father and the Son.
Which is adored and glorified together with the Father and the Son, and spoke through the prophets.
And in one holy Catholic and apostolic church.
I acknowledge one baptism for the pardoning of sins.
And I anticipate the resurrection of the dead.
And the life of the world to come.
Amen.

Eucharist

The second part of the Mass is begun by a statement of the liturgical interchange and the introduction to prayer. This leads straight into the Offertory (Item 11 in the table). Offertory chants used to be among the most elaborate chants of the Mass, but as the rituals of the offering (a procession, incensation of the altar, washing of hands, preparation of the bread and wine) were shortened, the chant became simpler. Originally, like the Introit, the Offertory was in the form of an antiphon with psalm verses. In the later Middle Ages the verses were dropped, and only the antiphon remained. The music of many Offertory chants is wide ranging and melismatic.

The Offertory for Pentecost (Ex. 4-11) is more neumatic than melismatic. It is in the form of several arches and reaches the outer limits of its range (D up to C) with unusual frequency. The chant ends on an E final, confirming a Mode-4, Hypophrygian, designation. But there are many phrases of the melody that pass into other modal areas, such as the phrase "quod operatus es in nobis," which suggests Mode 8, or the music for "reges munera," which moves momentarily into Mode 1. The text is proper to Pentecost, although, as is often the case with Offertory texts, it does not seem particularly apposite to the day. It does, however, refer to the offering of gifts, which suits an Offertory. Its first word ("Confirma") alludes to the sacrament of confirmation, which imparts the grace of the Holy Spirit; and it ends with the word "Alleluya," establishing its general appropriateness to the Easter season.

EXAMPLE 4-11   Offertory of the Mass for Pentecost.

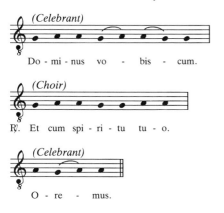

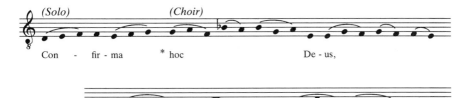

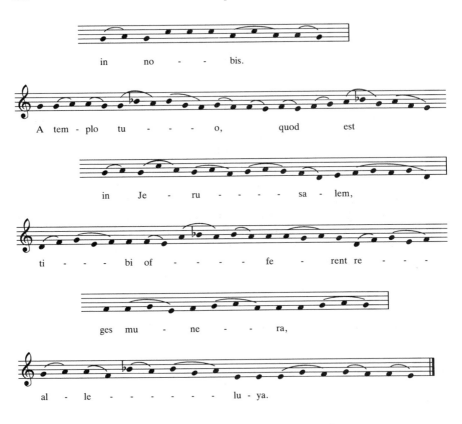

in   no - -   bis.

A tem - plo   tu - - - -   o,   quod   est

in   Je - ru - - - -   sa - lem,

ti - - -   bi of - - - -   fe -   rent re - - -

ges   mu -   ne - -   ra,

al - le - - - - - - -   lu - ya.

Dominus vobiscum.	The Lord be with you.
℟. Et cum spiritu tuo.	℟. And also with your spirit.
Oremus.	Let us pray.
Confirma hoc Deus, quod operatus es in nobis.	Confirm this, O God, that you have acted in us.
A templo tuo, quod est in Jerusalem,	From your temple, which is in Jerusalem,
tibi offerent reges munera,	there kings will bring you gifts,
alleluya.	alleluya.

The Secret (Item 12) is a prayer spoken in silence by the priest who is celebrating the Mass. It is usually quite short, and is concluded by the standard ending for prayers.

The Pentecost Secret (Ex. 4-12) refers to the Holy Spirit of the Pentecost celebration as well as to the offering which is a part of most Secret texts. The word "munera" ("gifts") connects the item with the Offertory text, as well as confirming the general spirit of offering of the second part (Eucharist) of the Mass. The last part of the standard ending (from "per omnia saecula" to the end) is recited aloud to mark the completion of the Secret, and the choir sings the response ("Amen").

EXAMPLE 4-12   Secret of the Mass for Pentecost.

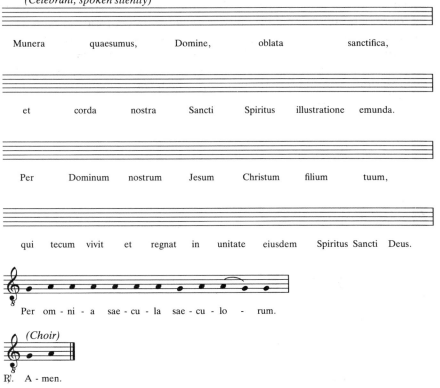

(Celebrant, spoken silently)

Munera   quaesumus,   Domine,   oblata   sanctifica,

et   corda   nostra   Sancti   Spiritus   illustratione   emunda.

Per   Dominum   nostrum   Jesum   Christum   filium   tuum,

qui   tecum   vivit   et   regnat   in   unitate   eiusdem   Spiritus Sancti   Deus.

Per om - ni - a   sae - cu - la   sae - cu - lo - rum.

(Choir)

℟.   A - men.

Munera quaesumus, Domine, oblata sanctifica,	Bless these gifts that we offer, we beseech you, O Lord,
et corda nostra Sancti Spiritus illustratione emunda.	and cleanse our hearts with the purification of the Holy Spirit.
Per Dominum nostrum Jesum Christum Filium tuum,	Through our Lord Jesus Christ, your Son,
qui tecum vivit et regnat in unitate eiusdem Spiritus Sancti Deus.	who lives and rules with you as God in the unity of the Holy Spirit.
Per omnia saecula saeculorum.	For ever and ever.
℟. Amen.	℟. Amen.

The Preface (Item 13) is also recited by the celebrant but is chanted aloud to a fairly elaborate recitational formula. Prefaces begin with a series of responses between priest and choir, directly after the final statement of the Secret. The Preface always has an open-ended conclusion (textually, though not musically) on the word "dicentes" ("saying").

The Pentecost Preface (Ex. 4-13) opens with words that are standard in all Prefaces, including the exchange of greetings between priest and choir; it becomes specific to the day at the phrase beginning "Qui." Here the Holy Spirit is compared to the anointing oil of consecration. The reciting formula is quite elaborate. Phrases begin with an upward skip of a minor third to the reciting tone on C; the half close is represented by a stepwise descent back down to A and a return to B, while the full close has an ornamental descent to G and ends on A, the pitch of the "Qui" opening. The text ends with the word "dicentes," which leads directly into the next item of the Mass, the Sanctus.

EXAMPLE 4-13   Preface of the Mass for Pentecost.

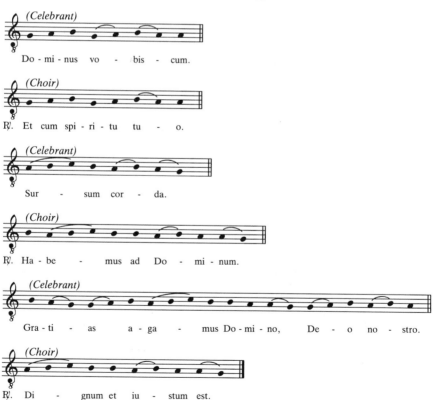

(Celebrant)

Ve - re di - gnum et iu - stum est, ae - quum et sa - lu - ta - re,

nos ti - bi sem - per et u - bi - que gra - ti - as a - ge - re,

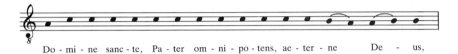

Do - mi - ne sanc - te, Pa - ter om - ni - po - tens, ae - ter - ne De - us,

per Chri-stum Do - mi - num no - strum.

Qui a - scen-dens su - per om-nes cae-los, se - dens-que ad dex - te - ram tu - am,

pro-mis-sum Spi - ri - tum San-ctum ho - di - er - na di - e in fi - li - os a - dop - ti - o -

nis ef - fu - dit.

Qua-prop-ter pro - fu - sis gau - di - is,

to - tus in or - be ter - ra - rum mun - dus ex - sul - tat.

Sed et su-per-nae vir-tu-tes at-que an-ge-li-cae po-te-sta-tes hym-num glo-ri-ae

tu - ae con - ci - nunt,

si - ne fi - ne di - cen - tes:

Dominus vobiscum.	The Lord be with you.
R⁊. Et cum spiritu tuo.	R⁊. And also with your spirit.
Sursum corda.	Lift up your hearts.
R⁊. Habemus ad Dominum.	R⁊. We hold them out to the Lord.
Gratias agamus Domino, Deo nostro.	Let us give thanks to the Lord, our God.
R⁊. Dignum et iustum est.	R⁊. It is worthy and just.

Vere dignum et iustum est, aequum et salutare,	Truly it is worthy and just, right and salutary,
nos tibi semper et ubique gratias agere,	for us to give thanks to you always and in all places,
Domine sancte, Pater omnipotens, aeterne Deus,	holy Lord, omnipotent Father, eternal God,
per Christum Dominum nostrum.	through Christ our Lord.
Qui ascendens super omnes caelos, sedensque ad dexteram tuam,	Who, ascending above all the heavens, and sitting at your right hand,
promissum Spiritum Sanctum hodierna die in filios adoptionis effudit.	has today poured out the promised Holy Spirit on the sons of the adoption.
Quapropter profusis gaudiis,	Therefore with rapturous joy
totus in orbe terrarum mundus exsultat.	let all mankind throughout the whole world exult.
Sed et supernae virtutes atque angelicae potestates hymnum gloriae tuae concinunt,	And the heavenly powers and the throngs of angels sing together a hymn of your glory,
sine fine dicentes:	endlessly saying:

The Sanctus (Item 14) is the fourth item in the Ordinary of the Mass. Its text falls into two main sections, both of which can be further subdivided. The first half of the text, from "Sanctus" to "gloria tua," is taken directly from the Jewish liturgy, where it plays an important role both in the daily services and in the additional service on the Sabbath. It is in two parts, beginning "Sanctus" and "Pleni" respectively. The second half, from "Hosanna" to the end, comes from St. Matthew and is in three parts:

Hosanna—Benedictus—Hosanna. This natural division of the text encouraged a sectional form of composition in Sanctus melodies, most of which are neumatic in construction.

The Sanctus of the Pentecost Mass (Ex. 4-14) begins with an intonation whose small arch built on G is also used to close the musical setting of the second word. The "Pleni" section is made up of two long descending lines. In the second half, the music for the "Benedictus" section begins as though it will parallel the music for the "Pleni" section (a common device in Sanctus settings), but this expectation is thwarted. The second "Hosanna" setting, however, reverses this device: the phrase begins differently, but ends up mirroring the first "Hosanna" setting. Thus the sectional division of the text is reflected in the music. The range of the chant is wide, encompassing an octave and a third. The melody is built as a long series of slowly descending curves, often balanced by short rises at the end of phrases. The mode is Mode 8, with a final on G. Cadences are on G, the final of the mode, or on C, the reciting tone, with the exception of the cadence at the end of the "Pleni" section, which is on E.

EXAMPLE 4-14   Sanctus of the Mass for Pentecost.

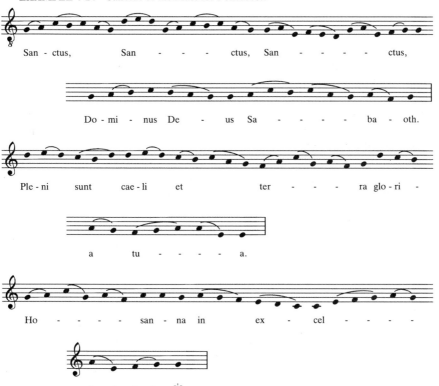

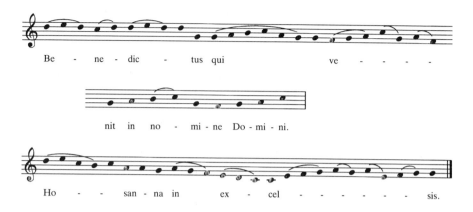

Be - ne - dic - tus qui ve - - -

nit in no - mi - ne Do - mi - ni.

Ho - - san - na in ex - cel - - - - - - sis.

Sanctus, Sanctus, Sanctus, Dominus Deus Sabaoth.	Holy, holy, holy, Lord God of hosts.
Pleni sunt caeli et terra gloria tua.	The heavens and the earth are full of your glory.
Hosanna in excelsis.	Hosanna in the highest.
Benedictus qui venit in nomine Domini.	Blessed is he who comes in the name of the Lord.
Hosanna in excelsis.	Hosanna in the highest.

The singing of the Sanctus by the choir is followed by the saying of the Canon (Item 15) silently by the priest (Ex. 4-15). The Canon comprises a large number of prayers, which cannot be given here. They involve petitions for acceptance of the offering, commemorations of the living and the dead, the consecration, declarations of unworthiness, and acceptance of the communion. They are accompanied by ritual actions and the taking of communion by the priest. (Sometimes the length of silence involved in the saying of the Canon encouraged the practice of singing the Sanctus, and occasionally also the following Agnus, during the Canon itself.)

EXAMPLE 4-15   Canon of the Mass for Pentecost.

[Silent prayers]

At the conclusion of the Canon the priest raises his voice to chant the Pater Noster (Item 16). This begins with a standard sentence ("Praeceptis salutaribus . . ."), which is itself introduced by the opening "Oremus" ("Let us pray"). Then follows the text of the Pater Noster with its series of petitions. The prayer ends with a response from the choir and an additional interchange between priest and choir. There are half a dozen melodies extant for this chant, but only one or two of them were in common use.

The music for the Pater Noster in the Mass for Pentecost (Ex. 4-16) opens with introductory recitational formulas for the "Oremus" and the beginning sentence and continues with a chant that is syllabic and simple. It is not far removed from an elaborate recitational formula itself. It centers on B for most of the text and then shifts to A near the end. Cadences are on A and G. A, the opening and ending pitch, is used for the full closes at the end of sentences, and G is used at half closes. The melody moves within a narrow range, and although the beginnings of phrases are varied, the internal music is closely related from phrase to phrase, reflecting the structure of the text.

EXAMPLE 4-16 Pater Noster of the Mass for Pentecost.

O - re - mus.

Prae-cep-tis sa - lu - ta - ri - bus mo - ni - ti, et di - vi - na in - sti - tu - ti - o - ne for - ma - ti,

au - de - mus di - ce - re:

Pa - ter no - ster, qui es in cae - lis,

sanc - ti - fi - ce - tur no - men tu - um.

Ad ve - ni - at re - gnum tu - um,

fi - at vo - lun - tas tu - a,

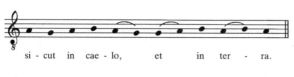

si - cut in cae - lo,   et   in ter - ra.

Pa - nem no - strum quo - ti - di - a - num da no - bis ho - di - e,

et di - mit - te no - bis de - bi - ta no - stra,

si - cut et nos di - mit - ti - mus de - bi - to - ri - bus no - stris.

Et ne nos in - du - cas in ten - ta - ti - o - nem,

(Choir)

℟. sed li - be - ra nos a ma - lo.

(Celebrant)

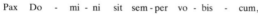

Pax Do - mi - ni sit sem - per vo - bis - cum,

(Choir)

℟. et cum spi - ri - tu tu - o.

Oremus.	Let us pray.
Praeceptis salutaribus moniti, et divina institutione formati, audemus dicere:	Guided by salutary precepts, and taught by divine counsel, we dare to say:
Pater noster, qui es in caelis, sanctificetur nomen tuum.	Our Father, you who are in heaven, may your name be made holy.

Adveniat regnum tuum,	May your kingdom come,
fiat voluntas tua,	and your will be done,
sicut in caelo, et in terra.	on earth as it is in heaven.
Panem nostrum quotidianum da	Grant us today our daily bread,
nobis hodie,	
et dimitte nobis debita nostra,	pardon our sins,
sicut et nos dimittimus debitoribus	just as we pardon those who have
nostris.	sinned against us.
Et ne nos inducas in tentationem,	And do not lead us into temptation,
℟. sed libera nos a malo.	℟. but free us from evil.
Pax Domini sit semper vobiscum,	May the peace of the Lord be always
	with you,
℟. et cum spiritu tuo.	℟. and also with your spirit.

The Agnus Dei (Item 17) is the final item among the main chants of the Ordinary of the Mass. Like the Kyrie and the Sanctus, the text of the Agnus Dei contains threefold invocations and falls into clearly defined sections. This encouraged the composition of sectional musical settings, as can be seen in the many Agnus Dei chants that were composed. Most are neumatic in style.

The Pentecost Agnus Dei (Ex. 4-17) uses the same music for the first two sections, thus clearly marking the parallelism of the text. The third section has a new phrase, but the endings of all three sections are linked, despite the change of text, by the same cadence formula. The range of the chant is an octave on D, with an extension downwards of a single tone in the last section. The mode is Mode 8, Hypomixolydian. All of the sections have a firm cadence on G, the final of the mode, approached both from above and below. The skip upwards of a fourth in the opening intonation is echoed at later points in the chant and also balanced by the appearance of some downward skips of a fourth, from D down to A as well as from C down to G.

EXAMPLE 4-17   Agnus Dei of the Mass for Pentecost.

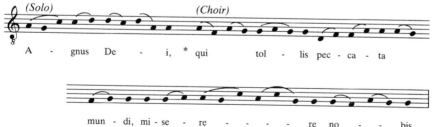

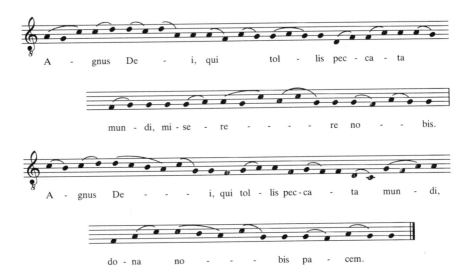

Agnus Dei, qui tollis peccata mundi,	Lamb of God, you who remove the sins
miserere nobis.	of the world, have pity on us.
Agnus Dei, qui tollis peccata mundi,	Lamb of God, you who remove the sins
miserere nobis.	of the world, have pity on us.
Agnus Dei, qui tollis peccata mundi,	Lamb of God, you who remove the sins
dona nobis pacem.	of the world, grant us peace.

The Communion chant (Item 18) is sung during the partaking of the bread and wine by those other than the priest. Like the Offertory, the Communion used to be constructed in the form of an antiphon with a variable number of verses to allow for adjustment to the time required. Later the verses were dropped, and only the antiphon remained. The melodic style of Communion chants ranges from the simple to the elaborate. The texts are proper and are drawn from the psalms or the Gospels.

The Communion for Pentecost (Ex. 4-18) takes its text from the reading of the Epistle for the day (see Ex. 4-5, third, fourth, sixth, and last lines), but the textual summary appears here with completely different effect. Two short sentences present the central facts of the miracle. The music is neumatic with several syllabic passages. The opening of the chant is striking, with its leap of a fifth upwards in the intonation answered by the corresponding leap downwards. The sudden downward leap is unexpected and was surely inspired by the word which it sets: "repente" ("suddenly"). Similarly the word "sonus" ("sound") is set to the highest and most prominent pitches in the whole chant. This kind of reflection of textual meaning in the music is rare in plainchant. The fifth G–D is a strong signal for the Mixolydian mode, Mode 7. The reciting tone of that mode, D, plays a significant role in both the first and the second ("Et repleti sunt . . .") phrase of the chant. The second phrase even begins with an ornamented version of the opening leap, though without the sudden downward echo. The two main cadences at the text divisions are on the G final, and indeed both of these cadences (on the "alleluya" at the mid-point and on the final "alleluya") have the same music. As if to stress the fact that the words "alleluya" are appended to the scriptural text, the music before these words also ends on G.

EXAMPLE 4-18 Communion of the Mass for Pentecost.

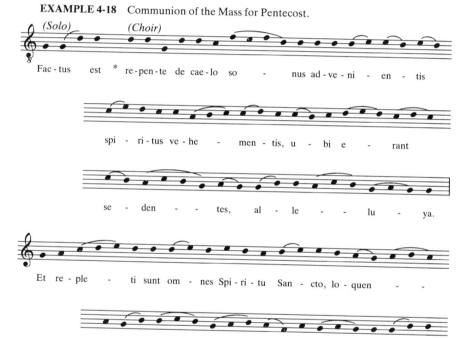

| Factus est repente de caelo sonus adve-nientis spiritus vehementis, ubi erant sedentes, alleluya. | And suddenly there came a sound from heaven, as though a powerful wind were coming, where they were sitting, alleluya. |
| Et repleti sunt omnes Spiritu Sancto, loquentes magnalia Dei, alleluya, alleluya. | And they were all filled with the Holy Spirit, speaking of the great acts of God, alleluya, alleluya. |

The conclusion of the communion portion of the Mass is marked by the chanting of the Post-Communion prayer (Item 19). Its text is proper and is sung to the same simple recitational chant as the Oratio and the ending of the Secret.

The Pentecost Post-Communion chant (Ex. 4-19) has a text appropriate to the day, with a petition for the purifying power of the Holy Spirit, and is sung to the same simple recitational formula as the Oratio in the Fore-Mass (see Ex. 4-4). It is preceded by the interchange between celebrant and choir and the brief invitation to prayer and concludes with the standard ending and the response by the choir ("Amen").

EXAMPLE 4-19   Post-Communion of the Mass for Pentecost.

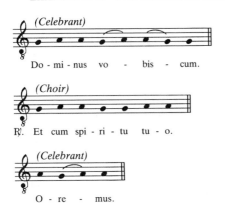

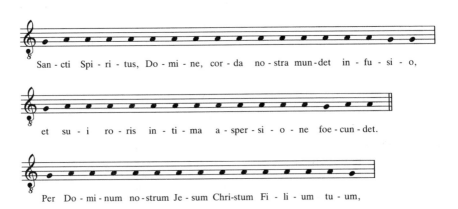

qui te-cum vi - vit et re-gnat in u - ni - ta - te e - ius-dem Spi - ri - tus San-cti De - us.

Per om - ni - a sae - cu - la sae - cu - lo - rum.

(Choir)

R̷. A - men.

Dominus vobiscum.
R̷. Et cum spiritu tuo.
Oremus.

Sancti Spiritus, Domine, corda
  nostra mundet infusio,

et sui roris intima aspersione foecun-
  det.
Per Dominum nostrum Jesum Christum Filium tuum,
qui tecum vivit et regnat in unitate
  eiusdem Spiritus Sancti Deus.
Per omnia saecula saeculorum.
R̷. Amen.

The Lord be with you.
R̷. And with your spirit.
Let us pray.

May the purification of the Holy
  Spirit, O Lord, cleanse our
  hearts,
And fertilize them with the secret
  sprinkling of its dew.
Through our Lord Jesus Christ, your
  Son,
who lives and rules with you as God
  in the unity of the Holy Spirit.
For ever and ever.
R̷. Amen.

The final item of the whole Mass is the dismissal chant, Ite, Missa Est (Item 20), which is sometimes considered an additional item of the Ordinary, though in penitential times its text is replaced by the words Benedicamus Domino. There are several melodies for this item, most of which are neumatic. It is sung by the celebrant and responded to by the choir with a repetition of the same melody.

The dismissal chant for Pentecost (Ex. 4-20) is sung to a melismatic melody which is taken from the first phrase of the Kyrie of this same Mass (see Ex. 4-2). This was not an uncommon practice in the later Middle Ages, establishing a cyclical sense for the Mass as a whole. The melody is clearly in Mode 1, Dorian, beginning on the reciting tone A, stressing that pitch, and descending to a firm cadence on D. The melody is repeated for the choir's response, "Deo gratias" ("Thanks be to God").

EXAMPLE 4-20   Ite Missa Est of the Mass for Pentecost.

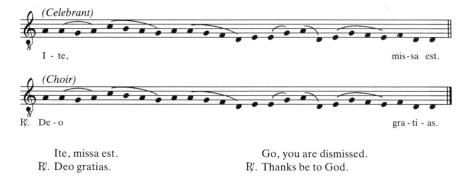

Ite, missa est.	Go, you are dismissed.
℟. Deo gratias.	℟. Thanks be to God.

In reconstructing this Mass for Pentecost, we may have compiled one that was never sung at any particular place in any particular year during the Middle Ages, for, as has been mentioned, customs and practices varied from country to country, from town to town, and from church to church. Similarly, the nature of the service and the form of some of the items changed during the long history of the development of the medieval liturgy. Moreover, no attempt has been made to describe the processions, ritual movements, clothing, books, plates, and cups, or the statuary, paintings, carvings, and architectural details of the Church, all of which provided ambience and meaning to the service. However, this examination has enabled us to gain a broad overview of the structure of the Mass in general, the types of chant that were used in the various items in the Mass and their styles of performance, as well as the main places where variants could occur.

SUMMARY

The Mass developed over many hundreds of years, and its form and content changed over time as well as from place to place. By about the tenth or eleventh century, however, it had taken on a relatively stable form. This form includes texts that are specific to the day and occasion upon which the Mass was celebrated ("proper") and texts that are invariable ("common"). The music for a Mass ranges from the simplest recitational style to the most elaborately melismatic, the former being used mostly for scriptural and other readings and prayers, the latter for chants which on the whole do not accompany important liturgical actions.

Three of the chants (Introit, Offertory, and Communion) were originally in the form of an antiphon framing one or more psalm verses. Only the Introit retained this form; the Offertory and Communion were reduced to their antiphons only.

The most melismatic chants are the Gradual (sometimes replaced by an Alleluya) and the Alleluya (sometimes replaced by a Tract). These are called responsorial chants from the fact that their interior verses (as well as intonations) are sung by solo singers, to whom the choir responds with the remainder of the music.

Five of the musical items of the Mass, having common texts, are known collectively as the Ordinary of the Mass. These are the Kyrie, Gloria, Credo, Sanctus, and Agnus Dei. The dismissal formula, Ite, Missa Est, is occasionally also considered a part of the Ordinary although its text may change according to the season.

In the main items of the Ordinary, the musical style is closely tied to the form and length of the text. The Gloria and Credo, with very long texts, are primarily syllabic. They also share the distinction of having intonations that are sung by the priest officiating at the service (the "celebrant"). The other three items of the Ordinary are characterized by musical settings that usually point up the tripartite nature of their texts. The Kyrie is neumatic, and its three statements are each sung three times. The Sanctus is also neumatic, and its text, opening with a threefold acclamation, falls into clear sections which are often matched by musical parallelism and repetition. The three parallel statements of the Agnus Dei are also usually set to a neumatic chant which mirrors the structure of the text.

In the Mass, the use of silence for certain items, such as the Canon and the Secret, is particularly noticeable. Prayers, which are either said silently or recited to simple formulas, are often marked by standard short introductory or closing sentences, as well as the invitation "Oremus" ("Let us pray") and a closing response ("Amen"). The greeting or interchange between priest and choir—"Dominus vobiscum" ("The Lord be with you") answered by "Et cum spiritu tuo" ("And also with your spirit")—is used as the introduction to prayers (Oratio, Preface, Post-Communion). The interchange and "Oremus" also are used to open the entire second part of the Mass.

The Sequence, a late addition to the Mass, is inserted at the end of the Alleluya and before the Gospel. It is made of rhyming verse set to a syllabic melody, each phrase of which, repeated, serves for a pair of text lines.

Throughout the celebration of the Mass, different participants, distinguished by their rank, their clothing, their actions, and their physical position in relation to the altar, take part in the elaborate ceremony, which involves books, vessels, draperies, gesture, scent, movement, and music.

Music is a central element in the whole service. It is music that articulates the Mass and that differentiates those chants that tell a story, those that are designed to present petitions, and those that encourage meditation. In the interweaving of texts that are constant from day to day and those that illuminate a specific occasion, music can make familiar words new and new words clear. It can present the same text either as a straightforward account of an event or as an opportunity for contemplation. (Compare the effect of the Epistle with that of the Communion.) Music reinforces the rhetorical as well as the spiritual content of the varied texts that occur in the Mass and adds clarity, solemnity, and intensity to them all.

DISCOGRAPHY

Example 4-1   Introit of the Mass for Pentecost.
Choir of the Monks of the Abbey of Saint-Pierre de Solesmes, *Gregorian Chant,* London LL 1463; also on Benediktinerabtei, Münsterschwarzach, *Gregorianischer Choral: Die grossen Feste des Kirchenjahres,* Archiv 2723 084; Schola Cantorum of Amsterdam Students, *Gregorian Chant,* Columbia D3M 32329 (Side III); Choir of the Monks of the Abbey of Saint Pierre de Solesmes, *Gregorian Chant: Pentecost, Corpus Christi,* London 5241; and Chorus of the Frati Minori of Busto Arsizio, *Gregorian Masses,* Musical Heritage Society MHS 1912.

Example 4-2   Kyrie of the Mass for Pentecost.
Ensemble Organum, *Léonin: Ecole Notre-Dame,* Harmonia Mundi HM 1148; also on *Opus Musicum: The Mass,* Arno Volk Verlag OM 201/03 (Side I, Band 1); Benediktinerabtei, Münsterschwarzach, *Gregorianischer Choral: Die grossen Feste des Kirchenjahres,* Archiv 2723 084 (Side I); and *History of European Music, Part One: Music of the Early Middle Ages,* vol. I, Musical Heritage Society OR 349 (Side I, Band 8).

Example 4-3   Gloria of the Mass for Pentecost.
Benediktinerabtei, Münsterschwarzach, *Gregorianischer Choral: Die grossen Feste des Kirchenjahres,* Archiv 2723 084 (Side I).

Example 4-4   Oratio of the Mass for Pentecost.
Nuns-Choir of the Benedictine Abbey of Our Lady of Varensell, *Missa in Festo Pentecostes,* Archive ARC 73203.

Example 4-5   Epistle of the Mass for Pentecost.
Nuns-Choir of the Benedictine Abbey of Our Lady of Varensell, *Missa in Festo Pentecostes,* Archive ARC 73203.

Example 4-6   Alleluya, *Spiritus Sanctus*
TAPE ONE, SIDE ONE.

Example 4-9   Gospel of the Mass for Pentecost.
Nuns-Choir of the Benedictine Abbey of Our Lady of Varensell, *Missa in Festo Pentecostes,* Archive ARC 73203.

Example 4-10   Credo of the Mass for Pentecost.
Choir of the Monks of L'Abbaye St. Pierre de Solesmes, *Gregorian Chant,* London 5632; also on Choir of the Monks of the Benedictine Abbey of St. Martin, Beuron, *Liturgia Paschalis,* Archiv 3088/90 (Side VI); and Chor der Mönche der Benediktiner-Erzabtei St. Martin, Beuron, *Tertia Missa in Nativitate Domini Nostri Jesu Christi,* Archiv 198 036.

Example 4-11   Offertory of the Mass for Pentecost.
Schola Cantorum of Amsterdam Students, *Gregorian Chant,* Columbia D3M 32329 (Side III); also on Benediktinerabtei, Münsterschwarzach, *Gregorianischer Choral: Die grossen Feste des Kirchenjahres,* Archiv 2723 084 (Side VIII); Choir of the Monks of the Abbey of Saint Pierre de Solesmes, *Gregorian Chant: Pentecost, Corpus Christi,* London 5241; and Chorus of the Frati Minori of Busto Arsizio, *Gregorian Masses,* Musical Heritage Society MHS 1912.

Example 4-12   Secret of the Mass for Pentecost.
Nuns-Choir of the Benedictine Abbey of Our Lady of Varensell, *Missa in Festo Pentecostes,* Archive ARC 73203.

Example 4-13   Preface of the Mass for Pentecost.
Nuns-Choir of the Benedictine Abbey of Our Lady of Varensell, *Missa in Festo Pentecostes,* Archive ARC 73203.

Example 4-16   Pater Noster of the Mass for Pentecost.
Choir of the Monks of the Benedictine Abbey of St. Martin, Beuron, *Liturgia Paschalis,* Archiv 3088/90 (Side VI); also on Chor der Mönche der Benediktiner-Erzabtei St. Martin, Beuron, *Prima Missa in Nativitate,* Archiv 198 153.

Example 4-18   Communion of the Mass for Pentecost.
Schola Cantorum of Amsterdam Students, *Gregorian Chant,* Columbia D3M 32329 (Side III); also on Benediktinerabtei, Münsterschwarzach, *Gregorianischer Choral: Die grossen Feste des Kirchenjahres,* Archiv 2723 084 (Side VIII); Choir of the Monks of the Abbey of Saint Pierre de Solesmes, *Gregorian Chant: Pentecost, Corpus Christi,* London 5241; and Chorus of the Frati Minori of Busto Arsizio, *Gregorian Masses,* Musical Heritage Society MHS 1912.

Example 4-19   Post-Communion of the Mass for Pentecost.
Nuns-Choir of the Benedictine Abbey of Our Lady of Varensell, *Missa in Festo Pentecostes,* Archive ARC 73203.

BIBLIOGRAPHICAL NOTES

The best study in English of the Mass is Joseph A. Jungmann *The Mass of the Roman Rite: Its Origins and Development,* trans. Francis A. Brunner, 2 vols. (Westminster, Maryland: Christian Classics, 1986).

The musical history of the Mass is summarized in the article "Mass" in *The New Grove Dictionary of Music and Musicians* (London: Macmillan Publishers Ltd., 1980). *The New Grove* also includes articles on most of the major items of the Mass.

Several anthologies have included music for the Mass for Easter Sunday. These include Richard H. Hoppin (ed.), *Anthology of Medieval Music* (New York: W. W. Norton and Co., Inc., 1978); Claude V. Palisca (ed.), *Norton Anthology of Western Music,* vol. 1, 2nd edition (New York: W. W. Norton and Co., Inc., 1988); Harry B. Lincoln and Stephen Bonta (eds.), *Study Scores of Historical Styles,* vol. 1 (Englewood Cliffs, New Jersey: Prentice Hall, Inc., 1986); and W. Thomas Marrocco and Nicholas Sandon (eds.), *Medieval Music: The Oxford Anthology of Music* (London and New York: Oxford University Press, 1977). This latter presents the Easter Mass as it was celebrated at the great cathedral of Salisbury in England in the late Middle Ages. Included are rubrics, or directions, to the participants, which provide a picture of some of the actions, movements, and rituals surrounding the service.

The music for the Mass for Pentecost is far less easily available. Some of it may be found in the *Liber Usualis,* a modern compilation of medieval and later chants, which has been published in several editions. Perhaps the most accessible is *The Liber Usualis with Introduction and Rubrics in English* (Tournai: Desclée and Co., 1938).

FIVE
THE OFFICE

The main form of worship in the Middle Ages other than the Mass is known as the Office (or Divine Office), a word deriving from the Latin *officium,* meaning "function" or "duty." The Office is actually a series of services, which took place at more or less fixed times of the day. In a monastic community the performance of the office was the main function of the monks. It occupied a large amount of their time, for it was their work— *opus Dei,* "the work of God."

In the early centuries, there was a considerable difference between the form of the Office as it was performed in churches by "secular" clergy and that performed in monasteries by "regular" clergy. Secular clergy were those who lived "in the world" (from the Latin *seculum*—"age," or "world") and might be attached to a particular church. Regular clergy were those who lived under a "rule" (Latin *regula*) in a monastic community. These differences became less marked from the fourth century on, as the monastic form of the Office was increasingly adopted in public churches and cathedrals. Some distinctions—mostly concerning the number of items performed in each part of the Office—remained as the Office developed during the Middle Ages, but the details of these are beyond the scope of this book. Again, as with the Mass, the exact nature of the services changed over time and differed from place to place. If anything the situation was even more complicated with the Office than with the Mass. Here we shall restrict ourselves to an overview of the types of service in the Office, and the examination of one of the most important of them from the musical point of view. First, however, a brief look at the development of monasticism in the Middle Ages will place the Office in its proper social and historical perspective.

MONASTICISM IN THE MIDDLE AGES

The word "monk" is derived from the Latin *monachus,* meaning a solitary person. The earliest monks were hermits who lived entirely alone and practiced a life of self-denial and spirituality in the deserts of the Middle East. The most renowned of these was St. Anthony (c. 260–350), who gave away a large fortune and retired into the desert in seclusion. Gradually other men of similar mind gathered around him, and he formed a community of monks who lived in solitude except for worship and meals.

The first set of rules governing a monastic community was written by St. Basil (c. 330–379), who left an active intellectual student life in Athens to devote himself to contemplation and worship. He was eventually appointed Bishop of Caesarea, a position that had influence over much of the Eastern Church. The Rule of St. Basil encouraged communal living, obedience to certain forms of behavior, and manual work, in contrast to the sometimes spectacular conduct of some of the Eastern hermits. (St. Simeon, for example, lived for thirty-five years on a small platform supported high above the ground on a column.)

The most widespread and influential form of monasticism in Europe was established in the early sixth century by St. Benedict. He too was born into an aristocratic family and went to Rome to study. He rejected the worldly life and became a hermit, living alone in a cave in the Italian countryside. Many others were attracted to this holy man, and after three years he began organizing a community of monks. Later he left his original community to found the first Benedictine monastery, at Monte Cassino in central Italy. This monastery was organized according to a set of principles known as the Rule of St. Benedict, one of the most important documents of the Middle Ages and remarkable for its moderation, humanity, and common sense. Benedictine monasteries spread throughout Europe, and monasticism in the West became synonymous with Benedictine practice. For centuries, literacy and learning, together with the works of Classical literature and Jewish scholarship, were preserved for the Christian world almost exclusively by Benedictine monks.

Although most of the Benedictine establishments were for men, some were founded for women. These nunneries or convents were adminis-

A tenth-century illumination depicts the founding of the monastery at Monte Cassino by St. Benedict, Biblioteca Apostolica Vaticana, Rome.

tered in very much the same way as the monasteries, with similar duties and a similar liturgy. The attendance of a priest, however, was required for the celebration of Mass.

The monastery was conceived as a lifelong family, dedicated to worship. (Larger establishments were known as abbeys and were headed by an abbot.) Each member of the community took vows of chastity, poverty, and obedience. Most monasteries were self-supporting, and the work of growing and preparing food, maintaining the buildings, organizing the library, and copying manuscripts was done by the monks themselves.

The monastery buildings were centered upon a church and included a dormitory, a refectory, and a library. There was usually a central courtyard surrounded by a cloister (from the latin *claustrum,* "enclosed"), intended both as a covered means of access to the various buildings and as a

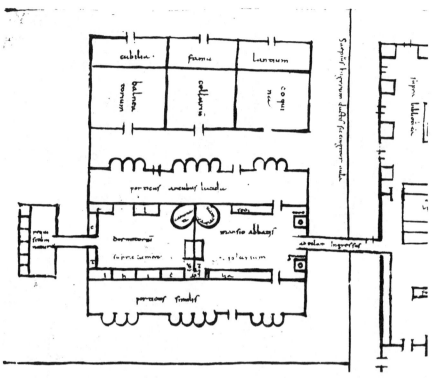

Portion of ground-plan from the ninth-century monastery of St. Gall, Stiftsbibliothek, St. Gall.

place for walking and meditation. The buildings were ringed by an outer wall and set close to or surrounded by cultivated land.

In his Rule, St. Benedict established in full the daily organization and running of a monastery, concerning himself with the smallest details of daily life. The arrangement of the dormitories, the washing of the towels, the rationing of the wine: all came under his consideration. The weekly servers in the kitchen are to be allowed an additional portion of bread and drink one hour before meals, so that they may serve their brethren "without murmuring or great labor." The sick must be looked after with the greatest care and should be allowed to take frequent baths and eat meat until they are recovered. During meals silence is observed, and one of the monks is designated to read aloud; he must be given a little bread and wine beforehand "lest it be too hard for him to fast for so long." Afterwards he may take his meal with those who are working as the cooks and servers for the week. Monks who are skilled at crafts should be allowed to pursue their talents. The monk designated as porter should be wise enough to know how to give and receive an answer, and old enough so that he does not feel like wandering about.

Artist's rendition of the cloister and surrounding buildings at St. Gall. From Lorna Price, *The Plan of St. Gall in Brief* (Berkeley: University of California Press, 1982). Copyright © 1982 Lorna Price, Walter Horn and Ernest Born. Used by permission.

Above all in importance, however, is the Divine Office:

At the time of the Divine Office, as soon as the signal is heard, let every one, leaving whatever he may have in hand, hasten to the church with the utmost speed—and yet with seriousness, so that there be no occasion for levity.
Let nothing be preferred to the work of God.[1]

[1]*Regula Benedicti*, Capitulum XVI.

The set of services that the Benedictine Rule established for the Office became the norm for the Middle Ages. With revitalizing reforms at Cluny in the tenth century and with the Cistercian movement in the twelfth, the Benedictines continued to represent the main focus of monastic life and accomplishment until the thirteenth century, when new religious orders evolved, based not on settled and cloistered living but on outside activity. The members of these new orders, known as friars, played a vital role in the intellectual life of the growing towns of Europe in the later Middle ages.

STRUCTURE OF THE OFFICE

As St. Benedict established it, and as it took its fixed form from the fourth and fifth centuries onwards, the Office was made up of eight services. Each of these was assigned to a particular time of the day or night, and the entire round of services was performed every day of the week. One of the most important of the Office services (or "hours" as they are sometimes called) was Matins, which took place in the middle of the night and usually lasted until dawn. This was immediately followed by Lauds. The day itself was marked every three hours by short services known as the "Little Hours"—Prime, Terce, Sext, and None. Another important service, Vespers, took place at sunset. Compline was performed before retiring for the night. Mass was also celebrated at least once a day, usually after Terce or Sext.

The following table summarizes the daily round of the Office. The times given are approximate, for they differed according to the geographical latitude of the church or monastery and according to the season of the year. Matins is so called from the Latin *matutinus*—early in the morning. Lauds is the English form of the word *laudes,* meaning praises, from the group of psalms of that name which were usually sung during the daybreak service. The Little Hours take their name from the Roman system of counting time—Prime is the first Roman hour, Terce the third, Sext the sixth, and None the ninth. *Vesperae* means evening in Latin, and Compline is derived from *completa,* meaning finished.

THE OFFICE

Matins		2 or 3 a.m.
Lauds		Daybreak
Prime		6 a.m.
Terce		9 a.m.
	[Mass]	
Sext		Noon
None		3 p.m.
Vespers		Sunset
Compline		Bedtime

The length of the Office services was variable, the longest being Matins, which could last between two and three hours. (The Mass might take about an hour and a half.) Next in importance were Vespers and Lauds, which celebrated the beginning and end of daytime; each might last three quarters of an hour. Compline focused on sleep and protection, and lasted about half an hour. The little hours took perhaps fifteen or twenty minutes each. These estimates are fairly conservative. In some establishments or on special feasts the services could be considerably extended.

The content of the various parts of the Office differed according to the time of day, as mentioned already. It also changed if there was a special feast to be celebrated. The main function of the Office, however, was to provide a forum for the recitation of the psalms. Early in the history of the Church the psalms were taken over from the Jewish liturgy as a rich and varied source of worship, and their recitation formed a central element in the Office. The practice developed of reciting the entire Psalter (the book of 150 Psalms) over a given period of time. In some early monastic communities this period was fixed at a day or a few days. Sometimes the recitation was continual, with groups of monks alternating in shifts. Ultimately, however, the pattern was established of distributing the psalms over a week, with some being repeated in particular services owing to their relevance to a particular hour of the day (the *laudes* psalms at Lauds, for example). Each week, then, the entire Psalter would be covered, while a distinction as to the hour of the day and the day of the week could still be maintained.

While the psalms are the central focus of the Office services, the structure of each service is slightly different. Matins, the most important, will be considered in detail below. Lauds and Vespers are similar to each other in intent (marking the beginning and end of daylight) and also in structure. Each contains five psalms,[2] a reading, a responsory (a chant in responsorial style), and a hymn. Each then continues with the singing of a canticle—a passage from scripture that has the form of a psalm but is not from the Psalter. Lauds has the canticle *Benedictus* (Luke I, 68–79), which speaks of "giving light to those who sit in darkness and in the shadow of death." Vespers has the canticle *Magnificat* (Luke I, 46–55), Mary's song of thanksgiving to the Lord. Both services end with prayers and the concluding exchange "Benedicamus Domino—Deo gratias."

The little hours all begin with a hymn and continue with a group of three psalms. Then there is a short reading, followed by prayers and the concluding exchange.

Compline, the bedtime service, begins with a group of three psalms and continues with a hymn. A reading follows and then a short responsory. The canticle for Compline is *Nunc dimittis* (Luke II, 29–32), which requests

---

[2] In Lauds one of the psalms is replaced by a canticle.

eternal peace. Compline too ends with prayers and the "Benedicamus Domino."

The musical styles of most of these items are ones we have encountered in the Mass and range from the simple to the elaborate. The psalms are chanted to recitational formulas and are framed by antiphons.[3] The prayers and readings are recited to simple formulas. The hymns, with their metrical poetic texts, are usually set to syllabic or slightly neumatic melodies, the same music serving for each stanza of the poetry. The canticles are treated like psalms, with their own antiphons, but they have more elaborate recitational formulas than the psalms. The most elaborate music of all is reserved for the responsories, which, like the responsorial chants of the Mass—the Gradual and the Alleluya—divide their music between soloists and choir. The concluding "Benedicamus Domino—Deo gratias" exchange is set to one of several short but wide-ranging melodies.

We shall examine one service of the medieval Office in detail, to gain an idea of how music functions in the service and how it serves to articulate the different elements of the liturgy. Since Matins was the most important of the Office services in the Middle Ages, we shall look at a Matins service. We shall begin by describing the general structure of Matins, and then analyze the Matins service on one of the great feasts of the year—Christmas, or, as it was called in the Middle Ages, the Nativity. As with our discussion of the Mass, it must be borne in mind that we shall not be examining an exact historical service as it might have been performed in a given year in a particular church or monastery, but a generalized structure that includes the main items and rationalizes a highly complex set of variants into a clearly understandable pattern.

MATINS FOR THE NATIVITY

Matins is divided into five sections: an introduction, three middle sections, which contain the psalms for the day, and a conclusion. The three middle sections, which are called Nocturns, are all alike in form. Each contains three psalms, each with its own antiphon; a short versicle; and three readings from scripture ("lessons"), each reading being followed by a responsory. The versicle, a short phrase with a response, serves to separate the psalms from the lessons. The form of each Nocturn is therefore as follows:

> Three psalms, each framed by an antiphon
> Versicle
> Three lessons, each followed by a responsory

[3]In Matins, Lauds, and Vespers, each psalm has its own antiphon. In Compline and the little hours the psalms are sung as a group, with only one antiphon framing the group.

The introduction contains the opening chants, the singing of Psalm 94 (which is known as the Invitatory Psalm from its standard position at the beginning of Matins), and a concluding hymn. Then come the three Nocturns. The conclusion contains the Te Deum (a long and highly rhetorical text with one well-known melody), and the Benedicamus Domino. This structure is given in full in the following table:

MATINS

Item	Style	Text
Introduction		
Domine Labia Mea	Recitational	Common
Deus in Adiutorium	Recitational	Common
Invitatory psalm (94)	Recitational	Common
with antiphon	Neumatic	Proper
Hymn	Syllabic/Neumatic	Proper
Nocturn I		
Psalm	Recitational	[4]
with Antiphon	Syllabic/Neumatic	Proper
Psalm / with Antiphon	*ditto*	
Psalm / with Antiphon	*ditto*	
Versicle	Recitational/Neumatic	Proper
Lesson	Recitational	Proper
Responsory	Neumatic/Melismatic	Proper
Lesson / Responsory	*ditto*	
Lesson / Responsory	*ditto*	
Nocturn II		
as above		
Nocturn III		
as above		
Conclusion		
Te Deum	Syllabic/Neumatic	Common
Benedicamus Domino	Neumatic	Common

[4]The psalms are chosen according to the weekly cycle.

Introduction

The opening two chants of Matins are common to all the services of the Office; they are preparatory to prayer and contain petitions for aid. Both are sung to the same extremely simple formula, and both divide their music between priest and choir.[5]

Christmas Matins opens with the first of these two recitations (Ex. 5-1). Then follows the Deus In Adiutorium chant (Ex. 5-2), which contains the Doxology and ends with the word "Alleluya" (during the festive season).

The Invitatory psalm, Psalm 94, stands at the beginning of every Matins service. Its choice must have been determined by the opening text: "Come, let us exult in the Lord, let us rejoice in God." Its method of performance is unusual, for it shares characteristics both of ordinary psalm singing and of responsorial chant, with some particular features of its own.

The text of the Invitatory psalm is divided into five sections (six with the Doxology), all of which are sung by soloists. An antiphon is sung at the beginning and end of the psalm (at the beginning it is sung first by soloists), and also between each of the psalm sections. (After sections 1, 3, and 5 the whole antiphon is sung; after sections 2, 4, and 6 only the second half is sung.) The alternation between soloists and choir is that of responsorial chant, and the framing of the psalm by an antiphon is taken from regular psalmody. However, the sectional division of the text and the insertion of the antiphon between these divisions are features which are distinctive to this chant. All of this is summarized in the following diagram:

Antiphon (complete)	First by soloists, repeated by choir
Psalm—Section 1	Soloists
Antiphon (complete)	Choir
Psalm—Section 2	Soloists
Antiphon (second half)	Choir
Psalm—Section 3	Soloists
Antiphon (complete)	Choir
Psalm—Section 4	Soloists
Antiphon (second half)	Choir
Psalm—Section 5	Soloists
Antiphon (complete)	Choir
Section 6 (Doxology)	Soloists
Antiphon (second half)	Choir

---

[5]In the monastic Office the chants designated for the priest were sung by one of the monks assigned to the task for the week (the "hebdomadary"). Certain specific singing roles were reserved for the Abbot, such as the Gospel reading and the opening of the Te Deum.

EXAMPLE 5-1 Domine, Labia Mea.

(Solo)

Do - mi - ne, la - bi - a me - a a - pe - ri - es.

(Choir)

R̵. Et os me - um an - nun - ti - a - bit lau - dem tu - am.

Domine, labia mea aperies,
R̵. Et os meum annuntiabit laudem
tuam.

O Lord, open my lips.
R̵. And my mouth will announce your
praise.

EXAMPLE 5-2 Deus In Adiutorium.

(Solo)

De - us in ad - iu - to - ri - um me - um in - ten - de.

(Choir)

R̵. Do - mi - ne ad ad - iu - van - dum me fe - sti - na.

Glo - ri - a Pa - tri, et Fi - li - o, et Spi - ri - tu - i San - cto.

Si - cut e - rat in prin - ci - pi - o, et nunc, et sem - per, et in sae - cu - la sae - cu - lo - rum.

A - men. Al - le - lu - ya.

Deus in adiutorium meum intende.
R̵. Domine ad adiuvandum me festina.
Gloria Patri, et Filio, et Spiritui
Sancto.
Sicut erat in principio, et nunc, et
semper, et in saecula saecu-
lorum. Amen. Alleluya.

O God, come to my assistance.
R̵. O Lord, make haste to help me.
Glory to the Father, and to the Son,
and to the Holy Spirit.
As it was in the beginning, both now
and always, and for ever. Amen.
Alleluya.

The Invitatory psalm for Christmas Matins (Ex. 5-3) is provided with an antiphon clearly appropriate to the day: "Christ is born for us. Come, let us adore him." The music is formed from a series of arches and is in Mode 4. The first half of the melody ("Christus natus est nobis") ends on G, the second half ("Venite, adoremus") on the final of the mode, E. The division of the text is marked by these two cadences and by the fact that both halves begin with a stepwise ascent from D.

The recitational formula for the psalm itself is very elaborate and approaches the freedom of a syllabic melody in its own right. Its reciting tone shifts from A to G. The music for the ending of the recitational formula for each of the sections of the psalm (on "iubilemus ei," "ipse conspicit," "pascuae eius" etc.) is the same as that used for the ending of the first phrase of the antiphon ("natus est nobis"). This provides a ready transition either to the second half of the antiphon or to the beginning of the first half, both of which share the ascending stepwise movement within the fifth D–A. As in regular psalm singing, the two halves of each psalm verse are clearly represented by the music.

EXAMPLE 5-3   Invitatory psalm.

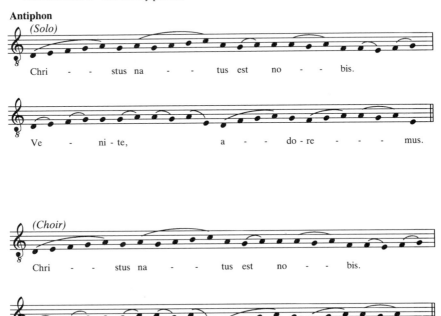

Psalm 94
Section I

Ve - ni - te, ex-sul-te-mus Do - mi - no,

iu - bi - le - mus De - o, sa - lu - ta - ri no - stro.

Prae-oc-cu-pe - mus fa-ci-em e - ius in con-fes - si-o - ne,

et in psal-mis iu-bi - - - le-mus e - i.

Antiphon
(Choir)

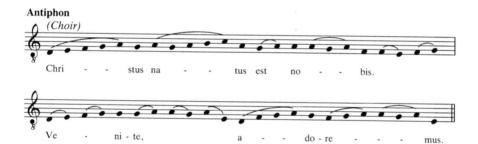

Chri - - stus na - - tus est no - - bis.

Ve - ni - te, a - - do - re - - - mus.

Section II
(Solo)

Quo - ni - am De - us ma-gnus Do - mi - nus,

et Rex ma - gnus su - per om - nes de - os.

Quo-ni-am non re-pel-let Do - mi-nus ple-bem su - am; qui-a in ma-nu e - ius

sunt om - nes fi - nes ter - rae,

et al - ti-tu - di-nes mon - ti-um ip - - se con - spi -

cit.

Antiphon
(Choir)

Ve - ni - te, a - - - do - re - - - mus.

Section III
(Solo)

Quo - ni - am ip - si - us est ma - re, et ip - se fe - cit il - lud,

et a - ri-dam fun - da - ve - runt ma - nus e - ius.

Ve - ni - te, a - do - re - mus, et pro-ci-da-mus an - te De - um; plo - re - mus

co - ram Do - mi - no, qui fe - cit nos, qui - a ip - se est

Do - mi - nus De - us no - ster.

Nos au – tem po – pu-lus e – ius, et o – ves pas – –

cu – ae e – – – ius.

Antiphon

(Choir)

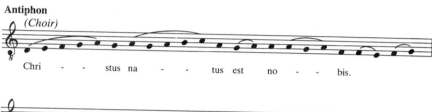

Chri – – stus na – – tus est no – – bis.

Ve – ni - te, a – – do - re – – – mus.

Section IV

(Solo)

Ho – di – e, si vo - cem e – ius au - di - e – ri - tis,

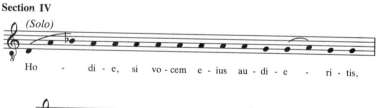

no - li – te ob - du - ra - re cor – da ve - stra.

Si - cut in ex - a - cer - ba - ti - o – ne se-cun-dum di – em ten - ta - ti - o -

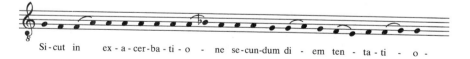

nis in de - ser – to, u - bi ten-ta - ve - runt me pa - tres ve - stri;

pro - ba - ve - runt et vi - de - runt o - - pe - ra

me - - a.

Antiphon

(Choir)

Ve - ni - te,   a - - do - re - - - mus.

Section V

(Solo)

Qua - dra - gin - ta an - nis prox - i - mus fu - i,

ge - ne - ra - ti - o - ni hu - ic, et di - xi; Sem - per hi er - rant cor - de.

Ip - si ve - ro non co - gno - ve - runt vi - as me - as, quibus iu - ra - vi in

i - ra me - a,

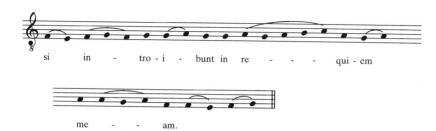

si in - tro - i - bunt in re - - - qui - em

me - - am.

Antiphon

(Choir)

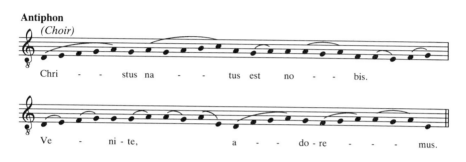

Chri - - stus na - - tus est no - - bis.

Ve - ni - te, a - - do - re - - mus.

Section VI

(Solo)

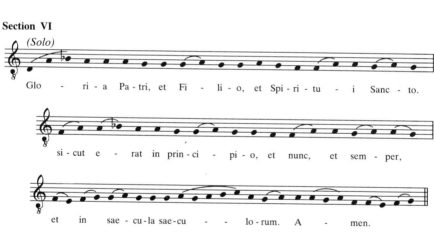

Glo - ri - a Pa - tri, et Fi - li - o, et Spi - ri - tu - i Sanc - to.

si - cut e - rat in prin - ci - pi - o, et nunc, et sem - per,

et in sae - cu - la sae - cu - - lo - rum. A - men.

Antiphon

(Choir)

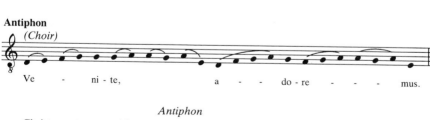

Ve - ni - te, a - - do - re - - mus.

Antiphon

Christus natus est nobis.   Christ is born for us.
Venite, adoremus.   Come, let us adore him.

Christus natus est nobis.   Christ is born for us.
Venite, adoremus.   Come, let us adore him.

Psalm 94

Section I

Venite, exsultemus Domino,
  iubilemus Deo, salutari nostro.

Come, let us exult in the Lord,
  let us sing joyfully to God, our salvation.

Praeoccupemus faciem eius in confessione,
  et in psalmis iubilemus ei.

Let us enter his presence with thanksgiving,
  and sing joyful psalms to him.

Antiphon

Christus natus est nobis.
Venite, adoremus.

Christ is born for us.
Come, let us adore him.

Section II

Quoniam Deus magnus Dominus,
  et Rex magnus super omnes deos.
Quoniam non repellet Dominus plebem
  suam; quia in manu eius sunt omnes
  fines terrae,
  et altitudines montium ipse conspicit.

For the Lord is a great God,
  and a great King over all gods.
For the Lord does not reject his people;
  in his hand are all the boundaries of
  the earth,
  and within his sight are the mountain-
  tops.

Antiphon

Venite, adoremus.

Come, let us adore him.

Section III

Quoniam ipsius est mare, et ipse fecit
  illud,
  et aridam fundaverunt manus eius.

For the sea is his, he himself made it,

  and his own hands fashioned the dry
  land.

Venite, adoremus, et procidamus ante
  Deum; ploremus coram Domino,
  qui fecit nos, quia ipse est Dominus
  Deus noster.

Come, let us adore him, and throw
  ourselves down before God; let us
  weep in the presence of the Lord
  who made us, for he is the Lord
  our God.

Nos autem populus eius, et oves pascuae eius.

We are his people and the sheep of his
  flock.

Antiphon

Christus natus est nobis.
Venite, adoremus.

Christ is born for us.
Come, let us adore him.

Section IV

Hodie, si vocem eius audieritis,
  nolite obdurare corda vestra.
Sicut in exacerbatione secundum diem
  tentationis in deserto, ubi ten-
  taverunt me patres vestri;
  probaverunt et viderunt opera mea.

If you hear his voice,
  do not harden your hearts today.
As you did at the time of the challenge in
  the desert, when your forefathers
  challenged me;
  they tested me and saw my powers.

Antiphon

Venite, adoremus.

Come, let us adore him.

Section V

Quadraginta annis proximus fui, generationi huic, et dixi: Semper hi errant corde.	For forty years I was angry with that generation, and I said: These people will always err in their hearts.
Ipsi vero non cognoverunt vias meas, quibus iuravi in ira mea, si introibunt in requiem meam.	And indeed they did not know my ways, and I swore to them in my anger, they would not enter the abode of my peace.

Antiphon

Christus natus est nobis.	Christ is born for us.
Venite, adoremus.	Come, let us adore him.

Section VI

Gloria Patri, et Filio, et Spiritui Sancto,	Glory to the Father, and to the Son, and to the Holy Spirit.
sicut erat in principio, et nunc, et semper,	As it was in the beginning, both now and always,
et in saecula saeculorum. Amen.	and for ever. Amen.

Antiphon

Venite, adoremus.	Come, let us adore him.

The introductory portion of Matins ends with the singing of a hymn. Benedict had prescribed the singing of one hymn in each of the services of the Office, and certain hymns became associated with particular seasons or occasions of the year. The hymn sung at Christmas Matins is *Christe, Redemptor Omnium* (Ex. 5-4). The text is in seven stanzas of four lines each. (Only the first two and the last two stanzas are given in the example.) Each line contains eight syllables in iambic (short-long) meter. In much medieval hymn writing this iambic meter is used very flexibly, with frequent substitutions of long accents for short and the reverse. The standard pattern contains four iambic "feet" in each eight-syllable line, as follows:

$$\smile - \mid \smile - \mid \smile - \mid \smile -$$

($\smile$ = a short syllable; $-$ = a long syllable).

Christe, Redemptor Omnium, however, has variants of this pattern in almost every line of its poetry, which lends interest and impulse to the meter.

The first stanza, for example, contains the following patterns for its four lines:

– ∪ | ∪ – | ∪ – | ∪–
Chris-te Re-demp-tor om-nium,

∪ – | ∪ – | ∪ – | ∪ –
Ex pa-tre pa-tris u-ni-ce,

– ∪ | – ∪ | ∪ – | ∪ –
So-lus an-te prin-ci-pi-um

– ∪ | – ∪ | ∪ – | ∪ –
Na-tus in-eff-a-bi-li-ter

The meter in the other stanzas of the hymn also varies slightly, although all the lines maintain the eight-syllable count and the overall loose iambic pattern.

Four phrases of music are used to set the four lines of each stanza, and the same music is repeated for each of the stanzas of the hymn. The four phrases end on D, A, E, and D. As with sequences in the Mass, which are also written in verse, hymns are not as clearly susceptible of modal classification as some other chants. In this hymn the mode must be classified as Mode 1, Dorian, because of its final, although the lower fourth, D–G, of the Hypomixolydian mode is stressed in the first and last phrases. The second phrase contrasts with the first by rising an octave within a short space, and cadences on the reciting tone, A, of the Dorian mode. The third phrase moves into the realm of the Phrygian mode with its descent from B and cadence on E. This descending phrase serves as a balance to the rise of phrase 2. As is fairly common in hymn melodies, the last phrase is a (near) repetition of the music of the first.

The balanced phrases, with their syllabic setting of the text interspersed with two- or three-note neumes, clearly reflect the form of the poetry, with its four matching lines of verse. This parallelism is reinforced by the opening of three of the phrases on the same pitch (C), the overall shape of the melody with its climax in the center, and the repetition of phrase 1 as phrase 4 to lend closure to each stanza.

The final stanza in this hymn is a brief form of doxology, as it is in many hymns. The chant ends with an "Amen" to a cadence formula for the Dorian mode.

The Nocturns

As we have seen, the central portion of Matins consists of three Nocturns, each of which has the same pattern (see p. 147). Here we shall ana-

EXAMPLE 5-4 Hymn, *Christe, Redemptor Omnium,* stanzas 1, 2, 6, and 7 only.

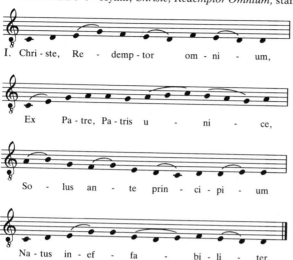

I. Chri - ste, Re - demp - tor om - ni - um,

Ex Pa - tre, Pa - tris u - ni - ce,

So - lus an - te prin - ci - pi - um

Na - tus in - ef - fa - bi - li - ter.

I. Christe, Redemptor omnium, Ex Patre, Patris unice, Solus ante principium Natus ineffabiliter.	O Christ, Redeemer of all, Only Son of the Father, You alone before the beginning Were born and cannot be described.
II. Tu lumen, tu splendor Patris, Tu spes perennis omnium, Intende, quas fundunt preces Tui per orbem servuli.	You are the light, the splendor of the 　　Father, An everlasting hope to all. Hear the prayers poured out to you, By your servants throughout the 　　world.
VI. Nos quoque qui sancto tuo Redempti sanguine sumus Ob diem natalis tui Hymnum novum concinimus.	And we, who by your holy blood Have been redeemed, On this day of your birth Sing together a new hymn.
VII. Gloria tibi Domine, Qui natus es de Virgine Cum Patre et sancto Spiritu In sempiterna saecula. Amen.	Glory to you, O Lord, Who were born from a Virgin, And to the Father and the Holy 　　Spirit, For ever and ever. Amen.

lyze only the first Nocturn of the Christmas Matins service. The second and third Nocturn differ in the texts of the psalms sung, the lessons read, and the music of the responsories. Their overall musical and textual structure, however, follows that of the first Nocturn.[6]

[6]The main difference between the secular and monastic uses concerned the number of psalms sung in each Nocturn of the Matins services. This could also vary from weekdays to Sundays and from Sundays to feast days.

Since the singing of psalms forms the central core of each of the services in the Office (and also plays an important role in some of the chants of the Mass, as we have seen), we should have a clear understanding of the way psalms are sung in the Office and the influence they had on the music of the liturgy as a whole. Before turning to the Nocturns of Christmas Matins, therefore, let us consider psalmody of the Office in general.

The parallelism of the poetry of the psalms has been described earlier (see pp. 41 and 51). This structure encouraged a method of performance which emphasized the balance of the verses by a division of the choir into two groups, which alternated in singing the verses of the psalms. This antiphonal type of performance must have been encouraged by the physical layout of both monastic and secular churches in the Middle Ages, with the choir stalls divided into two sections facing each other across the chancel, or altar area.

Facing choirstalls with monks singing at a liturgical service, British Library, London.

All the verses were performed in this way, including the Gloria Patri, which was added to the end of every psalm. Formulaic recitational chants were developed for the singing of these psalms, and, as we have seen, they were designed to put forth the texts as clearly as possible and by brief melodic inflections to articulate the grammar and structure of the poetry. Despite the differing line lengths, each line could be fitted to the recitation. The inflection that marks the beginning, the half close, and the full close of each line remains the same, while the remainder of the text, however short or long it is, is chanted to the reciting tone.

Early in the history of psalm singing, additional texts with their own melodies were added to the performance. These became known as "antiphons" because of their association with the psalms. This is a confusing term, unfortunately, for antiphons are *not* performed antiphonally, but, after the usual solo intonation, by the whole choir singing together. Antiphons are usually fairly simple melodies, syllabic or slightly neumatic, and their texts are quite short, often drawn from a biblical source or from a psalm verse (either part of the psalm to which they are attached, or some other psalm).

In the early Middle Ages it seems as though the antiphon was sung after every single verse of the psalm, as well as at the beginning and end. This practice survives in some special situations, for example in the Invitatory psalm, which we have just examined. But with the general expansion of the liturgy which took place over the centuries, the system simply became too time-consuming and antiphons were restricted to opening and closing each of the psalms with which they were associated.

The pattern of psalm singing with the framing antiphon is shown below:

> Antiphon (Full choir)
> Psalm (Alternating half choirs)
> Antiphon (Full choir)

There are a very large number of melodies for antiphons, although scholars have discovered that many of them are related to each other and can be traced back to common originals. With the reorganization of the liturgy in the eighth and ninth centuries, and the consequent emphasis upon regularity and modal categories, antiphons and the recitational formulas for psalms were adapted to one another so that together they would fit into the modal patterns. The ending of an antiphon has to have a cadence on the final of the mode, and the beginning of a psalm formula has to proceed smoothly from the ending of the antiphon. Similarly, the ending of the psalm formula has to tie in smoothly with the beginning of the antiphon when it is sung at the very end of the psalm. This concentration on conformity to the modes resulted in the assignation of various antiphons to particular modes, and the manipulation particularly of the ending inflection of psalm formulas to fit all the eight modes. Psalm formulas were arranged in books according to the numbering of the modes, and their distinctive endings (*differentiae*) written out in full. This passion for organizational clarity even affected the liturgy itself, with antiphons and psalm formulas being chosen by their numerical modal category. In Matins for example, the first psalm and antiphon would be in Mode 1, the second in Mode 2, and so on. Different patterns and arrangements of the modal numbers are seen in the late medieval liturgy, especially in new services or additions to services, such as those for new saints or for other new feasts.

The first psalm for the first Nocturn of Christmas Matins is Psalm 2 (Ex. 5-5). This is framed by an antiphon clearly appropriate to the day, with the text "The Lord said to me: You are my son. Today did I engender you," which is taken from the seventh verse of the psalm itself. The antiphon is in Mode 8, Hypomixolydian, with a final on G. The reciting tone of Mode 8 is C, and the melody utilizes the tension created by approaching C from both the half step below and the whole step above. This is emphasized by the three-note neumes that open the first and third phrases ("Dom[inus]" and "e[go]"). Descending skips of a third comprise a unifying motif throughout the melody, occurring three times in the first phrase, three in the second (two in succession), and four in the third phrase. The structure of the text, with its three short sentences, is reinforced by the similarity of the endings of the first two phrases, with their rise from A to C and descent from D to B, the half step below the reciting tone.

The final cadence of the antiphon makes a smooth transition to the opening of the recitation formula for the psalm, with its rise from G to A to the reciting tone on C. The half close is marked by a whole-step move to D and a return to C. The full close ends the same way but is preceded by a descending-third skip to A (which must have been the impetus for the incorporation of this motif so pervasively in the antiphon melody).

All further verses of the psalm omit the opening G and A and begin directly on the reciting tone. The last "verse" (actually, of course, the last line of the Gloria Patri) ends with the "Amen" on C, which prepares the return of the antiphon with its C–B–C initial neume.

EXAMPLE 5-5   Psalm 2 with antiphon.

Antiphon
(Solo)   *(Choir)*

Do - mi - nus   *   di - xit ad   me:

Fi - li - us me - us es tu.

E - go ho - di - e ge - - - nu - i te.

Psalm

(Half Choir 1)

Qua - re fre - mu - e - runt gen - tes,

et po - pu - li me - di - ta - ti sunt i - na - ni - a?

(Half Choir 2)

A - sti - te - runt re - ges ter - rae, et prin - ci - pes con - ve - ne - runt in u - num,

ad - ver - sus Do - mi - num, et ad - ver - sus Chri-stum e - ius.

(Half Choir 1)

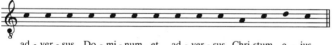

Di - rum - pa - mus vin - cu - la e - o - rum,

et pro - ii - ci - a - mus a no - bis iu - gem ip - so - rum.

(Half Choir 2) etc.

Qui ha - bi - tat in cae - lis, ir - ri - de - bit e - os,

et Do - mi - nus sub - san - na - bit e - os.

Tunc lo - que - tur ad e - os in i - ra su - a,

et in fu - ro - re su - o con - tur - ba - bit e - os.

E - go au - tem con - sti - tu - tus sum Rex ab e - o su - per Si - on, mon-tem san-ctum e - ius,

prae - di - cans prae - cep - tum e - ius.

Do - mi - nus di - xit ad me:

Fi - li - us me - us es tu, e - go ho - di - e ge - nu - i te.

Po - stu - la a me, et da - bo ti - bi gen - tes hae - re - di - ta - tem tu - am,

et pos - ses - si - o - nem tu - am ter - mi - nos ter - rae.

Re - ges e - os in vir - ga fer - re - a,

et tam-quam vas fi - gu - li con - frin - ges e - os.

Et nunc, re - ges, in - tel - li - gi - te,

e - ru - di - mi - ni, qui iu - di - ca - tis ter - ram.

Ser - vi - te Do - mi - no in ti - mo - re,

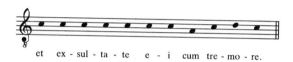

et ex - sul - ta - te e - i cum tre - mo - re.

Ap - pre - hen - di - te di - sci - pli - nam, ne - quan - do i - ra - sca - tur Do - mi - nus,

et pe - re - a - tis de vi - a iu - sta.

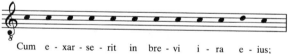

Cum e - xar - se - rit in bre - vi i - ra e - ius;

be - a - ti om - nes qui con - fi - dunt in e - o.

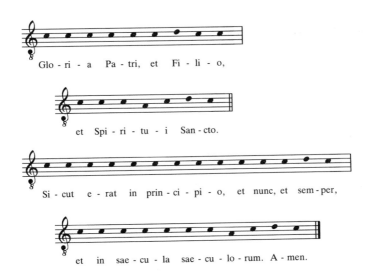

Antiphon

Antiphon

Dominus dixit ad me: The Lord said to me:
Filius meus es tu.   You are my son,
Ego hodie genui te.   Today did I engender you.

Psalm

Quare fremuerunt gentes,	Why did the nations conspire,
et populi meditati sunt inania?	and the people imagine empty things?
Astiterunt reges terrae, et principes	The kings of the earth set themselves up,
convenerunt in unum,	and the princes came together,
adversus Dominum, et adversus	against the Lord and against his
Christum eius.	Christ.
Dirumpamus vincula eorum,	Let us break their chains,
et proiiciamus a nobis iugem ipsorum.	and throw their yoke from us.
Qui habitat in caelis, irridebit eos,	He who lives in the heavens will laugh at them,
et Dominus subsannabit eos.	and the Lord will scorn them.
Tunc loquetur ad eos in ira sua,	Then he will speak to them in his anger,
et in furore suo conturbabit eos.	and in his fury he will confound them.
Ego autem constitutus sum Rex ab eo	For I have been appointed King by him
super Sion, montem sanctum eius,	over Zion, his holy mountain,
praedicans praeceptum eius.	speaking his decree.
Dominus dixit ad me:	The Lord said to me:
Filius meus es tu, ego hodie genui te.	You are my son, today did I engender you.
Postula a me, et dabo tibi gentes	Ask me, and I shall give you the nations
haereditatem tuam,	as a heritage,
et possessionem tuam terminos terrae.	and the ends of the earth for your possession.
Reges eos in virga ferrea,	You shall beat the kings with an iron rod,
et tamquam vas figuli confringes eos.	and break them like a pot of clay.
Et nunc, reges, intelligite,	Now therefore, kings, understand,
erudimini, qui iudicatis terram.	be warned, you who rule the earth.
Servite Domino in timore,	Serve the Lord in fear,
et exsultate ei cum tremore.	and exult with him in trembling.
Apprehendite disciplinam, nequando	Take heed, lest the Lord be angry,
irascatur Dominus,	
et pereatis de via iusta.	and you perish on the way.
Cum exarserit in brevi ira eius;	For his anger flares up in an instant;
beati omnes qui confidunt in eo.	blessed are all who trust in him.
Gloria Patri, et Filio,	Glory to the Father, and to the Son,
et Spiritui Sancto.	and to the Holy Spirit.
Sicut erat in principio, et nunc, et semper,	As it was in the beginning, both now and always,
et in saecula saeculorum. Amen.	and for ever. Amen.

Antiphon

Dominus dixit ad me:	The Lord said to me:
Filius meus es tu.	You are my son,
Ego hodie genui te.	Today did I engender you.

The second psalm in the first Nocturn of the Matins service for Christmas is Psalm 18 (Ex. 5-6). This is framed by a short and simple antiphon, which, like the first antiphon in the Nocturn, is also in Mode 8. The antiphon text is taken from the second half of the fifth verse of the psalm. Its relevance to the Christmas season is suggested by the image of God as a bridegroom. The melody forms a single arch and rises from the opening G to the reciting tone C, falling quickly again to G, which provides the connection for the beginning of the singing of the psalm.

The recitation formula for the psalm begins as did the previous one (G–A–C), and the half close is the same. The full close, however, is different, allowing for a seamless link with the return of the antiphon. The close of the psalm formula falls to G, the opening note of the antiphon.

EXAMPLE 5-6   Psalm 18, verses 1–3 and 15–16 only, with antiphon.

Et e-runt ut com-pla-ce-ant e-lo-qui-a o-ris me-i,

et me-di-ta-ti-o cor-dis me-i in con-spec-tu tu-o sem-per.

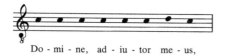

Do-mi-ne, ad-iu-tor me-us,

et re-demp-tor me-us.

Glo-ri-a Pa-tri, et Fi-li-o,

et Spi-ri-tu-i San-cto.

Si-cut e-rat in prin-ci-pi-o, et nunc, et sem-per,

et in sae-cu-la sae-cu-lo-rum. A-men.

Antiphon

 (Choir)

Tam-quam spon-sus Do-mi-nus pro-ce-dens de tha-la-mo su-o.

Antiphon

Tamquam sponsus Dominus procedens de thalamo suo.	The Lord is like a bridegroom, coming from his bedchamber.

Psalm

Caeli enarrant gloriam Dei,	The heavens speak the glory of God,
et opera manuum eius annuntiat firmamentum.	and the universe proclaims the work of his hands.
Dies diei eructat verbum,	One day announces the word to another day,
et nox nocti indicat scientiam.	and one night reveals the knowledge to another night.
Non sunt loquelae, neque sermones,	These are not spoken sounds, nor speeches,
quorum non audiantur voces eorum. . . .	their voices can not be heard. . . .
Et erunt ut complaceant eloquia oris mei,	And may my utterances please you,
et meditatio cordis mei in conspectu tuo semper.	and the meditation of my heart be always pleasing in your sight.
Domine, adiutor meus,	O Lord, my helper,
et redemptor meus.	and my redeemer.
Gloria Patri, et Filio,	Glory to the Father, and to the Son,
et Spiritui Sancto.	and to the Holy Spirit.
Sicut erat in principio, et nunc, et semper,	As it was in the beginning, both now and always,
et in saecula saeculorum. Amen.	and for ever. Amen.

Antiphon

Tamquam sponsus Dominus procedens de thalamo suo.	The Lord is like a bridegroom, coming from his bedchamber.

The third psalm in the Nocturn is Psalm 44 (Ex. 5-7); part of its third verse is taken to form the text of the framing antiphon. The antiphon ("Diffusa est") is in Mode 1, Dorian. It opens by approaching the reciting tone A from a third below and again from a whole step below. The first phrase cadences on the final, D. The second phrase begins on the D, rises to the reciting tone again, and descends to C, one step below the final, before cadencing on the final again. The gentle double arch form of each of these phrases serves to articulate the two short sentences of the text.

The psalm formula rises stepwise through the third F–G–A with which the antiphon had begun in staggered fashion. Its reciting tone is A, and the half close is formed by a half step from above (the B♭) and a whole step from below. The full close descends two steps to F and ends with the distinctive two-note neume G–A. This makes a rational transition to the F–A–G–A opening of the antiphon when it returns—a less obvious transition than the common-tone links of the previous two psalms but equally smooth in performance.

EXAMPLE 5-7   Psalm 44, verses 1–4 and 19–20 only, with antiphon.

Antiphon

Dif - fu - sa est gra - ti - a * in la - bi - is tu - is,

prop - te - re - a be - ne - di - xit te De - us in ae - ter - num.

Psalm

E - ruc - ta - vit cor me - um ver - bum bo - num,

di - co e - go o - pe - ra me - a Re - gi.

Lin - gua me - a ca - la - mus scri - bae,

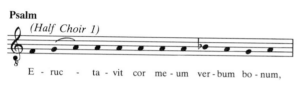

ve - lo - ci - ter scri - ben - tis.

Spe - ci - o - sus for - ma prae fi - li - is ho - mi - num, dif - fu - sa est gra - ti - a in la - bi - is tu - is,

prop - te - re - a be - ne - di - xit te De - us in ae - ter - num.

Ac - cin - ge - re gla - di - o tu - o su - per fe - mur tu - um,

po - ten - tis - si - me. . . .

Me - mo - res e - runt no - mi - nis tu - i,

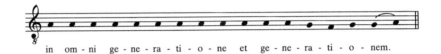

in om - ni ge - ne - ra - ti - o - ne et ge - ne - ra - ti - o - nem.

Prop - te - re - a po - pu - li con - fi - te - bun - tur ti - bi in ae - ter - num,

et in sae - cu - lum sae - cu - li.

Glo - ri - a Pa - tri, et Fi - li - o,

et Spi - ri - tu - i San - cto.

Si - cut e - rat in prin - ci - pi - o, et nunc, et sem - per,

et in sae - cu - la sa - cu - lo - rum. A - men.

Antiphon
(Choir)

Dif - fu - sa est gra - ti - a in la - bi - is tu - is,

prop - te - re - a be - ne - di - xit te De - us in ae - ter - num.

Antiphon

Diffusa est gratia in labiis tuis,	Grace is spread about on your lips,
propterea benedixit te Deus in aeternum.	therefore God has blessed you for eternity.

Psalm

Eructavit cor meum verbum bonum,	My heart has uttered a good word,
dico ego opera mea Regi.	I speak the deeds of my King.
Lingua mea calamus scribae,	My tongue is like the pen of a scribe,
velociter scribentis.	who writes quickly.
Speciosus forma prae filiis hominum,	You surpass all the sons of men in
diffusa est gratia in labiis tuis,	beauty, grace is spread about on your lips,
propterea benedixit te Deus in aeternum.	therefore God has blessed you for eternity.
Accingere gladio tuo super femur tuum,	Strap on your sword at your side,
potentissime. . . .	O most powerful one. . . .
Memores erunt nominis tui,	They will remember your name,
in omni generatione et generationem.	for generation after generation.
Propterea populi confitebuntur tibi in aeternum,	Therefore the people will praise you to eternity,
et in saeculum saeculi.	and for ever.
Gloria Patri, et Filio,	Glory to the Father, and to the Son,
et Spiritui Sancto.	and to the Holy Spirit.
Sicut erat in principio, et nunc, et semper,	As it was in the beginning, both now and always,
et in saecula saeculorum. Amen.	and for ever. Amen.

Antiphon

Diffusa est gratia in labiis tuis,	Grace is spread about on your lips,
propterea benedixit te Deus in aeternum.	therefore God has blessed you for eternity.

The brief versicle (short sentence or part of a sentence) in each Nocturn in Matins is chanted by the priest and responded to by the choir. This is a small item but it serves to articulate the service and to separate the group of psalms from the group of lessons. The versicle in the first Nocturn (Ex. 5-8) has the same text as the second antiphon, thus creating a certain unity within the service. The music is different, however, and thus the textual echo is given variety by a new musical setting. The recitation takes place on a single pitch with an ornamental cadential flourish. The choral response repeats the music of the priest's statement, as it does in many of the other dialogue or exchange chants we have examined.

EXAMPLE 5-8   Versicle, *Tamquam Sponsus.*

(Priest)

Tam-quam spon - sus,

(Choir)

R̸. Do - mi - nus pro - ce - dens de tha - la - mo su - o.

Tamquam sponsus,	The Lord is like a bridegroom,
R̸. Dominus procedens de thalamo suo.	R̸. Coming from his bedchamber.

After the versicle come the three lessons and the three responsories. Each Nocturn is given a distinctive literary and intellectual character by the nature of the readings (lessons) assigned to it. Generally, the first Nocturn has readings from the Old Testament, such as passages from the Prophets or the five books of Moses. The second Nocturn contains readings illuminating the meaning of the feast or season, usually from one of the patristic writers such as Augustine or Jerome. The readings in the third Nocturn are also usually by one of the great figures of church history but are specific commentaries on passages from the Gospels and are preceded by a reading of those passages. Each lesson begins with a request by the reader of the lesson for a blessing, answered by a short blessing by the priest, and ends with a brief statement, "Tu autem, Domine, miserere nobis" ("And may you, O Lord, have mercy on us") and a response by the choir, "Deo gratias" ("Thanks be to God").

The lessons of the first Nocturn of Christmas Matins are passages from Isaiah which were interpreted by Christian commentators as prefiguring the Nativity. The reciting formula for lessons based on the Old Testament prophets is very distinctive, with a half-step drop to B at the half close and a steep drop to F at the full close. The unusual clash—a tritone—between the B ending of the half close and the F ending of the full close even suggests something of the generally stern nature of the prophetic texts.

The first lesson (Ex. 5-9) is from Isaiah, Chapter 9. It is a famous passage, set by many composers during and since the Middle Ages, not the least of whom was Handel: "The people who walked in darkness have seen a great light . . . For a child is born for us . . . and he will be called admired Counsellor . . . Prince of peace." The ending of the lesson is marked by a slightly different formula for the last line of the reading, then the brief exchange "Tu autem . . . Deo gratias" between reader and choir.

EXAMPLE 5-9   First lesson.

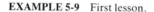

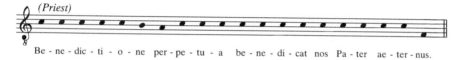

Ha - bi - tan - ti - bus in re - gi - o - ne um - brae mor - tis,

lux or - ta est e - is.

Mul - ti - pli - ca - sti gen - tem,

et non ma - gni - fi - ca - sti lae - ti - ti - am.

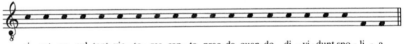

Lae - ta - bun - tur co - ram te, si - cut qui lae - tan - tur in mes - se,

si - cut ex - sul - tant vic - to - res, cap - ta prae - da, quan - do di - vi - dunt spo - li - a.

Iu - gum e - nim o - ne - ris e - ius, et vir - gam hu - me - ri e - ius,

et scep-trum ex - ac - to - ris e - ius su - pe - ra - sti si - cut in di - e Ma - di - an.

Qui - a om-nis vi - o - len-ta prae-da - ti - o cum tu-mul-tu, et ve -sti-men-tum mis-tum san-gui-ne,

e - rit in com - bu - sti - o - nem, et ci - bus i - gnis.

Par - vu - lus e - nim na - tus est no - bis, et fi - li - us da - tus est no - bis,

et fac - tus est prin - ci - pa - tus su - per hu - me - rum e - ius.

Et vo - ca - bi - tur no - men e - ius, ad - mi - ra - bi - lis Con - si - li - a - ri - us, De - us for - tis,

Pa - ter fu - tu - ri sae - cu - li, Prin - ceps pa - cis.

Tu au - tem, Do - mi - ne, mi - se - re - re no - bis.

(Choir)

R̶. De - o gra - ti - as.

Iube Domine benedicere.	Provide, O Lord, a blessing.
Benedictione perpetua benedicat nos Pater aeternus.	May the eternal Father bless us with endless blessing.
R̶. Amen.	R̶. Amen.
Primo tempore alleviata est terra Zabulon, et terra Nephtali,	Formerly the land of Zabulon and the land of Nephtali were spurned,
et novissimo aggravata est via maris trans Jordanem Galilaeae gentium.	but recently the way of the sea has been glorified, the land across Jordan of the nations of Galilee.
Populus, qui ambulabat in tenebris, vidit lucem magnam.	The people who walked in darkness have seen a great light.
Habitantibus in regione umbrae mortis, lux orta est eis.	For those who live in the region of the shadow of death a light has arisen.

Multiplicasti gentem,	You have multiplied the nation,
et non magnificasti laetitiam.	and you have not reduced their joy.

Laetabuntur coram te, sicut qui
laetantur in messe,

They will rejoice in your presence,
like those who rejoice at the
harvest,

sicut exsultant victores, capta
praeda, quando dividunt
spolia.

like victorious soldiers who exult
as they divide the spoils of
war.

Iugum enim oneris eius, et virgam
humeri eius,

The yoke of his burden, the rod on
his shoulder,

et sceptrum exactoris eius su-
perasti sicut in die Madian.

and the staff of his oppressor—
these you have smashed as on
the day of Madian.

Quia omnis violenta praedatio cum
tumultu, et vestimentum mistum
sanguine,

For every violent and noisy attack,
every bloody piece of clothing,

erit in combustionem, et cibus
ignis.

will be put to the fire and food for
the flames.

Parvulus enim natus est nobis, et
filius datus est nobis,

For a child is born for us, and a son is
given to us,

et factus est principatus super hu-
merum eius.

and the burden of leadership will
fall on his shoulder.

Et vocabitur nomen eius, admirabilis
Consiliarius, Deus fortis, Pater
futuri saeculi, Princeps pacis.

And he will be called admired Counsellor, mighty God, Father of
the world to come, Prince of
peace.

Tu autem, Domine, miserere nobis.

And may you, O Lord, have pity on
us.

℟. Deo gratias.

℟. Thanks be to God.

Each lesson in each of the Nocturns is followed by a responsory, a chant involving alternation between solo singers and the whole choir. In most of the other services of the Office the responsories are quite short and simple. In Matins, however, they are lengthy and elaborate and contain some of the richest music of the entire Office (to distinguish them from the smaller variety they are sometimes known as Great Responsories). They are sung to music with a formal design similar to that of the Gradual or the Alleluya of the Mass. In the opening section (the "respond"), the intonation is sung by soloists and the continuation by the choir. The interior section (the "verse") is for the soloists, and then the opening music is repeated by the choir. This pattern may be represented as follows·

Respond	**Verse**	**Respond**
Soloists–Choir	Soloists	Choir

There are a couple of complicating factors in the performance of responsories. First, in addition to the middle section, sometimes a second

A group of monks gathers round a large choirbook. In this fifteenth-century miniature, the leader wears spectacles. British Library, London.

"verse" is sung in the form of the first line of the Doxology.[7] The respond is sung after both of these solo sections, giving the form:

Respond	Verse	Respond	Doxology	Respond
Soloists-Choir	Soloists	Choir	Soloists	Choir

Second, since the elaborate music and the additional solo section resulted

---

[7]Normal medieval practice was to add the Doxology only to the third responsory in each Nocturn. The importance of the feast, however, encouraged the addition of the Doxology to the first responsory also.

in a rather lengthy item, the respond was usually shortened upon its returns, with only the second half being sung. This modified the form as follows:

R (complete)   **V**   **R** (second half)   **D**   **R** (second half)

This became the standard form for the first and third responsories. The second responsory retained only a single verse.

The texts for the responsories are taken from the Prophets, the five books of Moses, the Gospels, and early church writings; only occasionally are they excerpts from the psalms. There are many hundreds of responsory melodies in the medieval manuscripts, perhaps even more than a thousand. The melodies for the responds are mostly highly neumatic, sometimes melismatic, and are characterized by internal repetition of motifs. The verses are sung to standard melodies, which often stay close to the reciting tone of the mode, thus giving them the appearance of very elaborate recitation formulas.

The first responsory for Christmas Matins (Ex. 5-10) has a rich neumatic setting in which the long text is divided into five clear phrases, coinciding with the natural breaks in its grammatical structure. The music is in Mode 5, Lydian. It oscillates between the version with the B♮ and the alternative version with B♭. At the opening the B is avoided altogether: the words "Hodie nobis" are sung to a clear, unambiguous Mode-5 outline, stressing the reciting tone C, touching A, and cadencing on the F final. The remainder of the phrase, up to "dignatus est," introduces the B♭ and, with one brief exception, stays entirely within the lower fifth, F–C, of Mode 5, with another cadence on the final. By contrast, the next phrase, "ut hominem . . . revocaret," moves higher in the modal range and fills out the upper fourth, C–F, before cadencing on A. This suggests a move to a new mode, and indeed the next phrase, "Gaudet exercitus angelorum," moves to the realm of the Dorian by opening with a stepwise ascent up the fifth A–E, which is the Dorian fifth transposed, and by cadencing on A (the transposed final). The Lydian mode, however, is re-established by the music for "quia salus aeterna," which stresses the Lydian fifth once more, and does so by using virtually the same cadential pattern that appeared at the opening on "nobis." The final phrase of the respond, "humano generi apparuit," reconfirms the Lydian and cadences on the final, F. A unifying motif of the chant is the descending fourth, occurring stepwise, and analysis of the occasions when some form of B appears shows that when this motif descends to F the B♭ is used, so that the tritone may be avoided. B♭ also occurs when the lower portion of the mode is stressed, or when the music is centering on A and the step upward is only momentary.

The music for the verses focuses on the reciting tone C. The first phrase moves within a narrow range, touching on the D above the reciting tone only as a means of centering on, and ultimately cadencing on, the C.

The second phrase begins at the outset on the lower F but then continues within the same narrow range. The descending-fourth motif appears again at the close, and the cadence reiterates music from the respond ("[ange]-lorum"). The close on A allows a smooth transition to the part of the respond that is repeated ("Gaudet . . ."), with its stepwise ascent from A to E.

The two phrases of the music for the verses fit both the "Gloria in excelsis" and the "Gloria Patri" grammatically, for both texts fall into two clauses joined by the conjunction "et" ("and"). After the second verse (the Gloria Patri), the second half of the respond is sung once more to end the responsory.

EXAMPLE 5-10   Responsory, *Hodie Nobis Caelorum.*

qui - a   sa - lus   ae - ter - - - na,

hu - ma - no ge - ne - ri   ap - - - - - - - - - - - - -

pa - ru - - - - - - it.

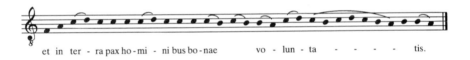

℣. Glo - ri - a   in ex - cel - sis   De - - - - o,

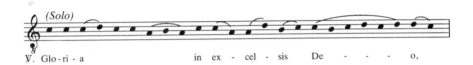

et in ter - ra pax ho - mi - ni bus bo - nae   vo - lun - ta - - - - - tis.

℞. Gau - det ex - er - ci - tus an - ge - lo - - - rum,

qui - a   sa - lus   ae - ter - na,

hu - ma - no ge - ne - ri   ap - - - - - - - - - - - - -

pa - ru - - - - - - it.

℣. Glo - ri - a Pa - tri, et Fi - li - o,

et Spi - ri - tu - i Sanc - to.

℟. Gau - det ex - er - ci - tus an - ge - lo - rum,

qui - a sa - lus ae - ter - na,

hu - ma - no ge - ne - ri ap - pa - ru - it.

Hodie nobis caelorum Rex de virgine
    nasci dignatus est,

ut hominem perditum ad caelestia
    regna revocaret.

Gaudet exercitus angelorum,
quia salus aeterna
humano generi apparuit.

℣. Gloria in excelsis Deo,
    et in terra pax hominibus bonae
      voluntatis.

℟. Gaudet exercitus angelorum,
quia salus aeterna
humano generi apparuit.

℣. Gloria Patri, et Filio,
    et Spiritui Sancto.

℟. Gaudet exercitus angelorum,
quia salus aeterna
humano generi apparuit.

Today the King of the heavens
    deigned to be born for us from a
    virgin,
so that he might summon back man-
    kind from its wanderings to the
    kingdom of heaven.
The crowd of angels rejoices,
for eternal salvation
has appeared for the human race.

℣. Glory to God in the highest,
    and on earth peace to men of good
    will.

℟. The crowd of angels rejoices,
for eternal salvation
has appeared for the human race.

℣. Glory to the Father, and to the Son,
    and to the Holy Spirit.

℟. The crowd of angels rejoices,
for eternal salvation
has appeared for the human race.

The text of this first responsory is obviously appropriate to the day, since it refers to the birth of Jesus. The first solo verse is the message of the angels which appears as the opening of the Gloria in the Mass. Again we find an example of the same text appearing in the liturgy on two quite different occasions. And once again it is the musical setting that creates the atmosphere and provides the relevant context for the words.

The texts of responsories are often so arranged that repetition of only the second half of the respond still makes grammatical sense. Sometimes this procedure is more successful than at other times; here the sense is perfectly consecutive. The verbal link is reinforced by the musical link between the A which ends the music for the verses, and the A which begins the music for the second half of the respond.

The second lesson of Christmas Matins (Ex. 5-11) is preceded by the traditional blessing. The text of the lesson is from a different part of Isaiah, and it too is well known from its association with the Christmas season. "Be comforted, my people, ... Every valley will be raised up, and every mountain and hill will be made low. . . . the word of our Lord lasts for ever." It concludes with the standard ending and the response of the choir. The same recitation formula is used as in the previous lesson.

EXAMPLE 5-11   Second lesson, beginning and end only.

Lo - qui - mi - ni   ad   cor   Je - ru - sa - lem,

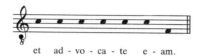

et   ad - vo - ca - te   e - am.

Quo - ni - am com - ple - ta est ma - li - ti - a   e - ius,

di - mis - sa   est   i - ni - qui - tas   il - li - us,

su - sce - pit de ma - nu Do - mi - ni du - pli - ci - a pro om - ni - bus pec - ca - tis su - is. . . .

Ex - sic - ca - tum est foe - num, et   ce - ci - dit flos,

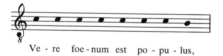

qui - a   spi - ri - tus Do - mi - ni   suf - fla - vit   in   e - o.

Ve - re   foe - num est   po - pu - lus,

ex - sic - ca - tum est foe - num, et   ce - ci - dit flos,

ver - bum au - tem Do - mi - ni no - stri ma - net   in   ae - ter - num.

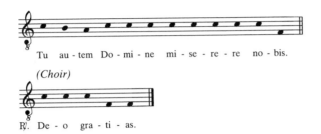

Tu au - tem Do - mi - ne mi - se - re - re no - bis.

(Choir)

℟. De - o gra - ti - as.

Iube Domine benedicere.
Benedictione perpetua benedicat nos
 Pater aeternus.
℟. Amen.

Consolamini, consolamini, popule
 meus,
  dicit Deus vester.
Loquimini ad cor Jerusalem,
 et advocate eam.
Quoniam completa est malitia eius,
 dimissa est iniquitas illius,
 suscepit de manu Domini duplicia
 pro omnibus peccatis suis. . . .

Exsiccatum est foenum, et cecidit
 flos,
 quia spiritus Domini sufflavit in eo.

Vere foenum est populus,
exsiccatum est foenum, et cecidit flos,

verbum autem Domini nostri manet
 in aeternum.

Tu autem Domine miserere nobis.

℟. Deo gratias.

Provide, O Lord, a blessing.
May the eternal Father bless us with
 endless blessing.
℟. Amen.

Be comforted, be comforted, my
 people,
 says your God.
Speak to the heart of Jerusalem,
 and advise them.
For their evil time is over,
 and their wrongdoing is pardoned,
 and they have received from the
 hand of the Lord double pun-
 ishment for all their sins. . . .

The grass has withered, and
 the flower has fallen,
 for the breath of the Lord has blown
 upon it.
Truly the people are like grass;
 the grass has withered, and the flower
 has fallen,
but the word of our Lord lasts for
 ever.

And may you, O Lord, have pity on
 us.

℟. Thanks be to God.

The responsory that follows the second lesson (Ex. 5-12) is in Mode
8, Hypomixolydian. Both the respond and the verses stay primarily within
the upper fifth of the mode, G–D, and the music is mostly neumatic. The
text of the respond, a beautiful metaphor of spring and renewal, is divided

by the music into four phrases, corresponding to the natural breaks in the sense. The first musical phrase opens with a syllabic reiteration of the final, G, and cadences on the reciting tone, C. The second makes the reverse movement from a stress on the reciting tone to a cadence on the final. The third phrase begins very much like the second but retains a feeling of incompletion by ending on F, the note below the final. The last phrase opens on G, and the music for its ending ("sunt caeli") is the same as that which ended the second phrase ("descendit"). There is thus a careful balance and parallelism in the music of this respond.

    This second responsory has only a single verse, which presents both a subtle contrast to, and a unity with, the respond. The descent from the reciting tone to the final (C to G) that is found several times in the respond reappears here, but more directly and twice in the first part of the verse ("Hodie illuxit . . . redemptionis novae."). The second part ("reparationis . . . aeternae") contains the reiterated G from the intonation of the respond and a variant of the same ending motif. The repeat of the respond is tied to the end of the solo verse (the second half of the respond opening on C, the verse ending on G) in the same way as the end of the respond (G) is tied to the beginning of the verse (C). Again music echoes textual structure, for all three main textual divisions (both halves of the respond and the opening of the verse) begin with the same word, "Hodie" ("Today").

EXAMPLE 5-12   Responsory, *Hodie Nobis De Caelo.*

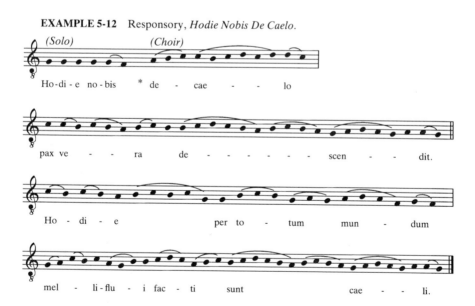

℣. Ho - di - e   il - lu - xit   no - bis di - es

re - demp - ti - o - nis   no - vae,

re - pa - ra - ti - o - nis an - ti - quae, fe - li - ci - ta - - - - tis

ae - ter - - - - - - - nae.

(Choir)

℞. Ho - di - e   per to - tum   mun - dum

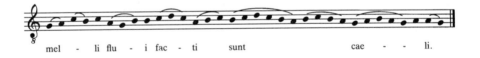

mel - li flu - i fac - ti   sunt   cae - - li.

Hodie nobis de caelo
pax vera descendit.
Hodie per totum mundum
melliflui facti sunt caeli.

℣. Hodie illuxit nobis dies redemptionis
     novae,
  reparationis antiquae, felicitatis
     aeternae.

℞. Hodie per totum mundum
  melliflui facti sunt caeli.

Today from the heavens
true peace has come down for us.
Today throughout the whole world
the heavens resound sweetly.

℣. Today the day of our new redemption
     shines for us,
  a day of ancient restoral, of eternal
     happiness.

℞. Today throughout the whole world
  the heavens resound sweetly.

The third lesson (Ex. 5-13), from Isaiah, Chapter 52, is again introduced by the blessing and ended by the interchange between reader and choir. The text celebrates the freedom of the people and city of Jerusalem, released from captivity. The reciting formula is the same as before.

EXAMPLE 5-13   Third lesson, portions only.

(Reader)

Iu - be Do - mi - ne be - ne - di - ce - re.

(Priest)

Be - ne - dic - ti - o - ne per - pe - tu - a be - ne - di - cat nos Pa - ter ae - ter - nus.

(Choir)

R̹. A - men.

(Reader)

Con - sur - ge, con - sur - ge, in - du - e - re for - ti - tu - di - ne tu - a, Si - on, in - du - e - re ve -

sti - men - tis glo - ri - ae tu - ae, Je - ru - sa - lem, ci - vi - tas sanc - ti,

qui - a non ad - ii - ci - et ul - tra ut per - tran - se - at per te in - cir - cum - ci - sus et im - mun - dus. . . .

Et nunc quid mi - hi est hic, di - cit Do - mi - nus, quo - ni - am ab - la - tus est po - pu - lus me - us gra - tis? . . .

Prop - ter hoc sci - et po - pu - lus me - us no - men me - um, in di - e il - la,

qui - a e - go ip - se qui lo - que - bar: Ec - ce ad - sum.

Tu   au - tem Do - mi - ne   mi - se - re - re   no - bis.

(Choir)

℟. De - o   gra - ti - as.

Iube Domine benedicere.	Provide, O Lord, a blessing.
Benedictione perpetua benedicat nos Pater aeternus.	May the eternal Father bless us with endless blessing.
℟. Amen.	℟. Amen.
Consurge, consurge, induere fortitudine tua, Sion, induere vestimentis gloriae tuae, Jerusalem, civitas sancti,	Arise, arise, put on your strength, O Zion, put on the garment of your glory, O Jerusalem, the holy city,
quia non adiiciet ultra ut pertranseat per te incircumcisus et immundus. . . .	for no longer shall the uncircumcised and unclean invade and trample you. . . .
Et nunc quid mihi est hic, dicit Dominus, quoniam ablatus est populus meus gratis? . . .	And now what do I have, said the Lord, seeing that my people have been taken away from me? . . .
Propter hoc sciet populus meus nomen meum, in die illa,	For this reason my people will know my name, on that day,
quia ego ipse qui loquebar: Ecce adsum.	for I myself shall say: Behold, I have come.
Tu autem Domine miserere nobis.	And may you, O Lord, have pity on us.
℟. Deo gratias.	℟. Thanks be to God.

The third lesson is followed by a responsory (Ex. 5-14), whose text is in the dramatic form of a dialogue, a particularly appropriate form for a responsory, with its solo-choir alternation. The music is in Mode 4, which, with its reciting tone on A—a reciting tone which it shares with Mode 1—is a particularly flexible mode; and indeed the opening phrase suggests the Dorian, Mode 1, with its intonation beginning and ending on D and the continuation of the phrase rising from D to cadence on A. The feeling of Mode 1 is strengthened in the second phrase ("Annuntiate . . . ") with its opening rising leap, but begins to dissolve as the phrase continues. The cadence is on F, an unexpected rising half-step cadence that coincides with a question in the text. Interestingly enough, the same rising half step is used for a question in the recitation formula of the lesson preceding this responsory. With the phrase "Natum vidimus," the definitive answer to the question, the music finally enters the realm of Mode 4 and has an unambiguous cadence on the E final, preceded by a stepwise descending fourth from the reciting tone. The last phrase both begins and ends on E, the final of the mode, and has an intermediate cadence on E (the last syllable of "angelorum"). The melody centers on the lower part of the mode for the first half of the phrase, finally reaching up to the B at the top of the Mode-4 octave before the confirmatory cadence on the E final.

EXAMPLE 5-14   Responsory, *Quem Vidistis, Pastores.*

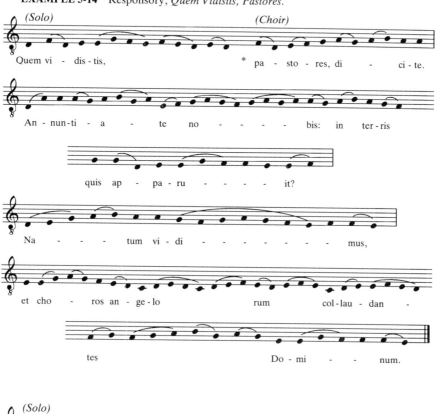

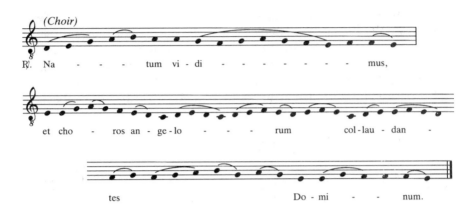

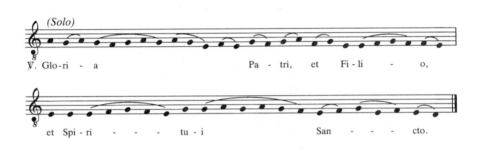

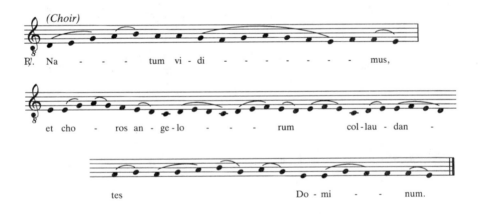

Quem vidistis pastores, dicite.	Tell, O shepherds, whom you have seen.
Annuntiate nobis: in terris quis apparuit?	Announce to us: who appeared to you in the countryside?
Natum vidimus, et choros angelorum collaudantes Dominum.	We saw a child, and choruses of angels praising the Lord.

℣. Dicite quidnam vidistis,
  et annuntiate Christi nativitatem.

℟. Natum vidimus,
  et choros angelorum collaudantes
    Dominum.

℣. Gloria Patri, et Filio,
  et Spiritui Sancto.

℟. Natum vidimus,
  et choros angelorum collaudantes
    Dominum.

℣. Tell us what you have seen,
  and announce the birth of Christ.

℟. We saw a child,
  and choruses of angels praising the
    Lord.

℣. Glory to the Father, and to the Son,
  and to the Holy Spirit.

℟. We saw a child,
  and choruses of angels praising the
    Lord.

As if to compensate for the ambiguity of the respond, the first part of the music for the solo verse ("Dicite . . . ") is almost a textbook Mode-4 melody, moving between the reciting tone and the final, making the descent twice, and clearly cadencing on E. The second part of the verse, however, needs to make a transition to the repeated section of the respond, which begins at "Natum" on D, and so, although it begins ("et annuntiate") with reiterated Es, it ends with a descent from the A reciting tone common to both Mode 4 and Mode 1 to a cadence on D.

This third responsory, like the first, contains a second solo verse in the form of the Doxology, and thus includes a second repetition of the concluding portion of the respond.

Immediately after the completion of the first Nocturn, the second Nocturn begins, with the antiphon for its first psalm. We shall not, however, look in detail here at the second and third Nocturns, as they follow the pattern of the first. Each contains three psalms with their antiphons, and a versicle, and continues with three lessons, each of which is followed by a responsory. Of course, each Nocturn has its own character as a result of the choice of psalms, the melodies for the antiphons, the literary style and content of the lessons, and the elaborate and distinctive music of the responsories. The constantly changing nature of the words and the music, within the set format of the Nocturn structure, help to give Matins its particular quality and make it one of the great manifestations of the medieval liturgy.

Conclusion

The concluding portion of the Matins service consists mainly of the singing of the Te Deum (Ex. 5-15).[8] This is an invariable text, traditionally sung at the conclusion of Matins (with the exception of some penitential seasons) and sometimes used on other liturgical and para-liturgical occasions such as processions and thanksgiving services. There is only one basic

---

[8]Sometimes in the Middle Ages, and regularly in modern times, the Te Deum would be sung in the place of the final responsory.

melody for the Te Deum, although manuscripts from the Middle Ages differ in detail as to its exact shape and some of its inflections. The text is very long and appears to have been made up from several different sources. It includes some paraphrases of psalm verses and a quotation of part of the Sanctus of the Mass. Its most striking feature, however, is its constant rhetorical repetition of the word "Te" or "Tu" ("You") at the beginnings of most of the lines. The chant is addressed directly to God. "It is you, God, we praise. It is you, Lord, we acknowledge. It is you, eternal Father, that all the world worships. It is to you that all the angels . . ."

The melody is primarily syllabic, though it contains a few short neumatic passages. It is written in Mode 4, Hypophrygian, and the intonation rises unusually quickly from the opening E through the reciting note A up to C and then ends on the A again. The choral continuation makes the same motion from the E through G to A. The parallelism of the text structure is matched by a repetitiveness in the musical phraseology, and this melodic gesture makes several reappearances ("omnis terra," "tibi caeli," "incessabili," etc.). Half closes are on A; full closes are on G. The syllabic pattern is broken briefly for the threefold "Sanctus," although the melodic statements are but ornamental versions of the cadence to the reciting tone at the opening of the chant, and the third "Sanctus" is both a reiteration of that cadence and a neumatic rendering of the E–G–A motif. On "Patrem" and "Sanctum" the neumatic pattern from "Sanctus" is repeated, thus drawing attention to those words by a technique we have seen used in the Gloria and Credo of the Mass. The melody of the Te Deum, with its syllabic setting and formulaic nature, may thus be seen as a derivation both from recitational psalm formulas and from the setting of hymns.[9] Its repetitiveness, both textual and musical, and simple syllabic melody enlivened by occasional neumatic groups explain the popularity of this chant throughout the Middle Ages.

EXAMPLE 5-15   Te Deum.

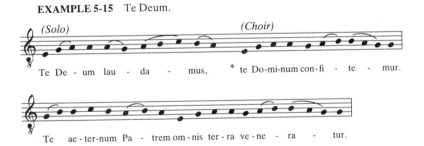

---

[9]The Te Deum is not, properly speaking, a hymn in the sense in which we now use the word: its text is prose and not strophic verse. Nor is its music exactly in the style of a recitational psalm formula: the music is derived from psalm formulas, but it incorporates positioned motifs and a shift in style halfway through the chant.

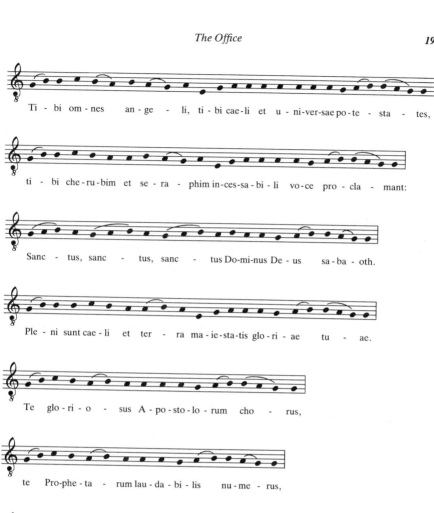

Ti - bi om - nes an - ge - li, ti - bi cae - li et u - ni-ver-sae po - te - sta - tes,

ti - bi che-ru-bim et se - ra - phim in-ces-sa-bi - li vo-ce pro - cla - mant:

Sanc - tus, sanc - tus, sanc - tus Do-mi-nus De - us sa - ba - oth.

Ple - ni sunt cae - li et ter - ra ma-ie-sta-tis glo - ri - ae tu - ae.

Te glo - ri - o - sus A - po-sto-lo-rum cho - rus,

te Pro-phe - ta - rum lau - da - bi - lis nu - me - rus,

te Mar-ty-rum can - di - da - tus lau-dat ex - er - ci - tus.

Te per or-bem ter - ra - rum sanc-ta con-fi-te-tur ec - cle-si - a,

Pa - trem im-men-sae ma - ie - sta - tis.

Ve - ne - ran-dum tu - um ve - rum et u - ni - cum Fi - li - um,

San - ctum quo - que Pa - ra - cli - tum   Spi - ri -   tum.

Tu,   Rex glo - ri - ae   Chris - te,

tu Pa - tris sem - pi - ter - nus es   Fi - li - us.

Tu, ad li - be - ran - dum sus-cep-tu-rus ho - mi - nem, non hor-ru - is - ti Vir - gi - nis   u - te-rum.

Tu de - vic-to mor-tis a - cu - le - o, a - pe - ru - is - ti cre-den-ti-bus re - gna coe - lo - rum.

Tu ad dex - te - ram De - i se - des in glo - ri - a   Pa - tris.

Iu - dex cre - de - ris es - se ven - tu - rus.

Te er-go quae-su-mus, tu-is fa-mu-lis sub-ve - ni, quos pre-ti - o - so san-gui-ne re-de - mi - sti.

Ae - ter - na   fac   cum san-ctis tu - is in glo - ri - a nu - me - ra - ri.

Sal-vum fac po-pu-lum tu-um, Do-mi-ne, et be - ne-dic hae-re - di-ta-ti tu - ae.

Et re - ge e - os, et ex - tol - le il - los us-que in ae - ter - num.

Per sin - gu - los di - es be - ne - di - ci - mus te.

Et lau - da - mus no-men tu - um in sae - cu - lum et in sae - cu - lum sae - cu - li.

Di - gna - re, Do - mi - ne, di - e i - sto si - ne pec - ca - to nos cus - to - di - re.

Mi - se - re - re no - stri, Do - mi - ne, mi - se - re - re no - stri.

Fi-at mi-se-ri-cor-di-a tu-a, Do-mi-ne, su-per nos, quem-ad-mo-dum spe-ra - vi-mus in te.

In te, Do - mi-ne, spe - ra - vi, non con - fun - dar in ae - ter - num.

Te Deum laudamus, te Dominum confitemur.	It is you, God, we praise. It is you, Lord, we acknowledge.
Te aeternum Patrem omnis terra veneratur.	It is you, eternal Father, that all the world worships.

Tibi omnes angeli, tibi caeli et universae
potestates,

tibi cherubim et seraphim incessabili
voce proclamant:
Sanctus, sanctus, sanctus Dominus Deus
sabaoth.
Pleni sunt caeli et terra maiestatis gloriae tuae.
Te gloriosus Apostolorum chorus,

Te Prophetarum laudabilis numerus,

Te Martyrum candidatus laudat exerci-
tus.
Te per orbem terrarum sancta confitetur
ecclesia,
Patrem immensae maiestatis.
Venerandum tuum verum et unicum
Filium,
Sanctum quoque Paraclitum Spiritum.
Tu, Rex gloriae Christe,
tu Patris sempiternus es Filius.
Tu, ad liberandum suscepturus
hominem, non horruisti Virginis
uterum.
Tu, devicto mortis aculeo, aperuisti
credentibus regna caelorum.

Tu ad dexteram Dei sedes in gloria
Patris.
Iudex crederis esse venturus.

Te ergo quaesumus, tuis famulis sub-
veni, quos pretioso sanguine
redemisti.
Aeterna fac cum sanctis tuis in gloria
numerari.
Salvum fac populum tuum, Domine, et
benedic haereditati tuae.
Et rege eos, et extolle illos usque in
aeternum.
Per singulos dies benedicimus te.
Et laudamus nomen tuum in saeculum et
in saeculum saeculi.
Dignare, Domine, die isto sine peccato
nos custodire.
Miserere nostri, Domine, miserere
nostri.

It is to you that all the angels, to you that
the heavens and the powers of the
universe,
to you that the cherubim and seraphim
endlessly proclaim:
Holy, holy, holy is the Lord God of
hosts.
The heavens and the earth are full of the
majesty of your glory.
It is you that the glorious chorus of
Apostles,
You that the praiseworthy group of
Prophets,
You that the gleaming band of Martyrs
praises.
It is you that the holy church acknowl-
edges throughout the world,
Father of infinite majesty.
Also your honored, true, and only Son,

and the Holy Spirit, the Comforter.
You, O Christ, King of glory,
you are the eternal Son of the Father.
You did not spurn the Virgin's womb
when you took up the task of free-
ing mankind.
You, having overcome the pain of death,
opened the realms of heaven to all
believers.
You sit at the right hand of God in the
glory of the Father.
We believe that you are the judge who
will come.
It is you therefore that we beg to help us,
your servants, whom you redeemed
with your precious blood.
Let them be counted with your saints in
eternal glory.
Save your people, O Lord, and bless
your heritage.
And rule them, and raise them up for
eternity.
We bless you every single day.
And we praise your name for ever and
ever.
Deign, O Lord, to keep us this day without sin.
Have mercy on us, O Lord, have mercy
on us.

Fiat misericordia tua, Domine, super nos, quemadmodum speravimus in te.	Let your mercy be upon us, O Lord, according as we have hoped in you.
In te, Domine, speravi, non confundar in aeternum.	I have hoped in you, O Lord, let me never be confounded.

The final item in Matins is the Benedicamus Domino, which closes all services in the Office.[10] It is sung by the priest, and the choir responds with "Deo gratias" ("Thanks be to God") to the same melody, as in the closing item of Mass. The chant (Ex. 5-16) is short and neumatic, with one arch formed on D, and then a slow descent from A down to the final on D.

EXAMPLE 5-16 Benedicamus Domino.

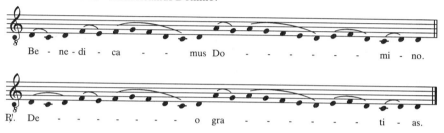

Be - ne - di - ca - - - mus Do - - - - - - - mi - no.

R⁷. De - - - - - - - o gra - - - - - ti - as.

Benedicamus Domino.	Let us bless the Lord.
R⁷. Deo gratias.	R⁷. Thanks be to God.

SUMMARY

This concludes our analysis of the complete medieval Matins service for Christmas. It is a lengthy service, with its central portion of three Nocturns, each containing psalms, lessons, and responsories, and its substantial introductory and concluding sections. As in the Mass, it is music that articulates and gives palpable form to the many disparate items in the service: clear and simple formulas for the readings and prayers; slightly more complex formulas for the poetry of the psalms; freer melodies for the antiphons which frame the psalms and for the "set pieces" such as the Invitatory psalm and the Te Deum; while the richest music is reserved for the responsorial chants, which follow the lessons and embody a dramatic alternation between solo and choral singing. Music gives length to short texts and shortens long ones; it provides "tempo" and rhythm for the service. Music distinguishes between meditation and narrative, commentary and petition. It draws attention to those parts of the liturgy that are the same for

---

[10]Sometimes the Matins service led straight into Lauds, in which case the concluding Benedicamus Domino was omitted.

every day and those that mark the occasion as special. In the work of God, intellect and music are one. As St. Benedict said:

> We believe that the Divine Presence is everywhere and that the eyes of the Lord behold the good and the evil in every place. We should be especially mindful of this when we participate in the work of God. . . . Let us therefore consider how we should behave in the sight of God and his angels, and participate in the Divine Office in such a way that our mind and our voice may accord together.[11]

DISCOGRAPHY

Example 5-1   Domine, Labia Mea.
Ensemble Organum, *Polyphonie aquitaine du XIIe siècle,* Harmonia Mundi HMC 1134.

Example 5-2   Deus in Adiutorium.
Ensemble Organum, *Polyphonie aquitaine du XIIe siècle,* Harmonia Mundi HMC 1134.

Example 5-3   Invitatory Psalm.
Ensemble Organum, *Polyphonie aquitaine du XIIe siècle,* Harmonia Mundi HMC 1134; also on Benediktiner der Abtei St. Maurice & St. Maur, Clervaux, *Gregorianischer Gesänge: Weihnachtsmusik,* Philips A 02092 L.

Example 5-4   Hymn, *Christe, Redemptor Omnium.*
Ensemble Organum, *Polyphonie aquitaine du XIIe siècle,* Harmonia Mundi HMC 1134; also on Choir of the Vienna Hofburg Kapelle, *Gregorian Chant for Christmas,* Turnabout TV 34181S.

Example 5-7   Antiphon only.
Choeur des Moines de l'Abbaye Saint Pierre de Solesmes, *Chant Gregorien,* London A4501.

Example 5-9   First Lesson.
Ensemble Organum, *Polyphonie aquitaine du XIIe siècle,* Harmonia Mundi HMC 1134; also on Capella Antiqua de Munich, *Chants grégoriens pour le temps de Noël,* Harmonia Mundi HM 5112.

---

[11]*Regula Benedicti,* Capitulum XIX.

Example 5-10   Responsory, *Hodie Nobis Caelorum.*
Pro Cantione Antiqua, *Medieval Music: Sacred Monophony,* Peters International PLE 114 (Oxford University Press OUP 161); also on Ensemble Organum, *Polyphonie aquitaine du XIIe siècle,* Harmonia Mundi HMC 1134; and Benediktiner der Abtei St. Maurice & St. Maur, Clervaux, *Gregorianischer Gesänge: Weihnachtsmusik,* Philips A 02092 L.

Example 5-14   Responsory, *Quem Vidistis, Pastores.*
Choeur des Moines de l'Abbaye Saint Pierre de Solesmes, *Chant Gregorien,* London A4501.

Example 5-15   Te Deum.
Pro Cantione Antiqua, *Medieval Music: Sacred Monophony,* Peters International PLE 114 (Oxford University Press OUP 161) (end of Side II); also on Capella Antiqua de Munich, *Ave Maria,* Harmonia Mundi HM B 5115.

BIBLIOGRAPHICAL NOTES

An accessible and illuminating edition of Benedict's Rule is Timothy Fry et al. (eds.), *R. B. 1980: The Rule of St. Benedict in Latin and English with Notes* (Collegeville, Minnesota: The Liturgical Press, 1981).

Lorna Price, *The Plan of St. Gall in Brief* (Berkeley: University of California Press, 1982) is a beautifully printed study of the monastery of St. Gall, with facsimiles, drawings, and a scholarly and readable text.

A sketch of the origins and structure of the Office, together with a comparison between the regular and the secular forms, is given in Roger E. Reynolds, "Divine Office," in *Dictionary of the Middle Ages,* vol. 4 (New York: Charles Scribner's Sons, 1984). There are also some useful articles on the development of the Office in Part Two, Section V, of *The Study of Liturgy,* ed. Cheslyn Jones, Geoffrey Wainwright, and Edward Yarnold (New York: Oxford University Press, 1978).

The music for some of the services in the Office is given in the *Liber Usualis* (see the Bibliographical Notes to Chapter 4). Only four Matins services are printed, including that for Christmas. The music for a Vespers service is collected in Claude V. Palisca (ed.), *Norton Anthology of Western Music,* vol. 1, 2nd edition (New York: W. W. Norton and Co., 1988).

Helpful summaries by Ruth Steiner of the various services include "Divine Office," "Matins," "Lauds," "Little Hours," and "Vespers," in *The New Grove Dictionary of Music and Musicians* (London: Macmillan Publishers Ltd., 1980).

SIX

900–1200: THE LATIN TRADITION

CHANT AFTER CHARLEMAGNE

The composition of plainchant did not come to a halt after the synthesis of Roman and Frankish liturgical practices, which Charlemagne had brought about, prevailed over much of Europe in the ninth century. Indeed, perhaps because of the relative stability of the repertoire, or the spread of musical notation, the tenth to the twelfth centuries saw a considerable increase in the amount of plainchant that was composed. This took two primary forms: additions to already existing items and newly composed pieces. In many instances the distinction between these two forms is not at all clear cut, as we shall see.

The medieval penchant for *elaboration* may be seen in almost any aspect of life in the Middle Ages: in social ritual, scholarly commentary, the writing of history, the decoration of manuscripts. From the beginning of the tenth to the end of the twelfth centuries this penchant became a passion. And the liturgy, though it had already been elaborated in church and monastery sufficiently to fill the day and the night, presented one of the foremost areas of opportunity.

How could an established liturgy, by now fairly stable in form and content, comprising a twenty-four-hour cycle of services including at least one Mass (several on major feasts) and the eight services of the Office, be subject to further elaboration? This was just the kind of problem that appealed to the medieval mind. And several solutions were found.

In the first place this period experienced a proliferation of new feasts, honoring the growing number of new saints and reflecting an intensified emphasis upon the Virgin Mary as a focus of worship. Gradually the calendar became filled with new feasts and saints' days, and each new feast required new chants for both Mass and Office, which had to be made appropriate to the occasion. For Marian feasts the texts could be taken from scriptural sources; for the saints' feasts texts were usually adaptations of, or quotations from, the large numbers of quasi-historical documents (*vitae*) that related in edifying detail events from the lives of the saints.

The concentrated focus on Mary in this period provided several opportunities for new compositions. In the eleventh century it became common practice to celebrate a Mass for the Virgin on Saturdays. Other new music is found in the Marian antiphons, chants devoted to the Virgin Mary. The four most important of these are *Alma Redemptoris Mater*; *Ave, Regina Caelorum*; *Regina Caeli*; and *Salve, Regina,* which praise Mary as mother and queen. It is important to realize that the Marian antiphons, despite their name, are not linked with psalms. They are separate chants, completely independent of psalm singing. They are, however, a part of the Office and were sung traditionally at Compline, the service held before retiring for the night.

In the new Marian antiphons, the music is clearly constructed to conform to the theoretical descriptions of the modes. The entire range of the mode is carefully filled, with a focus on the appropriate fifth and fourth and the correct reciting tone. The almost self-conscious style of this music may be seen in the Marian antiphon *Alma Redemptoris Mater* ("Nurturing Mother of the Redeemer"), with its perfect balance, exact F–F octave range (only once is the G above sounded), strict outlining of proper fifth and fourth, and clear cadence on the final (Ex. 6-1). Every phrase begins on the final, F, (or its octave) or the reciting tone, and every phrase ends on the final, the reciting tone, or the note a third above the final (A). A more correct Mode-5 melody would be hard to compose.

In the Office, new chants could be composed at several points in the services: hymns could be newly written, entire responsories could be new, and new and proper antiphons could be composed for the psalms of the day. The Mass provided fewer opportunities for new texts. The Ordinary items of the Mass, however, their texts familiar to everybody, offered constant musical challenges. A large number of new Ordinary settings were composed—individually for each item, not as a group (though sometimes

EXAMPLE 6-1 Marian antiphon, *Alma Redemptoris Mater.*

(Solo) (Choir)

Al - - - - - - - - - - ma * Re-demp-to - ris

Ma - ter,

quae per - vi - a cae - li por - - ta ma - - - nes,

et stel - - - la ma - ris,

suc - cur - re ca - den - - ti sur-ge - re qui cu - rat po - pu - lo.

Tu quae ge - nu - i - sti, na - tu - ra mi - ran - - te,

tu - um sanc - tum Ge - ni - to - rem.

Vir - - go pri - - - us ac po - ste - ri - us,

Ga-bri - e - lis ab o - re su - mens il - lud A - ve, pec-ca - to - rum

mi - se - re - re.

Alma Redemptoris Mater,	Nurturing Mother of the Redeemer,
quae pervia caeli porta manes,	you who are the transparent door to heaven,
et stella maris,	and star of the sea,
succurre cadenti surgere qui curat populo.	help your falling people who are struggling to rise up.
Tu quae genuisti, natura mirante,	You who gave birth, wonder of nature,
tuum sanctum Genitorem.	to your holy Creator.
Virgo prius ac posterius,	Virgin before and after,
Gabrielis ab ore sumens illud Ave,	receiving from the mouth of Gabriel that
peccatorum miserere.	"Hail," have mercy on us sinners.

they are found in the manuscripts in pairs: Kyrie-Gloria and Sanctus-Agnus). These too show more conformity to modal principles than the earlier settings. It was the shorter texts of the Ordinary that encouraged more settings: the Gloria, and especially the Credo, were usually passed over in favor of the Kyrie, Sanctus, or Agnus Dei.

TROPES

A different way of elaborating the liturgy also became popular in this period—adding to or inserting new material into pre-existing chants. The name given to this important form of elaboration is *troping*. The word trope—*tropos* in Greek (Latin *tropus*)—means a turn of phrase or figure of speech by means of which the language is embellished. Similarly a trope in the liturgy is an embellishment of the liturgy—either by music alone, or by music and words together.

In the Mass, tropes were added mostly to the Introit, Offertory, and Communion, and also to the items of the Ordinary except the Credo, which, perhaps because it is a statement of faith, was not considered an appropriate vehicle for troping. In the Office, antiphons, versicles, responsories, and Benedicamus Domino chants were the most frequent items to receive tropes.

Textually, tropes were used in two different ways. Either they served as introductions to the chants to which they were appended, or they were added as interpolations between the lines of the chant, commenting upon or explaining the original text. This latter function may be seen as a musical parallel to a favorite form of medieval intellectual endeavor known as "glossing"—writing examples or explanations above words or sentences in a manuscript, or in the margins, in order to elucidate the text. Similarly, troping was a technique of providing both a musical and textual commentary to a chant.

A "glossed" text from the fifteenth century. The original appears in lines of heavy writing on the right; above these lines (in very fine script) and in a column on the left, explanations and commentary appear. University Library, Uppsala. From Anders Piltz, *The World of Medieval Learning,* tr. David Jones (Totowa, NJ: Barnes and Noble Books, 1981). Used by permission.

The Mass Introit was a common place for tropes. Here, often the first kind of trope is found, the introductory type. The Introit for the Mass for Christmas, for example, begins with the words "Puer natus est" ("A child is born"). One trope for this Introit adds the introductory words "*Let us rejoice today, for God has descended from the heavens, and on earth on our behalf*: (A child is born)" (Ex. 6-2).

EXAMPLE 6-2 Introit, *Puer Natus Est,* with trope.

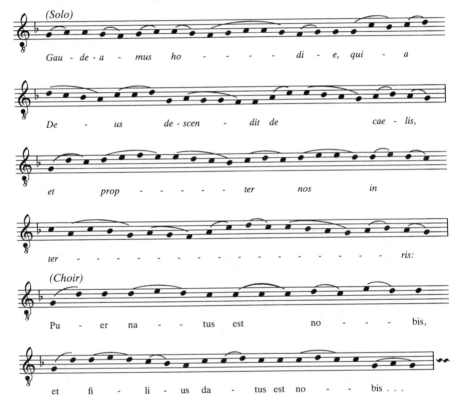

Gaudeamus hodie, quia Deus descendit de caelis,	Let us rejoice today, for God has descended from the heavens,
et propter nos in terris:	and on earth on our behalf:
Puer natus est nobis, et filius datus est nobis . . .	A child is born for us, and a son has been given to us . . .

Thirteenth-century manuscript with the Christmas Introit *Puer Natus Est* (cf. Example 6-2), Bibliothèque Nationale, Paris.

Tropes were usually sung by a soloist, so that a distinction between trope and original chant was maintained in performance, for after the singing of the trope the choir would begin the words of the Introit itself.

Musically, tropes were designed to complement the chant to which they were added. The introductory trope to "Puer natus est" is a clear Mode-7 melody, using the note below the final, reaching up to the reciting tone and beyond to F, and finally making a firm cadence on the final, G, preceded by the descending Mixolydian fifth D–G. Thus it fits well with the Introit itself, which is classically Mode 7, with its skip of the Mixolydian fifth G–D (repeated on "et [filius]")—which is anticipated in the trope at the beginning of the second phrase ("et [propter]")—and its focus upon D as the reciting tone and G as the final.

In the interpolated type of trope, the added musical phrases are often designed to echo or anticipate the phrases that precede or follow them. They must also make smooth transitions at their beginnings and endings. In Example 6-3, a troped Gloria (also in Mode 7), the interpolated text lines are printed in italics, the original lines in Roman type. The first added line (line 10, "Spiritus et alme orphanorum Paraclite") is given a phrase which is syllabic with a few neumes, like most of the original chant. Also like the original, it covers a wide range within a short space—the modal octave plus the note below the final. (Compare it with the music for line 7, "Gratias agimus tibi propter magnam gloriam tuam".) In order to make a seamless juncture with both the preceding and following phrases, it begins on D and ends on G, respectively the ending and beginning pitches of those two phrases.

The second added line (line 12) does not open on the previous pitch, but with one that is melodically consonant with it, the upper G of the modal octave. It also borrows music from the preceding phrase to make its close. (Compare *"virginis Matris"* with "Filius Patris.") The musical rhyme was here perhaps suggested by the verbal rhyme.

The remainder of the insertions follow similar principles, with the last three (lines 18, 20, and 22, which are textually parallel in structure) drawing progressively closer to the phrases they follow. The final one (line 22, *"Mariam coronans"*) uses, with one small adjustment for the number of syllables, exactly the same music as the phrase that precedes it.

Textually too, these tropes complement their surroundings, adding ornaments of praise to the list of Christ's attributes. They also expand the text to include mention of the Virgin Mary, who does not appear in the original Gloria chant. Five of the six added phrases include the name of Mary.

Sometimes a trope consists of music interpolated without any words. Such interpolations often occur in the responsories of the Office, where a melisma is inserted in the final appearance of the respond. This

EXAMPLE 6-3 Troped Gloria. Trope from Peter Wagner, *Einführung in die gregorianischen Melodien: Ein Handbuch der Choralwissenschaft,* vol. 3 (Leipzig: Breitkopf und Härtel, 1921).

1 Glo - ri - a in ex - cel - sis De - o.

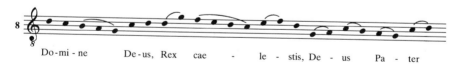

2 Et in ter - ra pax ho - mi - ni - bus bo -nae vo -lun -ta - tis.

3 Lau - da - mus te.

4 Be - ne - di - ci - mus te.

5 A - do - ra - mus te.

6 Glo - ri - fi - ca - mus te.

7 Gra -ti - as a - gi -mus ti - bi prop -ter ma -gnam glo - ri - am tu - am.

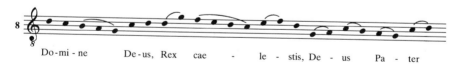

8 Do -mi - ne De -us, Rex cae - le - stis, De - us Pa - ter

om - ni - po - tens.

18 Ma - ri - am sanc - ti - fi - cans.

19 Tu so - lus Do - mi - nus,

20 Ma - ri - am gu - ber - nans.

21 Tu so - lus Al - tis - si - mus,

22 Ma - ri - am co - ro - nans,

23 Je - su Chri - ste.

24 Cum San - cto Spi - ri - tu, in glo - ri - a De - i Pa - - tris.

25 A - - - - - - - - - men.

1. Gloria in excelsis Deo.
2. Et in terra pax homnibus bonae voluntatis.
3. Laudamus te.
4. Benedicimus te.
5. Adoramus te.
6. Glorificamus te.
7. Gratias agimus tibi propter magnam gloriam tuam.

1. Glory to God in the highest.
2. And on earth peace to men of good will.
3. We praise you.
4. We bless you.
5. We adore you.
6. We glorify you.
7. We give thanks to you on account of your great glory.

8. Domine Deus, Rex caelestis, Deus Pater omnipotens.	8. O Lord God, heavenly King, God the omnipotent Father.
9. Domine Fili unigenite, Jesu Christe.	9. O Lord the Son, only-begotten Jesus Christ.
10. *Spiritus et alme orphanorum Paraclite.*	10. *Spirit and nurturing Protector of orphans.*
11. Domine Deus, Agnus Dei, Filius Patris,	11. O Lord God, Lamb of God, Son of the Father,
12. *Primogenitus Mariae, virginis Matris,*	12. *First-born son of Mary, the virgin Mother,*
13. Qui tollis peccata mundi, miserere nobis.	13. You who take away the sins of the world, have pity on us.
14. Qui tollis peccata mundi, suscipe deprecationem nostram,	14. You who take away the sins of the world, hear our plea,
15. *ad Mariae gloriam.*	15. *to the glory of Mary.*
16. Qui sedes ad dexteram Patris, miserere nobis.	16. You who sit at the right hand of the Father, have pity on us.
17. Quoniam tu solus sanctus,	17. Since you alone are holy,
18. *Mariam sanctificans.*	18. *sanctifying Mary.*
19. Tu solus Dominus,	19. You alone are the Lord,
20. *Mariam gubernans.*	20. *guiding Mary.*
21. Tu solus Altissimus,	21. You alone are the Most-High,
22. *Mariam coronans,*	22. *crowning Mary,*
23. Jesu Christe.	23. Jesus Christ.
24. Cum Sancto Spiritu, in gloria Dei Patris.	24. With the Holy Spirit, in the glory of God the Father.
25. Amen.	25. Amen.

practice had two interesting consequences. First, there appears to have grown up a whole repertory of melismas which could be added to responsories. These were grouped by mode so that the correct melisma could be used with the responsory of a given mode. This is an important phenomenon, because it suggests the beginning of a slightly more flexible attitude towards plainchant on the part of composers of the time: the melismas constituted a separate corpus of melodies, independently conceived and interchangeable among different pieces. Second, it seems as though the added melismas were not always newly composed but were sometimes taken from other chants. Again, a rather less restrictive view of the musical nature of chant appears, and a freer hand in the manipulation of musical materials may be seen at work.

A quite striking melisma is found in the second responsory of the second Nocturn of the Matins service for the feast of Corpus Christi (Ex. 6-4). Placed towards the end of the respond, on the word "corpus," the melisma stands out from the surrounding predominantly neumatic music.

Corpus Christi was one of the new feasts added to the liturgical calendar in the later Middle Ages, and the music for its services displays many of the characteristics typical of late-medieval chant. The responsory in Example 6-4, for example, has a slightly wider range than is common in most of the earlier repertory. It is also modally conceived in a self-conscious, almost "textbook" manner. Clearly, it was composed to fit an existing pattern (Mode 5, Lydian). It also has wider leaps and longer stepwise chains than is customary in chant from the earlier period. The melisma added to "corpus" covers the modal octave (plus a note above) twice in the course of its flow, and does so by large leaps upwards and a lengthy descending chain which touches upon every note in the entire range of the chant.

EXAMPLE 6-4   Responsory, *Coenantibus Illis,* with added melisma.

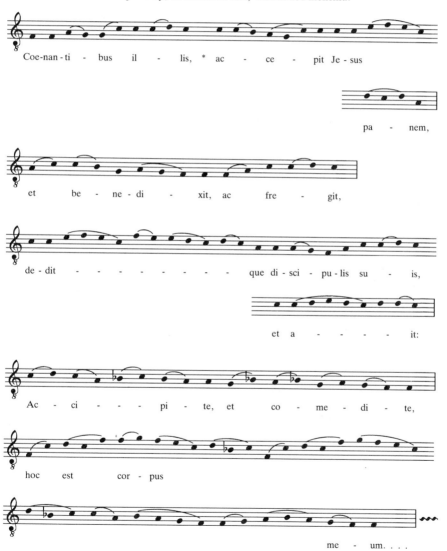

Coenantibus illis, accepit Jesus panem,

et benedixit, ac fregit,
deditque discipulis suis, et ait:
Accipite, et comedite,
hoc est corpus meum. . . .

And while they were dining, Jesus took
  the bread,
and blessed it, and broke it,
and give it to his disciples, and said:
Take this, and eat it,
this is my body. . . .

The arrangement of the chants for the new feast of Corpus Christi also reveals the late medieval preoccupation with modal assignment, for the nine responsories of Matins are arranged in numerical order. The first is in Mode 1, the second in Mode 2, and so on up to Mode 8. The ninth responsory uses Mode 1 again.[1]

PROSULAS

A different form of addition to plainchant was the adding of words to passages that were originally melismatic. This is a curious phenomenon, for it obviously changes quite drastically the balance between music and text. It may nevertheless be seen as another aspect of the desire for expansion and elaboration of the liturgy, as well as an opportunity for the creation of new liturgical texts.

The added text was known as a *prosula*. Prosulas were applied mostly to those items in both Mass and Office where the music was the most melismatic. In the Mass the best opportunities were provided by the Kyrie, Offertory verses, and the Alleluya. In the Office, in a typically medieval technique of elaborating upon elaboration, the new melismas added to responsories were themselves often given prosula texts.

The addition of words to pre-existing melismas usually results in a syllabic setting of the new text. With most prosulas all of the original words are retained; Kyrie prosulas, however, often omit the word "Kyrie" itself in the first and third phrase. Example 6-5 is a Kyrie with prosula. The original Kyrie chant is given as Example 4-2 on p. 92. The added text turns the originally neumatic and melismatic openings of the phrases into completely syllabic settings; the neumatic endings of the phrases on "eleison" remain. Textually, the simple addresses to "Lord" ("Kyrie") in the first and last sections, and to "Christ" ("Christe") in the middle section, have been re-

---

[1]The responsories for Trinity Sunday, another late feast, are also in modal order, with the ninth responsory being in Mode 4.

placed with elaborate descriptions and appeals. However, the distinction between the sections—between the Father in the outer sections and the Son in the middle section—is retained.

Prosula texts are often very carefully written so that the words reflect upon and illuminate the liturgical context into which they are placed. This is less true of prosulas for the Kyrie, which is part of the Ordinary of the Mass, than of prosulas for proper items.

EXAMPLE 6-5 Kyrie with prosula.

I. 1. *Cuncti-po-tens Ge-ni-tor, De-us, om-ni-um cre-a-tor, e - - - - - le - i - son.*
2. *Fons et o-ri-go bo-ni, pi-e lux-que pe-ren-nis, e - - - - - le - i - son.*
3. *Sal-vi-fi-cet pi-e-tas tu-a nos, bo-ne Rec-tor, e - - - - - le - i - son.*

II. 1. *Chri-ste, De-i for-ma, vir-tus Pa-tris-que so-phi-a, e - - - le - i - son.*
2. *Chri-ste, Pa-tris splen-dor, or-bis lap-si Re-pa-ra-tor, e - - - le - i - son.*
3. *Ne tu-a dam-ne-mur, Je-su, fac-tu-ra, be-ni-gne, e - - - le - i - son.*

III. 1. *Am-bo-rum sa-crum spi-ra-men, ne-xus a-mor-que, e - - - - le - i - son.*
2. *Pro-ce-dens fo-mes vi-tae, fons pu-ri-fi-cans nos, e - - - - le - i - son.*

3. *Pur-ga-tor cul-pae, ve-ni-ae lar-gi-tor op-ti-me, of-fen-sas de-le, sanc-to nos*

mu-ne-re re-ple, e - - - - - le - i - son.

I. 1. *Cunctipotens Genitor, Deus, omnium creator,* eleison.
   2. *Fons et origo boni, pie luxque perennis,* eleison.

   3. *Salvificet pietas tua nos, bone Rector,* eleison.

II. 1. *Christe, Dei forma, virtus Patrisque sophia,* eleison.

I. 1. *Omnipotent Father, God, creator of all,* have mercy.
   2. *Fountain and origin of all good, holy and eternal light,* have mercy.

   3. *May your holiness bring us salvation, O good Leader,* have mercy.

II. 1. *Christ, appearance of God, power and wisdom of the Father,* have mercy.

2. *Christe, Patris splendor, orbis
    lapsi Reparator*, eleison.

3. *Ne tua damnemur, Jesu, factura,
    benigne*, eleison.

III. 1. *Amborum sacrum spiramen,
        nexus amorque*, eleison.
     2. *Procedens fomes vitae, fons
        purificans nos*, eleison.
     3. *Purgator culpae, veniae largitor
        optime, offensas dele, sancto
        nos munere reple*, eleison.

2. *Christ, splendor of the Father,
    Savior of a fallen world*, have
    mercy.

3. *Let us not be condemned by your
    judgement, O benevolent Jesus,*
    have mercy.

III. 1. *Sacred breath of both, and com-
        bined love*, have mercy.
     2. *Active former of life, fountain
        purifying us*, have mercy.
     3. *Redeemer of sin, greatest
        dispenser of pardon, remove
        our misdeeds, fill us with holy
        reward*, have mercy.

Offertory prosulas are common in manuscripts from the tenth and eleventh centuries. It was mentioned before that the Offertory chant of the Mass used to be quite lengthy, with several interior verses, often in highly melismatic style. It was these verses that attracted prosulas, and they demonstrate well the careful and artistic way in which text was matched to melody. Example 6-6 shows a long melisma from an Offertory verse together with its prosula. The text begins with the same words as those to which the melisma is set ("Cor meum"), and the sense is continuous. Throughout the new setting, words are designed to coincide more or less with the neumes of the original melisma. The endings of many of the words match the sound of the syllable ("-e-") which they replace, and the last word of the prosula ("eternum") rhymes with the original word of the chant ("meum"), thus confirming the place of the prosula textually within the chant. Text phrases (separated by commas in the text) also take advantage of the parallelism of the music of the melisma. Most of the phrases that belong together end on E—the last note of the melisma and the final of the mode of the entire chant, Mode 3, Phrygian. Others are linked by ending on G, an important subsidiary note in the Phrygian mode.

EXAMPLE 6-6 Offertory prosula and original melisma. After Ruth Steiner, "Prosula," in *The New Grove Dictionary of Music and Musicians* (London: Macmillan, 1980).

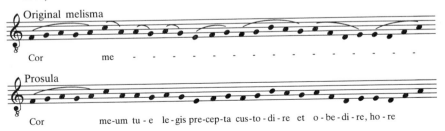

Original melisma

Cor   me -   -   -   -   -   -   -   -

Prosula

Cor   me-um tu - e le-gis pre-cep-ta cus-to-di-re et o-be-di-re, ho-re

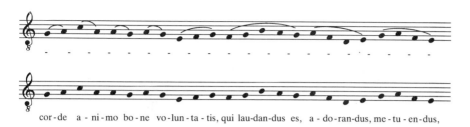

cor-de a-ni-mo bo-ne vo-lun-ta-tis, qui lau-dan-dus es, a-do-ran-dus, me-tu-en-dus,

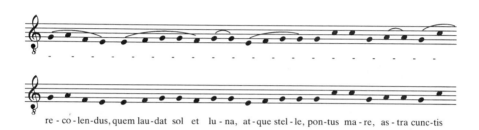

re-co-len-dus, quem lau-dat sol et lu-na, at-que stel-le, pon-tus ma-re, as-tra cunc-tis

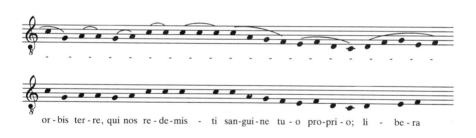

or-bis ter-re, qui nos re-de-mis - ti san-gui-ne tu-o pro-pri-o; li - be-ra

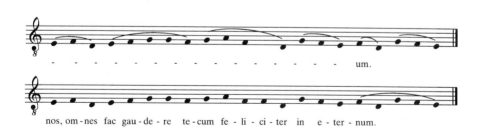

nos, om-nes fac gau-de-re te-cum fe-li-ci-ter in e-ter-num.

um.

Original: Cor meum.

Prosula: Cor meum tue legis precepta custodire et obedire, hore corde animo bone voluntatis, qui laudandus es, adorandus, metuendus, recolendus, quem laudat sol et luna, atque stelle, pontus mare, astra cunctis orbis terre, qui nos redemisti sanguine tuo proprio; libera nos, omnes fac gaudere tecum feliciter in eternum.

Original: My heart.

Prosula: My heart follows and obeys the precepts of your law, with a heart and soul of good will, for you are to be praised, adored, feared and worshipped, and the sun and moon praise you, and the stars, the sea, the stars of the whole world, for you redeemed us with your own blood; free us, make us all rejoice happily with you for ever.

The Alleluya, as one of the most melismatic chants of the Mass, also offered many opportunities for the insertion of prosulas. These could be written either for the jubilus, or for melismas in the florid solo verse section. Here too the prosula commented or expanded up on the original text of the chant, and transformed the wordless melisma into a syllabic setting.

SEQUENCES

As we have noted earlier (see pp. 107–8), the Alleluya of the Mass was the site of one of the most important additions to the liturgy in the later Middle Ages: the sequence. It is possible that the sequence began as a melismatic musical trope to the Alleluya, to which words were later added. However, it very soon took on independent life and became a unit separable from the Alleluya. For three hundred years it offered a major opportunity for both poetic and musical composition.

Many thousands of sequences were composed in the later part of the Middle Ages. The main development may be divided into two periods, the first from about 850 to the year 1000, the second from 1000 to about 1150. As with all historical groupings, these periods are approximate and artificial. Nonetheless, some important general distinctions may be made between the early and late phases of sequence composition. In the first phase, sequences appear sporadically in the manuscripts or gathered into small groups. They are mostly written in couplets, each line of which has an equal number of syllables, but without regular meter or rhyme. In the second phase, sequences are found increasingly in large collections and are written in systematic metrical and rhyme schemes.

The name most commonly associated with the early sequence is that of a Benedictine monk at the abbey of St. Gall. As mentioned earlier (p. 76), St. Gall was one of the most prominent and influential monasteries in Europe in the ninth and tenth centuries. Though the monastery was suppressed in 1805, the monastic church was revived as a cathedral in the mid-nineteenth century, and the rich holdings of the library, including some of the most important sources for the history of music, have been preserved.

Among the historians, poets, theologians and scholars who lent their brilliance to the cultural and intellectual life of St. Gall was the author, poet, and composer Notker Balbulus (c. 840–912). From his output have survived some accounts of the lives of saints (including that of St. Gall himself), an idealized history of Charlemagne (*The Deeds of Charles the Great*), poems, and letters. But from the musical point of view, Notker's most significant contribution was a book containing some thirty sequences. From this book, and from the other ninth- and tenth-century sources of the repertoire, a general picture may be drawn of the early sequence. The text is formed by pairs of lines, each line in the pair having the same syllable count. Usually the first and last lines are single. Although both lines in a couplet share the same number of syllables, the rhythm of the accented and unaccented syllables is irregular from one line to the next. Rhyme is not used, though a flexible assonance (matching of syllable sounds) appears in many of the texts.

Musically, each single line or couplet is set to a new melodic phrase, with the text distributed almost entirely syllabically throughout. Since the lines or couplets of text may differ considerably in length, the length of the musical phrases also is very variable. The melody is artfully constructed, with different profiles within a generally narrow range. Modal focus is sharp, and phrases usually end on the reciting tone or the final of the mode.

The careful construction and subtle matching of text to music in the early sequence may be demonstrated by Notker's sequence *Scalam Ad Caelos* (Ex. 6-7). There are eleven musical phrases, each setting a pair of text lines, except for the first line which is single. Most of the phrases are fairly short, with the exception of phrase 4, which is divided into two sections. The sequence is built in the Dorian mode, and D is the cadential note for most of the first part (phrases 2, 3, 4) and last part (phrases 8, 9, 10, 11) of the piece. The central part (phrases 5, 6, and 7) creates a sense of departure, with its cadences a fifth higher, on the reciting tone A. These phrases also reach higher in the modal range than the opening or closing phrases. A sense of unity is provided, however, by the opening pitch of the phrases throughout the piece, all of which (except 1 and 7) begin on A.

The sequence is in praise of women. It contains striking images, from a ladder reaching to heaven in its opening line (inspired by Jacob's dream in Genesis), to a dragon, an Ethiopian with drawn sword, and Eve and the serpent. The first main text division, at the period after "sumere," coincides with the end of the first part of the music (the end of phrase 4). There is also a sentence break between the second and third parts (at the end of phrase 7). This linking of text and music is made at the most detailed level, too, for throughout the composition accented syllables of the words are set to higher pitches in the music. The second line of each couplet is carefully designed to follow the accentuation pattern of the first. Each line contains a subtle use of assonance in the language: the sounds of the consonant "c" and the syllable "am" in the first line, for example, or the vowel "i" in couplet 7. From the rich and symbolic imagery of the text to the overall design of the music to the smallest details of construction, this early sequence shows evidence of great artistry and both musical and poetic accomplishment.

The most important change in the style of the sequence from the earlier repertory to the later was in the structure of the texts. This in turn influenced the musical settings. The irregular accent rhythms and flexible assonance of the early sequence gave way in the eleventh and twelfth centuries to more rigid schemes of recurring metrical patterns and strict rhymes in lines of equal length. The regularity of rhythm and rhyme in the later repertory made some of the eleventh- and twelfth-century sequences extremely popular. Perhaps the best known of all the late sequences, thanks to its many settings in the later history of music, is the Sequence from the Mass for the Dead, *Dies Irae,* whose first line is given here:

$$- \smile - \smile \quad - \smile - \smile \quad - \smile - \quad \smile - \smile - \smile \quad - \smile - \smile - \quad \smile - \smile$$

Dies irae, dies illa, / solvet saeclum in favilla, / teste David cum Sibylla.

The thoroughgoing application of the rhyme in this sequence (each segment of this first line ends with the "illa" sound) is less typical of the late

EXAMPLE 6-7 Notker Balbulus, sequence, *Scalam Ad Caelos*. From Richard L. Crocker, *The Early Medieval Sequence* (Berkeley: University of California Press, 1977).

1

Sca - lam ad cae - los sub - rec - tam tor - men - tis cin - ctam,

2

Cu - ius i - ma dra - co ser - va - re cau - tus in - vi - gi - lat iu - gi - ter,
Ne quis e - ius vel pri - mum gra - dum pos - sit in - sau - ci - us scan - de - re,

3

Cu - ius as - cen - sus ex - trac - to Ae - thi - ops gla - di - o ve - tat ex - i - ti - um mi - ni - tans,
Cu - ius su - pre - mis in - ni - xus iu - ve - nis splen - di - dus ra - mum au - re - o - lum re - ti - net:

4

Hanc er - go sca - lam i - ta Chri - sti a - mor fe - mi - nis fe - cit per - vi - am,
Per om - ne ge - nus tor - men - to - rum cae - li a - pi - cem que - ant ca - pe - re,

ut dra - co - ne con - cul - ca - to et Ae - thi - o - pis gla - di - o tran - si - to,
et de ma - nu con - for - tan - tis re - gis au - re - am lau - re - am su - me - re.

5

Quid ti - bi pro - fe - cit, pro - fa - ne ser - pens, quon - dam u - nam de - ce - pis - se mu - li - e - rem,
Cum vir - go pe - pe - re - rit in - car - na - tum De - i Pa - tris u - ni - cum do - mi - num Je - sum?

6

Qui prae - dam ti - bi tu - lit et ar - mil - la ma - xil - lam fo - rat,
Ut e - gres - sus E - vae na - tis fi - at, quos te - ne - re cu - pis.

7

Nunc er - go te - met vir - gi - nes vin - ce - re cer - nis, in - vi - de,
Et ma - ri - ta - tas pa - re - re fi - li - os de - o pla - ci - tos.

8

Et vi - du - a - rum ma - ri - tis fi - dem nunc in - ge - mis in - te - gram,
Qui cre - a - to - ri fi - dem ne - ga - re per - sua - se - ras vir - gi - ni.

9

Fe - mi - nas nunc vi - des in bel - lo con - tra te fac - to du - ces e - xi - ste - re,
Quae fi - li - os su - os in - sti - gant for - ti - ter tu - a tor - men - ta vin - ce - re.

10

Quin et tu - a va - sa me - re - tri - ces do - mi - nus e - mun - dat,
Et haec si - bi tem - plum di - gna - tur ef - fi - ce - re pur - ga - tum.

11

Pro his nunc be - ne - fi - ci - is in com - mu - ne Do - mi - num nos glo - ri - fi -
Qui et stan - tes cor - ro - bo - rat et pro - lap - sis dex - te - ram por - ri - git ut

ce - mus et pec - ca - to - res et iu - sti,
sal - tem post fa - ci - no - ra sur - ga - mus.

1. Scalam ad caelos subrectam tormentis cinctam,
2. Cuius ima draco servare cautus invigilat iugiter,
   Ne quis eius vel primum gradum possit insaucius scandere,
3. Cuius ascensus extracto Aethiops gladio vetat exitium minitans,

   Cuius supremis innixus iuvenis splendidus ramum aureolum retinet:
4. Hanc ergo scalam ita Christi amor feminis fecit perviam,
   ut dracone conculcato et Aethiopis gladio transito,
   Per omne genus tormentorum caeli apicem queant capere,
   et de manu confortantis regis auream lauream sumere.
5. Quid tibi profecit, profane serpens, quondam unam decepisse mulierem,
   Cum virgo pepererit incarnatum Dei Patris unicum dominum Jesum?

1. A ladder raised up to the heavens, surrounded by torments,
2. Whose base is carefully guarded by a vigilant dragon,
   So that no-one can approach even the first step unharmed,
3. And whose ascent is denied by an Ethiopian with drawn sword, threatening death,
   But at whose top a radiant youth offers a golden bough—
4. This ladder Christ's love makes accessible to women,
   so they can trample the dragon and pass by the Ethiopian,
   Ignore all the torments and reach the peak of heaven,
   and receive the golden laurel from the hand of the comforting king.
5. What use was it, unholy serpent, to have once deceived one woman,

   When a virgin can bear the only lord Jesus, incarnate of God the Father?

6. Qui praedam tibi tulit et armilla maxillam forat,

Ut egressus Evae natis fiat, quos tenere cupis.

7. Nunc ergo temet virgines vincere cernis, invide,
Et maritatas parere filios deo placitos.

8. Et viduarum maritis fidem nunc ingemis integram,

Qui creatori fidem negare persuaseras virgini.

9. Feminas nunc vides in bello contra te facto duces existere,
Quae filios suos instigant fortiter tua tormenta vincere.

10. Quin et tua vasa meretrices dominus emundat,
Et haec sibi templum dignatur efficere purgatum.

11. Pro his nunc beneficiis in commune Dominum nos glorificemus et peccatores et iusti,
Qui et stantes corroborat et prolapsis dexteram porrigit ut saltem post facinora surgamus.

6. He who has taken away your prize and pierced your jaw with his spear,
So that there may be salvation for the sons of Eve, whom you tried to hold captive.

7. But now you know that virgins have overcome you, jealous one,
And that wives bring forth sons pleasing to God.

8. Now you lament the unbending loyalty of widows to their husbands,
You who persuaded a virgin to deny her faith to her creator.

9. Now you see women outstanding in the battle waged against you,
Women who bravely urge their sons to vanquish your torments.

10. The Lord even purifies your vessels, the whores,
And makes them worthy to be a perfect temple for Himself.

11. Let us now, both righteous and sinners alike, praise the Lord for his bounties,
Who strengthens the upright and stretches out his hand to the fallen, so that afterwards we may all rise again.

sequence than the change of rhyme in the similarly popular *Veni Sancte Spiritus*:

    ‾ ͜ ‾   ͜   ‾ ͜ ‾   ͜ ͜ ‾ ͜ ‾ ͜ ‾   ‾ ͜ ‾ ‾ ‾ ͜ ‾
Veni sancte spiritus, / et emitte caelitus / lucis tuae radium.

Here the change of rhyme (from "-itus" in the first two segments to "-ium" in the third) is more representative of the style as a whole. There is also a shift of accent in the second segment, which does not occur in the very regularly patterned *Dies Irae*. These later sequences usually have lines with alternating stressed and unstressed syllables. Each line is divided into segments of seven or eight syllables, the first two of which are linked by end-rhyme. The third segment has a new ending which rhymes with the ending of the next complete line. Thus each individual line is unified by internal rhyme (a-a-b), while also being linked to the next line of the couplet (c-c-b).

We find the same concern with careful melodic outline, modal propriety, and overall shape in the later sequence as in the earlier. The musical phrases, however, are more regular in length, matching the regularity of the verse, and there is an increasing use of repetition of small melodic motifs to unify the composition on a large scale. Short neumes appear more frequently.

The matching of musical form to that of the text remains the same. Both lines of a couplet receive the same music, and the melody begins afresh for each couplet; but opening and closing lines in a sequence usually stand alone.

The most famous composer of late sequences was the poet known as Adam of St. Victor (c. 1080–1150). Adam was an official of the cathedral at Paris and lived the last part of his life at the Abbey of St. Victor, an establishment of canons regular of the Augustinian order, which was founded in the eleventh century. (Canons regular lived in a community under a rule—hence "regular"—but were not cloistered like monks.) Adam was a distinguished figure in Parisian religious and intellectual circles, and was a skilled musician as well as a learned and powerful poet. He was probably the composer of *Laudes Crucis Attollamus* (Ex. 6-8), a well-known sequence that was already famous in its own day; its melody was used as the basis for many other twelfth-century sequences.

As a whole, the melody of this sequence ranges widely, but each phrase has its own character, shape, and affect, with pitch accent both coinciding with and presenting a counterpoint to the accentuation of the text. A great diversity of musical construction is in evidence in this piece, as can be gauged simply by comparing the opening gestures of each of the phrases. Certain motifs recur, such as the cadential motifs for phrases 1, 2, and 4; the same motif occurs as a cadential figure in the middle of phrase 3 ("vite dari munera" / "rubens agni sanguine"). The descending thirds in phrase 8 are balanced by ascending thirds in phrases 10, 11, and 12. The text employs many varied poetic devices within the overall sequence structure: double verse lines appear in phrase 3; for phrase 9, the opening segments of both lines contain internal rhyme ("scripturis/figuris," "latent/patent," "credunt/cedunt," "cruce/duce"); and the number of segments in each line expands in phrases 10 and 11 from three to four, and finally, in phrase 12, to five. In this poem of praise to the Cross, the word for "cross" appears no fewer than fifteen times (apart from all the metaphorical references to trees, wood, branches, ships, and ladders). Throughout the sequence, unity and variety are in perfect balance, and the rich poetry of the text, with its regular but changing rhythms, finds both confirmation and intensification through the carefully constructed melodic architecture.

EXAMPLE 6-8 Adam of St. Victor, sequence, *Laudes Crucis Attollamus*. After E. Misset and Pierre Aubry, *Les Proses d'Adam de Saint Victor: Texte et musique* (Paris: H. Welter, 1900).

1. Lau-des cru-cis at-tol-la-mus, nos qui cru-cis e-xul-ta - mus spe-ci-a-li glo-ri-a.
   Nam in cru-ce tri-um-pha-mus, hos-tem fe-rum su-pe-ra - mus vi-ta-li vic-to-ri-a.

2. Dul-ce me-los tan-gat ce - los, dul-ce li-gnum dul-ci di-gnum cre-di-mus me-lo-di-a;
   Vo-ce vi-ta non dis-cor - det cum vox vi-tam non re-mor-det, dul-cis est sim-pho-ni-a.

3. Ser-vi cru-cis cru-cem lau-dent, qui per cru-cem si-bi gau-dent vi-te da-ri mu-ne-ra
   O quam fe-lix, quam pre - cla - ra hec sa-lu-tis fu-it a-ra, ru-bens a-gni san-gui-ne,

Di-cant om - nes et di-cant sin-gu-li A - ve, sa - lus to-ti-us se-cu-li,
A-gni si - ne ma - cu-la, qui mun-da - vit se - cu-la

ar-bor sa-lu-ti-fe-ra.
ab an-ti-quo cri-mi-na!

4. Hec est sca-la pec-ca-to - rum per quam Chris-tus rex ce-lo-rum ad se tra-xit om-ni-a;
   For-ma cu-ius hoc o-sten-dit que ter-ra-rum com-pre-hen-dit qua-tu-or con-fi-ni-a.

5. Non sunt no-va sa-cra-men-ta, nec re-cen-ter est in-ven-ta cru-cis hec re - li-gi-o:
   Is-ta dul-ces a-quas fe-cit, per hanc si-lex a-quas ie-cit Mo-y-sis of - fi-ci-o.

6. Nul-la sa - lus est in do-mo ni-si cru-ce mu-nit ho - mo su-per-li-mi-na-ri-a;
   Ne-que sen - sit gla-di - um, nec a-mi-sit fi-li-um quis-quis e-git ta - li-a.

7

Li - gna   le-gens in Sa - rep - ta   spem sa - lu - tis est a-dep-ta   pau-per mu-li - - er-cu-la;
Si - ne   li-gnis fi - de - - i   nec le-chy-tus o - le - i   va - let, nec fa - ri-nu-la.

8

Ro - ma   na-ves u-ni-ver-sas   in pro-fun - dum vi - dit mer-sas   u - na cum Ma-xen-ti-o;
Fu - si   Tra-ces, ce-si Per-se,   sed et par - tis   dux ad-ver - se   vic-tus ab E - ra-cli-o.

9

In scrip-tu - ris sub fi - gu - - ris   is-ta la-tent, sed iam pa-tent   cru-cis be-ne-fi - ci - a;
Re-ges cre-dunt, hos-tes ce - - dunt,   so-la cru-ce, Chri-sto du - ce,   ho-stis fu-gat mi-li - a.

10

Is - ta su - os for-ti - o - res   sem-per fa - cit et vic-to-res,   mor-bos sa-nat et lan-guo-res,
Dat cap-ti - vis li-ber-ta-tem,   vi - te con-fert no-vi-ta-tem,   ad an-ti-quam di-gni-ta-tem

re - pri-mit de - mo-ni - a;
crux re-du - xit om-ni - a.

11

O crux, li-gnum tri-um-pha-le,   mun-di ve-ra sa-lus, va-le,   in - ter li-gna nul-lum ta-le,
Me-di - ci-na chri-sti - a-na,   sal-va sa-nas, e-gros sa-na,   quod non va-let vis hu-ma-na

fron-de, flo - re,   ger-mi-ne;
fit in tu - o   no-mi-ne.

12

Ad - si - sten - tes cru - cis lau - di, Con - se - cra - tor cru - cis, au - di, at - que ser - vos tu - e cru - cis
Quos tor - men - to vis ser - vi - re, fac tor - men - ta non sen - ti - re, sed cum di - es e - rit i - re,

post hanc vi - tam ve - re lu - cis trans - fer ad pa - la - ti - a;
no - bis con - fer et lar - gi - re sem - pi - ter - na gau - di - a.

1. Laudes crucis attollamus, / nos qui crucis exultamus / speciali gloria.

   Nam in cruce triumphamus, / hostem ferum superamus / vitali victoria.

2. Dulce melos tangat celos, / dulce lignum dulci dignum / credimus melodia;
   Voce vita non discordet / cum vox vitam non remordet, / dulcis est simphonia.

3. Servi crucis crucem laudent, / qui per crucem sibi gaudent / vite dari munera. Dicant omnes et dicant singuli / Ave, salus totius seculi, / arbor salutifera.

   O quam felix, quam preclara / hec salutis fuit ara, / rubens agni sanguine, Agni sine macula, / qui mundavit secula / ab antiquo crimina!

4. Hec est scala peccatorum / per quam Christus rex celorum / ad se traxit omnia;

   Forma cuius hoc ostendit / que terrarum comprehendit / quatuor confinia.

1. Let us raise up praises to the cross, we who exult in the special glory of the cross, for we triumph in the cross, and conquer the fierce enemy with living victory.

2. Let sweet music touch the heavens, for we believe that the sweet wood is worthy of sweet melody; and let our lives not be discordant with our voices, since when voices mirror lives, the harmony is sweet.

3. Let the servants of the cross praise the cross, who by means of the cross rejoice in the gifts of life. Let them all say one and all: Hail, salvation of the world, tree that brings salvation.

   O how happy, how splendid was the altar of salvation, red with the blood of the lamb, A lamb without stain, who purified the world from its ancient sin.

4. This is the ladder of sinners, by means of which Christ, king of heaven, brought all things to himself; the form of which includes and displays the four corners of the earth.

5. Non sunt nova sacramenta, / nec recenter est inventa / crucis hec religio:

    Ista dulces aquas fecit, / per hanc silex aquas iecit / Moysis officio.

6. Nulla salus est in domo / nisi cruce munit homo / superliminaria;

    Neque sensit gladium, / nec amisit filium / quisquis egit talia.

7. Ligna legens in Sarepta / spem salutis est adepta / pauper muliercula; Sine lignis fidei / nec lechytus olei / valet, nec farinula.

8. Roma naves universas / in profundum vidit mersas / una cum Maxentio;

    Fusi Traces, cesi Perse, / sed et partis dux adverse / victus ab Eraclio.

9. In scripturis sub figuris / ista latent, sed iam patent / crucis beneficia;

    Reges credunt, hostes cedunt, / sola cruce, Christo duce, / hostis fugat milia.

10. Ista suos fortiores / semper facit et victores, / morbos sanat et languores, / reprimit demonia;

    Dat captivis libertatem, / vite confert novitatem, / ad antiquam dignitatem / crux reduxit omnia.

11. O crux, lignum triumphale, / mundi vera salus, vale, / inter ligna nullum tale, / fronde, flore, germine;

    Medicina christiana, / salva sanos, egros sana, / quod non valet vis humana / fit in tuo nomine.

12. Adsistentes crucis laudi, / Consecrator crucis, audi, / atque servos tue crucis / post hanc vitam vere lucis / transfer ad palatia;

---

5. These are not new sacraments, nor is this worship of the cross newly invented:

    it made the waters sweet, and drew water from the rock, through Moses' action.

6. There is no safety in a house unless a man protects his household with a cross;

    no one felt the sword, nor lost a son, who did so.

7. Gathering sticks in Sarepta the poor woman gained hope of salvation; without the wood of faith, neither the jar of oil nor the small amount of grain has any power.

8. Rome saw all her ships sunk in the sea together with Maxentius;

    the Thracians fled, the Persians yielded, and the leader of the enemy force was conquered by Heraclius.

9. In the scriptures these benefits of the cross lie hidden under metaphors, but now they are revealed; kings believe, enemies yield, and by the force of the cross alone, with Christ as leader, a host of the enemy retreats.

10. The cross makes its adherents stronger and always victorious, cures the sick and feeble, repels the devil;

    frees captives, bestows new life, restores everything to its former greatness.

11. O cross, victorious wood, true salvation of the world, farewell; among woods, none with leaf or flower or seed is like you; Christian medicine, save the healthy, cure the sick; what human power cannot do can happen in your name.

12. O Consecrator of the cross, hear those standing by the cross in praise, and after this short life take the servants of your cross to the palaces of the true light;

Beginning of the sequence *Laudes Crucis Attollamus* in a twelfth-century manuscript (see Example 6-8), British Library, London.

Quos tormento vis servire, / fac tormenta non sentire, / sed cum dies erit ire, / nobis confer et largire / sempiterna gaudia.

Make those whom you wish to condemn to torment unable to feel its pain, but when the day of wrath is here, grant us and bestow on us eternal joys.

LATIN SONGS

Other forms of new Latin poetry also were set to music in the tenth, eleventh, and twelfth centuries. These were mostly known by the names *versus* and *conductus*, names that cover a very wide range of format and content. From the palace of Charlemagne to the Frankish monasteries, learning and culture were now beginning to spread to the newly settled towns and cities, to be disseminated gradually from the cathedral schools in these centers. Latin poetry had made an important transition from the Classical meters of antiquity to the newly fashionable regularity of rhyme and accented rhythm (as we have seen in the late sequence). Other sacred poetry took the form of verses to elaborate the last item of Matins—the Benedicamus Domino—or as informal additions to the liturgy on feast days.

A great deal of secular poetry of various sorts also was written in rhythmical, rhyming Latin: satires, epics, moralizing poems, and especially lyrics. The lyrical poems themselves cover a wide range of subjects, from love to nature, from drink to dawn, and these topics found expression in the local languages (as we shall see in Chapter Seven), as well as in Latin.

The words *versus* and *conductus* were originally confined to serious poetry, mostly of a sacred nature. *Versus* is a general term for most of this repertoire, whereas *conductus* designated a song to accompany a procession, of which there were many in the Middle Ages of a para-liturgical nature: processions from one church to another, processions from the main altar to a side chapel, processions around the town on feast days. The music for all of these new poems is primarily syllabic, with musical phrases matching the lines of verse and reflecting the structure of the poetry.

The strophic versus *Gaudeamus* (Ex. 6-9), a celebration of the Christmas season, begins with a refrain which is repeated between each of the stanzas of the poem. Each stanza has its own rhyme and is made up of three pairs of lines of different length, the first pair with lines of eight syllables, the second with lines of eleven syllables, and the last pair with lines of seven syllables. Within each stanza, the paired lines are each set to the same music, except for the last pair, which are independently set. The descending fifth of the refrain is balanced by the music of the stanzas, the first three phrases of which project a simple arch on D. The climax of the melody is reached at the beginning of the last phrase, with the highest pitch, B, and a descending melisma. All of the phrases, with their rhyming text words, display varied ways of approaching the same final.

The Latin poem set to music without direct connection with the official liturgy represented an important opportunity for composers. This genre opened the way for many types of poetry and music, starting with para-liturgical texts in Latin and then spreading to both sacred and secular texts in Latin and in the local languages. A distinction needs to be made here between the designations liturgical and sacred. A liturgical piece is one that takes its place within the official liturgy of the Church. A sequence, for example, though newly composed, has its proper position within the celebration of Mass. But a piece may be sacred—may deal with a sacred subject—and not be actually liturgical. This distinction first began to appear in the versus and conductus. And soon Latin poems were being written with texts of a decidedly secular nature.

EXAMPLE 6-9 Versus, *Gaudeamus*, Paris, Bibliothèque Nationale, latin 1139.

Gau - de - a - mus no - va cum le - ti - ci - - a!

Ful - get di - es ho - di - er - na
Na - ta lu - ce sem - pi - ter - na.

No - va di - es, no - va na - ta - li - ci - a,
No - vus an - nus, no - va hec sol - lem - ni - a:

No - va de - cent gau - di - a,

No - ve lau - dis can - ti - ca.

Gaudeamus nova cum leticia!

I. Fulget dies hodierna
   Nata luce sempiterna.
   Nova dies, nova natalicia,
   Novus annus, nova hec sollemnia:
   Nova decent gaudia,
   Nove laudis cantica.

   Gaudeamus nova cum leticia!

II. Speciali gaude coro,
    Maritali iuncta toro,
    Suo Deus sempiterno filio
    Ecclesiam copulat conubio:
    Viduata, Domino
    Anne gaude gaudio.

    Gaudeamus nova cum leticia!

Let us rejoice with new joy!

I. This day shines
   With a new-born everlasting light.
   New day, new birth,
   New year, new festivities:
   These things deserve new joys,
   New songs of praise.

   Let us rejoice with new joy!

II. Rejoice with a special dance,
    On this wedding day,
    For God has joined his eternal
    Son in marriage to the church:
    Let all rejoice with the Lord
    With seasonal joy.

    Let us rejoice with new joy!

III. Prius gaude naturali,
    Senex etas ac senili
    Da se visum Simeoni veteri,
    Mittunt aquas sub enyte pueri:
    Novitas miraculi,
    Quo mittuntur iaculi.

Gaudeamus nova cum leticia!

IV. Omnis etas ergo gaude,
    Sed tu, Virgo, prius plaude,
    Virgo parit filium prudentie.
    Novum genus mirum hoc potentie:
    Partum esse femine
    Sine viri semine.

III. Rejoice first with natural joy,
    For the old year has gone
    And Simeon recognized the sight
    When he saw the infant:
    A new miracle,
    For which banners must be raised.

Let us rejoice with new joy!

IV. Let every age rejoice,
    And the Virgin first of all,
    For she it was who bore the son.
    A new and wondrous power:
    To give birth
    Without the seed of a man.

Musically, the distinction between song and chant was not clear cut. The music of the new poetry is written in a similar style to that of hymns or sequences. The melodies are modally cast, with a conscious use of half and full closes, and display an artistic structural approach to motivic cross-reference and the overall shape of each composition. Quite often melodies are actually shared between liturgical chant and lyric poem.

Many collections of such poems survive, although they are often preserved without their music. Some ninth- and tenth-century songs with music show simple, syllabic melodies with occasional small neumatic groups. They include laments (known as *planctus* in Latin), songs of praise for rulers, and celebrations for coronations. They are usually set strophically, and some have recurring refrains. In the eleventh and twelfth centuries the number of collections increased. Some of the later songs are anonymous, but others have been safely attributed to some of the most important figures of the period. There is a mingling of sacred and secular elements both in the texts and in the music. Some of the songs use chant melodies; others show a tendency to move away from simple strophic settings to elaborate and continuous through-composition.

One collection of Latin songs is contained in an eleventh-century manuscript now in the University Library at Cambridge. Many of these so-called "Cambridge Songs," which deal with topics of love, imperial flattery, the glory of God, and comic insult, are written in the form of the sequence. Other English and continental manuscripts transmit songs that mix strophic and sequence forms.

Perhaps the most famous collection is that known as *Carmina Burana,* which means "Songs of Benediktbeuern" after the monastery in southern Germany where the manuscript was found. The collection is large, and contains songs from a wide geographical area composed over a period of some two hundred years. There are serious moralistic poems, drinking songs, and love lyrics. All display a freshness, a frankness, and an immediacy that have made the collection both famous and notorious. These stanzas from two different poems suggest the flavor of the originals:

> Let's forget studying,
> It's more fun to fool around.
> Let's enjoy the sweet things
> That come with youth;
> Serious concerns are for
> Old folks.
> (Refrain:) *Studies are a waste of time,*
> *Much more fun are women and wine.*

> The golden god of love
> Has power over all.
> I put out my hands:
> What shall I get? . . .
> He gave me a girl.
> I'll give *her* something
> She'll never forget.

Love was not the only subject. There are also songs to Christ, elegies to the seasons, and virulent satirical attacks on decadent and unprincipled clerics. Many of the songs must have been written by the so-called Goliards, those scholars, poets, and students who were not attached to a particular court or institution but wandered in groups from place to place. Their existence is a manifestation of the reaction against the settled system of monasteries and courts in favor of the less orderly and more disparate life of the towns.

In the twelfth century the composition of Latin songs attracted several of the most famous personalities of the period. They included Peter Abelard, Hildegard of Bingen, and Walter of Châtillon.

Peter Abelard (c. 1080–1142) was a philosopher, theologian, and teacher who studied and taught in Paris. When he was about forty years old he fell in love with one of his students, a young woman of twenty named Heloise, who was the niece of an official at the cathedral. Their affair resulted in the birth of a son, and they were secretly married. The uncle of Heloise was outraged and hired two thugs to break into Abelard's room one night and castrate him. The pair was separated, and Abelard joined a monastery, while Heloise became a nun at a nearby convent. Abelard continued his philosophical writings and became renowned as a philosopher and theologian. Later he founded a new convent, for sixty nuns, where Heloise served as abbess and which Abelard visited from time to time as a teacher. He was buried there, and Heloise, his "former wife, now sister in Christ," was later buried beside him.

Abelard was one of the most influential writers of the twelfth century. His commentaries and treatises were widely read, and his teaching drew students from all over Europe. An autobiography survives, as well as a vivid series of letters between him and Heloise, through which the strength of their love still shines.

We know that Abelard was also a composer. Heloise describes a considerable number of lovesongs, which were "charming and sweet in both language and music, with soft melodies"; he also wrote hymns and planctus. Unfortunately much of his music has been lost, but the texts and melodies for a hymn and six planctus on Old Testament themes have survived.

One of Abelard's planctus is the lament of King David over the death of Saul, the warrior, and Jonathan, David's closest friend ("more than a brother, and sharing one soul"), who was also killed in battle. Abelard takes the story from the Books of Samuel, Chronicles, and Kings, and the poem moves from political to personal misfortune with exquisite strength and timing. The form of the text is reminiscent of that of the late sequence, with a similar metrical and rhyming scheme and matched pairs of lines. The music is mostly in Mode 7, Mixolydian, but it opens and closes in the plagal, Hypomixolydian, and thus covers a wide range of an octave and a half. Unusually wide range is a characteristic of planctus melodies. The style of the lament establishes a highly expressive contrast between syllabic and melismatic styles.[2]

Another famous twelfth-century abbess who was herself a writer and composer was Hildegard of Bingen (1098–1179). She founded a convent in Germany, near Bingen in the valley of the Rhine, and became famous as a prophet and mystic. She was the author of treatises on science and medicine, accounts of the lives of saints, and visionary revelations. As a composer she is represented by a large number of lyric poems with music in the form of antiphons, hymns, sequences, and responsories for feasts of the Virgin Mary and other saints, especially women. Hildegard also wrote the earliest surviving morality play with music. Known as the *Ordo Virtutum* ("Play of the Virtues"), it may have been written for the founding of her convent in 1152 and depicts the struggle between the Devil and the sixteen Virtues (Humility, Charity, Fear of God, Obedience, etc.) for possession of a (female) soul. The play is rich in imagery and drama, and contains an elaborate and symbolic use of both text and music.

---

[2]A transcription and analysis of the *Planctus David* may be found in Lorenz Weinrich, "Peter Abaelard as Musician—II," *The Musical Quarterly* LV (1969): 464–486. For recordings, see the Discography at the end of this chapter.

Beginning of Walter of Châtillon's song *Sol Sub Nube Latuit* in thirteenth-century measured notation (see Example 6-10), Herzog-August-Bibliothek, Wolfenbüttel.

Walter of Châtillon was a French poet and intellectual who served in the English royal court and is known to have been active in Italy as well. He was born in 1135 and died (possibly of leprosy) in 1190. The author of a historical epic in ten books on the life of Alexander the Great, he also wrote a considerable number of Latin lyric songs, some of which are monophonic, while others survive in later collections with polyphonic settings. Representative of his style is the song *Sol Sub Nube Latuit* (Ex. 6-10), which is in six stanzas, the last of which is a repetition of the third. It is set for two voices and survives in one of the earliest manuscripts with measured notation. The text is an allegorical discussion of the Father, the Sun, and the Son, with shifting rhyme scheme and complex word play.

Of all the types of Latin song, perhaps the most striking is the planctus. This was a widespread genre throughout this period and beyond into the later Middle Ages, although the extant examples are more remarkable for their style than they are numerous. These laments take as their theme the death of a contemporary personage, or the death of a historical or biblical figure. The music is highly expressive, often with a wide range, and is written in deliberate contrast to the prevailing style of plainchant with its subtlety and restraint.

The earliest planctus that survives was written on the death of Charlemagne. Later subjects included Rachel's lament over her children, and Mary's lament for her Son. Abelard's six planctus on Old Testament stories are the best known of the twelfth-century examples.

EXAMPLE 6-10 Walter of Châtillon, *Sol Sub Nube Latuit*. From Janet Knapp, *Thirty-five Conductus for Two and Three Voices*, Collegium Musicum, no. 6 ([New Haven]: Yale University Department of Music, 1965).

Quod a car - ne   De - i - tas   Non fu - it   cor - rup - - - - - -

i - - - - - - - - - - - - - - - ta.

I.   Sol sub nube latuit,
     Sed eclypsis nescius,
     Cum se carni miscuit
     Summi Patris filius.

II. Maritari noluit
     Verbum Patris altius;
     Nubere non potuit
     Caro gloriosius.

III. *Gaude, nova nupta!*
     Fides est et veritas,
     Quod a carne Deitas
     Non fuit corrupta.

IV. Qui solus eternus est
     Et qui regit omnia,
     Quod non erat factus est,
     Nec tamen res alia.

V.   Illum, qui solutus est,
     Stricta ligat fascia,

     Iacet, qui immensus est,
     Inter animalia.

VI. *Gaude, nova nupta!*
     Fides est et veritas
     Quod a carne deitas
     Non fuit corrupta.

I.   The sun hid under a cloud,
     But was not eclipsed,
     When the Son of the greatest Father
     Became flesh.

II. The word of the Father on high
     Did not want to be coupled;
     The glorious flesh
     Could not marry.

III. *Rejoice, new bride!*
     It is the true faith,
     For the Godhead was not
     Corrupted by becoming flesh.

IV. He who alone is eternal
     And governs everything
     Has become what He was not
     And yet is unchanged.

V.   He who was free
     Is now bound by the chains of
          humanity,
     And He who was boundless
     Now walks among mortals.

VI. *Rejoice, new bride!*
     It is the true faith,
     For the Godhead was not
     Corrupted by becoming flesh.

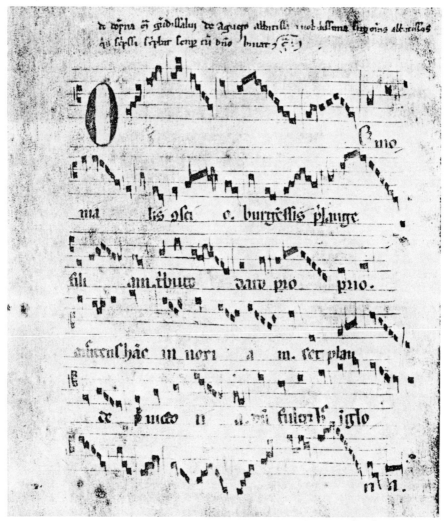

Original notation of the planctus *O Monialis Concio* showing its striking opening and closing melismas (see Example 6-11), Monasterio de las Huelgas, Burgos.

The vitality of the genre is indicated by the existence of several monophonic planctus in a thirteenth-century manuscript (containing mostly polyphonic music), that comes from the Las Huelgas convent near Burgos in the Iberian peninsula. Its planctus mourn the death of King Alfonso VII, who died in 1157, and other members of the royal family. One, *O Monialis Concio,* given as Example 6-11, was written as a lament on the death of the abbess of the convent, Maria Gonzalez de Aguero. The music is through-composed, with a pitch center on G, though standard modal

EXAMPLE 6-11 Planctus, *O Monialis Concio,* Burgos, Monasterio de las Huelgas.

O monialis concio	O convent dwellers
Burgensis, plange filiam,	Of Burgos, weep for this daughter,
Tributo dato proprio,	You have paid a heavy price
Amittens hanc innoxiam.	And lost a true innocent.
Set plaude pro victoria	Yet celebrate your victory,
Dum fulget haec in gloria.	For she shines in true glory.

construction is not in evidence. The cascades of descending melismas contrast vividly with the syllabic setting of other parts of the text and are particularly remarkable in the original notation (see illustration). The lament is framed by the wide-ranging and expressive melismas on "o" in the first and last words of the poem. Indeed, the range of the piece, an octave and a fifth from D to A, is quite unusual even for planctus. The poem is written in six eight-syllable lines, each of which ends with a cadence on G, reinforcing the form of the text, with the exception of the third line ("Amittens hanc innoxiam"), which lies in a higher range than the other lines and cadences on E.

THE RHYMED OFFICE

The popularity of rhymed and rhythmical verse strongly influenced liturgical texts even apart from the sequence in the tenth to the twelfth centuries. The technique infiltrated the liturgy wherever new texts were needed, primarily the Office services created for newly designated saints. The antiphons for the psalms and the responsories could all receive tropes to make them proper, as we have noted above, but increasingly they were newly written in the new poetic style. These rhymed Office services have not yet been adequately studied, partly because scholars for a long time regarded later chant and the new services as debased forms of the liturgy, partly because the sheer quantity and the scattered nature of the sources make research difficult. Rhymed Office texts and music continued to be composed into the fifteenth century, and the increasingly localized nature of saints' worship meant that many texts and chants were used in one place only.

What is notable about these services is the use of the written histories of saints' lives as material for the liturgical texts. These accounts, or *vitae,* as they were known, became extremely popular in the Middle Ages, as indeed the lives of the holy men and women themselves widely affected those among whom they lived. Disciples flocked to them; crowds lined the routes they travelled. Large numbers of people from all social classes attended their funerals, and sometimes churches squabbled over their relics or remains. The possession of the relics of an important saint could make a church lastingly famous: Santiago de Compostela in the Iberian peninsula grew into a city of splendor and influence because of its shrine, later a cathedral, built on a site designated as the tomb of the apostle St. James. Ultimately Santiago became one of the most famous centers and sought-after places of pilgrimage in the entire Middle Ages.

LATIN DRAMA

The lives of saints also affected another form of medieval culture in which music played an important role: the drama. Medieval drama developed in three directions from the eleventh century to the beginning of the Renaissance. One of these took its impetus from the current fascination with the lives of the saints and led to the type of drama known as the miracle play, from the collections of miracles associated with each saint. (At the end of a saint's *vita* is usually appended a list of miracles wrought by the saint during life or by calling upon the saint's name after death.) The two other types of drama are the mystery play, based upon scriptural episodes such as the Resurrection, the Creation, or the Day of Judgment; and the morality play, which usually had a moral or allegorical tale as its basis. An early example of the morality play is the *Ordo Virtutum* of Hildegard of Bingen (see p. 236), although the morality play as a genre did not become popular until later in the Middle Ages.

In medieval drama, even more than with most other medieval musical forms, the surviving manuscripts can give us no more than the barest idea of the richness of the original presentation. Details about costumes and stage settings, stage directions, and even much of the music are missing from many of the dramas that have come down to us. From the evidence of other sources, historical and literary, however, we gather that they could be highly elaborate productions, full of visual spectacle and musical allusion.

The origins of medieval drama were probably far less pretentious. A lively tradition of theater had lasted into the early Middle Ages from Antiquity, but it had disappeared from the written sources by the sixth century. For the next five hundred years the evidence is circumstantial, but it points to a wide variety of dramatic activity in court and countryside, involving music and acting, sometimes also dance, often on standard topics already known to the audience (knight encounters shepherdess, clown mocks king) and performed by professional travelling troupes of minstrels.

To this tradition must be added another important strand of drama in the Middle Ages—the drama surrounding the liturgy. With processions in and around churches, representations of the Nativity and the Resurrection, and enactments of scenes from the life of Mary, the liturgy presented a wealth of material for dramatic representation. In a time when most people could not read, a play could tell a story far more effectively than a book.

These two elements, the minstrel plays and scenes from the liturgy, form the principal background for medieval drama as it has survived in written form. Again, what has survived is partly a matter of chance, but it gives us a glimpse of what must have been the state of affairs from the tenth to the end of the twelfth centuries. As in our discussion of songs of the period, the division of the subject into Latin and vernacular traditions is somewhat artificial. There are Latin plays on subjects clearly in the vernacular tradition (*Interludium de Clerico et Puella*—"The Play about the Cleric and the Girl"), and many of the plays in local languages include plainchant. One aspect that does seem to distinguish the Latin dramas of this period is the fact that they are sung throughout, whereas the vernacular plays often include spoken passages.

Latin drama had one favorite topic, which was known as the *Visitatio Sepulchri* ("The Visit to the Tomb"). In its earliest versions this appears as a simple dialogue, which was performed on Easter Sunday as part of a procession before Mass. The three Marys visit the tomb of Christ and are told by angels that he has risen from the dead. This dialogue is sung to a melody in the style of plainchant (Ex. 6-12). Its range is wide, covering the tenth from D to F, and its final is G. All four of the speeches end on G, and there are internal cadences on G at some of the other textual divisions. The only other cadence pitches used are F and A, for instances of less finality, and these provide a focus for the G. There is a careful balance and parallelism in the music. The opening of the second phrase ("Jesum Nazarenum . . .") uses motifs—the rising thirds F–A–C, the F–G neume, and the A–G neume—that are taken directly from the first phrase; and at the endings of both of these phrases the music for the parallel forms of address—"O christicole" ("O followers of Christ") and "O celicole" ("O dwellers in heaven")—is the same. The final cadence of the dialogue picks up the F–G–G ending formula from these earlier phrases.

EXAMPLE 6-12 *Visitatio Sepulchri* dialogue. After John Stevens, "Medieval Drama," in *The New Grove Dictionary of Music and Musicians* (London: Macmillan, 1980).

Angels:

Quem que - ri - tis in se - pul - chro, O chri - sti - co - le?

Marys:

Je - sum Na - za - re - num cru - ci - fi - xum, O ce - li - co - le.

Angels:

Non est hic; sur - re - xit si - cut pre - di - xe - rat.

I - te nun - ci - a - te qui - a sur - re - xit.

Marys:

Al - le - lu - ya, re - sur - re - xit Do - mi - nus.

Ho - di - e re-sur-re - xit le - o for - tis, Chri - ste fi - li - us De - i,

De - o gra - ti - as.

Di - ci - te: e - i - a!

Angels:
Quem queritis in sepulchro, O christicole?

Marys:
Jesum Nazarenum crucifixum, O celicole.

Angels:
Non est hic; surrexit sicut predixerat.
Ite nunciate quia surrexit.

Marys:
Alleluya, resurrexit Dominus.
Hodie resurrexit leo fortis, Christe filius
Dei, Deo gratias.
Dicite: eia!

Angels:
Whom do you seek in the tomb, O followers of Christ?

Marys:
Jesus of Nazareth who was crucified, O
dwellers in heaven.

Angels:
He is not here; he has risen as he foretold.
Go and announce that he has risen.

Marys:
Alleluya, the Lord has risen.
Today the strong lion has risen, Christ the
son of God, thanks be to God.
Say: hurrah!

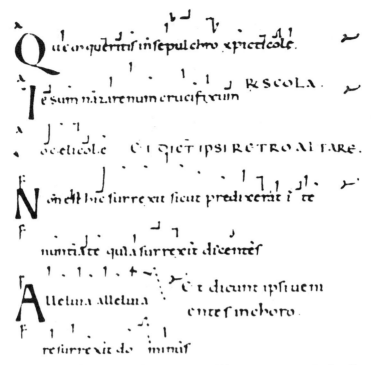

The *Visitatio Sepulchri* dialogue in an early twelfth-century manuscript (see Example 6-12). The words in large letters are stage directions. Biblioteca Capitolare, Pistoia.

The *Visitatio Sepulchri* dramas soon became more elaborate, with an expansion of the dialogue between the Marys and the angels, or the addition of more roles, such as those for the apostles or for Christ. Musically the dramas often included the singing of chants traditionally associated with Easter Sunday, such as antiphons, hymns, or the Easter sequence. Also found in some expanded versions are planctus sung by the Marys at the opening of the drama.

Parallel to the resurrection dramas are those based on the Nativity. Again the origin was a simple dialogue. The shepherds are asked "Whom do you seek?," and they reply "The infant Christ." The parallelism of the Christmas dialogue with that for Easter is reinforced by similar opening lines: the opening of the Easter dialogue is "Quem queritis in sepulchro?" ("Whom do you seek in the tomb?"); the Christmas dialogue begins "Quem queretis in presepe?" ("Whom do you seek in the crib?").

The Christmas dramas also expanded into more elaborate forms, including additional roles, such as those for Herod and the three Kings, and the singing of antiphons for the season, as well as hymns and sequences.

These dramas for Easter and Christmas are clearly based on scriptural sources and thus fall into the category of mystery plays. By far the majority of mystery plays deal with these two topics. A few, however, are based on other subjects. *The Play of Daniel,* telling the story of the learning and the integrity of Daniel and his safe escape from the lions' den, comes from the twelfth century. There are also plays on the conversion of St. Paul, the story of Abraham and Isaac, and the raising of Lazarus from the dead.

The most important manuscript of medieval drama is known as the Fleury Playbook. The manuscript was compiled in the thirteenth century in a Benedictine monastery in north central France, but it contains a retrospective collection of many different items. One section of the manuscript contains ten different plays, four of which may be categorized as miracle plays since they deal with the achievements of St. Nicholas, who saved the three daughters of a poor man from an ignominious life by giving them each a bag of gold and restored to life three small boys who had been chopped into pieces and pickled by a butcher; he also rescued a boy from kidnapping by a pagan king.

A type of drama that might be considered both mystery and miracle play took events from the life of Mary as subject matter. Since Mary was considered the central figure among the saints, plays about her life are miracle plays, strictly speaking, and yet they dramatize events from scripture, the domain of the mystery play. The main Marian feasts offered the best opportunities for this kind of drama, several of which have survived, treating subjects such as the Annunciation and the Presentation at the Temple.

The texts for Latin drama show the same shift of emphasis displayed by liturgical texts and Latin songs from the tenth to the late twelfth century—from prose towards rhymed and metrical verse. Many plays contain a mixture of the two forms. Sometimes, if a metrical scheme is adopted, it is used throughout the play as a means of textual unification.

Musically the Latin plays are diverse. The style is primarily syllabic with some neumatic groups, like plainchant. The actual chant items, such as antiphons and sequences, retain their traditional melodies. Texts with metrical verse may have been rhythmically sung to match the accents of the words. The most melismatic items are the planctus, which stand in deliberate contrast to their surroundings.

A few of the plays contain indications of instrumental performance. Instruments seem to have been used primarily for processional items—to accompany the entrance of regal characters or to symbolize movement from one place to another. Other directions in the manuscripts include links in the narrative, designations of speaker, acting gestures, and singing style. They are usually brief but direct: "Then Herod, having seen the prophecy, is overwhelmed by fury and throws away the book"; "Immediately King Darius appears with his princes, and the instrumentalists and princes walk before him, chanting these words . . . ." The vocabulary for singing style is quite rich, including such directions as "authoritatively," "smoothly," "querulously," "weepingly," as well as many words for loud and soft.

An edict was issued by the pope in 1210 forbidding the clergy from acting on a public stage. Before this time the roles in medieval drama were taken by monks and clerics, and performances took place mostly in and around the church. From the altar platform to the churchyard was a small step, and from the churchyard to the town square was also no great distance. This move, however, marked a change in medieval drama—a change in language and a change in personnel. Latin was gradually replaced by the local languages, and control of the drama shifted to the professional players, who had long been travelling from marketplace to court to marketplace, with their situation comedies, miming acts, and juggling shows.

SUMMARY

Chant composition continued at an increased pace during the tenth to the twelfth centuries. New pieces were composed for the new Marian feasts and for services dedicated to the newly created saints. New hymns, antiphons, and responsories were written for the Office, and new musical settings were composed for the invariable texts of the Mass. These chants tended to reflect an absorption with the modal system of melodic construction. Old chants were elaborated by the process of troping, textually by addition or interpolation, musically by the insertion of melismas. Melismas, both new and old, could have texts added to them, thus turning a melismatic passage into a syllabic one. Sequences, syllabic settings of newly written poems, became immensely popular during this period and went through two main stages of development, of which the most important representatives were Notker Balbulus and Adam of St. Victor. Meter and rhyme were the hallmarks of the later sequence, as well as of the large quantity of other Latin verse set to music in this period. These poems were devoted equally to liturgical, sacred, and secular subjects. The most florid of the new musical genres was the planctus, the lament song. Latin drama in this period included the genres of miracle, mystery, and morality play. In two simple dialogues, one for Easter and one for Christmas, the Latin mystery play found a rich source of inspiration for further elaboration and development. Other stories were taken from the Old and the New Testaments. Miracle plays, based on the lives of saints, were also popular, while an intermediate genre dramatized events in the life of Mary. The Latin tradition of musical composition flourished alongside a different tradition, which grew up during this same era: a tradition based on the growth of local languages in the different regions of Europe. This gradual shift of emphasis from an international culture to one of self-conscious regionalism will be examined in the next chapter.

DISCOGRAPHY

Example 6-1 Marian antiphon, *Alma Redemptoris Mater.*
Capella Antiqua de Munich, *Ave Maria,* Harmonia Mundi HM B 5115; also on Purcell Consort of Voices/Musica Reservata, *Music of the Early Renaissance,* Turnabout TV 4058/TV 340588.

Example 6-2 Introit, *Puer Natus Est,* with trope.
Ensemble Organum, *Léonin: Ecole Notre-Dame,* Harmonia Mundi HMC 1148; also (without trope) on Chor der Mönche der Benediktiner-Erzabtei St. Martin, Beuron, *Tertia Missa in Nativitate Domini Nostri Jesu Christi,* Archiv 198 036; and Benediktinerabtei, Münsterschwarzach, *Gregorianischer Choral: Die grossen Feste des Kirchenjahres,* Archiv 2723 084 (Side III).

Example 6-3 Gloria (without trope).
Chor der Mönche der Benediktiner-Erzabtei St. Martin, Beuron, *Prima Missa in Nativitate Domini Nostri Jesu Christi,* Archiv 198 153.

Example 6-5 Kyrie with prosula.
History of European Music, Part One: Music of the Early Middle Ages, vol. I, Musical Heritage Society OR 349 (Side I, Band 8).

Example 6-8 Adam of St. Victor, sequence, *Laudes Crucis Attolamus*
TAPE ONE, SIDE ONE.

Example 6-10 Walter of Châtillon, *Sol Sub Nube Latuit.*
TAPE ONE, SIDE ONE. Studio der frühen Musik, *Vox Humana: Vokalmusik aus dem Mittelalter,* EMI Reflexe 1C 069-46 401.

Example 6-11 Planctus, *O Monialis Concio.*
TAPE ONE, SIDE ONE. Studio der frühen Musik, *Planctus,* EMI Reflexe 1C 063-30 129; also on Sisters of the Cistercian Monastery of Santia María la Real de las Huelgas, *Las Huelgas Codex (12th–14th Centuries), History of Spanish Music, Volume V,* Musical Heritage Society MHS 3052.

Latin songs, together with French lais (see Chapter Seven), appear on Sequentia, *Spielmann und Kleriker (um 1200)*, Harmonia Mundi 1C 067-99 921 T. Several songs from the *Carmina Burana* collection have been recorded on Studio der frühen Musik (Early Music Quartet), *Carmina Burana aus der Original-Handschrift, um 1300*, Telefunken SAWT 9455-A and *Carmina Burana (II): 13 Songs from the Benediktbeurn Manuscript, circa 1300*, Telefunken SAWT 9522-A Ex; also on The New London Consort, *Carmina burana vol. 1*, L'Oiseau-lyre 417 373-2.

Two planctus of Abelard, including the *Planctus David*, may be heard on Studio der frühen Musik, *Peter Abélard*, EMI Reflexe 1C 063-30 123. The *Planctus David* is also on Paul Hillier, *Troubadour Songs and Medieval Lyrics*, Hyperion A 66094. The *Ordo Virtutum* of Hildegard of Bingen is available on Sequentia, *Hildegard von Bingen: Ordo Virtutum*, Harmonia Mundi 19-9942-3 (7 49249 8). Other music by Hildegard may be heard on Sequentia, *Hildegard von Bingen: Symphoniae (Geistliche Gesänge)*, Harmonia Mundi 067 19 9976 1 (7 49251 2).

Recordings of Latin dramas are as follows. The Play of Herod: French National Radio Ensemble, *Play of Herod*, Nonesuch 71181; Pro Cantione Antiqua of London, *The Play of Herod*, Peters International PLE-114. The Play of Daniel: New York Pro Musica, *The Play of Daniel*, MCA 2504; Clerkes of Oxenford, *Play of Daniel*, Nonesuch 78003 (Calliope CAL 1848). The Plays of Nicholas: New York Ensemble for Early Music, *Four Saint Nicolas Plays: Filius Getronis*, Musical Heritage Society MHS 824437 (Musicmasters MM 20049/50); Studio der frühen Musik, *Ludi Sancti Nicolai*, EMI Reflexe 1C 065-30 940.

BIBLIOGRAPHICAL NOTES

A clear summary of the history of tropes is given in Ruth Steiner, "Trope (i)," in *The New Grove Dictionary of Music and Musicians* (London: Macmillan Publishers Ltd., 1980). Paul Evans, *The Early Trope Repertory of Saint Martial de Limoges* (Princeton, New Jersey: Princeton University Press, 1970) presents a valuable discussion of the beginning of the practice of troping as well as a large amount of the music.

The early sequence is discussed and the repertory analyzed with sensitivity and insight in Richard L. Crocker, *The Early Medieval Sequence* (Berkeley: University of California Press, 1977). The late sequence is the subject of a thorough study in Margot Fassler, "Musical Exegesis in the Sequences of Adam and the Canons of St. Victor," (Ph. D. dissertation, Cornell University, 1983). A complete edition of the sequences of Adam of St. Victor is E. Misset and Pierre Aubry, *Les proses d'Adam de Saint Victor: Texte et musique* (Paris: H. Welter, 1900).

The large number of Latin songs from this period and the chants of the rhymed Office have not yet been adequately surveyed.

The music for the Play of Herod from the Fleury Playbook is edited in *Medieval Music: The Oxford Anthology of Music,* ed. W. Thomas Marrocco and Nicholas Sandon (London: Oxford University Press, 1977), with the music and original stage directions.

An edition of the *Ordo Virtutum* of Hildegard of Bingen, together with planctus by Abelard and an illuminating discussion of medieval poetry and drama is given in Peter Dronke, *Poetic Individuality in the Middle Ages* (Oxford: Oxford University Press, 1970).

Medieval drama in general, both Latin and vernacular, is surveyed in John Stevens, "Medieval Drama," in *The New Grove Dictionary of Music and Musicians* (London: Macmillan Publishers Ltd., 1980).

SEVEN
THE VERNACULAR TRADITION: 1000–1300

The period between 1000 and 1300 was marked by a vital development in European history, one that has influenced literature in particular
and culture in general throughout the Western world. This was the gradually increasing use of local languages for literary purposes. These languages
are known as vernacular languages from the Latin word *vernaculus,* meaning native or indigenous. Many of the regions in Europe that had formed
part of the Roman Empire came to use Latin as their language; but this
spoken Latin developed slightly differently in different locations, becoming the related vernaculars that are known as Romance languages (such as
French, Spanish, and Italian). In other places, such as Germany and England, where the Latin influence was not as strong, the original language
persisted or was replaced by that of other invaders.

The beginning of this period was characterized by the simultaneous
existence of a large number of regional dialects throughout Europe. Gradually some of the dialects prevailed and formed the basis for the future vernaculars of Europe. These emerging languages were enriched from many
sources, including local elements, borrowings from other dialects, and the

imposition of a new culture upon an old one. The invasion of England by William the Conqueror in the eleventh century, for example, brought a heavy infusion of Norman French into English.

The vernacular languages grew in importance between the twelfth and the fourteenth centuries and were used increasingly as vehicles for literary expression. The *Chanson de Roland,* Thomas' *Tristan,* and the chivalric *Parzifal* were all produced in this period and were written in vernacular languages (Old French, Anglo-Norman, and Middle High German respectively).

SOUTHERN FRANCE

The first vernacular language to produce literary works of major consequence to the history of music was Occitan[1] (in literary scholarship it is often called Provençal), and the region in which it developed was the whole of what is now southern France, including the Auvergne, Toulouse, Narbonne, and Provence, reaching nearly as far north as the Loire, and bounded on the southwest by the Pyrenees. This region was rich in natural resources and also was involved in lively trade with North Africa across the Mediterranean and with the luxurious East by way of the Italian city-states. Each count and duke and lord had his fiefdom, and each vied with the others not only in territorial claims but also in the elegance and sophistication of his court. Their clothes and colors, Arabian horses, perfumes, hairstyles, and lavish displays of wealth made these southern aristocrats the butt of mockery and scarcely veiled envy on the part of contemporary (northern) chroniclers.

Into this elegant and highly developed society a new type of poetry was born, a type which had enormous influence on Western literature and society from the Middle Ages until the present day. This new poetry drew on the Latin lyric for some of its forms and images, it took musical elements from plainchant, and it stylized courtly conventions of its own time. All three of these aspects were blended with the prevailing Christian ethic of spiritual love and the cult of the Virgin to create a new lyric form, infused with the ideals of "courtly love."

In a society in which marriage was a political arrangement and women of noble birth presided over courts of luxury and elegance, courtly love was both a code of manners and a literary convention. The concept

---

[1]The name of the language (Occitan, the language of "oc") was distinguished from that of northern France (the language of "oïl") by the different forms of the words for "yes"— "oc" in the South, "oïl" in the North (present-day "oui").

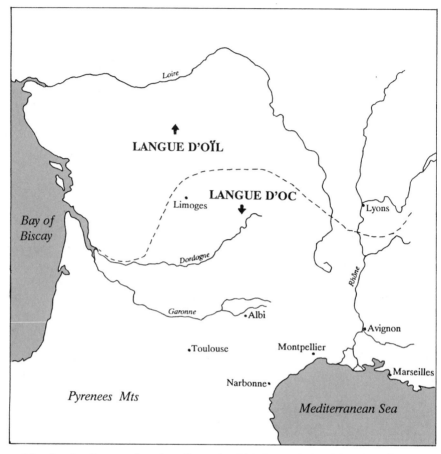

Map showing the area of southern France in which the troubadours flourished, and indicating the linguistic boundary between the languages of north and south.

involved worship from afar of an unattainable ideal woman (the Christian element is particularly evident here), the pursuit of acts of heroism and courage on her behalf (knightly conduct stylized), and the transmutation of the lover's sufferings into verse. Feudalism lent images to this concept: the lover was a "vassal," the lady his "liege mistress."

Courtly love was the primary topic of the new lyric poetry, but it was not the only one. The poems also reflect other aspects of the society for which they were composed: service to a noble lord, literary conceits, travel, treason, and loyalty. Some genres were taken over from Latin lyric: the dawn song, for example, or the celebration of a season.

The composers of this poetry were occasionally nobles themselves. William IX of Aquitaine, Prince Jaufre Rudel, and other lords and ladies were among the active poets. But mostly they were professional artists who were accepted into the highest social circles as a result of their talent. They were known as *trobadors* (in English, troubadours) from the Occitan word *trobar,* meaning to invent or compose. They might on occasion have performed their own poems in the courts and banquet halls of their patrons, but usually the actual performance was left to the minstrel or *joglar,* the professional singer and musician, distinctly lower in the social order. An ambitious and gifted *joglar* might become accepted as a *trobador* through his talent. Sometimes circumstances forced a *trobador* to earn his living as a *joglar.*

Some of the troubadours and even a few of the joglars were women. The female joglars traveled, played, and sang for a living, like their male counterparts. The female troubadours were mostly members of the nobility, returning the compliment of poetic flattery in verse. Occasionally a truly personal tone may be heard in the poems of the female troubadours. One of the most famous is the love song of Beatriz de Dia, a countess and the wife of Guillem II of Poitiers, who, in a twist on the usual theme, laments the disdain shown her by her lover:

> A chantar m'es al cor que non deurie
> Tant mi rancun de lui cui sui amie,
> Et si l'am mais que nule ren qui sie;
> Non mi val ren beltat ni curtesie
> Ne ma bontaz ne mon pres ne mon sen;
> Altresi sui enganade et tragide
> Qu'eusse fait vers lui desavinence.

> I must sing, whether I wish it or not,
> For the pain I have from him whose friend I am.
> I love him more than anything.
> Yet my beauty and manners, my goodness,
> Virtue, and wit are of no use.
> I feel despised and betrayed
> As though I had no attractions for him at all.

As so often in cultural history, the art was dependent upon the patronage of princes, and the songs reflect the life of the myriad small courts of the kings and counts and lords and ladies of the region. Other evidence about that society and the way the troubadours fitted into it comes from the *vidas,* accounts of the lives of the poets that have been preserved in the manuscripts of their compositions.

The Countess Beatriz de Dia in a miniature from one of the troubadour manuscripts, Bibliothèque Nationale, Paris.

The vidas are in many ways stylized, with notable literary influences from the *vitae* of saints and the brief introductions to collections of Latin poetry that were common in the schools. Nonetheless, they provide a unique glimpse of the life, views, and attitudes of the time. The vidas are often quite brief. Here is the vida of a troubadour named Guillem Ademar:

> Guillem Ademar was from Gevaudan, from a castle called Meyrueis. He was a nobleman, the son of a poor knight, and the Lord of Meyrueis made him a knight. He was a very worthy and eloquent man, and knew well how to compose poetry. He was unable to support his rank as a knight, so he became a joglar. And he was greatly honored by the whole of high society.

The vida of Arnaut de Marueil, given below, illustrates well the part played by the lady in these courtly intrigues. Here she is both object of worship and patroness. The final twist in the tale reminds us that the topic of the suffering lover, pining and dependent upon the whim and goodwill of the lady, if it had antecedents in Classical and medieval Latin lyric, became systematic in troubadour poetry and from there influenced the entire course of later love poetry in the West.

> Arnaut de Marueil was from the bishopric of Perigord, from a castle called Marueil, and he was a humble cleric. Because he was unable to live from his learning, he traveled around the world. He was a fine composer of poetry.
> Fortune took him to the court of the Countess of Burlatz. And the Countess favored him and honored him. And he fell in love with her and composed songs about her. But he did not dare tell anyone that he had composed them himself; he said that someone else had composed them.

But Love made him compose a song in which he revealed his love for the Countess. The Countess did not shun him, but welcomed his words and was pleased with them. And she gave him fine clothing and honored him and encouraged him to write more poems about her.

So he composed many good songs, which reveal that he received both very good and very bad treatment from her.

The fact that troubadour poetry is closely tied to music is demonstrated in several ways: from the poems themselves, from contemporary evidence about their performance, and from the *chansonniers*—the manuscripts that have transmitted the poems, often with music. Chronicles and romances of the time are full of descriptions of musical entertainment. An educated person was knowledgeable in music and capable of singing and performing on one or several instruments. A feast or banquet was not complete without the joglars. Sometimes it is clear that a poem might be sent in writing, but the method of delivery *par excellence* was by performance.

The poetry of the troubadours flourished from the late eleventh century until the early part of the thirteenth century. The main period of activity was the second half of the twelfth century, a period from which a considerable number of poets' names have come down to us as well as many compositions with music. They include Bernart de Ventadorn, Giraut de Borneill, Peirol, Gaucelm Faidit, and Raimon de Miraval.

The *vidas* of all these troubadours have survived and tell us something of their lives as well as the stylized circumstances of their careers. For example, according to his vida, Bernart de Ventadorn (c. 1140–1190) was of humble birth, but his lord grew fond of him and admired his musical talents and honored him. Bernart fell in love with his lord's wife and composed songs about her and her great merits. The lord found out about it and banished Bernart from his court. He left and went to the Duchess of Normandy (Eleanor of Aquitaine), who received him well and was pleased by his poems. He fell in love with her and she with him, and he composed many songs about her. But King Henry II of England took Eleanor for his wife and she departed for England. Bernart grieved for her and joined a monastery, where he died.

Forty-five of Bernart's poems survive, eighteen with music, and the fame and popularity of his works is attested to by the fact that several of them were used as the basis for imitations by other composers. One of these songs is *Can Vei La Lauzeta Mover* ("When I see the lark moving"), whose exquisitely controlled melody and opening image made it one of the most famous compositions of the period, as well as one of the most imitated (Ex. 7-1).

The overall form is strophic, as each stanza of the poem is sung to the same melody, but each line within the stanza receives its own phrase of the melody. The mode is Dorian, and the piece begins and ends on D. The cadences are very carefully organized. D does not appear as a cadential pitch except at the end of the fourth phrase and the last (eighth) phrase. This has the effect of dividing each stanza into two half stanzas (phrases 1–4 and 5–8), corresponding both to the rhyme scheme and to the grammatical structure of the verse. (Notice that every stanza except the first has a period at the end of the fourth line.) The last four phrases have a slowly descending series of cadences towards the final (G, F, E, D).

The upper part of the octave is carefully balanced against the prevailing lower fifth, and the top D is reached on only two occasions. Only in the last line does the note below the final appear, which reinforces the last cadence and the return to the lower D. Neumatic groups are carefully distributed within the otherwise syllabic setting, often appearing on penultimate or final syllables of poetic lines. The shape of the neumatic groups is artfully contrasted throughout.

EXAMPLE 7-1   Bernart de Ventadorn, *Can Vei La Lauzeta Mover*. From Hendrik van der Werf, *The Extant Troubadour Melodies: Transcriptions and Essays for Performers and Scholars*. Texts ed. Gerald A. Bond. (Rochester, NY: Author, 1984).

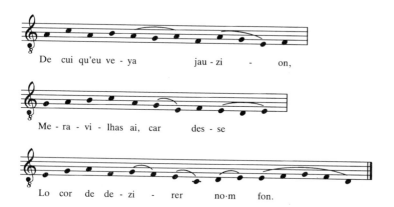

De cui qu'eu ve - ya   jau - zi - on,

Me - ra - vi - lhas ai, car   des - se

Lo cor de de - zi - rer   no·m   fon.

I. Can vei la lauzeta mover
   De joi sas alas contra·l rai

   Que s'oblid' e·s laissa chazer

   Per la doussor c'al cor li vai,
   Ai! tan grans enveya m'en ve
   De cui qu'eu veya jauzion,
   Meravilhas ai, car desse

   Lo cor de dezirer no·m fon.

II. Ai las! tan cuidava saber

    D'amor, e tan petit en sai,
    Car eū d'amar no·m posc tener
    Celeis don ja pro non aurai.
    Tout m'a mo cor, e tout m'a me,
    E se mezeis e tot lo mon;
    E can se·m tolc, no·m laisset re

    Mas dezirer e cor volon.

III. Anc non agui de me poder
     Ni no fui meus de l'or' en sai
     Que·m laisset en sos olhs vezer

     En un miralh que mout me plai.
     Miralhs, pus me mirei en te,

     M'an mort li sospir de preon,
     C'aissi·m perdei com perdet se
     Lo bels Narcisus en la fon.

I. When I see the lark moving
   Its wings joyfully against the rays of
   the sun,
   And then abandon itself and let it-
   self fall
   Because of the bliss in its heart,
   Oh! such envy do I feel
   For those that are happy,
   That I am amazed that my heart
   does not
   Instantly melt with longing.

II. Alas! I thought I knew so much
    about
    Love, but know in truth so little,
    For I cannot help myself loving
    One who gives me nothing in return.
    My whole heart, myself,
    Herself, and the whole world
    She has taken from me, and left me
    nothing
    But desire and a yearning heart.

III. I lost all strength and
     Self-possession
     From the time she let me gaze into
     her eyes—
     A mirror that pleases me so.
     O mirror, since I was mirrored in
     you,
     My sighs have slain me,
     For I am lost, just as
     Handsome Narcissus was lost in the
     pool.

IV. De las domnas me dezesper;
     Ja mais en lor no·m fiarai;
     C'aissi com las solh chaptener,
     Enaissi las deschaptenrai.
     Pois vei c'una pro no m'en te

     Vas leis que·m destrui e·m cofon,

     Totas las dopt' e las mescre,
     Car be sai c'atretals se son.

V.   D'aisso's fa be femna parer
     Ma domna, par qu'e·lh o retrai,

     Car no vol so c'om deu voler,

     E so c'om li deveda, fai.

     Chazutz sui en mala merce,
     Et ai be faih co·l fols en pon;

     E no sai per que m'esdeve,

     Mas car trop puyei contra mon.

VI. Merces es perduda, per ver,
     Et eu non o saubi anc mai,
     Car cilh qui plus en degr'aver
     No·n a ges, et on la querrai?

     A! can mal sembla, qui la ve,

     Qued aquest chaitiu deziron
     Que ja ses leis non aura be,
     Laisse morir, que no l'aon!

VII. Pus ab midons no·m pot valer

     Precs ni merces ni·l dreihz qu'eu ai,

     Ni a leis no ven a plazer
     Qu'eu l'am, ja mais no·lh o dirai.

     Aissi·m part de leis e·m recre;
     Mort m'a, e per mort li respon,

     E vau m'en, pus ilh no·m rete,

     Chaitius, en issilh, no sai on.

IV. I despair of ladies;
     Never again shall I trust them;
     Just as I used to defend them,
     Now shall I accuse them.
     Since I see that not one of them will
       help me
     Against her who is destroying and
       ruining me,
     I fear and distrust them all,
     For I know that they are all the
       same.

V.   My lady shows that she is just like
     Other women, and I reproach her
       for that,
     For she does not want what she
       should want,
     And what is unreasonable, she
       does.
     I have fallen into disfavor,
     And have acted like the fool on the
       bridge;
     And I do not know why this hap-
       pened,
     Unless perhaps I attempted too
       much.

VI. Mercy is lost, surely,
     And I never knew why,
     For she who should have the most
     Has none, and where else should I
       look?
     Ah! how wretched it seems to every-
       one
     That this poor hopeless being
     Who has no happiness without her
     She will let die, and refuse to offer
       him help!

VII. Since nothing has any effect on my
       lady,
     Neither prayers nor mercy nor the
       rights I have,
     Nor does it please her
     That I love her, I shall speak of it no
       more.
     So I shall leave her and her service;
     She has put me to death, and I reply
       with death,
     And I shall go away, since she does
       not hold me back,
     Hopeless, into exile, I know not
       where.

Tornada:	*Tornada:*
Tristans, ges no·n auretz de me,	Tristan, you will hear no more from me,
Qu'eu m'en vau, chaitius, no sai on.	For I am going away, sadly, I know not where.
De chantar me gic e·m recre,	I shall stop my singing,
E de joi e d'amor m'escon.	And flee from joy and love.

The poem itself is created with great skill, evoking the cruelty and indifference of the lady as contrasted with the lark's soaring swoop. Classical and mythical allusions combine with poetic images and down-to-earth realism in a poem of considerable verbal power. What today seems like conventionality of text and simplicity of musical line cannot disguise the beauty and artfulness of this song.[2]

Example 7-1 is a *canso*—a song with courtly love as its subject. The form is quite simple, as can be seen by analyzing the poetry. Each stanza contains eight lines of eight syllables each, and the rhyme scheme is *ababcdcd*. Each stanza follows this same syllable count and rhyme scheme. A final half stanza stands at the end of the poem; this is known as the *tornada*. Tornadas are always addressed directly to someone (either real or mythical) as a "parting shot" to complete the sentiments of the poem. Here the poet addresses the mythical lover Tristan, who figured prominently in contemporary vernacular literature. The tornada provides a sense of compression and climax, as it uses the rhymes of the last half of the stanza and is set to the concluding portion of the music.

Not all cansos are as simple in form as this one. Often the lengths of lines vary within a stanza, and rhyme schemes may be more complex. It is even possible to find cansos in which the rhyme scheme is *abcdef* etc.—that is to say there is no rhyme within a stanza. The following stanzas, however, pick up the pattern of the first, either in the same order, or, sometimes, with the order rearranged. Rearranging the order of the rhymes or introducing new ones is a practice found also in the simpler poems. The poetic art of the troubadours is subtle and varied, and each poem may have its own design.

The construction of the melodies is as artful as that of the poems. They lie mostly within an octave and are primarily syllabic settings enlivened by small neumatic groups. Although the music is usually without repetition, there are often unifying motifs or pitch levels within the melody. Sometimes these occur in reinforcement of the rhyme scheme, sometimes in deliberate counterpoint to it. The cadence structure is carefully manipu-

---

[2]Nathaniel B. Smith has analyzed and translated the poem with great sensitivity in " 'Can vei la lauzeta mover': Poet vs. Lark," *South Atlantic Bulletin* XL (1975): 15–22.

lated to provide a sense of departure and return. The melodies also display a flexible approach to the modal patterns of plainchant. Chromatic inflections appear more often than in chant, and unexpected finals and reciting tones are sometimes found. Mixture of authentic and plagal versions of a mode is common, as is a shift within the melody from one mode to another.

There are other types of troubadour poetry, which are distinguished by their subject matter. The *sirventes* ("song of service") has political or satirical content and is based on the form and melody of someone else's song. The *descort* ("discord") is a deliberate muddle of rhymes, with stanzas disagreeing, and often written in several languages, to represent the confusion brought about by love. There are dance songs known as *dansas,* and a form of dramatic dialogue between roving knight and innocent shepherdess called the *pastorela.* The Occitan equivalent to the Latin planctus is the *planh,* a lament on the death of a patron or other important personage. Another parallel to Latin song is found in the *alba,* the dawn song, in which lovers are forced to part at daybreak. Finally, there are poems written in the form of debates—between the troubadour and Love personified, or between two poets. The latter version often involves much intellectual parrying and rivalry, with criticisms of each other's work. Sometimes the alternating stanzas are actually written in turn by the two poets. The name for this type of debate poem was *tenso* ("argument") or *joc-parti* ("shared game").

The form of the poetry in these different genres is generally strophic. In two important ways, however, the poetic genre is reflected in the verse and music. The *descort,* with its varied stanzas, is through-composed, with new music for each of the stanzas. Both *dansa* and *alba* often have refrains—the same text, always set to the same music, recurring as part of every stanza, or it may be a single phrase or word, such as the word for dawn itself ("alba") recurring at the end of each stanza of an *alba.*

One of the best known of the albas is that by Giraut de Borneill (c. 1140–1200) called *Reis Glorios* (Ex. 7-2). His vida tells us that Giraut was from Limousin, a man of low birth who worked in the castle belonging to the Viscount of Limoges. He was a great troubadour and was greatly honored by those who understood love: worthy men and ladies. He spent winters teaching in school and summers traveling to the courts with two singers who sang his songs. He never wanted a wife, and he gave all the money he earned to his poor relatives and to the church of the village where he was born.

The poem is made up of seven stanzas of five lines each. The poet addresses God at the approach of day and asks him to protect his sleeping friend from the wrath of his rival. The tension set up by the situation in the text is intensified by the recurring refrain. The lines are of ten syllables each (unaccented final syllables are not considered in the syllable count) except the refrain line, the last in each stanza, which has seven. The musical phrase for the first line of the poem is repeated for the second line, which reflects the rhyme ("clartatz"/"platz"). This phrase opens with a striking upward skip and hovers around the reciting tone A, with a cadence on that pitch. The phrase for the third text line descends in two curves from the A to the note below the final, C. This C opens the next phrase, which is formed as an arch and cadences on the note above the final, E. Thus these two lines, which also rhyme ("ajuda"/"venguda"), are both linked and contrasted. The last phrase, for the refrain, begins as a variant of the previous phrase and descends to a cadence on the final D, which has been avoided cadentially thus far and is focused (C and E) by the previous two cadences.

EXAMPLE 7-2   Guiraut de Borneill, *Reis Glorios*. From Hendrik van der Werf, *The Extant Troubadour Melodies: Transcriptions and Essays for Performers and Scholars.* Texts ed. Gerald A. Bond. (Rochester, NY: Author, 1984).

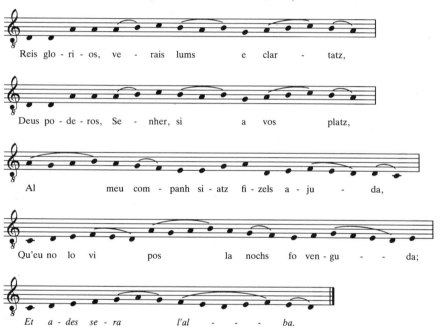

I. Reis glorios, verais lums e clartatz,

    Deus poderos, Senher, si a vos platz,

    Al meu companh siatz fizels ajuda,

    Qu'eu no lo vi pos la nochs fo venguda;
       Et ades sera l'alba.

I. Glorious King, true light and illumination,

    Powerful God, Lord, if it pleases you,

    Be a faithful friend to my companion,

    Whom I have not seen since the night came;
       And soon it will be dawn.

II. Bel companho, si dormetz o
        velhatz?
     No dormatz plus, suau vos ressidatz,
     Qu'en orien vei l'estela creguda
     C'amena·l jorn, qu'eu l'ai be cono-
        guda;
        Et ades sera l'alba.

III. Bel companho, en chantan vos apel;

     No dormatz plus, qu'eu auch chan-
        tar l'auzel
     Que vai queren lo jorn per lo bos-
        chatge;
     Et ai paor que·l gilos vos assatge;

        Et ades sera l'alba.

IV. Bel companho, issetz al fenestrel

     E regardatz las estelas del cel:
     Conoisseretz si·us sui fizels mes-
        satge.
     Si non o faitz, vostres n'er lo dam-
        natge;
        Et ades sera l'alba.

V.   Bel companho, pos me parti de vos,
     Eu no·m dormi ni·m moc de
        genolhos,
     Ans preiei Deu, lo filh Santa Maria,

     Que·us me rendes per leial com-
        panhia;
        Et ades sera l'alba.

VI. Bel companho, la foras als peiros

     Me preiavatz qu'eu no fos dor-
        milhos,
     Enans velhes tota noch tro al dia;

     Era no·us platz mos chans ni ma pa-
        ria;
        Et ades sera l'alba.

VII. "Bel dous companh, tan sui en ric
        sojorn
     Qu'eu no volgra mais fos alba ni
        jorn,
     Car la gensor que anc nasques de
        maire
     Tenc et abras, per qu'eu non prezi
        gaire
        Lo fol gilos ni l'alba."

II. My fine companion, are you asleep
        or awake?
     Sleep no longer, be vigilant,
     For in the east I see the morning star
     That brings the day, I know it well;

        And soon it will be dawn.

III. My fine companion, I call you in my
        song;
     Sleep no longer, for I have heard the
        bird singing
     That flies in search of day through-
        out the woods;
     And I fear your jealous rival will
        come upon you;
        And soon it will be dawn.

IV. My fine companion, open the win-
        dow
     And look at the stars in the sky:
     You can see if my message is true.

     If you do not act, the fault will be
        yours;
        And soon it will be dawn.

V.   My fine companion, since I left you,
     I have not slept or left my knees,

     I have prayed to God, to the Son of
        Mary,
     To give me back my loyal compan-
        ion;
        And soon it will be dawn.

VI. My fine companion, here on the
        stones outside
     You begged me not to sleep,

     To keep watch for you throughout
        the night to the day;
     I know my loyalty and my songs do
        not please you;
        And soon it will be dawn.

VII. "My fine dear companion, I am tast-
        ing such joy
     That I never want to see the dawn or
        day again,
     For the sweetest lady that ever was
        born
     I hold in my arms, and I do not give a
        damn
           For my crazy rival,
           nor for the dawn!"

The castle in the southern part of France where Giraut de Borneill lived. From Margarita Egan, *The Vidas of the Troubadours,* Garland Library of Medieval Literature, vol. 6, series B (New York: Garland, 1984). Used by permission.

The beauty and clarity of this song led to its imitation by other troubadours. They wrote new poems to fit Guiraut's melody. One version, with the melody only slightly varied, draws attention to the homage done to Guiraut de Borneill by starting with the same two words: "Reis glorios."

About seventeen poems by the troubadour Peirol (c. 1160–1221) have survived with their music. His vida describes him as a poor knight who was supported by the Dauphin of Auvergne. Peirol wrote love poems about the Dauphin's sister, but the Dauphin, finding the strength of their relationship excessive, withdrew his support and banished him. Peirol was forced to travel around the courts as a joglar and to receive his clothing and money and horses from his patrons.

Two of Peirol's poems contain historical allusions and may be dated approximately. One is a *tenso,* a debate with Love personified as to whether the poet should join a crusade or stay and honor his lady. The other was written in Jerusalem, where Peirol must have traveled in the service of a crusade, and where be probably died.

One of Peirol's poems was written together with Gaucelm Faidit (c. 1150–1220), a troubadour from the Limousin region. Gaucelm's vida, which is amusingly realistic, though almost certainly embroidered, relates that he was the son of a burgher.

> And he sang worse than anyone in the world, but he composed many good melodies and good poems. He became a joglar because he lost everything he owned in a game of dice. He was a very big man and was very greedy both in eating and drinking. That is why he became extremely fat. And he wandered around the world from place to place for twenty years, because no-one wanted either him or his songs.
>
> Later he married an actress, who was very clever and very beautiful, and she became as big and fat as he was. And the Marquis of Monferrat provided money and clothing for him and honored both him and his songs.

A large number of the poems of Gaucelm Faidit have survived, more than a dozen of them with music. One of his cansos has a melody that is based on that for *Can Vei La Lauzeta Mover* by Bernart de Ventadorn. Perhaps the best known of his songs is *Fortz Chauza* (Ex. 7-3), a planh written in honor of Richard the Lion-Heart,[3] who died in 1199. This song must have been highly regarded in the Middle Ages, for it appears in a large number of the chansonniers. It was also used as a basis for a sirventes by a later anonymous composer.

The heightened rhetoric of the poetry and grief-stricken distraction of the poet are reflected in the unusually fragmented nature of the melody. None of the phrases begins on the same pitch on which a previous phrase has ended. Indeed, there are some unexpected clashes between the cadence pitch of certain phrases and the opening pitch of the next phrase. For example, line 7 ends on B, and line 8 begins on F, a tritone away. And between the end of line 8 and the beginning of line 9 there is a leap of a sixth. For the nine lines five different cadence pitches are used (D, E, C, G, and B), and every line cadences lower than it begins. Throughout the mel-

---

[3]Richard was the son of Henry II and Eleanor of Aquitaine, whom we have come across already in the vida of the troubadour Bernart de Ventadorn. Upon his father's death Richard succeeded to the English throne as Richard I. A famous legend relates how Richard was rescued from captivity in Germany by means of a song. A poet in his service wandered from castle to castle singing a song that only he and Richard knew. The King heard him and sang the refrain, whereupon the poet was able to tell the English army of his whereabouts.

ody there are more leaps than usual, especially descending leaps. An expressive downward leap of a fifth is used to set the name "Richartz" in the first stanza.

EXAMPLE 7-3 Gaucelm Faidit, *Fortz Chauza*. Music from Hendrik van der Werf, *The Extant Troubadour Melodies: Transcriptions and Essays for Performers and Scholars*. Texts ed. Gerald A. Bond. (Rochester, NY: Author, 1984). Text from Erhard Lommatzsch, *Leben und Lieder der provenzalischen Troubadours* (Munich: Wilhelm Fink, 1972).

Fortz chau - za es que tot   lo ma - jor   dan

E·l ma - jor dol,   las! qu'ieu anc   mais a - gues,

E   so don   dei   tos-temps plan - her plo - ran,

M'a - ven a   dir   en chan - tan   e re - trai - re;

Car   selh   qu'e - ra de va - lor caps e pai - re,

Lo rics va - lenz Ri - chartz, reys   des En - gles,

Es   mortz! a - - i, Dieus!   quals per - d'e quals dans   es!

Quant es - trangz   motz,   quan sal - vatge   a   au - zir!

Ben a dur cor totz   hom qu'o pot   suf - frir.

I. Fortz chauza es que tot lo major dan
E·l major dol, las! qu'ieu anc mais agues,
E so don dei tostemps planher ploran,
M'aven a dir en chantan e retraire;

Car selh qu'era de valor caps e paire,
Lo rics valenz Richartz, reys des Engles,
Es mortz! ai, Dieus! quals perd'e quals dans es!
Quant estrangz motz, quan salvatge a auzir!
Ben a dur cor totz hom qu'o pot suf-frir.

Tornada:
Ai! senher Dieus, vos qu'etz vers perdonaire;
Vers dieus, vers hom, vera vida: merces;
Perdonatz li, que ops e cocha l'es,
E non gardetz, Senher, al sieu falhir,
E membre vos com vos anet servir!

I. It is very hard, the greatest loss
And the greatest sorrow, alas! that I have ever had,
One which I shall always lament in tears,
That I must tell and recount in my song;

For he who was the leader and fa-ther in valor,
The brave and powerful Richard, king of the English,
Is dead! oh God! what a loss, what a calamity!
What cruel words, how painful to hear!
A heart of stone must the man pos-sess who can bear it.

Tornada:
Ah! Lord God, you who offer true forgiveness;
True God, true man, true life: have mercy;
Pardon him, for he is truly in need,
And do not look upon his sins, O Lord,
But remember how he went to serve you!

The scope of this book prevents our printing all the stanzas of every song that will be discussed. However, in each case a summary of the text will be given and an indication of the length of the song as a whole. *Fortz Chauza* has six stanzas and a concluding tornada. The text continues in the tone of this first stanza, lamenting the loss of the king and praising his deeds of valor.

One of the last troubadours from the central period of troubadour activity was Raimon de Miraval (c. 1160–1215). His vida describes him as a lesser noble who shared a small castle with his brothers. Because of his beautiful discourse and poetry, and because he knew more about love and gallantry and gracious deeds than most people, he received the patronage of many counts and kings and lords. He died in a Cistercian convent.

More than twenty of Raimon de Miraval's songs have been pre-served in the chansonniers with music. Repetition of musical phrases is quite common, especially at the beginning of each stanza, and several songs contain lines of different length. One song contains a reference to the historical events that marked the sudden end of the brief but spectacular flourishing of the art of the troubadours and the society that had encouraged and sustained it.

Between 1208 and 1229 a series of wars in southern France, resulting from an attack known as the Albigensian Crusade, devastated the region and put an end to a way of life in which wealthy patrons had been able to support sophisticated courtly entertainment. The political and religious reasons for this assault on the south were complicated. The region was one of the areas in which a religious group known as the Cathars were particularly numerous. One of their centers was the town of Albi in the county of Toulouse (see map on p. 254), from which they were also known as Albigenses and whence the crusade received its name. The Cathars believed in the coexistence of good and evil and led ascetic lives, espousing ultimately a belief in suicide. They preached widely in the region and encouraged many converts, including some important local figures. The Church denounced the Cathars as heretics, and in 1208, when a papal envoy was murdered in the area, the Pope declared a crusade against them. Northern leaders and a Spanish king saw the opportunity for territorial acquisition, and the resulting wars dragged on for twenty years. Eventually a treaty gave the county of Toulouse to the King of France, but Catharism continued for another hundred years. It was finally suppressed through constant preaching by the friars—traveling members of new religious organizations—and by means of that murderous but effective political institution, begun in 1233, known as the Inquisition.

Raimon de Miraval laments the loss of his home to the Albigensian crusaders in the deliberately conventional context of the song *Bel M'es Q'ieu Chant E Coindei* (Ex. 7-4). The king addressed in the seventh stanza is Pedro II of Aragon, one of the heroes of the south against the French

EXAMPLE 7-4   Raimon de Miraval, *Bel M'es Q'ieu Chant E Coindei*. From Hendrik van der Werf, *The Extant Troubadour Melodies: Transcriptions and Essays for Performers and Scholars*. Texts ed. Gerald A. Bond. (Rochester, NY: Author, 1984).

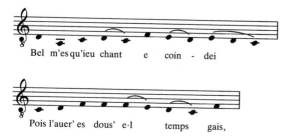

E per ver - giers e per   plais

Aug lo re - tint   e·l ga - bei

Que fant l'au - zei - llet me - nut

En - tre·l blanc e·l vert e·l vai - - - - - re;

A - doncs se deu - ri' a - trai - - - - re

Cel qe vol c'a - mors   l'a - jut

Vas chap - te - nen - ssa de   drut.

I. Bel m'es qu'ieu chant e coindei
    Pois l'auer'es dous' e·l temps gais,

    E per vergiers e per plais
    Aug lo retint e·l gabei
    Que fant l'auzeillet menut
    Entre·l blanc e·l vert e·l vaire;

    Adoncs se deuri' atraire
    Cel qe vol c'amors l'ajut
    Vas chaptenenssa de drut.

I. It pleases me to sing and be gay
    Since the breeze is sweet and the
        weather fine,
    And in the orchards and hedgerows
    I hear the warbling and twittering
    Of the birds
    Amongst the green and white and
        other colors;
    So he who wishes
    For Love's help
    Must act like a lover.

VII. Chanssos, vai me dir al rei,   VII. O song, go and tell the king,
    Cui jois guid'e vest e pais,   Who is the provider and ornament
                            of all joy,

Q'en lui non a ren biais,	That he is fully worthy,
C'aital cum ieu vuoill lo vei;	That I see him as an ideal;
Ab que cobre Montagut,	May he recover Montagut
E Carcasson'el repaire,	And return to Carcassonne,
Pois er de pretz emperaire	Then will he be a revered emperor
E doptaran son escut	And his shield will be feared
Sai Frances e lai Masmut.	Here by the French and abroad by the Mohammedans.

Tornada I: *Tornada I:*

    Dompn'ades m'avetz valgut   Lady, you have always been so worthy,

    Tant que per vos sui chantaire;   That I sing for you;
    E no·n cuiei chanson faire   And I never thought of composing a song

    Tro·l fieu vos agues rendut   Without offering you the rights
    De Miraval q'ai perdut.   To Miraval, which I have lost.

Tornada II: *Tornada II:*

    Mas lo reis m'a convengut   But the king has promised
    Que·l cobrarai anz de gaire,   To recover it for me soon,
    E mos Audiartz Belcaire: And Beaucaire for my Audiartz;
    Puois poiran dompnas e drut   Then will ladies and lovers
    Tornar el joi q'ant perdut.   Recover the joy they lost.

armies from the north. The poem is made up of seven nine-line stanzas with an *abbacddcc* rhyme scheme and two five-line tornadas which use the rhyme scheme (and the music) of the last five lines of the stanzas. Each of the lines has seven syllables, although lines 6 and 7 have additional unaccented final syllables. The melody is very simple, with neumatic groups concentrated towards the end of phrases. Unity is achieved by similarity among the opening gestures of many of the phrases, by the linking of the end of one phrase to the beginning of the next by a common tone (lines 1/2, 2/3, 3/4, 4/5, 7/8, and 8/9), and by the repetition of a musical phrase for lines 6 and 7. This musical repetition matches the rhyme ("vaire"/"atraire"), although previous opportunities for such parallelism (e.g., lines 2 and 3) are deliberately not taken. A subtle sense of closure is created by having the opening of the last phrase descend, the only one to do so since the first phrase of the melody.

The art of the troubadours did not die completely. It survived in the work of some late troubadours who were dispersed to foreign courts and continued to compose in their traditional forms and language, and, most importantly, in the influence the repertoire had on the development of secular song and poetry in other Romance languages.

In the thirteenth century two prolific troubadours writing in Occitan found favor in Spanish courts. Peire Cardenal (c. 1180–1278) worked as a clerk in the court of the Count of Toulouse before the Albigensian crusade, and later traveled from court to court with his own joglar. He specialized in sirventes, many of which are angry denunciations of the turbulent life of the times, and he ultimately gained support from King Jaime of Aragon.

Guiraut Riquier (c. 1230–1300) is thought of as the last of the troubadours. His late position ensured the survival of nearly fifty of his poems with music. Many of them contain autobiographical details or references, and a famous letter by him survives from 1274; in it he begs for increased respect and remuneration for troubadours and joglars. He found service with two Spanish nobles, among them the King of Castile, Alfonso X.

The songs of Guiraut Riquier show an increasing tendency towards the use of repetition schemes, especially the repetition of the first phrase or phrases of the melody, thus giving the rough equivalent of an overall *AAB* musical form (here the upper-case letters indicate sections of the music). Such patterns of repetition in later troubadour songs had important consequences, especially in other repertoires of vernacular song.

Finally, the history of the troubadours would not be complete without mention of the poets of other nationalities who imitated the style and wrote in the language of the troubadours. The most important of these was Sordello (c. 1180–1269), an Italian poet who wrote in Occitan and borrowed themes from the poetry of southern France. He was one of many Italians who imitated the troubadour style. Especially influential was a school of poetry which flourished at the court of Frederick II in Sicily and which was responsible for the transition to a purely Italian repertoire of lyric poetry. Sordello is honored with a place in the *Divine Comedy* of Dante, himself a beneficiary of the art of the troubadours.

Occitan and its several dialects produced many important literary works apart from the songs of the troubadours and their vidas. These include the epic poem *Girart de Roussillon* and two romances, *Jaufre* and *Flamenca*. Over the next two centuries, the main productions were several treatises on poetic technique, and dramas, both serious and comic. The language is still spoken in areas of southern France today, and a literary revival has produced several modern works.

The birth of the art of the troubadours had far-reaching and eventful consequences. It was the first vernacular literature to establish the concept of courtly love, with its topics of the pining lover, unattainable lady, and faithful friend—topics central to European literature ever since. Its other poetic genres, such as the joc-parti and the pastorela, were also imitated in different languages and cultures. Its artful poetic constructions are set to subtle musical forms, in which control of pitch focus, counterpoint between text rhyme and musical repetition, use of small melodic motifs, appearance of refrains, and strophic format play major roles of balance, structure, and projection. The compositions of the troubadours laid the foundation for other vernacular song repertories for several centuries to come.

NORTHERN FRANCE

In northern France the situation was different from that in the south. After the Carolingian dynasty had begun to disintegrate in the tenth century, the repeated raids of the Vikings from Scandinavia threatened to put northern Europe back into the turbulence and chaos from which it had only recently emerged. Local dukes and feudal lords vied constantly for control and became increasingly powerful. In 987 the nobles chose Hugh Capet, one of the dukes of Francia (the region around Paris), as king of France. Gradually the Capetian monarchs increased their control of the area, extended their territory, and brought prosperity to the region. The towns increased in size, and commercial activity flourished in the local fairs. A succession of French kings in the eleventh and twelfth centuries made Paris the political center of Europe. In the eastern part of the kingdom, at Cluny, a religious reform movement begun in the tenth century had spread through the Benedictine world and given new force to monastic learning, art, and architecture. The French kings also became involved in the Crusades, partly as a result of the desire to increase their own prestige, partly because they needed to find employment for the large number of nobles without land who belonged to the military and social class called knights. French ideals and manners spread throughout Europe, both by aggression and by emulation.

The language spoken in the northern part of France was known as the *langue d'oïl*, now called Old French. This had several dialects, including Picard, Norman, and Francien. As the power of the French kings increased and Paris became more and more the center of French political activity, Francien, the dialect of Francia, gained in importance and prevailed over the other dialects. It is the ancestor of the modern French language.

Of all the European languages, Old French was perhaps the most international, for it came into widespread use in trading, military, and courtly circles, and some of its literary forms were the basis for many of the poetic accomplishments in other tongues. Old French developed from Latin as a vehicle for literary expression in the eleventh century, and by the twelfth century many masterpieces of literature had been produced. The earliest writings were in the heroic and military mold, reflecting the mythic status of Charlemagne and catering to the contemporary taste for glory and daring exploits. Epic poems of many thousands of lines were written, celebrating nobility, adventure, and warfare. These were called *chansons de geste* ("songs of deeds") and were formed of ten- to twelve-syllable lines, linked by assonance and (later) by rhyme. The most famous of the chansons de geste, and one of the earliest, is the *Chanson de Roland* (c. 1100), which tells the story of the battle between Roland, one of Charlemagne's generals, and the Saracens, the Muslim invaders of Europe. Roland is killed, but the battle is won by Charlemagne's return to the field.

The chansons de geste were sung by minstrels for the entertainment of their noble audiences. The mode of delivery may have been similar to that employed by the singers of heroic narrative poems nearly two thousand years earlier. Homer's *Iliad* and *Odyssey* were probably sung to simple declamatory formulas which could support an epic poem of thousands of lines, just as the chansons de geste were sung at knightly banquets by the twelfth-century minstrels.

Another literary form which appeared in the northern vernacular in the twelfth century was the *romance*. This seems to have become popular simultaneously in the north and the south of France. Two Occitan romances, *Jaufre* and *Flamenca,* have been mentioned above. The romance was a long narrative poem, like the chanson de geste, but its subject matter involved chivalry and love. The *Roman de la Rose,* from the thirteenth century, is a highly developed example of the form. It is an elaborate and complex disquisition on love in over twenty thousand lines of eight-syllable couplets.

Other prose and verse genres were allegories and animal fables, with many stories that derived directly from the old Greek tales of Aesop and the *Metamorphoses* of Ovid. Most important from the musical point of view was a new poetic form known as the *lai,* whose invention is traditionally associated with Marie de France (c. 1140–1190). Marie wrote over a dozen lais, which are in rhyming couplets and reflect the background of the legend of King Arthur and other material of Celtic origin. Unfortunately no music survives for these works.

Later twelfth- and thirteenth-century lais address the topics of love for the Virgin and earthly love with equal ease. The form of the poems is very disparate, but often the verse is divided into stanzas of equal length, with about twenty eight-syllable lines in each. The music, like that for the narrative poems, is made up of a few simple formulas used over and over again to provide a vehicle for the words.

Another genre native to the northern tradition was the *chanson d'histoire,* a song which tells a story. The story is a standardized one, in which the lady sits spinning or weaving and laments the absence of her lover. Often these begin with the name of the lady and a description of her whereabouts. Two well-known chansons d'histoire begin "Bele Yolanz en ses chambres seoit" ("The beautiful Yolanz was sitting in her room") and "Bele Doette as fenestres se siet" ("The beautiful Doette sat by the window"). The first one goes on to describe the lover's return; the second tells of the lover's death in a tournament and the founding of an abbey in his name. Both are written in four-line stanzas, with simple musical phrases matching the lines, and have reiterated refrains.

In other respects the poetry and songs of northern France were strongly influenced by the art of the troubadours. The lyric effusions of Old French may have begun before the Albigensian Crusade, but even then the model was provided by Occitan lyric. The boundary between the *langue d'oc* and the *langue d'oïl* was real enough, but it was primarily a linguistic boundary, and troubadours and joglars must certainly have traveled to northern courts. After the Albigensian Crusade, the main achievements in vernacular song were in the north. The main period of troubadour activity was in the second half of the twelfth century, while Old French lyric began to flourish in the last two decades of the twelfth century and continued to the end of the thirteenth.

In many respects the equivalents between the two repertoires are exact. The poets of Old French called themselves *trouvères*, and the performing minstrels were known as *jongleurs*. There were noble trouvères, such as Thibaut, King of Navarre, and the social lines between composer and performer were distinct. The audiences sat in courts and banquet halls, the patrons were wealthy nobles, just as in the south. Many of the genres were transferred to their new locale and language intact. The canso became the *chanson d'amour* ("song about love"), the joc-parti was now *jeu-parti,* pastorela was called *pastourelle;* only the subtle sirventes did not survive.

But if the themes of the troubadours seemed new and alive to them, for the trouvères they had become standard topics, worthy of rhetorical exploitation but less reflective of current society than of literary convention. Towards the middle of the thirteenth century, groups of trouvères were formed to evaluate and discuss each other's work, and these groups also included educated clerics and middle-class citizens. Popular elements entered the poetry, and the verse forms were simplified. The music shows an increasing tendency towards repetition and unification. Motifs are commonly used to unify a composition, and the favorite large-scale repetition form is tripartite (AAB), in which the first pair of musical phrases is repeated before a contrasting new section. Refrains become more frequent, either within the stanzas, like the refrains in troubadour music, or between them. The latter style is used especially in the many dance songs found in the trouvère repertory. Sometimes refrains, being repetitive and recognizable, are quoted intact by the composer of a new song. Other more complex dance forms are seen in the later part of the century, and these eventually crystallized into the standard forms of songs in the fourteenth and fifteenth centuries, the *formes fixes* ("fixed forms"), which will be discussed later.

Much more music has survived from the trouvères than from the troubadours. Although the amount of extant poetry is about the same in both cases, nearly ten times as many trouvère melodies have come down to us in the manuscripts. The relationship between poetry and music remained the same: poem and melody were created together and were designed to be performed together. A similar attitude towards imitation is also seen among the northern composers. Famous old poems could provide the basis for new ones; if the new one had the same verse patterns as the old one, the well-known melody could be retained, to provide both a sense of recognition for the audience and a respectful sign of homage to the other composer. Many trouvère songs are imitations of famous compositions from the troubadour repertory; others imitate contemporary songs by other trouvères.

Finally, a new element is found in the songs of northern France which reflects both the historical climate and the rather more public nature of the repertoire. This new element is overt religious content, either in the form of songs to Mary or songs for the crusades. The Marian element in the growth of twelfth-century love poetry has been discussed before; but in the Occitan poems it was subsumed into the courtly love ideals of the troubadours. In the northern repertory the devotion to Mary is explicit, and songs in her honor became a separate genre. Songs supporting the crusades are both another aspect of explicit religious content in northern vernacular song and a clear reflection of the political demands of the times.

Among the large number of trouvères whose names have come down to us, a few may be selected as representative of general or particular trends in the Old French song repertoire. They may be divided into two groups: a group representing activity from the whole of northern France, and a group centered upon a particular town which seems to have attracted and encouraged many trouvères. The town was Arras, a flourishing commercial center in the northern part of the country which in 1180 was granted a special charter by the French king. Here many trouvères lived and worked, and a literary society was founded to perform and judge their songs. The society was known as a *puy* and although many towns had *puys,* the one at Arras was particularly well known. It had its origins in a local guild of jongleurs, and was founded by the wealthy merchants of the town. It held annual song recitations and contests, the winner being crowned a "prince" as a mark of honor and respect for his work.

The group of trouvères from areas other than Arras includes Gace Brulé, Colin Muset, and Gautier de Coincy.

Gace Brulé (c. 1160–1220) was one of the earliest of the trouvères. He was active at the court of the Count of Brittany, who was also the patron of several important troubadours. A jeu-parti between Gace Brulé and the Count is extant (though unfortunately without music). Gace may himself have been a knight with property: one of the chansonniers shows him in full armor, brandishing his sword and striped shield (see below). His poetry and music are typical of the early period in trouvère work. Both verse and musical structures are derived from those of the troubadours, with frequent occurrence of repetition of the first pair of musical phrases for the second pair of lines. Settings are primarily syllabic with neumatic groups towards the end of phrases. The song *Biaus M'est Estez* (Ex. 7-5) is representative

Gace Brulé in a miniature from one of the trouvère manuscripts, Biblioteca Apostolica Vaticana, Rome.

of his style. The poem is divided into six eight-line stanzas, with a final parting couplet. (In Old French this final section was known as the *envoi*.) The
music for the first pair of lines is repeated for the second pair, while the last
half of the stanza receives new phrases. The very beginning is reminiscent
of the famous *Can Vei La Lauzeta Mover* of Bernart de Ventadorn (see p.
258). The envoi is set to the music of the last two lines. The text is an exploration of the standard theme of the chanson d'amour—love for an unattainable lady, her disdain, and the poet's pain—with an opening that praises
the beauties of nature.

The conventionality of the text is reflected in the straightforward
rhyme scheme of the poetry and in the regular phrasing and design of the
music. The rich rhyme schemes of the troubadours are here replaced by a
simple pattern: *abab{}abba*. And the first two phrases (repeated as phrases 3
and 4) are balanced by the opposition of an "open" ending for the first
phrase (on F) and a "closed" ending for the second phrase (on D). The mid-
point of the stanza is marked by a higher range in the music (phrase 5),
which fills out the upper fourth (A–D) of the mode. The second half
(phrases 5–8) of the melody is also made to fall into two sections by the use
of a slight variant of the "closed" phrase from the first half to set line 6. The
music is thus characterized throughout by balance and regularity of form.

EXAMPLE 7-5   Gace Brulé, *Biaus M'est Estez*. From Samuel N. Rosenberg, Samuel
Danon, and Hendrik van der Werf, *The Lyrics and Melodies of Gace Brulé*, Garland
Library of Medieval Literature, vol. 39, series A (New York: Garland, 1985).

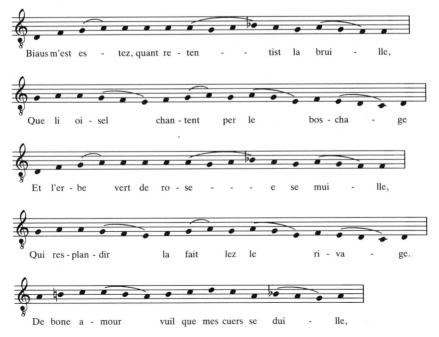

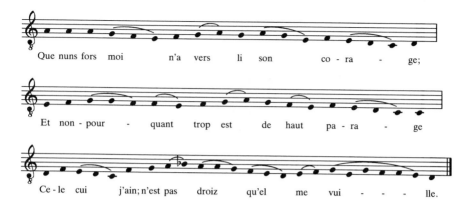

I. Biaus m'est estez, quant retentist la
   bruille,
   Que li oisel chantent per le bos-
   chage
   Et l'erbe vert de rosee se muille,
   Qui resplandir la fait lez le rivage.
   De bone amour vuil que mes cuers
   se duille,
   Que nuns fors moi n'a vers li son
   corage;
   Et nonpourquant trop est de haut
   parage
   Cele cui j'ain; n'est pas droiz qu'el
   me vuille.

III. De bien amer Amors grant sen me
   baille,
   Si me trahit s'a ma dame n'agree.

   La voluntez pri Deu que ne me
   faille,
   Car mout m'est bon quant ou cuer
   m'est entree;
   Tuit mi panser sunt en li, ou que
   j'aille,
   Ne riens fors li ne me puet estre mee
   De la dolor dont sopir a celee.

   A mort me rent, ainz que longues
   m'asaille.

Envoi:
   Gui de Pontiaux, Gasçoz ne set que
   dire:
   Li deus d'amors malement nos con-
   soille.

I. I love the summer, when the woods
   resound,
   When the birds sing in the trees

   And the green grass is soaked with dew
   And gleams along the river bank.
   I want my heart to be taken over by
   good love,
   For no one but myself approaches
   love with courage;
   And yet she is of too noble birth,

   The one I love; it is not right for her
   to want me.

III. Love gives me the ability to love
   well,
   But has betrayed me if I cannot
   please my lady.
   I pray to God that my courage not fail,

   For I am glad that love has entered
   my heart;
   All my thoughts are of her, wherever I go,
   And no one but she can cure me
   Of the pain from which I secretly
   sigh.
   I shall surrender to death, which has
   beseiged me so long.

Envoi:
   Guy de Ponceaux, your Gace does
   not know what to say:
   The god of love advises us badly.

Colin Muset (c. 1200–1250) appears to have risen from the rank of jongleur to become a trouvère. He was active in the county of Champagne and the duchy of Lorraine, both of which were important and independent regions in the northeastern part of the country. Champagne was ruled by the counts of Blois in the eleventh and twelfth centuries and only came under the jurisdiction of the king of France in 1314; it was prosperous and renowned as an international trading center. Great commercial fairs were held at Troyes, where many regulations governing trade were developed, including the standard weight for gold, still called troy weight. One of the counts of Champagne—Thibaut, later also king of Navarre—was himself an active and prolific trouvère.

The incorporation of popular elements into Old French vernacular song may be seen in Colin Muset's song *Sire Cuens* (Ex. 7-6), which describes the situation of the musician who is dependent upon the goodwill of a noble audience for his livelihood. All five stanzas of the song are provided in the example. The animation and freshness of the poetry, with its immediacy of direct speech and realistic, down-to-earth details, are brought out by a simple melody of narrow range and repeated notes, with syllabic text setting. The musical phrases for the first two lines are repeated for lines 3 and 4, and phrases 5 and 7, with adjustments for line length, are almost identical.

EXAMPLE 7-6   Colin Muset, *Sire Cuens*. After Pierre Aubry, *Trouvères and Troubadours: A Popular Treatise*, trans. Claude Aveling (New York: Cooper Square, 1969). Additional text from Joseph Bédier, *Les Chansons de Colin Muset*, 2nd ed. (Paris: Librairie Ancienne Honoré Champion, 1938).

Si - re Cuens j'ai vi - e - le

De - vant vous en vostre os - tel,

Si ne m'a - vez riens do - ne

Ne mes ga - ges a - qui - te:

C'est vi - la - ni - e!

Foi que doi san - te Ma - ri - e,

En - si ne vous sieur - re mi - e.

M'au-mos-niere est mal gar - ni - e

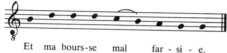

Et ma bours-se mal far - si - e.

I. Sire Cuens j'ai viele
   Devant vous en vostre ostel,
   Si ne m'avez riens done
   Ne mes gages aquite:
   C'est vilanie!
   Foi que doi sante Marie,
   Ensi ne vous sieurre mie.
   M'aumosniere est mal garnie
   Et ma boursse mal farsie.

II. Sire Cuens, car conmandez
    De moi vostre volente.
    Sire, s'il vous vient a gre,
    Un beau don car me donez.
    Par courtoisie!
    Car talent ai, n'en doutez mie,
    De raler a ma mesnie.
    Quant g'i vais boursse desgarnie,

    Ma fame ne me rit mie.

III. Ainz me dit: "Sire Engele,

     En quel terre avez este,
     Qui n'avez riens conqueste?
     Trop vos estes deporte
     Aval la ville.
     Vez com vostre male plie!
     Ele est bien de vent farsie!
     Honiz soit qui a envie
     D'estre en vostre compaignie!"

I. Mister Count, I've played the fiddle
   For you in your house,
   Yet you've given me nothing
   Nor paid my wages.
   That's just unfair!
   By the faith I owe holy Mary,
   I won't be in your employ any more.
   My lunchbox is empty
   And my wallet is thin.

II. Mister Count, you can order me
    To play anything you want.
    But Mister, please,
    Give me a little something.
    It's only right!
    Believe me, I'd really rather
    Go home.
    But when I get there with an empty
       wallet,
    The old lady will give me a hard
       time.

III. She'll say to me: "Well, Mister
     Thickhead,
     What have you been up to,
     And brought nothing back?
     You've been having a drink or two
     Down in the town.
     Look how your wallet bulges!
     It's full of wind!
     Good luck to whoever
     Wants *you* around!"

IV. Quant je vieng a mon ostel
     Et ma fame a regarde
     Derrier moi le sac enfle,
     Et je, qui sui bien pare
     De robe grise,
     Sachiez qu'ele a tost jus mise
     La quenoille, sanz faintise:
     Ele me rit par franchise,
     Ses deus braz au col me plie.

IV. But when I come home
     And my wife sees me
     With a sack full of gifts,
     And me all slicked out
     In a nice gray robe,
     You can bet she'll put down
     Her sewing, quick as that:
     She'll laugh out loud
     And fling her arms around my neck.

V.   Ma fame va destrousser
     Ma male sanz demorer;
     Mon garçon va abuvrer
     Mon cheval et conreer;
     Ma pucele va tuer
     Deus chapons pour deporter
     A la jansse alie;
     Ma fille m'aporte un pigne
     En sa main par cortoisie.
     Lors sui de mon ostel sire
     A mult grant joie sanz ire,
     Plus que nuls ne porroit dire.

V.   She'll empty out
     My sack right away;
     The boy will water
     And stable the horse;
     The maid will kill
     A couple of capons for a feast
     With fresh garlic sauce;
     My daughter will bring me a comb
     In her hand, sweet as anything.
     Then I'll be the lord of the manor,
     And all will be laughter and joy,
     Better than I can even describe.

Gautier de Coincy (c. 1177–1236) is important as the composer of the enormous narrative poem known as the *Miracles de Nostre Dame* ("Miracles of Our Lady"), which tells of the miracles associated with the Virgin Mary. The poem contains many religious songs, some of which are based on melodies by other trouvères. The close association of the sacred and secular worlds in the Middle Ages, discussed earlier, is demonstrated by the life and work of Gautier. Both trouvère and monk, later abbot, he happily adopted secular melodies to serve his religious songs. The distinction between "ma dame" ("my lady"—the mistress in courtly love) and "nostre dame" ("our lady"—the Virgin Mary) was at this time not very great. Both were objects of respect and adoration. Gautier wrote in many forms; the song to the Virgin, *Royne Celestre* (Ex. 7-7), is a lai, with three long stanzas, only the first of which is given here. The text celebrates the status of the Virgin as mother and saint; the repetition of part of the opening of the stanza as the last line provides effective closure. The music falls into four main sections, each of which is repeated with new text. Each of the sections is further subdivided into phrases with parallel shapes and open and closed cadences. This lai is untypical in that all three stanzas are designed to be set to the same music.

EXAMPLE 7-7 Gautier de Coincy, *Royne Celestre.* After Jacques Chailley, *Les Chansons à la Vierge de Gautier de Coinci 1177(78)–1236,* Publications de la Société française de Musicologie (Paris: Heugel, 1959).

A.

1. Ro - y - ne ce - les - tre, Buer fus - ses tu ne - e,
2. Tant es de haut es - tre, Pu - ce - le sa - cre - e,

Quant port' et fe - nes - tre Du ciel es nom - me - e.
Qu'el ciel a sa des - tre T'a Dieus cou - ron - ne - e:

B.

1. Car de ta ma - me - le, Qui tant est em - mie - le - e,
2. Hau - te da - moi - se - le, Vir - ge be - ne - u - re - e,

Fu sa bou - che be - le Pe - ue et a - be - vre - e.
Touz li mons t'a - pe - le, Par - tout es re - cla - me - e.

C.

1. Hau - te pu - ce - le pu - r'et mon - de, De toi sourt la rou - se - e.
2. Dont es tou - te la riens du mon - de Nou - rrie et a - rou - se - e.

D.

1. Ro - yn' en - nou - re - e, Buer fus - ses en - gen - re - e, Car plus es douc' et plus ple - sanz
2. Cer - tes, qui ne be - e De tou - te sa pen - se - e A toi ser - vir tout en a - pert,

Et plus sa - de cent mil - le tanz Que mielz en fres - che re - e:
Puis bien di - re que s'a - me pert Et qu'el' en iert damp - ne - e;

Riens qu'a sa - veur Sans ta sa - veur Ne m'est a - sa - vou - re - e.
Mes qui te sert, Dieu en de - sert: Que buer fus - ses tu ne - e.

A. 1. Royne celestre, Buer fusses tu
      nee,
      Quant port'et fenestre Du ciel es
      nommee.
   2. Tant es de haut estre, Pucele
      sacree,
      Qu'el ciel a sa destre T'a Dieus
      couronnee:

B. 1. Car de ta mamele, Qui tant est
      emmielee,
      Fu sa bouche bele Peue et
      abevree.
   2. Haute damoiselle, Virge beneu-
      ree,
      Touz limons t'apele, Partout es
      reclamee.

C. 1. Haute pucele pur'et monde, De
      toi sourt la rousee.
   2. Dont es toute la riens du monde
      Nourrie et arousee.

D. 1. Royn' ennouree, Buer fusses
      engenree,
      Car plus es douc'et plus plesanz
      Et plus sade cent mille tanz

      Que mielz en fresche ree:
      Riens qu'a saveur Sans ta saveur

      Ne m'est asavouree.
   2. Certes, qui ne bee De toute sa
      pensee
      A toi servir tout en apert, Puis
      bien dire que s'ame pert
      Et qu'el' en iert dampnee;
      Mes qui te sert, Dieu en desert:

      Que buer fusses tu nee.

A. 1. Heavenly Queen, you were born
      at a good time,
      For you are called the door and
      window to heaven.
   2. You are of such great worth,
      sacred maiden,
      That God has crowned you in
      heaven at his right hand.

B. 1. For at your breast, which is as
      sweet as honey,
      Was his glorious mouth nour-
      ished and fed.
   2. Royal lady, benevolent virgin,

      The whole world calls to you,
      everywhere are you hailed.

C. 1. Royal maiden, pure and chaste,
      from you comes the dew,
   2. Which nourishes and gives life to
      the whole world.

D. 1. Honored Queen, you were
      conceived at a good time,
      For you are more sweet and
      pleasing, and a hundred
      thousand times more beauti-
      ful,
      Than the freshest honeycomb:
      Nothing that is sweet is sweet to
      me
      Without your sweetness.
   2. Certainly he who does not com-
      letely bend his thoughts
      To serve you fully and openly will
      surely lose his soul
      And see it damned;
      But he who serves you is deserv-
      ing of God,
      For you were born at a good
      time.

The group of trouvères who were active in the town of Arras included Moniot d'Arras, Jehan Bretel, and Adam de la Halle.

Moniot d'Arras (c. 1200–1239) was a monk at a monastery in the
town (his name means "the little monk of Arras"). He wrote both religious
and secular songs, including pastourelles, jeux-partis, and chansons d'a-
mour. He was obviously quite well known, for he is named in a jeu-parti by
a contemporary; several of his poems are addressed to important nearby
courts and nobles; and some of his songs served as models for those of other
trouvères. The song *Bone Amor* (Ex. 7-8) was imitated no less than four

times, inspiring one spring song, two chansons d'amour, and a song to the Virgin. Each of the five stanzas has eight lines of seven syllables (final "e" at the end of a line does not count). Each phrase of the melody is artfully shaped, with descending lines balanced by arches. The center of the melody (lines 5 and 6) reaches the highest pitch (C). Cadences away from the final (D) are on E, G, and C, and there is a sense of pairing of phrases provided by the alternation of open and closed endings (phrases 1 and 2, 5 and 6, and 7 and 8). The phrase pairing is also confirmed at a higher level by the division of the stanza into half stanzas. The remainder of the poem goes on

EXAMPLE 7-8   Moniot d'Arras, *Bone Amor*, Paris, Bibliothèque de l'Arsenal, 5198.

I. Bone amor sanz tricherie
   Servirai sanz losengier,
   Car aillors servir ne qier,
   Ne d'autre amor n'ai envie.
   Du tout sui en sa baillie;
   S'or mi voloit fere aie
   Ma dame d'un seul besier,
   Bien seroit l'amor merie.

I. A fine love without deceit—
   This shall I serve faithfully,
   For I cannot serve elsewhere,
   Nor do I want any other love.
   I am entirely under her power;
   If she wanted to help me,
   My lady could grant me but a single kiss,
   Then she would surely deserve my love.

to praise the lady's beauty and simultaneously to lament her harsh treatment of her lover. Text and music reinforce each other throughout this delicate and supple song.

Jehan Bretel (c. 1210–1272) was also one of the best-known trouvères of the Arras circle. During one of the annual poetry competitions he was named prince of the *puy*. A small number of his chansons d'amour are extant, but by far the largest proportion of his output is represented by jeux-partis, in which he participated with many other poets of the Arras group. Since it was conventional to begin the first stanza of the jeu-parti with the name of the addressee, it is easy to discover the trouvères with whom Jehan worked in these joint compositions. They include many local poets and wealthy figures of the time, and one of these honored him in turn by beginning a poem with the salutation "prince."

Another of Jehan's colleagues, and the addressee of no fewer than eleven of his jeux-partis, is a composer whose work marks the end of the period of trouvère activity and the beginning of a new direction in music. His name is Adam de la Halle, and despite his position at a turning point in musical history, and the quantity and importance of his work, the dates of his birth and death are uncertain. He was born around the middle of the thirteenth century and lived until about 1290 or 1300. He was a member of the Arras circle but spent a considerable amount of time away from the town in the service of Charles Anjou, who was the brother of King Louis IX of France (Saint Louis). Charles took part in several crusades and fought in southern Italy and Sicily on the side of the pope, ultimately being crowned king of Sicily. Adam de la Halle was educated in Paris, so that with his experience in Italy and the time he spent in the French capital, he must have come into contact with several important musical trends of the time, both retrospective and progressive. In Italy he would have met local troubadours, both refugees from the south of France and native poets, and in Paris he must have heard the new developments in musical polyphony that were revolutionizing compositional style in France and elsewhere (see Chapter Nine).

This varied experience is reflected in the disparate nature of Adam's work. He wrote chansons d'amour and jeux-partis in the traditional monophonic format of the time, but he also composed polyphonic songs in three

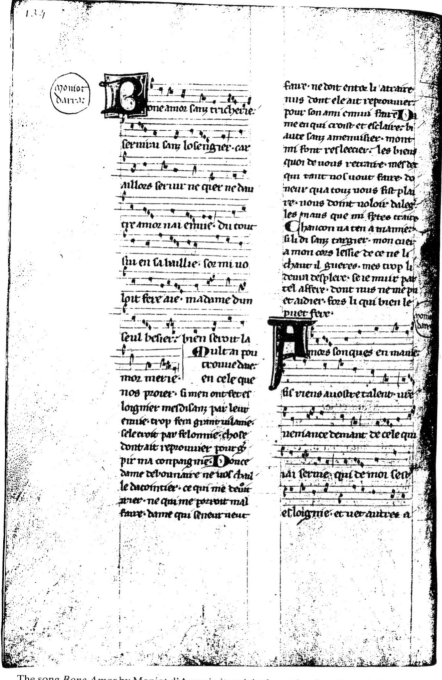

The song *Bone Amor* by Moniot d'Arras in its original notation (see Example 7-8). The composer's name is written in the top left margin. Bibliothèque Nationale, Paris.

voices, anticipating developments of the next century. Moreover, he wrote three-voice motets, with French lyric poems for the upper voices and a lower voice derived from chant, in the modern Parisian style, and he contributed broadly to the development of vernacular drama.

The significance and reputation of Adam de la Halle in his own time are attested to by the large number of manuscripts that preserve his work. One of them even contains a complete collection of his output, with the different types of composition arranged in groups.

The three-voice songs of Adam are given the name *rondeau*, for they contain a refrain and are probably derived from dance songs. In structure they anticipate the "fixed form" of the rondeau as it became known in the fourteenth century. The scheme is a sophisticated one, for it includes a refrain that appears both in complete and in partial form. In *A Dieu Commant Amouretes* (Ex. 7–9), which elaborates on the topic of "farewell" (a topic common to the works of many later poets), the refrain is made up of three lines, two of which recur in the middle of the poem.

Adam gives this poem a simple polyphonic setting, with the main melody in the middle voice and the other voices in counterpoint against it. The upper voice incorporates the same rhythms as the main melody and moves primarily in contrary motion. The lower voice is in longer note values and is very simple, with a range of only a third and motion more or less in parallel fifths with the middle voice. By itself, the main melody could easily stand as a monophonic song directly in the trouvère tradition, and indeed it may well have been composed as such before the addition of the other voices. The rhythmic patterns of the song are those which were developed in Paris in the late twelfth century for coordinating the voices in polyphonic compositions. (This important development will be examined more fully in Chapter 9). The music is in only two sections, and the text of the whole refrain (lines 1–3, 6–7, and 11–13), as well as that of the stanza (lines 4–5 and 8–10), is distributed between them. All three voices sing the same text.

The *musical* form of the rondeau may be represented by an alphabetical scheme in which the letter "a" stands for the first section of the music, and the letter "b" for the second section. If recurring text (refrain) occurs with the music, an upper-case letter is used; if new text occurs, a lower-case letter is used. The rondeau then is represented as follows: ABaAabAB.

Of the half-dozen motets by Adam de la Halle, some use quotations from his songs in one of the upper voices. In the thirteenth century this was quite a common device. The audience would have been expected to recognize the quotation and enjoy the reference to a song with which they were all familiar. This is similar to the technique of quoting in a new song the refrain of an earlier one by another trouvère—a popular technique, as we have seen. In motets too it is the refrain of a song that is usually quoted, the

EXAMPLE 7-9 Adam de la Halle, *A Dieu Commant Amouretes.* From Nigel Wilkins, *The Lyric Works of Adam de la Halle,* Corpus Mensurabilis Musicae, vol. 44 ([Rome]: American Institute of Musicology, 1967).

A Dieu commant amouretes,
Car je m'en vois,
Souspirant en terre estrainge.
Dolans lairai les douchetes
Et mout destrois.
A Dieu commant amouretes,
Car je m'en vois.
J'en feroie roinetes
S'estoie roys.
Comment que la chose empraigne:
A Dieu commant amouretes,
Car je m'en vois,
Souspirant en terre estrainge.

I commend my loves to God,
For I am going away,
To sigh in a foreign land.
I must leave the sweet things
Grieving, and much distressed.
I commend my loves to God,
For I am going away.
I would make them all queens
If I were king.
But whatever happens:
I commend my loves to God,
For I am going away,
To sigh in a foreign land.

part that would be the most familiar because of its constant repetition. In
the motet given as Example 7-10, the refrain from the rondeau *A Dieu
Commant* (printed in italics) appears in the middle voice—the first two
lines at the opening of the piece, the last line at the end. The intervening
lines of the new poem are deliberately written to merge with the sense of
the original refrain. A different poem is sung simultaneously in the upper
voice. The lower voice uses a melody from plainchant (a setting of the
words "Super te"), which is repeated starting at measure 27. The notes of
this voice that accompany the refrain (measures 1–6 and 48–52) are very
similar to those used in the lower voice of the original setting (Ex. 7-9).

Finally, one of Adam's most important contributions was in the
realm of drama. He wrote three dramas in Old French, one of which contains considerable amounts of music. This is the *Play of Robin and Marion*,
which is discussed in more detail below (see pp. 328–29). The music for the
play is in simple monophonic popular style, not very different from the
style of the main melody of the rondeau *A Dieu Commant.*

EXAMPLE 7-10   Adam de la Halle, motet, *A Dieu Commant/Aucun se Song/Super
Te.* From Nigel Wilkins, *The Lyric Works of Adam de la Hale,* Corpus Mensurabilis
Musicae, vol. 44 ([Rome]: American Institute of Musicology, 1967).

rer,   N'on-ques che - le   que j'a-moi - e   Ne me vaut mous -

si   four - me - ne Qu'il ni   queurt,   drois,   ne   lois.

trer   San - lant   ou   je me de - us - se   con - for - ter Ne

Gros   tour - nois   Ont   a - nu - les

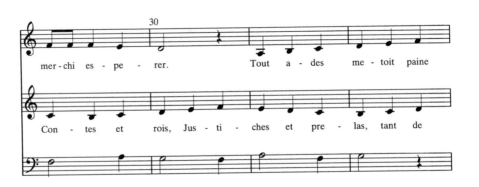

mer - chi es - pe - rer.   Tout   a - des   me - toit paine

Con - tes   et   rois, Jus - ti - ches et pre - las, tant de

a moi es - kie - ver; Trop m'i don - na a pen-ser Ains

fois Que main - te be - le com - pain - gne,

que je la peus-se ou - vli - er. Or voi je bien

Dont Ar - ras me - hain - gne, Lais - sent a -

sans dou -ter Que loi -aus hom est per - dus qui veut a - mer,

mis et mai - sons et har - nois, Et fui -

I. Aucun se sont loe d'amours,
   Mais je m'en doi plus que nus blas-
      mer,
   C'onques a nul jour
   N'i poi loiaute trouver,
   Je cuidai au premiers
   Avoir amie par loiaument
   Ouvrer,
   Mais g'i peusse longuement
   Baer,
   Car quant je miex amai,
   Plus me convient maus endurer,

I. There are some who praise love,
   But I must curse it more than any-
      one,
   For not for a single day
   Have I found loyalty.
   I thought at first
   That my own loyalty would
   Suffice,
   But I would have had to wait
   Forever,
   For the more faithful I was,
   The more pain I had to endure,

N'onques chele que j'amoie
Ne me vaut moustrer
Sanlant ou je me deusse conforter
Ne merchi esperer,
Tout ades metoit paine a moi
　　eskiever;
Trop m'i donna a penser
Ains que je la peusse ouvlier.
Or voi je bien sans douter
Que loiaus hom est perdus qui veut
　　amer,
Ne nus, che m'est vis, ne s'en doit
　　mesler
Fors cil qui bee a servir de guiller.

And she whom I loved
Never threw me
A comforting glance
Or gave me any hope for pity.
She took great pains to avoid me,

And gave me much trouble
Before I could forget her.
Now I see clearly
That a loyal man in love is lost,

And that in my mind no one should
　　get involved
Unless he decides to act deceitfully.

II. *A Dieu commant amouretes,*
Car je m'en vois
Dolans pour les douchetes,
Fors dou douc pais d'Artois,
Qui est si mus et destrois
Pour che que li bourgois
Ont este si fourmene
Qu'il n'i queurt, drois, ne lois.

Gros tournois
Ont anules
Contes et rois,
Justiches et prelas, tant de fois
Que mainte bele compaigne,
Dont Arras mehaingne,
Laissent amis et maisons et harnois,

Et fuient, cha deus, cha trois,
Souspirant en terre estrainge.

III. Super te.

II. *I commend my loves to God,*
For I am going away,
Grieving for the sweet things,
Far from the land of Artois,
Which is so silent and distressed
Because its inhabitants
Have been so afflicted
That they have no more courts,
　　rights, or laws.
The great tournaments
Have been cancelled
By counts and kings,
Judges and priests, so many times
That many of the finest people,
Those whom Arras disdains,
Have left their friends, their houses,
　　and their belongings,
And flee in twos and threes,
To sigh in a foreign land.

III. Over you.

A page from an Italian *lauda* manuscript, showing the beginning of Jacopone da Todi's *O Cristo* (see Example 7-12). The large decorated initial "O" has been cut out of the manuscript by some vandal. Biblioteca Nazionale Centrale, Florence.

ITALY

In Italy vernacular song developed under two main influences: the art of the troubadours and a local tradition of dance songs. Both influences were strong in the thirteenth century; before that time there is only sporadic evidence of music outside the plainchant repertoire.

Dance songs evolved from simple repetitive forms into more sophisticated, stylized structures for art songs (a common evolution in the history of music). The most popular of these was the *ballata* (from the Italian *ballare,* to dance). The ballata incorporated solo verses alternating with a choral refrain. The music was cast in two sections and the text was distributed between them according to the following scheme: AbbaA. (Again each section of the music is represented by a letter, upper case if sung with the refrain, lower case if sung with new text.) During the thirteenth century all ballatas seem to have been monophonic; not until the fourteenth century did they begin to appear in polyphonic settings (usually for three voices). The texts are mostly based on themes of love or contain moralistic advice.

The sacred song type called *lauda* (plural *laude*), was also in ballata form. The lauda ("song of praise") became particularly popular in the second half of the thirteenth century as a result of two social phenomena. The first was the activity of the Franciscan friars, a religious order founded in 1223 within the lifetime of St. Francis himself (1182–1226). The spread of the Franciscans in the thirteenth century was extraordinary. Their life in the outside world as opposed to a monastery, their espousal of a poor and simple way of life, and their zealous missionary activity soon made them visible throughout the Italian peninsula. The second phenomenon was a sudden rise of penitential fervor in the towns of northern Italy. Crowds of people would march about the town and countryside, beating themselves and heralding the end of the world. They were often known in contemporary writings as the flagellants.

The laude of this time are mostly simple syllabic settings of texts addressing the Virgin or describing aspects of the life of Christ or St. Francis. Cast in ballata form, with its repeated refrain, they lent themselves well to public performance. (One manuscript from the time, however, contains much more complex neumatic melodies and exemplifies the artistic elaboration to which these simple devotional songs were subject.) *A Tutta Gente* (Ex. 7-11) is only slightly neumatic and represents a style halfway between the two extremes. The text is in praise of the third-century Saint Margarita

EXAMPLE 7-11 Lauda, *A Tutta Gente*. After Fernando Liuzzi, *La lauda e i primordi della melodia italiana,* 2 vols. ([Rome]: Libreria dello Stato, [1935]).

I. *A tutta gente faccio prego e dico*

   Che laudi meco Margarita aulente.

   O vergine, che'n piccola etade
   A Dio videste e fecevi sua sposa,

   Et non voleste, per nobilitade,

   Che foss' en voi, esser del mondo
    rosa;
   Anci prendeste la fede Cristiana
   Che scaccia vana et fa a Dio ser-
    vente.
   A tutta gente . . .

IV. Si fosti piena e di virtu ornata,

   O gemma Margarita molto cara,
   Che chi vi'lege per sua avocata
   Guardata e da turbatione amara;
   Et accattate gratia di partire

   Da ogne dire o fare villanamente.
   A tutta gente . . .

I. *To all the world I make my prayer
   and say*

   *That they should praise with me the
   noble Margarita.*

   O virgin, who when you were young
   Dedicated yourself to God and be-
   came his spouse,
   And did not want, because of your
   nobility,
   To become a mere worldly orna-
   ment;
   You took up the Christian faith,
   Which disdains vain things, and be-
   came a servant of God.
   To all the world . . .

IV. You are so fully endowed with vir-
   tue,
   O Margarita, priceless pearl,
   That whoever is under duress of law
   Or is oppressed by bitter confusion
   May beg for your grace and protec-
   tion
   From all slander and evildoing.
   To all the world . . .

of Antioch, the daughter of a pagan priest, who as a young woman decided to adopt Christianity and remain a virgin all her life. Her relics were brought to Italy in the twelfth century, and as a result her cult became very popular there in the later Middle Ages. The poem is made up of five stanzas and commends the saint's virtue, calling upon the listeners to join in singing her praises. There is a pun on the name of the saint in the fourth stanza, as the word *margarita* in Italian also means a pearl. Each section of the music sets two lines of the text. The melody has a range of an octave plus the note below the final. The second section of the music is distinguished by starting at the top of the octave and making a quick descent to the final. This kind of contrast in range between the first and second sections is common to many of the two-part song forms both in Italian and in other vernacular languages. Although slight variants of ballata form appear in some of the laude, *A Tutta Gente* adheres exactly to the standard structure. The refrain (shown in italics) would be sung between each of the stanzas of the poem.

    One of the composers of the florid style of lauda was Jacopone da Todi (c. 1230–1306), a Franciscan who also contributed to the development of Italian vernacular drama by composing laude in dialogue form. The effectiveness of these dialogue laude is illustrated by Example 7-12, with its flexible approach to the ballata structure. The text is designed as a dialogue between Christ and an anonymous questioner. (The erring wife of the poem is an allegorical symbol both for the human soul and for the contemporary Church). The full poem is eighteen stanzas long. The refrain poses the question, and each stanza gives Christ's sad response. A higher pitch marks the beginning of the second section of the music (b), but there are variants in the repetition of this section (b'). The music of the refrain returns only in partial form (a') for the last two lines of each stanza: only the first and last phrases are used (the first slightly varied), giving a sense of compression to the melody. An inherent unity is imparted to the composition by the recurrence of descending neumes and by the sharing of cadences between sections.

EXAMPLE 7-12 Jacopone da Todi, lauda, *O Cristo*. After Fernando Liuzzi, *La lauda e i primordi della melodia italiana*, 2 vols. ([Rome]: Libreria dello Stato, [1935]).

b′
Di gio - ie   l'a - dor - na - - - - - i

Per a - ver - ne   ho - no - re;

a′
La - sciom-mi a dis - - o - no - re,

Fa - mi   gi - re   pe - na - to."

A
O Cri - sto 'ni - po - ten - te,

Do - ve   sie - te   in - vi - a - to,

Che si po - ve - - ra - men - - - - te

Gi - te   pel - le - - gri - na - to?

I. *O Cristo 'nipotente,*
Dove siete inviato,
Che si poveramente
Gite pellegrinato?
"Una sposa piglai,
Che datol' il mio core,
Di gioie l'adornai
Per averne honore;
Lasciommi a disonore,
Fami gire penato."
O Cristo 'nipotente, . . .

I. *O omnipotent Christ,*
Where are you going,
That you travel so poorly
In the guise of a pilgrim?
"I took a wife,
And gave her my heart,
I adorned her with joys,
So that I might have honor from her;
But she left me to dishonor,
And makes me wander in pain."
O omnipotent Christ, . . .

IBERIA

The Iberian peninsula, separated from the remainder of Europe by the Pyrenees, had a rich and diverse cultural development of its own during the Middle Ages. Invaded by tribes of Arabic and North African Muslims, known as the Moors, in the eighth century, the area soon became wealthy. Art, architecture, and scholarship flourished amid the tri-cultural groups of Muslims, Christians, and Jews. The southern cities of Seville, Cordoba, and Granada became centers of learning and artistic accomplishment. In the eleventh and twelfth centuries, northern Christian kings, regarding the Muslim presence as a constant offense, began the series of destructive assaults on the region known as the "reconquest." During this period Portugal gained its independence, and separate kingdoms such as Navarre, Aragon, Leon, and Castile were established in Spain. The political importance of Castile gradually made its dialect the prevalent language, and Castilian is still regarded as the standard form of Spanish today. In the thirteenth century, however, several dialects were still actively in use on the peninsula. One of these was Gallego-Portuguese (from Galicia and Portugal), which survived for several centuries as a poetic language even in Castilian areas. It was used for narrative poems such as the *cantigas de gesta* (the equivalent of the Old French *chansons de geste*) and for Iberian lyrics called *cantigas de amigo* ("songs of love").

Gallego-Portuguese is the language of two of the most important collections of Iberian vernacular song from the thirteenth century. The earlier and smaller collection is by a composer known as Martin Codax, who lived and worked during the early part of the thirteenth century in the town of Vigo on the northwestern coast above Portugal in Galicia. We know nothing of his life, and indeed the survival of his music at all is due to a lucky chance. Although the texts for his songs occur in two manuscripts, the music for them was only discovered in 1914, on a single parchment page in the binding of a book.

The collection of Martin Codax comprises seven songs, all *cantigas de amigo* and all written from the point of view of a woman, as was traditional with the genre. The woman sits in Vigo, looking out over the sea and awaiting the return of her lover. The songs are all of the same poetic form, which suggests that they might have been composed as a cycle. They all have three-line stanzas, made up of a rhyming couplet and a single-line refrain. From one stanza to the next, whole lines may be repeated intact or with just the final (rhyming) word changed. The melodies are simple and narrow in range, and make use of a varied first phrase for the rhyming couplet and a new phrase for the refrain.

In the first song of the collection, *Ondas Do Mar De Vigo* (Ex. 7-13), only four text lines apart from the refrain are used, sometimes with varied rhyming words, to make up the whole poem. The woman's double appeal—to the sea and to God—is profoundly moving in its artlessness (disguising the art of the poet). The musical phrases become progressively more ornate towards their endings. Very slight variants are introduced at the beginning and end of the second phrase, and the third phrase, after its opening, which subtly delineates the invocation to God, has a continuation that echoes the beginning of the song. All three phrases share the same cadence on G. The extreme simplicity of the materials, both textual and musical, belies the haunting beauty of this song.

EXAMPLE 7-13 Martin Codax, *Ondas Do Mar De Vigo.* After Higinio Anglés, *La música de las Cantigas de Santa María del Rey Alfonso el Sabio,* 3 vols. (Barcelona: Biblioteca Central, 1943–64).

I. Ondas do mar de Vigo,
   Se vistes meu amigo,
   E ay Deus! Se verra cedo!

II. Ondas do mar levado,
    Se vistes meu amado,
    E ay Deus! Se verra cedo!

III. Se vistes meu amigo,
     O por que eu sospiro,
     E ay Deus! Se verra cedo!

IV. Se vistes meu amado,
    Por que ey gran coidado,
    E ay Deus! Se verra cedo!

I. O waves of the sea of Vigo,
   If you have seen my friend,
   O God, let him come back quickly.

II. O waves of the rough sea,
    If you have seen my lover,
    O God, let him come back quickly.

III. If you have seen my friend,
     Him for whom I sigh,
     O God, let him come back quickly.

IV. If you have seen my lover,
    For whom I have great concern,
    O God, let him come back quickly.

The Iberian peninsula in the thirteenth century.

The second, larger collection of medieval Iberian vernacular song comprises one of the most remarkable repertoires of the period. It is also in Gallego-Portuguese and was compiled at the court of King Alfonso X (1221–1284), known as "El Sabio" ("The Wise"). In 1230, under Ferdinand III (Alfonso's father), the kingdoms of Leon and Castile had been united, and Alfonso gained the succession in 1252. Although he was a man of immense political ambition and his authoritarian practices led to rebellion of the nobles, revolts among his subjects, and civil war between his sons, Alfonso's reign was also marked by great cultural, scientific, and literary accomplishment. Under his guidance were produced the *Siete partidas*, a huge compilation of legal knowledge; the "Alfonsine tables," a collection of all known astronomical data; and several other scientific and historical works. Alfonso built up the schools at Seville and Salamanca, and he supported the cultural and scholarly contributions of the Jewish and Moorish populations within his realm.

The most enduring musical heritage of Alfonso the Wise is a collection of four hundred songs in honor of the Virgin Mary. These are known as the *Cantigas de Santa Maria* and are gathered in three beautifully illustrated manuscripts from the late thirteenth and early fourteenth centuries. The lavish production of these manuscripts and the careful organization of the collection make it clear that Alfonso intended the *Cantigas de Santa*

Maria to represent a monument to his reign as significant as his administrative and scientific achievements.

Every single song in the collection is devoted to the Virgin. Most of the Cantigas tell in narrative form stories of miracles performed by Mary on behalf of everyday people of the time: men and women, knights and nuns, merchants, robbers, an incestuous widow, a pregnant abbess. The first song, and every tenth song thereafter, is a general song of praise in honor of Mary.

All the Cantigas are in strophic form with a refrain; most have from six to eight stanzas. The poetry uses a rhyme scheme known as the *zajal,* a Moorish verse form in which a repeated rhyme in each stanza is differentiated from the rhyme in the refrain; the last line of the stanza, however, anticipates the return of the refrain. Musically, the form is like that of the Italian ballata: there are two sections of music, repeated in the pattern AbbaA.

The range of the melodies is not very great, but the subtlety and sophistication of their construction is considerable. Alfonso's court was an international cultural center, drawing upon the resources of troubadours scattered by the Albigensian crusade, northern French travelers, local chant traditions, and the colorful music of the kingdom's Jewish and Moorish citizens. The melodic construction of the Cantigas is dependent upon the modal patterns, which support the structure of the verse and the form of the music. Echoing the rhyme scheme, part of the music of the refrain is often used to set the last line of each stanza. Sometimes short motifs or whole phrases tie the refrain to the melody of the stanzas, thus unifying the whole.

Often, however, there is a deliberate tension or contrast between rhyme scheme and musical scheme. This kind of counterpoint between poetry and music makes the Cantigas constantly varied and fascinating. As in the repertoire of the troubadours and trouvères, both of which also make use of strophic songs with their constant repetition of the same music for each stanza, a direct and obvious correspondence between music and poetry is often avoided in favor of a subtle interplay between the two. Despite the large number of songs in the Cantigas collection, each one is an independently conceived artistic construction in its own right.

Example 7-14, an unusually extended composition of fourteen stanzas, illustrates the richness and scope of the Cantigas. The story tells how a pilgrim was tricked by the devil into committing suicide for a sin he had committed. The devil and St. James argue over his soul, which is ultimately restored to him by the intervention of the Virgin Mary.

A brief synopsis is placed at the head of the Cantiga in the original manuscript to introduce the story; then the refrain and first stanza are given with their music, and the remainder of the text is written out underneath.

The refrain is made up of two pairs of lines, the first line in each pair having eight syllables and the second having five syllables. Each pair is set to a single phrase of music, the first phrase having an open ending on F, the second having a closed ending on D. The second section of the music has only one phrase, which is sung twice to eleven-syllable lines and stresses the higher part of the range with reiterated notes on A before descending to another open cadence on F. The remainder of the stanza uses almost the same music (and has the same verse structure) as the refrain. Between each of the stanzas the refrain is repeated.

The quantity of musical material for this Cantiga is very small, being made up essentially of only three phrases. Even among these three phrases musical gestures are shared, such as the note repetition at the beginning of the refrain and the beginning of the stanza, the conjunct descent from A to D in the two phrases of the refrain, the F cadences, and the descending third skips. But the unfolding of the story, the setting both of repeated text and new text to the same music, the diverse line and phrase lengths, the mixture of syllabic and neumatic groups—all these contribute to a composition of great fascination and appeal.

EXAMPLE 7-14   Cantiga de Santa Maria, *Non E Gran Cousa*. After Higinio Anglés, *La música de las Cantigas de Santa María del Rey Alfonso el Sabio,* 3 vols. (Barcelona: Biblioteca Central, 1943–64).

5. Non e gran cou-sa se sa - be Bon jo - y - zo dar_____

A Ma - dre do que o mun-do Tod' a de jo - i - gar.

Esta e como Santa Maria juigou a alma do romeu que ya a Santiago, que sse matou na carreira por engano do diabo, que tornass' ao corpo et fezesse penedença.	This is how Holy Mary judged the soul of a pilgrim who was going to Santiago, who killed himself on the way through a trick of the Devil but was brought back to life and did penance.

I. *Non e gran cousa se sabe* *Bon joyzo dar* *A Madre do que o mundo* *Tod' a de joigar.* Mui gran razon e que sabia dereito Quen Deus troux' en seu corp', e de seu peito Mamentou, et d'el despeito Nunca foi fillar; Poren ue sen me sospeito Que a quis avondar. *Non e gran cousa . . .*	I. *It is no great marvel if She knows* *How to render good judgment,* *For She is the Mother of Him* *Who has to judge the entire world.* There is very good reason that She would know righteousness, For She carried God in her body and suckled Him At her breast, and was never Rejected by Him; Therefore did He grant to her An abundance of good sense. *It is no great marvel . . .*
III. Este romeu con bona voluntade Ya a Santiago de verdade; Pero d'esto fez maldade, Que ant'albergar Foi con moller sen bondade, Sen con ela casar. *Non e gran cousa . . .*	III. The pilgrim did indeed go To Santiago in good will; But on this occasion he committed a sin, For before lodging for the night He went with a woman of ill repute, With no intention of marrying her. *It is no great marvel . . .*

[The pilgrim is tricked into mutilating himself and committing suicide for his sin; the devil and St. James argue over possession of his soul; they agree to abide by the decision of the Virgin Mary.]

XIV. Este joyzo logo foi comprido, Et o romeu morto foi resorgido De que foi pois Deo servido. Mas nunca cobrar Pod' o de que foi falido Con que fora pecar. *Non e gran cousa . . .*	XIV. So Her judgment was carried out, And the pilgrim was brought back from the dead So that he might serve God thenceforth. But he never recovered The part that was missing With which he had sinned. *It is no great marvel . . .*

ENGLAND

In England the history of vernacular song is a complicated one, for much of the territory of the kingdom lay overseas, in what is now France. Before the Norman Conquest the language and literature of England was Anglo-Saxon, in which, between the seventh and twelfth centuries, a number of masterpieces of epic and narrative poetry were produced, including the heroic epic *Beowulf*. No lyric poetry was written in Anglo-Saxon, though the sagas (historical epics) and other poems may have been recited to simple melodic formulas.

When Norman French became the official language of the country (from the eleventh to the fourteenth centuries), romance and history became the dominant literary genres. Geoffrey Gaimer's two-part history of England, *Histoire des Bretons* and *Estorie des Engles,* was written in verse. One of the most important early sources of the Tristan legend, Thomas's *Tristan,* was written towards the end of the twelfth century. During this time, when commerce and other interchange (including royal marriage) was common between England and the continent, we must assume that courtly music was primarily French, and that trouvère music flourished in England as it did in France. King Richard I of England ("Richard the Lion-Heart") was the subject of trouvère songs, as we have seen, and was himself both a poet and a composer.

English, however, was not completely superseded by French during this period, and Anglo-Saxon evolved into Middle English, in which were created several poems, songs, and romances. The famous allegorical tale *The Owl and the Nightingale* depicts in verse a debate between a religious, monkish owl and a free-spirited, lively nightingale. Romances taken over from continental practice and infused with local traditions, especially the Arthurian legends, flourished in the twelfth and thirteenth centuries. A number of lyric poems are also extant from this time, on both secular and sacred themes.

The earliest Middle English lyric poems with music are supposed to have been written by the English hermit St. Godric around the middle of the twelfth century. One of these (Ex. 7-15) is a prayer to the Virgin Mary in rhyming verse set to a melody that mixes syllabic passages with short neumatic groups. These groups serve to unify the music, as they are almost all brief conjunct descending neumes of similar shape. The two stanzas that make up the whole song are set to similar but subtly varied music. Within each stanza the first three phrases have an open ending on A, while the last phrase descends to a closed cadence on D.

A few songs in Middle English survive from the thirteenth century. Their subject matter ranges from laments on the ephemeral nature of happiness to an exalted elegy on the joy of love. The first topic may be repre-

EXAMPLE 7-15 St. Godric, *Sainte Marie*. After E. J. Dobson and F. Ll. Harrison, *Medieval English Songs* (New York: Cambridge University Press, 1979).

I. Sainte Marie, viergene,
   Moder Jesu Christes Nazarene,
   Onfoo, schild, help thin Godric,

   Onfonge bring heyliche with thee in
   Godes riche.

II. Sainte Marie, Christes bur,
   Maidenes clenhad, moderes flur,

   Dilie min sinne, rix in min mod,
   Bring me to winne with the selfe
   God.

I. Holy Mary, Virgin,
   Mother of Jesus Christ of Nazareth,
   Receive, O Shield, and help your
   Godric,
   And once received bring him honor-
   ably with you to God's kingdom.

II. Holy Mary, bower of Christ,
   Purity of maidens, flower of moth-
   ers,
   Wipe out my sins, rule my spirit,
   Bring me to bliss with God himself.

sented by the song *Worldes Blis* (Ex. 7-16), which presents a sad and melancholy picture of life. Here, as in *Sainte Marie*, small melodic motifs are used
to bind the music together (a descending three-note neume appears
throughout), and parallel verse patterns are reflected in parallel musical
phrases. The phrase for the fourth line is a repetition of that for the second
(both have the rhyme *-on*), and lines 5 and 6, and 7 and 8, are paired by
rhyme and parallelism of construction. The range of the music is exactly
one octave from D, and G is used as the pitch goal, as it both opens the song
and ends it, as well as forming the cadence for five of the ten phrases.

The poem as a whole has seven stanzas. The remaining six urge the
adoption of a good life here on earth, for death comes soon, and all worldly
things are transitory compared to the eternity of heaven or hell.

EXAMPLE 7-16 *Worldes Blis.* After E. J. Dobson and F. Ll. Harrison, *Medieval
English Songs* (New York: Cambridge University Press, 1979).

Worldes blis ne last no throwe,	The joy of the world does not last a moment,
It went and wit awey anon.	It departs and disappears immediately.
The langer that ich hit iknowe,	The longer I know it,
The lass ich finde pris tharon.	The less do I value it.
For al it is imeind mid care,	For it is all mixed with worry,
Mid serwen and mid evel fare.	With sorrows, and with evil.
And atte laste povre and bare,	And at the last it leaves man poor and bare,
It lat man wan it ginth agon.	When it begins to disappear.
Al the blis this heer and thare,	All the joy that is both here and there,
Bilucth at ende weep and mon.	Comes at the end to weeping and moaning.

The simplicity and beauty of Middle English song can nowhere be seen better than in the exquisite strophic love song *Bryd One Brere* (Ex. 7-17). Here the artful alliteration, assonance, and rhythmical repetition of the verse are matched by a melody whose hypnotic intensity is confined almost entirely to the range of a sixth. The shape of the melody, the linking or separation of phrases by common tone or leap, and the definition and arrival at pitch goals are handled with great mastery and assurance.

Bryd One Brere survived by accident: it was found copied on the back of a papal edict. The notation makes use of the new rhythmic values of the time. This lovely piece shows that the composition of vernacular song was very much alive even in a country dominated by the language of the continent.

EXAMPLE 7-17 *Bryd One Brere.* After E. J. Dobson and F. Ll. Harrison, *Medieval English Songs* (New York: Cambridge University Press, 1979).

I. Bryd one breere, briht brid one brere,
   Kynd is come of Love, love to crave.

   Blithful brid, on me thu rewe
   Or greith, leef, greith thu me my grave.

II. Ich am so blith, so briht, brid one brere,
    Whan I see that hende in halle.
    Yhe is whit of lim, loveli, trewe,
    Yhe is fayr, and flur of alle.

III. Mihte ich hir at wille haven,
     Stedfast of love, loveli, trewe,
     Of mi sorwe yhe may me saven:
     Joy and bliss were er me newe.

I. Bird on a briar, bright bird on a briar,
   Man has come to beg love from Love.

   Gracious bird, have pity on me
   Or prepare, my beloved, prepare for me my grave.

II. I am so happy, so bright, bird on a briar,
    When I see that lady in the hall.
    She is white of limb, lovely and true,
    She is fair and flower of all.

III. If I could have her at will,
     Steadfast in love, lovely and true,
     She might save me from my sorrow:
     Joy and bliss would then ever be mine.

GERMANY

After the disintegration of Charlemagne's great empire in the ninth century, Germany remained divided into several small principalities, duchies, and independent free cities. An attempt at central authority was made in 962 by the coronation of Otto I as Holy Roman Emperor. Otto's aim was to revive the empire of Charlemagne, which was itself a revival of ancient glory. His success and that of later emperors was only partial: although the emperors owned territory in Lorraine, Sicily, and part of southern Italy, several German dukes (especially those of Bavaria, Saxony, and Franconia) retained considerable power. In addition, the emperors' divided role as both rulers of a dispersed empire and kings of Germany and their nominal dependence upon the pope weakened their authority. The growth of the feudal system, with its strict divisions between classes and its pattern of local allegiances, also tended to increase the power of local lords and dukes. In the twelfth and thirteenth centuries, however, and especially under the Hohenstaufen dynasty, the empire expanded eastwards, and a period of increased control stood out from the general turbulence. This period was short-lived; and in contrast to the increasing centralization of the kingdoms in France, Iberia, and England, Germany remained a collection of small territories of competing interests. In the cities, an increasingly prosperous middle class, made up of merchants, traders, and bankers, came more and more to influence German culture.

The German language in the Middle Ages may be classified into two categories: geographical and chronological. The German spoken in the hilly and mountainous regions of the south is known as High German; the language of the northern lowlands is called Low German. Historically, the divisions are as follows: the language spoken and written from approximately the eighth century to the eleventh is known as Old German; from the eleventh to the sixteenth century, Middle German.

Much of the literature of the central Middle Ages, and the literature that most affected the course of music history, was written in Middle High German. Epic poetry was influenced by the Old Norse legends and included poems such as *Gudrun* and the *Nibelungenlied* (both of these dating from the early thirteenth century). At about the same time were written the two great chivalric romances, *Parzival* by Wolfram von Eschenbach and the *Tristan* of Gottfried von Strassburg. Both of these were probably recited at banquets and courtly gatherings to simple melodic formulas like the Old French chansons de geste.

Gottfried's *Tristan* is as readable and gripping today as when it was first written. Music echoes throughout the story. Both Tristan and his lover, Isolde, are accomplished musicians. Both are praised for their mastery of singing and of several instruments, and for the sweetness and beauty of their musical gifts. They perform publicly to the delight of all their listeners, and they play and sing together at the great spiritual and erotic consummation of the story in the Lovers' Cave:

> When they tired of stories, they resumed their favorite pleasure of playing the harp and singing sadly and sweetly. They busied their hands and their voices in turn. They performed amorous *lais* and the accompaniments to them, varying the delight as it suited them: if one took the harp, the other sang the tune with wistful tenderness. And indeed the sounds of harp and voice, merging their sound in each other, echoed in the cave so sweetly, that it was dedicated to sweet love.

In the twelfth and thirteenth centuries, and as a clear parallel to the musical traditions of the troubadours and the trouvères, a German repertoire of vernacular lyric song developed; it had important individual qualities, but was also dependent upon earlier models. This repertoire is called *Minnesang* ("love song"), and its practitioners *Minnesinger*.

The development of Minnesang began in the late twelfth century. The travels of jongleurs and trouvères must have provided models for German courts, and the Hohenstaufen emperor Frederick I, who reigned from 1152 to 1190, married a French duke's daughter, who brought a French trouvère with her among her attendants. Soon Minnesang flourished in towns and courts all over Germany, French traditions mingling with native elements such as feudal metaphors and clarity of poetic structure.

Minnesang in general is categorized according to content; it has many parallels to the categories of the troubadours and trouvères. The alba has its counterpart in the *Tagelied* ("day song"), which depicts the separation of lovers at dawn. Courtly love songs, influenced by Occitan, Old French, and Gallego-Portuguese models, are found in the Middle High German lyric in two kinds: those from the point of view of the man, known as *Minnelied* ("love song"), and those from the point of view of the woman, called *Frauenlied* ("woman's song"). An interesting example of cross-fertilization of styles may be seen in the many Minnelieder that begin with a description of nature or the season. The tenso and jeu-parti of the troubadours and trouvères were modified in the German repertoire to present alternating stanzas, not from two different poets, but from the man and the woman in love. This genre is known as the *Wechsel* ("interchange"). Two other categories with direct parallels in other languages are the *Tanzlied* ("dance song") and *Kreuzlied* ("crusade song").

All of these types, though distinct in content, are poetically and musically in the same form: they are strophic songs. Within the music of each stanza, however, a repetition scheme that we have seen crystallizing in the songs of the troubadours and trouvères soon became standardized. This repetition scheme is known as *Bar* form and is simply represented by the

Walther von der Vogelweide in a miniature from one of the Minnesang manuscripts, Universitätsbibliothek, Heidelberg.

alphabetical format aab. The first two lines of the poetry are sung to the first section of the melody (a), which is then repeated for the second pair of lines. Then the last part of the stanza is sung to the second section of the melody (b). Sometimes the b section deliberately uses the same closing phrase as the a section; this is called "rounded" Bar form.

Two genres of Minnesang are not strophic; they are the *Leich,* the German equivalent of the lai, which is in several stanzas but is through-composed, and the *Spruch,* which is a single-stanza composition of moral, didactic, or political content. The Spruch began as an imitation of the Occitan sirventes, but as it grew in popularity in the German courts it gradually came to deal with a wider range of topics, including religion, social commentary, irony, and insult.

In the first main period of Minnesang, from about 1180 to 1220, the most accomplished of the Minnesinger was Walther von der Vogelweide (c. 1170–1230). He appears to have come from a poor family of the lower aristocracy and to have spent most of his life working for different dukes and nobles, and for three emperors. He was active in Vienna, then part of a separate dukedom in the eastern part of the empire and one of the many towns that were growing in importance as a result of their situation on the new trade route along the Danube. Walther was regarded by his contemporaries as the greatest poet of his time. In Gottfried von Strassburg's *Tristan* he is called a "nightingale," who sings in a high, clear voice over the countryside, and is the "leader of them all."

Before Walther von der Vogelweide, there was a distinction between the aristocratic composers, who wrote Minnelieder, and the lower-class musicians who were associated more with the Spruch. With the rise of the merchant class in Germany in the thirteenth century and the spreading of culture from the aristocracy to the middle classes, both genres became equally popular, and Walther was influential in bringing the Spruch to the same level of poetic artistry as the Minnelied.

Not many melodies for Walther's poems have survived, though some of them were clearly based on earlier troubadour models and can be sung to their melodies. One song that seems to have its own melody is the crusade song *Nu Alrest Lebe Ich Mir Werde* (Ex. 7-18), which describes Walther's joy at seeing the Holy Land. It has five stanzas and marvels at the sacred places, ending by claiming the rights of possession for Christianity. It may have been written while Walther was in the service of the emperor Frederick II, who led a crusade in 1228. The range of the music is an octave, with a final on D. It is in rounded Bar form, the b section using the same ending phrase as the a section. As is common in such two-part forms of the time, the b section is distinguished by its lying in the upper part of the melodic range, which has been left unclaimed by the a section. Neumes of two, three, and four notes are mixed with syllabic setting of the text. The fame of this song, later known as the *Palästinalied* ("Palestine Song"), led to its being used as a model for both Latin and German imitations.

EXAMPLE 7-18   Walther von der Vogelweide, *Nu Alrest Lebe Ich Mir Werde.* After Friedrich Gennrich, *Troubadours, Trouvères, Minne- und Meistergesang* (Cologne: Arno Volk-Verlag, 1951).

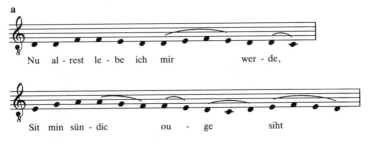

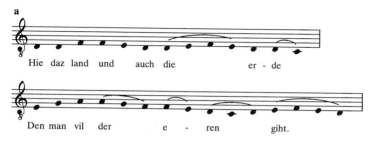

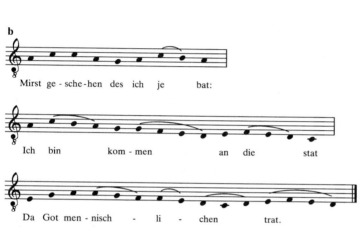

I.a	Nu alrest lebe ich mir werde,	I.a	Now is my life fully blessed,

<table>
<tr><td>I.a</td><td>Nu alrest lebe ich mir werde,
Sit min sündic ouge siht</td></tr>
<tr><td>a</td><td>Hie daz land und auch die erde
Den man vil der eren giht.</td></tr>
<tr><td>b</td><td>Mirst geschehen des ich je bat:</td></tr>
<tr><td></td><td>Ich bin kommen an die stat
Da Got mennischlichen trat.</td></tr>
<tr><td>II.a</td><td>Schoeniu lant rich unde here,</td></tr>
<tr><td></td><td>Swaz ich der noch han gesehen,</td></tr>
<tr><td>a</td><td>So bist duz ir aller ere.
Waz ist wunders hie geschehen!</td></tr>
<tr><td>b</td><td>Daz ein magt ein kint gebar!
Here über aller engel schar,
Was daz niht ein wunder gar?</td></tr>
</table>

<table>
<tr><td>I.a</td><td>Now is my life fully blessed,
Since my sinful eyes have seen</td></tr>
<tr><td>a</td><td>The Holy Land and the earth
Which has been so honored.</td></tr>
<tr><td>b</td><td>What I have always wanted has
happened:
I have come to the city
Where God appeared as man.</td></tr>
<tr><td>II.a</td><td>Of all beautiful lands, rich and
splendid,
That I have seen till now,</td></tr>
<tr><td>a</td><td>You are the most honored
What wonders happened here!</td></tr>
<tr><td>b</td><td>A virgin gave birth to a son!
Lord of all the angels,
Was that not a wonder of won-
ders?</td></tr>
</table>

The second main period of Minnesang (c. 1220–1300) saw a move away from the courtly ideals of the past and an increasing emphasis upon social realism, popular and rustic themes, and even parody of the whole topic of courtly love. Many poets were active during this period, the best known of whom are Neidhart von Reuental (c. 1180–1250), Tannhäuser (c. 1200–1270), and Heinrich von Meissen (c. 1250–1318). The difference in the backgrounds of these three Minnesinger is representative of the trends of the time. Neidhart von Reuental was a member of a family of knights serving the Duke of Bavaria and was himself later given land within the feudal system. Tannhäuser was an impoverished nobleman who traveled widely among the courts. Heinrich von Meissen was neither a noble nor a knight but a member of the middle class. His poetic and musical gifts, however, caused him to be accepted and highly regarded in the aristocratic circles in which he found employment.

Themes of irony, wit, and rustic humor are particularly pronounced in the songs of Neidhart von Reuental. They often begin with a description of nature and the season and then turn to some realistic incident, sometimes depicting a conversation in alternating stanzas. Girls complain about the difficulties of finding decent men or disdain the local country bumpkin in favor of a polished knight; men insult each other or moralize about life. Often the name of the poet himself appears in the last stanza, as the perfect suitor or companion, or as an outside observer or commentator. The language is lively and down-to-earth, and the scenes are realistically drawn, the favorite locale being a country dance.

The songs that begin with a description of nature usually fall into either a "summer" category or a "winter" category, and the Middle High German words *sumer* or *winder* frequently appear in the first line. Sometimes Neidhart deliberately satirizes even his own convention by starting a winter song with a reference to summer. ("Oh, dear summer, how your brightness is missed. Frost and snow now cover everything. . . .")

Neidhart's style marks a change in the history of vernacular song. No longer is the theme of courtly love self-sufficient. The country settings, conversational tone, ironic exchanges, and deliberately distancing shift to the poet's viewpoint all serve to undermine the standard conventions and bring a new realism to the poetry and music of the thirteenth century. The melodies are simply constructed and are primarily syllabic. They tend to use many more skips, usually of a third, and more repeated notes than troubadour or trouvère melodies, thus giving a squarer, less flexible impression. The settings continue to be strophic.

Neidhart's song *Meie, Din Liehter Schin* (Ex. 7-19), which has four stanzas altogether, contrasts the poet's unhappiness in love with the deliberately misleading opening image of springtime. Irony and sarcasm lend pungency to the poem. The setting, which is entirely syllabic throughout, is in Bar form, with one section of music for the first six lines of the poetry,

EXAMPLE 7-19   Neidhart von Reuental, *Meie, Din Liehter Schin.* After Wolfgang Schmieder, *Lieder von Neidhart (von Reuental),* Denkmäler der Tonkunst in Österreich, vol. 71 (Graz: Akademische Druck- und Verlaganstalt, 1960).

a

Mei - e,   din lieh - ter schin

Und diu klei - nen vo - ge - lin

Brin-gent vröu-den vol - len schrin.

Daz si   wil - le - ko - men sin!

Ich bin an den vröu-den min

Mit der werl - de kranc.

a

Al - le tag ist min klag,

Von der ich daz bes - te sag

Und ir hol - dez her - ze trag

Daz ich der niht wol be - hag.

Von den schul-den ich ver - zag

Daz mir nie ge - lanc,

b

Al - so noch ge - nuo - gen an ir die - nest ist ge - lun - gen,

Die nach guo - ter wi - be lo - ne hö - ve - schli-chen run - gen.

Nu han ich bei - du um sust ge - die - net und ge - sun - gen.

I.a Meie, din liehter schin Und diu kleinen vogelin Bringent vröuden vollen schrin. Daz si willekomen sin! Ich bin an den vröuden min Mit der werlde kranc.	**I.a** O May, your shining brightness And the little birds Bring a flood of joy. Welcome to you! As to my own joys, I am sick with the world.
a Alle tag ist min klag, Von der ich daz beste sag Und ir holdez herze trag Daz ich der niht wol behag. Von den schulden ich verzag Daz mir nie gelanc,	**a** Every day I lament That she of whom I speak so well And who has my heart Does not feel kindly towards me. I should leave For lack of success,
b Also noch genuogen an ir dienest ist gelungen, Die nach guoter wibe lone höves- chlichen rungen.	**b** For many others have been fortu- nate in her service, Who have sought rewards from the noble lady in a courtly man- ner.
Nu han ich beidu um sust ge- dienet und gesungen.	But I have served her and sung for her in vain.

repeated for the second six lines. The second section of the music is used for the last three lines, which are far longer than the earlier ones. The melody opens with striking upward leaps, and although the remainder of the music is mainly conjunct, a descending fourth marks the fourth phrase. The b section opens at the top of the octave and is thus clearly differentiated. One descending third and one ascending third are the only intervals that enliven the prevailingly conjunct motion of this section. The return in ensuing stanzas of the opening leaps thus retains its striking effect.

The Minnesinger known as Tannhäuser was involved in the fifth crusade and is the author of several examples of the Leich and Spruch as well as many Minnelieder. He continued the serious courtly song alongside the newer, parodistic style cultivated by Neidhart. Example 7-20 (*Est Hiut Ein Wunniclicher Tac*) is a song of penitence with a far longer b section than the a section. Only the first of four stanzas is given here. The range is narrow, staying mostly within a sixth, and many phrases are confined to a fourth. Parallelism of melodic structure ties many of the phrases together, and whole or partial phrases from the a section reappear towards the end of the melody.

EXAMPLE 7-20   Tannhäuser, *Est Hiut Ein Wunniclicher Tac.* After Ronald J. Taylor, *The Art of the Minnesinger: Songs of the Thirteenth Century Transcribed and Edited with Textual and Musical Commentaries* (Cardiff: University of Wales Press, 1968) and J. W. Thomas, *Tannhäuser: Poet and Legend, with Texts and Translations of His Works* (Chapel Hill: The University of North Carolina Press, 1974).

a

Est hiut' ein   wün - nic - li - cher tac.

Nu pfle - ge min   der al - ler din - ge wal - te,

Daz ich mit sael - den müe - ze we - sen

Unt ich ge - büe - ze mi - ne gro - ze schul - de.

a

Wand ich mich wol ge - hel - fen mac,

Al - so daz ich die se - le min be - hal - te,

Daz ich vor sün - den si ge - ne - sen.

Unt daz ich noch er - wer - be Go - tes hul - de.

b

Nu geb er mir so stae - ten muot,

Daz ez der lip ver - die - ne so,

Daz mir Got dan - ken müe - ze.

Daz mir daz en - de wer - de guot,

Unt ouch diu se - le wer - de vro.

Min schei-den wer - de süe - ze.

Daz mich diu hel - le gar ver - ber,

Des hel - fe mir der rei - ne.

Unt vüe - ge mir des ich da ger,

Daz mich diu hoeh - ste vröi - de si ge - mei - ne.

Als ich der ma - ge muoz en - bern, daz ich dort vriun - de vin - de,

Die mi - ner kunf - te wer - den vro, daz ich ge - hei - zen müg' ein

sael - den - ri - chez in - ge - sin - de.

I.a Est hiut' ein wünniclicher tac.
Nu pflege min der aller dinge
    walte,
Daz ich mit saelden müeze wesen
Unt ich gebüeze mine groze
    schulde.

a Wand ich mich wol gehelfen mac,
Also daz ich die sele min behalte,
Daz ich vor sünden si genesen.

Unt daz ich noch erwerbe Gotes

I.a Today is a wonderful day.
Please care for me, You who
    watch over all,
That I might live a blessed life
And repent me of my great of-
    fences.

a May the Lord provide me aid,
That I might save my soul
And receive redemption for my
    sins,
And still receive God's mercy.

b Nu geb er mir so staeten muot,

Daz ez der lip verdiene so,
Daz mir Got danken müeze.
Daz mir daz ende werde guot,
Unt ouch diu sele werde vro.
Min scheiden werde süeze.
Daz mich diu helle gar verber,

Des helfe mir der reine.
Unt vüege mir des ich da ger,
Daz mich diu hoehste vröide si gemeine.
Als ich der mage muoz enbern, daz ich dort vriunde vinde,

Die miner kunfte werden vro, daz ich geheizen müg' ein saeldenrichez ingesinde.

b May the Lord grant me a steady heart,

That is so deserving of his love
That God will reward me.
May I have a peaceful end,
And may my soul be happy.
Let my death be a gentle one.
May I escape from the jaws of hell,

Protected by my purity.
Provide for my needs,
That I may share in highest joy.

And when I have to leave my companions, may I find friends in the other world,
Who are so happy with my songs that I shall win fame amongst the knights in heaven.

The last member of this second group of Minnesinger was Heinrich von Meissen. His songs include the new themes of realism and nature but are of a more serious nature than those of most of his contemporaries. His many poems in the genre of the Spruch that were written in praise of courtly women and in praise of the Virgin earned him the name "Frauenlob" ("praiser of women"). He had both secular and ecclesiastical patrons, including the Archbishop of Mainz, and for the last part of his life he lived in Mainz, where his tombstone in the cathedral may still be seen.

The dark quality of Frauenlob's poetry is exemplified by the Spruch given as Example 7-21, which laments his approaching death and is provided here in full. The music uses rounded Bar form, with the last phrase of the b section repeating the final phrase of the a section. The second statement of the a section is slightly varied, to accommodate the changes in the poetry. There is also a considerable amount of motivic repetition between sections, especially of ascending and descending three-note neumes. The opening of the b section employs the upper part of the melodic range for the first time. Although much of the melody is conjunct, skips of a third are quite frequent, and the final phrase uses seven such skips, both ascending and descending. In the last phrase of each section a falling five-note melisma from C down to D is used to set the words "tot" ("death"), "iamirlichin" ("sad"), and again "tot," respectively. A flexible use of the Hypolydian mode is apparent, with a concentration on the lower fourth C–F and frequent repetition of the reciting note A, but with an irregular ending away from the final and uncharacteristic leaps and interval chains. The sense of wandering pitch focus reflects the despair of the text.

EXAMPLE 7-21 Heinrich von Meissen, *Myn Vroud 1st Gar Czugangyn.* After Heinrich Rietsch, *Gesänge von Frauenlob, Reinmar v. Zweter und Alexander,* Denkmäler der Tonkunst in Österreich, vol. 41 (Graz: Akademische Druck- und Verlaganstalt, 1960).

a Myn vroud ist gar czugangyn;
Nu horit iamirliche clag:
Mich rüwit myne sünde
Di ich begangyn han myn tage;
Der ist leydir also vil
Nu wil der tot mich breng der werld
   czu nichte.

a Myn lebyn wert nicht lange;
Der tot myn ende hot gesworn.
Waz ich an yn gesende
Das ist allis gar vorlorn,
Wen he mich myt ym nemyn wil.
Owe der iamirlichin czu vorsichte!

b Mich hilft nich vrey gamute,
Noch kundekeyt, noch obyrmüt,
Noch allir vrouwyn gute.
Myn tognt, myn kraft, myn synnyn:
Das ist allis gar vorlorn.
Der mich czu gesellin hot dyr korn
Das ist der tot, myt dem mus ich von
   hynnyn.

a My joy has completely vanished;
Listen now to my sad lament:
I repent of the sins
That I committed during my life;
There are indeed so many of them
That death will bring my life to
   nothing.

a I have not long to live;
Death has sworn my end.
Whatever pleas I make to him
Are all in vain,
For he wants to take me with him.
Alas for this sad certainty!

b Happiness does not help me,
Nor wisdom, nor pride,
Nor all the kindness of ladies.
My virtue, my strength, my senses:
All these are completely lost.
The one who has chosen me
Is Death, and with him must I de-
   part.

The tradition of monophonic vernacular song continued far longer in Germany than in the other European countries. It lasted into the fourteenth and even the fifteenth centuries, and was marked by standardization of poetic content and floridity of melodic style. Long melismas became common, some of twenty-five notes or more. Exponents of this style included Wizlav III of Rügen (who was a prince), the anonymous Monk of Salzburg, and Oswald von Wolkenstein (c. 1377–1445), whose colorful life included travel to many countries, litigious property disputes, and a love affair with a female member of the opposing side in these disputes. Oswald is sometimes considered the last of the Minnesinger, but Minnesang as a developing monophonic art with its roots in the great vernacular lyric of the troubadours had ended more than a hundred years earlier.

VERNACULAR DRAMA

The main history of vernacular drama belongs to the fourteenth and fifteenth centuries, but examples from the twelfth and thirteenth centuries laid the groundwork for the great flourishing of the genre that occurred later in Spain, Italy, England, and France. As with vernacular song, some of the early dramas mingled Latin with the local language before total emancipation was reached. In fact, the introduction into the dramas of plainchant, with its symbolic and allusive power, was particularly effective. Plays have survived in Occitan, Old French, Anglo-Norman, and Middle English, and most use Latin texts for the sung portions (the remainder of the play is spoken in the vernacular).

The earliest play in Occitan is based on the parable of the wise and foolish virgins from the Gospels. Although the Latin songs are not set to liturgical melodies, the rhyming and metrical texts give them the feeling of sequences or conductus. A later Occitan drama, the *Play of St. Agnes,* tells the story of the fourth-century saint's success in retaining her virginity despite Roman attempts to relieve her of it. The action is in the vernacular; stage directions and some musical portions are in Latin. The melodies used are from the liturgy of the Office for Virgins, but also, interestingly enough, from some of the well-known troubadour songs.

The miracle play was the popular genre in Old French, especially that dealing with miracles performed by the Virgin. Later, in the fourteenth and fifteenth centuries, mystery plays on biblical topics such as the Nativity became more common. The Nativity plays often contained extensive episodes for the shepherds—an early and long-lived element in French music and drama.

As mentioned earlier, there are three Old French dramas by Adam de la Halle, of which only *Le Jeu de Robin et de Marion* ("The Play of Robin and Marion") contains music in significant quantity. This is a play that stands outside the main tradition of vernacular drama, for it includes no Latin texts or chant melodies. It is a direct descendant of the pastourelle, that genre of song that told the story of a knight riding in the country and meeting a pretty shepherdess. Adam took this well-known theme and turned an inherently dramatic situation into an actual drama. Robin, a young man, and Marion, a shepherdess, are in love. They dance and sing together. A knight tries to abduct Marion, and in the process Robin gets beaten. Marion escapes, and the lovers celebrate together.

The Play of Robin and Marion is a delightful situation comedy which uses music of a popular nature to contribute to the pastoral atmosphere. Some of the melodies may have been borrowed by Adam from the common stock of local popular song; others he may have written himself in imitation of the popular style. Example 7-22 gives some of the happy tunes that permeate the play.

In Italy the lauda served as an impetus towards the growth of medieval Italian drama, for towards the end of the thirteenth century laude in dialogue form began to appear, as we have seen (pp. 299–301). Other *laude dramatiche* represented dramatic situations such as the events surrounding the Crucifixion.

No plays with music seem to have been written in the Iberian peninsula during this period, but the rich dramatic repertoire of the fifteenth cen-

EXAMPLE 7-22 Melodies from *The Play of Robin and Marion*. After Friedrich Gennrich, *Adam de la Halle: Le Jeu de Robin et de Marion, Li Rondel Adam*, Musikwissenschaftliche Studienbibliothek, vol. 20 (Langen: Author, 1962).

tury, which included Christmas, Easter, and Corpus Christi celebrations and a lively mixture of realistic and religious elements, cannot have been without precedents. The performance of Latin drama from elsewhere in Europe, especially France, may have prevented the development of local traditions, or accidents of survival may be distorting our historical perspective.

The twelfth-century *Play of Adam* is not by Adam de la Halle but is a drama about the biblical Adam and Eve. It is written in Anglo-Norman and may therefore have originated in England, where that language was used in official and literary circles. The power of the play (in which God himself is one of the *dramatis personae*) comes not just from the simple and archetypal conflicts of the story, but also from the inclusion of Latin lessons and responsories sung to the appropriate plainchant melodies. These obviously come from a Matins service and give the drama its seriousness of purpose and musical depth of expression. English vernacular drama enjoyed its most vigorous growth in the fifteenth century, when Passion plays and the great cycles of mystery plays, depicting the history of the world from Adam and Eve to the Last Judgment, flourished in the important towns such as Chester, Coventry, and York.

In Germany, vernacular drama was extensively produced from the thirteenth to the fifteenth centuries, but a full assessment of the music will have to await the publication of complete editions. The plays fall into three main categories: those for Easter, Christmas, and Corpus Christi. A specialty of German vernacular drama was the Easter play in which the musical highpoint was the *planctus* sung by Mary. These plays were known as *Marienklagen* ("Laments of Mary"). As with the dramatic repertoire of other languages, musical settings included plainchant in Latin for its allusive quality, as well as both religious and popular songs in the vernacular.

SUMMARY

The vernacular tradition began in the southern part of France with the sophisticated and courtly art of the troubadours, and the literary, social, and musical ideals of this art were widely influential. Mingling with local elements and transferred into the different languages, the concept of courtly love in both its heavenly and earthly versions was manifested in song and drama all over Europe. Reflecting the political and cultural currents of the time, the medieval languages began to assert their independence from Latin without fully cutting the ties that that ancient, now sacred, language had with the liturgy. Literary masterpieces were produced in the vernacular, while in plays other than the pastoral, Latin retained its symbolic power. The music for epic and narrative verse, drama, lament, and courtly song continued to be cast in monophonic melody, loosely tied to the modes of plainchant, but exhibiting new freedoms of pitch goals, interval formations, and cadential expectations. Formal structure became more rigid, with a two-section form becoming the norm, though several varieties of repetition pattern were available. The ability of the composer to balance these patterns with or against the corresponding patterns of the verse supplied a subtle and infinite variety and allowed the tradition of monophonic music to remain alive in Europe long after immensely fertile new directions had been taken elsewhere—directions which would change the course of Western music for the remainder of its history.

COMMENTS ON NOTATION AND PERFORMANCE

The manuscripts of the vernacular song repertories that have survived were mostly produced a century or more after the composition of the music they contain. They are thus written in a style of notation that is essentially anachronistic. As with plainchant, controversy about the performance of this repertoire has centered upon rhythm. Many manuscripts preserve the melodies in a metrical notation of the late thirteenth century, while most of the songs were actually composed during the twelfth century. The situation becomes complicated for those late songs whose date of composition actually overlaps with the period of production of the manuscripts. Is it only the notational style that has changed, or did the performance style also become more "up to date?"

The two main approaches to the rhythmic performance of vernacular song have been (1) to follow the metrical implications of the late notation, or (2) to base the rhythm of the song upon the accentuation and declamation of the text (which changes from stanza to stanza). The examples in this chapter have mostly been transcribed in the non-committal style used for chant, in which the pitches and note groupings are clear but in which no rhythmic indication is given. Some of the examples, however, representing later compositions, have been transcribed in modern rhythmic notation, following the free patterns of long and short notes indicated in the manuscripts, and without attempting to force the music into any regular meter.

The original manuscripts give only the texts of the songs and the melody, with no directions for instrumental accompaniment. There is, however, a great deal of evidence that suggests that instrumental accompaniments for the songs were invented by the musicians during performance. Descriptions of medieval celebrations and banquets often contain allusions to such performances, and some of the manuscripts themselves are decorated with pictures of a wide range of instruments. (Brief descriptions of the most important medieval instruments are given in Chapter Ten.)

The art of improvisation—an art cultivated by professional musicians from the beginnings of musical history through the nineteenth century—has been almost entirely lost by today's "classical" performers. In the Middle Ages, however, when most music was not written down, and almost everybody played or sang from memory, the art of improvisation was central to the performance of music. We have every reason to believe that accompaniments were devised for the performance of many of the types of song described in this chapter. They would have taken into account the structure of the melody, its range, open and closed cadences, the form of the poetry—including line length, accentuation, and rhyme—as well as the overall atmosphere of the song and its changing affect from stanza to stanza. The performers probably played preludes and postludes to introduce and sum up a song; they might have joined some stanzas and separated others by means of interludes; perhaps they played sparse accompaniments for some stanzas and complex ones for others, and they would have been able to speed up or slow down the delivery of the poetry by means of the accompaniment itself.

The whole shape of the performance could be regulated by a skilled and sensitive player. This might have been the singer, accompanying himself on a plucked or bowed instrument, or it might have been another, or indeed several others, playing the accompaniment as the song was sung. Certainly the performance was the result of a close interaction between singer and instrumentalist(s); and indeed the performance could have been different each time, depending upon different circumstances, different instruments, even different moods. A song was created afresh each time it was sung. We are used to music for which every detail of performance is predetermined, and in which performers strive for uniformity of presentation. In the Middle Ages the notation presented merely the skeleton of a composition; everything else—its flesh and blood, *its soul*—was provided by the performers.

DISCOGRAPHY

Example 7-1 Bernart de Ventadorn, *Can Vei La Lauzeta Mover.*
Tape One, Side One. Studio der frühen Musik, *Chansons der Troubadours: Lieder und Spielmusik aus dem 12. Jahrhundert,* Telefunken 6.41126 AS; also on Studio der frühen Musik, *Musik des Mittelalters,* Telefunken 6.35412 EX; Paul Hillier, *Troubadour Songs and Medieval Lyrics,* Hyperion A66094; and Ensemble für frühe Musik, Augsburg, *Trobadors, Trouvères, Minnesänger: Lieder und Tänze des Mittelalters,* Christophorus SCGLX 74 033.

Example 7-2 Guiraut de Borneill, *Reis Glorios.*
Paul Hillier, *Troubadour Songs and Medieval Lyrics,* Hyperion A66094; also on Clemencic Consort, *Troubadours,* Harmonia Mundi HMC 396/8; and Russell Oberlin, *Troubadour and Trouvère Songs,* Lyrichord EAS 12.

Example 7-3 Gaucelm Faidit, *Fortz Chauza.*
Tape One, Side One. Studio der frühen Musik, *Planctus,* EMI Reflexe 1C 063-30 129; also on The Early Music Consort of London, *Music of the Crusades,* Argo ZRG 673.

Example 7-4 Raimon de Miraval, *Bel M'es Q'ieu Chant E Coindei.*
Gérard le Vot, *Chansons des Troubadours: La Lyrique Occitane au Moyen Age, XIIe-XIIIe siècles,* Studio SM 30 1043.

Example 7-5 Gace Brulé, *Biaus M'est Estez.*
Tape One, Side One. Studio der frühen Musik, *Chansons der Trouvères: Lieder des 13. Jahrhunderts aus Nordfrankreich,* Telefunken 6.41275 AW; also on Studio der frühen Musik, *Musik des Mittelalters,* Telefunken 6.35412 EX.

Example 7-6 Colin Muset, *Sire Cuens.*
Tape One, Side One.

Example 7-7 Gautier de Coincy, *Royne Celestre.*
Trio LiveOak, *'Don Alfonso the Wise': Music of Mediaeval Spain.* Mnemosyne Mn-4.

Example 7-9 Adam de la Halle, *A Dieu Commant Amouretes.*
Sequentia, *Trouvères: Höfische Liebeslieder aus Nordfrankreich,* Harmonia Mundi 1C 3LP 157-1695013.

Example 7-10 Adam de la Halle, motet, *A Dieu Commant/Aucun Se Sont/ Super Te.*
Sequentia, *Trouvères: Höfische Liebeslieder aus Nordfrankreich,* Harmonia Mundi 1C 3LP 157-1695013.

Example 7-11 Lauda, *A Tutta Gente.*
History of European Music, Part One: Music of the Early Middle Ages, vol. II, Musical Heritage Society OR 350 (Side I, Band 4).

Example 7-12 Jacopone da Todi, lauda, *O Cristo.*
Storia della musica italiana, vol. I, RCA Italiana LM 40000 (Side I, Band 13).

Example 7-13 Martin Codax, *Ondas Do Mar De Vigo.*
TAPE ONE, SIDE TWO. Studio der frühen Musik, *Bernart de Ventadorn: Chansons d'amour; Martim Codax: Canciones de amigo,* EMI Reflexe 1C 063-30 118; also on Euterpe, *Cantigas de amigo,* Harmonia Mundi 1060; and *Medieval Courtly Monody, Arabian-Andalusian Music: History of Spanish Music, vol. II,* Musical Heritage Society MHS 1573.

Example 7-14 Cantiga de Santa Maria, *Non E Gran Cousa.*
TAPE ONE, SIDE TWO. Studio der frühen Musik, *Camino de Santiago I: Eine Pilgerstrasse, Navarra/Castilla,* EMI Reflexe 1C 063-30 107; also on Ensemble für frühe Musik, Augsburg, *Camino de Santiago: Musik auf dem Pilgerweg zum Hl. Jacobus,* Christophorus SCGLX 74 032.

Example 7-15 St. Godric, *Sainte Marie.*
The Hilliard Ensemble, *Sumer is icumen in: Chants médiévaux anglais,* Harmonia Mundi HMC 1154; also on Sequentia, *Worldes Blis: English Songs of the Middle Ages,* Harmonia Mundi 067 16 9604 1 (7 49192 2); *Medieval English Lyrics,* Argo ZRG 5443; Russell Oberlin, *English Medieval Songs,* Music of the Middle Ages, vol. V, Expériences Anonymes EA 0029; and *History of European Music, Part One: Music of the Early Middle Ages,* vol. II, Musical Heritage Society OR 350 (Side I, Band 6).

Example 7-16 *Worldes Blis.*
Sequentia, *Worldes Blis: English Songs of the Middle Ages,* Harmonia Mundi 067 16 9604 1 (7 49192 2); also on Paul Hillier, *Troubadour Songs and Medieval Lyrics,* Hyperion A66094; Russell Oberlin, *English Polyphony, 13th and Early 14th Centuries,* Lyrichord EAS 24; Russell Oberlin, *English Medieval Songs,* Music of the Middle Ages, vol. V, Expériences Anonymes EA 0029; *History of Music in Sound,* vol. II, RCA Victor LM-6015 (Side III, Band 1); and *History of European Music, Part One: Music of the Early Middle Ages,* vol. II, Musical Heritage Society OR 350 (Side I, Band 6).

Example 7-17 *Bryd One Brere.*
TAPE ONE, SIDE TWO. Early Music Quartet, *Secular Music circa 1300,* Telefunken SAWT 9504-A Ex; also on Sequentia, *Worldes Blis: English Songs of the Middle Ages,* Harmonia Mundi 067 16 9604 1 (7 49192 2); and Russell Oberlin, *English Medieval Songs,* Music of the Middle Ages, vol. V, Expériences Anonymes EA 0029.

Example 7-18 Walther von der Vogelweide, *Nu Alrest Lebe Ich Mir Werde.* TAPE ONE, SIDE TWO. Studio der frühen Musik, *Minnesänger & Spielleute,* Telefunken 6.35618 DX; also on Collegium Musicum, Krefeld, *Music of the Middle Ages,* Lyrichord LLST 785; The Early Music Consort of London, *Music of the Crusades,* Argo ZRG 673; and *History of European Music, Part One: Music of the Early Middle Ages,* vol. II, Musical Heritage Society OR 350 (Side I, Band 2).

Example 7-19 Neidhart von Reuental, *Meie, Din Liehter Schin.* TAPE ONE, SIDE TWO. Studio der frühen Musik, *Minnesänger & Spielleute,* Telefunken 6.35618 DX; also on Studio der frühen Musik, *Musik des Mittelalters,* Telefunken 6.35412 EX.

Example 7-21 Heinrich von Meissen, *Myn Vroud Ist Gar Czugangyn.* TAPE ONE, SIDE TWO.

Example 7-22 Melodies from *The Play of Robin and Marion.* TAPE ONE, SIDE TWO. Early Music Quartet, *Secular Music circa 1300,* Telefunken SAWT 9504-A Ex.

The love song of Beatriz de Dia, "A chantar," is recorded on Studio der frühen Musik, *Chansons der Troubadours: Lieder und Spielmusik aus dem 12. Jahrhundert,* Telefunken 6.41126 AS; also on Studio der frühen Musik, *Musik des Mittelalters,* Telefunken 6.35412 EX; and Hesperion XX, *Cansos de Trobairitz,* Odeon/Reflexe 1C 065-30941Q. A re-release of two of the recordings listed above by the Studio der frühen Musik is Studio der frühen Musik, *Troubadours & Trouvères,* Teldec 8.35519 ZA. Other troubadour recordings include Martin Best, *The Testament of Tristan: Songs of Bernart de Ventadorn (1125–1195),* Hyperion CDA 66211; and The Martin Best Mediaeval Ensemble, *The Dante Troubadours,* Nimbus NI 5002.

An excellent collection of music from northern France, including trouvère songs and chansons d'histoire, is Sequentia, *Trouvères: Höfische Liebeslieder aus Nordfrankreich,* Harmonia Mundi 1C 157 16 9501 3 (7 49387 8). Chansons d'histoire may also be heard on Esther Lamandier, *Chansons de Toile au temps du Roman de la Rose,* Alienor AL 11 (Harmonia Mundi, HM 69).

Other recordings of the Cantigas de Santa Maria include Esther Lamandier, *Alfonso El Sabio: Cantigas de Santa Maria,* Astrée E7707; and The Martin Best Mediaeval Ensemble, *The Cantigas of Santa Maria of Alfonso X El Sabio,* Nimbus NI 5081.

A recording which provides examples of the Spruch is Sequentia, *Spruch-dichter des 13. Jahrhunderts: Kelin und Fegfeuer,* Harmonia Mundi 1C 069 19 9994 1. Music of Oswald von Wolkenstein may be heard on Studio der frühen Musik, *Oswald von Wolkenstein,* EMI Reflexe 1C 063-30 101.

The entire *Play of Robin and Marion* is recorded on Early Music Quartet, *Secular Music circa 1300,* Telefunken SAWT 9504-A Ex.

BIBLIOGRAPHICAL NOTES

Studies of the art and milieu of the troubadours include L. T. Topsfield, *Troubadours and Love* (Cambridge: Cambridge University Press, 1975); Robert S. Briffault, *The Troubadours,* ed. Lawrence F. Koons (Bloomington: Indiana University Press, 1965); Peter Dronke, *The Medieval Lyric* (2nd edition, London: Cambridge University Press, 1977). For an essay on female composers and performers see Maria V. Coldwell, *"Jougleresses* and *Trobairitz:* Secular Musicians in Medieval France," in *Women Making Music: The Western Art Tradition, 1150–1950,* ed. Jane Bowers and Judith Tick (Urbana: University of Illinois Press, 1986). Some poems of female troubadours are available with translations in Meg Bodin, *The Women Troubadours* (New York: Paddington Press, 1976). The vidas may be read in translation in Margarita Egan, trans., *The Vidas of the Trou-badours,* Garland Library of Medieval Literature, vol. 6, series B (New York: Garland Publishing, Inc., 1984). An important analysis of the tradition of courtly love is C. S. Lewis, *The Allegory of Love: A Study in Medieval Tradition* (New York: Oxford University Press, 1936). The music for the troubadour songs is available in Hendrik van der Werf, *The Extant Trouba-dour Melodies: Transcriptions and Essays for Performers and Scholars.* Texts ed. Gerald A. Bond. (Rochester, New York: Author, 1984).

The trouvère repertory can be studied in Hendrik van der Werf, *Trouvères-Melodien,* Monumenta musicae medii aevi, vols. 11 and 12 (Kassel: Bärenreiter, 1977–9), or through individual editions of composers or particular manuscripts, or in anthologies such as Jean Maillard, *Anthologie de chants de trouvères* (Paris: Editions Aug. Zurfluh, 1967)' Hendrik van der Werf, *The Chansons of the Troubadours and Trouvères: A Study of the Melodies and Their Relation to the Poems* (Utrecht: A. Oosthoek, 1972); and Samuel N. Rosenberg and Hans Tischler, *Chanter m'estuet: Songs of the Trouvères* (Bloomington: Indiana University Press, 1981).

The best source for the Italian laude remains Fernando Liuzzi, *La lauda e i primordi della melodia italiana,* 2 vols. ([Rome]: Libreria dello Stato, [1935]).

For the music of the Iberian peninsula, the works of Martin Codax are available in C. Ferreira da Cunha, *O cancionero de Martin Codax* (Rio de Janeiro: [Departamento de Imprensa Nacional], 1956); and with facsimiles in Pedro

Vindel, *Martin Codax: Las siete canciones de amor* (Madrid, 1915; reprint, Monterrey, Mexico: Ediciones Sierra Madre, 1978); while the Cantigas de Santa Maria are printed in facsimile with complete transcriptions in Higinio Anglès, *La música de las Cantigas de Santa María del Rey Alfonso el Sabio,* 3 vols. (Barcelona: Biblioteca Central, 1943–64). A fine study of the Cantigas is Gerardo Victor Huseby, "The Cantigas de Santa Maria and the Medieval Theory of Mode" (Ph. D. dissertation, Stanford University, 1983).

The texts and music of the English songs have been edited and are discussed in detail in E. J. Dobson and F. Ll. Harrison, *Medieval English Songs* (New York: Cambridge University Press, 1979).

A fluent and readable translation of Gottfried von Strassburg's *Tristan* is A. T. Hatto (trans.), *Gottfried von Strassburg: Tristan* (Middlesex, England: Penguin Books, Ltd., 1960). The most complete edition of Minnesang is Ronald J. Taylor, *The Art of the Minnesinger: Songs of the Thirteenth Century Transcribed and Edited With Textual and Musical Commentaries* (Cardiff: University of Wales Press, 1968). The poems and some of the musical settings are available in individual editions of the manuscripts and of the most famous composers. An attractive anthology, published together with an illustrative recording, is Barbara Garvey Seagrave and Wesley Thomas, *The Songs of the Minnesingers* (Urbana: University of Illinois Press, 1966).

A broad overview of the development of medieval drama is provided by Richard Axton, *European Drama of the Early Middle Ages* (London: Hutchinson, 1974). The Play of Robin and Marion, with text and music, has been edited in Friedrich Gennrich, *Adam de la Halle: Le Jeu de Robin et de Marion, Li rondel Adam,* Musikwissenschaftliche Studienbibliothek, vol. 20 (Langen: Author, 1962).

Performance practice, especially for the Middle Ages, is not easy to describe in words. Three important contributions, however, should be consulted: Stanley Boorman (ed.), *Studies in the Performance of Late Mediaeval Music* (Cambridge: Cambridge University Press, 1983); Timothy McGee, *Medieval and Renaissance Music: A Performer's Guide* (Toronto: University of Toronto Press, 1985); and Christopher Page, *Voices and Instruments of the Middle Ages: Instrumental Practice and Songs in France, 1100–1300* (Berkeley: University of California Press, 1986). A highly practical guide, together with an anthology of pieces, is provided by Elizabeth V. Phillips and John-Paul Christopher Jackson, *Performing Medieval and Renaissance Music: An Introductory Guide* (New York: Schirmer Books, 1986). The most illuminating insights may be obtained by listening carefully to some of the recordings mentioned in the discography for this chapter and comparing some of the more imaginative performances with the bare scores given in these pages.

EIGHT
EARLY POLYPHONY

Polyphony means "many sounds," and the word is used to describe music which contains more than one composed part at a time. The whole repertory of plainchant, from its earliest manifestations to the late sequences and beyond, was expressed in monophonic music, which, although it may have been sung by several people at once, still produced only one note at a time. We have seen how extraordinarily sophisticated and complex this music might be, so it is not surprising that it satisfied the artistic and musical aims of composers and listeners for a thousand years and more. Even when secular songs were accompanied by instruments—which, as has been suggested, was a fairly common practice—the accompaniment was improvised according to the written line of music and was probably based closely upon it. The idea of composing a piece with more than one simultaneous line of music begins to appear about the year 850.

Two things should immediately be noted. First, it was a very long time before polyphony became the predominant form of composition. For centuries monophonic music continued to be composed and, as we have seen, it was the primary focus of composers and performers in chant and secular song. Polyphony represented a minute fraction of the music being composed and performed until at least the thirteenth century. Second, polyphony grew out of the same impetus that produced expansions of and accretions to the liturgy in the form of tropes and sequences. The earliest polyphonic compositions were liturgical addenda, ways of making the chant more intense and more elaborate, exactly like tropes. It is only in retrospect that polyphony seems to have been such a remarkable development; at the time, it was but one of several ways composers found to embellish and enrich the liturgy.

SOURCES TO THE TWELFTH CENTURY

Information about early polyphony has survived mostly in theoretical writings. These describe ways in which a new musical line can be added to one that already exists, usually in parallel motion to it. It is quite likely that this technique had been in existence for some time before it appeared in written theory, for it is very easy to do. Indeed, it can easily be applied to any chant example in this book. The result is a richer, fuller sound (especially with the pure intervals that can be achieved in singing) that thickens the texture of the chant without in any way changing other aspects of the music, such as the relationship between the notes and the words, or the shape and design of the melody.

In the earliest treatises the interval of the fourth is the one most often suggested for this parallel polyphony. Sometimes, however, the voices proceed in parallel fifths or octaves. Usually the added voice is placed below the original, so that the original chant is in the most prominent position.

The first treatise that contains actual musical examples is the *Musica Enchiriadis* ("Musical Handbook"), one of a group of treatises from about 900 which show how polyphonic music may be made by adding a line of music to the chant. Example 8-1 is taken from this treatise and is a setting in parallel fifths of a phrase from the *Te Deum*. The original chant is the upper voice, the added part is below. (In this and the following examples the added parts are notated in white note heads, the original chant in black, as before.)

There is nothing to suggest that the whole *Te Deum* could not have been sung in this way. Indeed, as an enhancement of certain parts of the liturgy, parallel polyphony must have been performed far more often than is suggested by the few brief didactic examples which survive.

The *Musica Enchiriadis* shows ways in which polyphony may be expanded to even more than two lines. If a voice sings a fifth below the chant (as in Ex. 8-1) and then both the chant and the added voice are doubled at the octave (one an octave above and the other an octave below), the result is four-part music, all in parallel motion, comprising intervals of a fourth, a fifth, and an octave simultaneously. The treatise gives a verse from one of the psalms (Ex. 8-2), illustrating such a method of performance.

EXAMPLE 8-1   *Te Deum*, phrase in parallel fifths, from *Musica Enchiriadis*. Text edition by Hans Schmid, *Musica et Scolica Enchiriadis*, Veröffentlichungen der Musikhistorisches Kommission, vol. 3 (Munich: Bayerische Akademie der Wissenschaften, 1981).

Tu Patris sempiternus es filius.   You are the eternal son of the Father.

EXAMPLE 8-2   Four-part parallel polyphony from *Musica Enchiriadis*. Text edition by Hans Schmid, *Musica et Scolica Enchiriadis*, Veröffentlichungen der Musikhistorisches Kommission, vol. 3 (Munich: Bayerische Akademie der Wissenschaften, 1981).

Sit gloria Domini in saecula;   May the glory of the Lord last forever;
laetabitur Dominus in operibus suis.   the Lord will rejoice in his works.

The richness of the sound of this early four-part polyphony must have appealed greatly to its ninth- and tenth-century performers and auditors. The ease with which it can be produced suggests that it occurred far more frequently than surviving records show. Indeed, the very fact that it can be sung with little or no preparation is itself a reason why it would have been considered unnecessary to write down any more than a few brief illustrations.

More deliberation, however, was required for polyphony departing from the strict parallel motion of the extracts given above. *Musica Enchiriadis* shows how polyphony may be created by having two voices begin on a unison and gradually diverge to a fourth, which interval is maintained until towards the end of the phrase, when a unison is reached again. The treatise offers as an example the first phrase of the sequence *Rex Caeli* (Ex. 8-3). The first three intervals are a unison, second, and third, by means of which the fourth is reached. Then the music stays in parallel fourths until the cadence, when two unisons are sounded again.

EXAMPLE 8-3 *Rex Caeli,* two-part polyphony, from *Musica Enchiriadis.* Text edition by Hans Schmid, *Musica et Scolica Enchiriadis,* Veröffentlichungen der Musikhistorisches Kommission, vol. 3 (Munich: Bayerische Akademie der Wissenschaften, 1981).

Rex cae - li,   Do - mi - ne,   ma - ris   un - di - so - ni,
Ti - ta - nis   ni - ti - di   squa - li - di - que   so - li.

Rex caeli, Domine, maris undisoni,   O Lord, King of Heaven, and of the
                                              sounding sea,
Titanis nitidi squalidique soli.   Of the shining sun and the dark earth.

The second musical phrase of the same sequence is also given as an example in the treatise (Ex. 8-4). Here more freedom in the choice of intervals is apparent, with a third, a unison, and a fifth occurring in the middle of the phrase—the fifth E/B being used to avoid the tritone F/B.

EXAMPLE 8-4 *Rex Caeli,* continued, from *Musica Enchiriadis.* Text edition by Hans Schmid, *Musica et Scolica Enchiriadis,* Veröffentlichungen der Musikhistorisches Kommission, vol. 3 (Munich: Bayerische Akademie der Wissenschaften, 1981).

Te   hu - mi - les   fa - mu - li,   mo - du - lis   ve - ne - ran - do   pi - is,
Se   iu - be - as   fla - gi - tant   va - ri - is   li - be - ra - re   ma - lis.

Te humiles famuli, modulis venerando   Your humble servants worship you in
   piis,   sacred songs,
Se iubeas flagitant variis liberare malis. And urge you to agree to free them from
                                              all their evils.

The sequence seems to have been a popular chant to sing in the polyphonic manner: the *Musica Enchiriadis* was written not long after the invention of the genre, and both it and later practical sources contain several examples of polyphonic sequences.

Not until the eleventh century, however, does the evidence for polyphonic performance of chant become more substantial, both in theoretical documents and in music manuscripts themselves. One theorist of major importance in this development, and indeed in the general history of music, was Guido of Arezzo, whom we have met earlier (see p. 66). The fame of this Italian monk in the later Middle Ages rivalled that of Boethius, for he was single-handedly responsible for some of the most influential innovations in the memorization, notation, and performance of both chant and polyphony.

It was Guido who developed the staff, with its lines and spaces to indicate relative pitches; letters on the staff (the forerunners of modern clefs) to denote exact pitch; and a sight-singing system which is the basis of modern solfeggio. Of his many writings the best-known is the treatise entitled *Mikrologus* ("Little Discussion"). This deals mostly with chant—its intervals, the modes, the formation of melodies, and the balancing of phrases—but one chapter discusses polyphony. From the evidence of this chapter, and another which gives musical examples, the new polyphonic style seems to have gained some flexibility in its construction by the beginning of the eleventh century. First, we notice that although the added voice begins below (or in unison with) the original chant, it is sometimes permitted to cross the chant and sound briefly above it. The mixture of intervals is greater than in the examples given in earlier treatises. Guido also regularizes the system of making cadences by having the parts converge to a unison through a third and a second (Ex. 8-5). Sometimes the added voice acts more or less as a drone, stressing mostly a single pitch below the chant melody (Ex. 8-6).

EXAMPLE 8-5 Polyphony from Guido's *Mikrologus*. Text edition by Joseph Smits van Waesberghe, *Guidonis Aretini Micrologus,* Corpus Scriptorum de Musica, vol. 4 ([Rome]: American Institute of Musicology, 1955).

De - vo - ti - o - ne com - mit - to.

Devotione committo.   I trust in your protection.

EXAMPLE 8-6 Polyphony from Guido's *Mikrologus*. Text edition by Joseph Smits van Waesberghe, *Guidonis Aretini Micrologus,* Corpus Scriptorum de Musica, vol. 4 ([Rome]: American Institute of Musicology, 1955).

Ve - ni   ad   do - cen - dum   nos   vi - am pru - den - ti - ae.

Veni ad docendum nos viam prudentiae.   Come and teach us the way of wisdom.

The few short examples in Guido's treatise are designed, as were the examples in the *Musica Enchiriadis,* to suggest a method of applying polyphony to many different kinds of chant. Both treatises are didactic sources, theoretical documents prescribing and analyzing practice. They certainly represent only a fraction of the polyphony that must have been actually sung at the time, either by improvisation or in a more contrived fashion.

It is from about the period when Guido wrote his *Mikrologus* (c. 1025), or even a little earlier, that the first sizeable body of actual polyphony for performance appears. This is contained in a manuscript preserving mostly Alleluyas, sequences, and tropes both in plainchant and in polyphony from the Old Minster in Winchester, England. Winchester was one of the most important centers of learning in the British Isles before the Norman Conquest, a focal point of scholarship and manuscript production, and the capital of the Anglo-Saxon kingdom of Wessex. From its place of origin and the nature of its contents the music manuscript is known as the Winchester Troper.

The Winchester Troper contains a large number of polyphonic pieces, most of which are Alleluya settings, responsories from the Office, and sequences. The style of the music reflects very closely the didactic precepts of Guido. The added voice lies below the original chant, although the voices occasionally cross. Almost all of the intervals up to a fifth appear, including the third and the second. Openings and cadences use the diverging and converging of parts that we have seen in the examples above. Passages with reiterated pitches in the added voice are common. In general the style displays a flexibility of treatment that shows that polyphony was by no means restricted to textbook examples in the early eleventh century. It is likely that the Winchester Troper contains only a small portion of a considerable body of polyphonic music from the period, most of which has not survived.

Example 8-7 is a polyphonic setting from the Winchester Troper of the Alleluya of the Mass for Two or More Martyrs. The single sentence of the verse is taken from the Te Deum (see Ex. 5-15). Notice the converging of the voices at cadences, the reiterated notes in the added voice, and the crossing of the voices. In its enrichment and embellishment of the original chant, this composition is certainly worthy to be included in a book of tropes.

EXAMPLE 8-7 Polyphonic Alleluya from the Winchester Troper. After W. Thomas Marrocco and Nicholas Sandon, *Medieval Music: The Oxford Anthology of Music* (London: Oxford University Press, 1977).

(Soloists)

Al – le – – – lu – – – ya.

℣. Te mar – ty – rum can – – – –

di – – da – – – tus lau – – – – –

dat ex – er – – – – – ci – – – – tus,

Do – – – – – – – – mi – – – ne.

Al – le – – – lu – – – ya.

Alleluya.	Alleluya.
Alleluya.	Alleluya.
℣. Te martyrum candidatus laudat exercitus, Domine.	℣. It is you that the gleaming band of martyrs praises, O Lord.
Alleluya.	Alleluya.

Apart from a fragmentary manuscript from the late eleventh century, which is from Chartres in northern France, most of the information about polyphony for the next hundred years comes from theoretical documents, giving us again no more than a glimpse of what must have been a widespread polyphonic tradition. The fragmentary Chartres manuscript contains several Alleluya settings. In these settings the acceptable intervals have expanded to include sixths, voice crossing is more frequent, and the added voices look more like independent melodies. Only the solo portions of the Alleluyas are provided with polyphony—the intonation and the solo verse.

Several theoretical treatises from about 1100 deal with polyphony. In some the subject appears only in passing, as though the author felt that a treatise on music would now no longer be complete without at least a mention of polyphony. On the other hand, some are devoted entirely to the new practice, and discuss at considerable length the allowable intervals, movement of the parts, openings, and cadences.

A further element appears in the treatises of this period: the division of polyphony into two styles: an older style, in which the parts are composed in a more or less note-against-note texture, and a newer style in which the added voice is permitted to indulge in short melismas against single notes of the chant. The names given to these two styles were *discant* (the note-against-note texture) and *organum* (the melismatic texture). This distinction was an important one, for it foreshadowed a development of major consequence in the future of polyphonic composition. In fact, although the treatises mention the stylistic distinction, actual music displaying the two styles is not found in them, but appears, most spectacularly, in the major practical sources of polyphony of the twelfth century.[1]

One further innovation that became important in all later polyphony was a change in the relationship between the chant and the added voice. Previously the chant had always stayed in the higher position, with the added voice below it (apart from some passages of crossing). Around 1100 this relationship changed, and the chant began to be used as the foundation of the composition, with the added voice written above it, thus gaining in prominence and independence.

---

[1]One confusing aspect of the terminology of the time is that the word "organum," indicating the melismatic style within a polyphonic composition, also was used to describe polyphony as a whole. Thus organum (polyphony in general) has two styles: discant (the note-against-note style) and organum (the melismatic style).

One of the main treatises of this period, and the one in which this shift in relationship first appears, is entitled *Ad Organum Faciendum* ("How to Make Polyphony"). This discusses the intervals and voice relationships to be observed in the fashioning of polyphonic music and gives many musical examples, among them a beautiful setting of the Alleluya *Iustus Ut Palma,* from the Mass for Abbots (Ex. 8-8). As in the Chartres manuscript, only the solo portions of the chant—the intonation and the solo verse—are set polyphonically, while the parts traditionally sung by the choir—the repetition of the first "Alleluya" with its jubilus, the closing words of the verse, and the final "Alleluya"—remain in monophonic chant. In the polyphonic sections the original melody is in the lower voice, while the new part is written above it, and the most frequent intervals between them are fourths and fifths; but unisons, thirds, and octaves are not uncommon, and there are occasional sixths. The music displays a carefully controlled mixture of parallel and contrary motion, and, in an effective contrast, the intonation begins on an octave and ends on a unison, while the solo verse does the opposite. The artistry of this polyphonic setting is quite apparent; no longer in the realm of simple improvisation, it is a fully created composition in its own right. That it obviously needed to be written down in full is confirmed by such details as the care with which the manuscript records the distinction between B♭ and B natural in the upper voice.

EXAMPLE 8-8 Polyphonic Alleluya from *Ad Organum Faciendum.* After W. Thomas Marrocco and Nicholas Sandon, *Medieval Music: The Oxford Anthology of Music* (London: Oxford University Press, 1977).

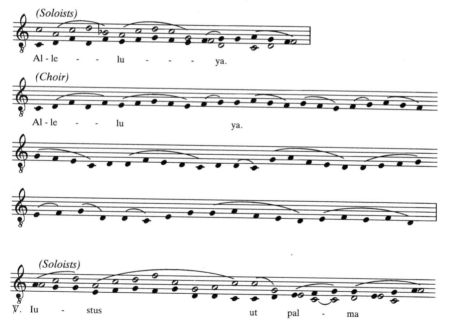

flo - re - - - - - - bit, et   si - cut

ce - - - - - - - - - - - - - - - - -

- - - drus

(Choir)

mul - ti - pli - ca - - bi - tur.

(Choir)

Al - le - lu - - - ya.

Alleluya.
Alleluya.

℣. Iustus ut palma florebit, et sicut ce-
drus multiplicabitur.

Alleluya.

Alleluya.
Alleluya.

℣. The righteous one will flourish like a
palm-tree, and will grow like a cedar.

Alleluya.

TWELFTH-CENTURY SOURCES

The twelfth century in Europe was a time of fertile developments: a rise in learning, the consolidation of cities, the growth of national economies, a restored self-assurance, the flowering of new forms of vernacular literature (as we have seen), the instigation of church reforms, and a sense of hope and renewal. The period has even been claimed to represent an early manifestation of the Renaissance. In polyphonic music the evidence suggests that throughout the century the trends in artistic construction, conscious design, and flexibility of approach that have been sketched above were coming together to produce repertories of polyphony that could finally rival the sophistication and subtlety of chant.

Several large manuscripts containing polyphony survive from the twelfth century. The provenance of some of them is not known, but there appear to have been two main centers for the composition of this new music. One was the area of southwestern France known as Aquitaine. In the twelfth century this duchy was one of the most powerful states in Europe. Under Eleanor of Aquitaine, the charismatic politician and renowned patron of the arts, wife of two kings and mother of two more, it became a center of culture and a scene of much troubadour activity. Some of the manuscripts which preserve polyphony from this region come from the Benedictine Abbey of St. Martial in Limoges, others from elsewhere in and around Aquitaine. Nonetheless, the polyphony in these manuscripts is composed in a fairly consistent manner, and the sources may therefore be considered as a group.

Aquitainian Polyphony

The types of composition that are set to polyphony in the Aquitainian sources are more varied than we have encountered so far. They include sequences, tropes, Benedicamus Domino settings (for the end of Mass or the Office), and many sacred songs that do not appear to have any narrowly liturgical function but were probably sung on any one of a number of possible occasions before, during, or after the services.

It is not only in the diversity of the repertoire but in the actual compositions themselves that Aquitainian polyphony is notable, for here the distinction in styles mentioned by the theorists of the early part of the century first appears. The music clearly displays a distinction between sections of polyphony in note-against-note style (discant) and sections in which melismas appear in the upper voice against single notes or small groups of notes in the lower voice (organum). Often the organum sections appear on penultimate syllables of text lines, and here a close relationship may be seen between the sacred polyphony of the period and its secular songs, for it is the penultimate syllables of text lines in troubadour and trouvère songs that also usually receive the most melismatic settings.

In Aquitainian polyphony the original chant is the lower of the two voices, and the new voice is written above it, as had now become the standard practice, although voice crossing still occurs. The variety of intervals has increased, including some quite prominent dissonances. And a more flexible approach to the composition of discant is evident, for the texture is less rigidly note-against-note and includes many places in which a small group of notes is set against another group, each group not necessarily including exactly the same number of notes. This "neume-against-neume" feature contributes to the intriguing nature and subtle appeal of Aquitainian polyphony. In Example 8-9, which gives the first three stanzas of a polyphonic setting of a versus from one of the Aquitainian manuscripts, this feature may be clearly seen. Neume combinations of two against three, three against four, and five against seven notes occur, although there are also note-against-note passages and moments (especially at the ends of phrases) where a long flourish appears in the newly composed upper voice against a single note below. The added voice sounds mostly above the original, though there are several instances where the voices cross. The last line of each stanza receives the most melismatic treatment. In the first two stanzas the preceding lines are set quite simply, but as the song progresses, they too become increasingly elaborate. The versus is through-composed, for each stanza has different music, both in the original voice and in the added voice.

EXAMPLE 8-9   Polyphonic versus, *Veri Solis Radius.* After Wulf Arlt, "Analytische Bemerkungen zu 'Veri solis radius,' " in *Bericht über den Internationalischen Musikwissenschaftlichen Kongress Berlin 1974* (Kassel: Bärenreiter, 1980).

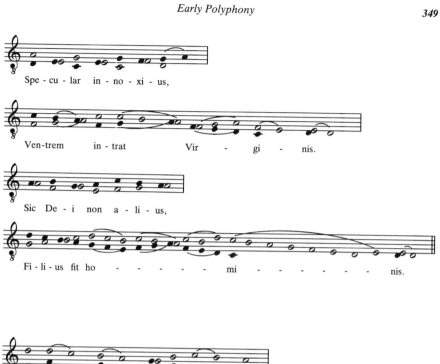

Spe - cu - lar in - no - xi - us,

Ven-trem in - trat Vir - gi - nis.

Sic De - i non a - li - us,

Fi - li - us fit ho - - - - - - mi - - - - - - nis.

II.

Ver - nis, qui sub ve - spe - re

Mun - di iu - bar e - xe - rit,

Ra - mum sic - cat he - de - re,

Quo se Jo - nas o - pe - rit.

Non in um - bra lit - te - - - - re

Spem sa - lu - tis in - - - - - - - - - - - - -

ge - - - - - rit.

Qua fo — — — — ve — tur Me - di - co,

Pro-pul-san — te vi - ci — a,

Qui ve - ge - bat Je - ri — — — — — cho,

Vi — a lap — — sus re — — — — — — —

gi — — — — — a,

Nec af - flic - tus mo - di - co,

Vi - te fle - bat spo — — — — — — — —

— — — li — — — — — — — a.

I. Veri solis radius
   Et sol pleni luminis,
   Specular innoxius,
   Ventrem intrat Virginis.
   Sic Dei non alius,
   Filius fit hominis.

II. Vernis, qui sub vespere
   Mundi iubar exerit,
   Ramum siccat hedere,
   Quo se Jonas operit.

I. A beam of the true sun,
   The sun of shining light,
   A ray of purity,
   Enters the womb of the Virgin.
   In just this way did God's Son
   Become the Son of man.

II. In spring, at fall of night,
   The world-star rises,
   And dries the ivy frond,
   Where Jonah hid.

| Non in umbra littere | It is not in the shadow of the word |
| Spem salutis ingerit. | That he holds out hope of salvation. |

III. Qua fovetur Medico,	III. It is nourished by the Physician
Propulsante vicia,	Who cures us of all sickness,
Qui vegebat Jericho,	And he who cultivated Jericho,
Via lapsus regia,	Led astray from the royal path,
Nec afflictus modico,	Full of grief,
Vite flebat spolia.	Lamented the ruins of his life.

Codex Calixtinus

The second major center of twelfth-century polyphony was Santiago de Compostela in Galicia in the northwestern corner of the Iberian peninsula—the same area whose importance we sketched earlier (see p. 302).

Santiago de Compostela was, after Jerusalem and Rome, the most popular destination for pilgrims in the entire Middle Ages. People flocked there from all over Europe to visit the cathedral, which was built over a tomb designated as that of St. James (Sant' Iago) the Apostle. The roads converging on Compostela from hundreds of miles away were filled with inns, taverns, and hostels catering to the travelers; and pickpockets, cut-purses, and highwaymen thrived on the throngs.

The early polyphonic music from Santiago de Compostela is contained in the *Codex Calixtinus,* named after Pope Calixtus II (1119–1124), who was supposed to have compiled the manuscript. The codex (meaning manuscript book) seems to have been compiled about 1170 and may still be seen in the library of the Cathedral of St. James in Santiago de Compostela. Polyphony represents only a small portion of the contents of this fascinating document. It also includes a whole series of plainchants for the new Office and Mass of St. James, a written account of twenty-two miracles performed by the saint, a satirical story of Charlemagne written in deliberately incorrect Latin, and a tourist guide about the main routes to Compostela, describing the inns to be sought out and those to be avoided by the unwary traveler.

The polyphonic music is contained in a supplement to the codex and consists mostly of settings of responsorial chants for the Mass and Office of St. James, Benedicamus Domino settings, and sacred songs. The structure of the music is not very different from that found in the Aquitainian manuscripts. The original melody is always in the lower voice, and both organum and discant styles are used. There appears, however, to be a more deliberate choice of styles according to the type of piece, for responsorial chants are mostly set as organum, while the sacred songs, with their metrical, rhyming texts, are composed in discant style. The discant sections, as in the Aquitainian polyphony, contain both note-against-note and neume-against-neume passages.

When the organum style has only a few notes in the upper voice against a note or two in the original chant, it closely approaches neume-against-neume discant style. Indeed, in some of the pieces from the Codex Calixtinus a merging of the two styles is apparent. In Example 8-10, which is a polyphonic setting of a troped Kyrie, there are several sections in clear-cut organum style, in which the upper voice has long melismas against single notes of the original chant; but some passages are not as clear-cut, the composer having chosen to let the music flow imperceptibly between one style and the other.[2]

EXAMPLE 8-10 Polyphonic troped Kyrie from Codex Calixtinus, Santiago de Compostela, Biblioteca de la Catedral.

[2]The metamorphosis of this Kyrie from its original plainchant setting to the troped version and then the polyphonic elaboration may be studied by comparing Examples 4-2 and 6-5 with Example 8-10.

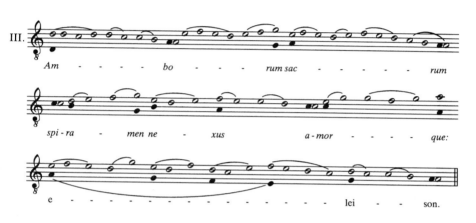

I. *Cunctipotens genitor, Deus omni-creator:* eleison.

II. *Christe, Dei forma, virtus Patrisque sophia:* eleison.

III. *Amborum sacrum spiramen nexus amorque:* eleison.

I. *Omnipotent Father, God, Creator of all,* have mercy.

II. *Christ, form of God, power and wisdom of the Father,* have mercy.

III. *Sacred breath of both, and combined love,* have mercy.

The discant style used in the Codex Calixtinus for regularly patterned verse texts is displayed in Example 8-11. *Nostra Phalans* is a strophic song with four stanzas in metrical, rhyming verse. The text is a sacred song to St. James, obviously designed to be sung by pilgrims visiting the shrine in Santiago de Compostela. A single refrain line ("*Angelorum in curia*") ends each stanza. The music is written in a discant style that incorporates both note-against-note and neume-against-neume passages. All phrases end on unisons or octaves, but they begin on octaves, fifths, or fourths. These intervals are consistently used for the places where single notes or the first notes of neumes coincide. Other intervals, such as thirds and sixths, and even seconds and sevenths, are formed as the notes within the neumes progress. Both voices appear to be newly composed and to have no basis in chant.

EXAMPLE 8-11 *Nostra Phalans,* Santiago de Compostela, Biblioteca de la Catedral.

No - stra pha - lans plau - dat le - ta

Hac   in di - - - e, qua   ath - le - - - ta

Cri - sti gau - det si - ne   me - ta,

Ja - co - bus   in glo - ri - - - - - - - a,

An - ge - lo - rum in   cu - ri - - - - - a.

I. Nostra phalans plaudat leta
    Hac in die, qua athleta
    Cristi gaudet sine meta,
    Jacobus in gloria,
    Angelorum in curia.

II. Quem Herodes decollavit,
    Et idcirco coronavit

I. Let our joyful group celebrate
    On this day, when James,
    The champion of Christ, in his glory
    Rejoices without limit
    In the court of the angels.

II. He whom Herod beheaded;
    And therefore Christ

Illum Christus, et ditavit	Crowned him and placed him
In celesti patria,	In his heavenly home,
Angelorum in curia.	*In the court of the angels.*

III. Cuius corpus tumulatur,
Et a multis visitatur,
Et per illud eis datur
Salus, in Gallecia,
Angelorum in curia.

III. His body is entombed,
And visited by many,
And for that reason they receive
Salvation, in Galicia,
In the court of the angels.

IV. Ergo festum celebrantes,
Eius melos decantantes,
Persolvamus venerantes
Dulces laudes Domino
Angelorum in curia.

IV. Therefore, celebrating his feast,
Singing his songs,
We give homage and offer
Sweet praises to the Lord
In the court of the angels.

SUMMARY

Polyphony began as an improvisatory technique designed to enrich plainchant by adding to it a further voice or voices in parallel intervals. The gradual appearance of more flexibility in the construction of the added voice and in the allowable intervals marks the establishment of polyphony as a compositional form. In the earliest surviving large repertoire, the Winchester Troper, the added voice still lies primarily below the original chant. By about 1100 two important changes had occurred: the appearance of two distinct textural styles and the placing of the newly composed voice above the chant. By the twelfth century, polyphony had developed into a conscious artistic device for intensifying both the liturgy and para-liturgical song. Nonetheless, monophonic chants for new feasts and new forms of plainchant such as tropes, prosulas, and sequences continued to be composed. It was also at this same time that monophonic vernacular song was reaching its height of expression and diffusion.

From the Aquitainian sources and the Codex Calixtinus, we are able to piece together a picture of the state of polyphonic music as it must have been in the second half of the twelfth century. Because of what must surely have been lost in the intervening years, and the little that was actually written down, the surviving music must represent only a small portion of the polyphonic music that was actually being composed and performed at this time. Almost certainly simple parallel polyphony continued to be sung. It is only in retrospect that the developments in composed polyphony seem of such importance, for these developments—the adding of a new voice above the chant, the types of chant in which this occurred, the control of the intervals formed between the voices, the manipulation of two different styles of polyphonic texture—turn out to be the necessary foundation for the creation of one of the most remarkable repertories of polyphonic music in the history of European culture—the music written for the Cathedral of Notre Dame in Paris.

DISCOGRAPHY

Example 8-1, Example 8-2, Example 8-3, Example 8-4   Examples of polyphony from *Musica Enchiriadis.*
Pro Cantione Antiqua, *Medieval Music: Ars Antiqua Polyphony,* Peters International PLE 115 (Oxford University Press OUP 164).

Example 8-7   Polyphonic Alleluya from the Winchester Troper.
Pro Cantione Antiqua, *Medieval Music: Ars Antiqua Polyphony,* Peters International PLE 115 (Oxford University Press OUP 164).

Example 8-8   Polyphonic Alleluya from *Ad Organum Faciendum.*
Pro Cantione Antiqua, *Medieval Music: Ars Antiqua Polyphony,* Peters International PLE 115 (Oxford University Press OUP 164).

Example 8-9   Polyphonic versus, *Veri Solis Radius.*
Ensemble Organum, *Polyphonie aquitaine du XIIe siècle: Saint Martial de Limoges,* Harmonia Mundi HMC 1134.

Example 8-10   Polyphonic troped Kyrie from Codex Calixtinus.
Opus Musicum: The Mass, Arno Volk Verlag OM 201/03 (Side I, Band 3).

Example 8-11   *Nostra Phalans.*
Tape One, Side Two.   Studio der frühen Musik, *Camino de Santiago II: Eine Pilgerstrasse, Leon/Galicia,* EMI Reflexe 1C 063-30 108.

Polyphonic performances of the opening chants and the first lesson of Christmas Matins (see Chapter Five) are contained on Ensemble Organum, *Polyphonie aquitaine du XIIe siècle,* Harmonia Mundi HMC 1134.

BIBLIOGRAPHICAL NOTES

Translations of some of the original theoretical treatises that discuss polyphony are included in Oliver Strunk, *Source Readings in Music History* (New York: W. W. Norton & Co., Inc., 1950); Hugo Riemann, *Polyphonic Theory to the Sixteenth Century,* trans. Raymond H. Haggh (Lincoln: University of Nebraska Press, 1962); Jay A. Huff, *Ad organum faciendum,* Musical Theorists in Translation, vol. 8 (Brooklyn: Institute of Mediaeval Music, 1969); and Warren Babb, *Hucbald, Guido, and John on Music: Three Medieval Treatises,* ed. Claude Palisca, Music Theory Translation Series, vol. 3 (New Haven: Yale University Press, 1978).

Bryan Gillingham, *Saint-Martial Polyphony,* Musicological Studies, vol. 44 (Henryville, Pennsylvania: Institute of Mediaeval Music, 1984) presents the Aquitainian repertory in metrical transcription.

W. M. Whitehill, J. Carro Garcia, and G. Prado, *Liber Sancti Jacobi: Codex Calixtinus,* 3 vols. (Santiago de Compostela: [n. p.], 1944) contains an edition of the whole of the manuscript, with facsimiles and transcriptions of the music.

NINE

THE NEW MUSIC OF PARIS

PARIS: ITS UNIVERSITY AND CATHEDRAL

As we have seen in the previous chapter, the twelfth century was a time of optimism and self-confidence. It was a time in which ambitious new architectural styles were born, painting took on a new vigor and depth, and the power of the intellect manifested itself in the charismatic personalities of famous teachers and lecturers.

During the course of the twelfth century, intellectual and artistic events began to center in one small area in France, comprising about twenty square miles in and around Paris. The great thinkers and teachers of the time gathered there, and the area became a focal point for philosophers and theologians from all over Europe. Politically, too, the time was one of ambition and consolidation, as Paris became the undisputed capital of France under the monarchs of the Capetian dynasty. Both Louis VII (1137–1180) and his successor, Philip Augustus (1180–1223), contributed to the growth of Paris: enlarging the city walls, paving the streets, and encouraging an enthusiastic building program, which included the first Louvre, the king's palace and fortress.

The European economy in general was on the rise, and a large and growing merchant population conducted business and trade in Paris. A weekly market took place in the city, and the river Seine carried a constant flow of barges loaded with goods from other commercial centers.

Paris was also the site of the first university in medieval Europe. From informal beginnings in the twelfth century, the University of Paris had become by the early thirteenth century one of the most important scholarly centers in the West. Students came from all over Europe to study there, to hear the great thinkers of the time lecture on the liberal arts and on philosophy and theology, and to equip themselves for careers as administrators in the burgeoning ecclesiastic and civil bureaucracies. Many of them stayed on in Paris to become teachers themselves.

The university as an institution caught on quickly. By the year 1300 about twenty universities had been established, from Seville to Cambridge, and from Angers to Salerno. Some became famous for particular specialties: Bologna for law, Paris for theology and logic, Montpellier for medicine. By the end of the Middle Ages, universities dotted the European

A lecturer on medicine from a mid-twelfth-century manuscript, British Library, London.

Map of universities in Europe before the year 1500 with dates of foundation. From Anders Piltz, *The World of Medieval Learning,* tr. David Jones (Totowa, NJ: Barnes and Noble Books, 1981). Used by permission.

landscape and formed an integral part of its economy, education, and culture.

Paris was particularly affected by its university. Schoolrooms and lecture halls sprang up on the south bank of the river (the "Left Bank"); teachers and students filled the lodging houses of the area; and bookshops, where manuscripts were copied and sold, did a thriving business. From administrative documents, legal proceedings, and other writings of the time we learn that academic life in the twelfth and thirteenth centuries was not very different from that of today. Students complained about the cost of housing and the price of books. Teachers complained about their wages. Local citizens complained about the rowdiness and irresponsibility of the students. The art of getting money out of parents was just as advanced then as it is today:

> To our very dear and respected parents, greetings from your sons.
>
> This is to inform you that by divine mercy we are living in good health in the city and are devoting ourselves wholly to study. We have good lodgings near the classrooms so that we can go to school every day without getting too wet. We also have good companions in the house with us, who study hard and have good habits. We appreciate this, for as it says in the Psalms, "With an upright man you will show yourself to be upright."
>
> To make sure that our studiousness continues, we beg our father to send us money—to buy parchment, ink, a desk, and the other things we need. God forbid that we should suffer deprivation, for we wish to complete our studies and return home with honor.
>
> We feel sure that you will also wish to send us clothes . . . and any news as well.

Apart from the university, one other important foundation was begun in Paris in the late twelfth century. This was a huge project, which was to result in the most splendid and awe-inspiring monument to God that had yet been seen: the Cathedral of Notre Dame, situated at the east end of an island (the Ile de la Cité) in the middle of the river Seine at the heart of medieval Paris. At the other end of the island was the palace of the king; next to the cathedral on the south side stood the Bishop's palace; and just across the river to the south and north respectively were the university and the commercial district of the city.

The concept for the cathedral came from the young new bishop of Paris, Maurice de Sully. Its realization required imagination and organizing ability, as well as tremendous ambition and faith—and a great deal of money. Maurice was a superb administrator, and his power, as bishop, rivalled that of the king. Funds were collected from every available source, from clergy and nobility, from rich and poor, and from the extensive revenues of the cathedral's land holdings. The cornerstone was laid in 1163. By 1182 the east end of the great cathedral—the choir (for that is where the members of the choir gathered and where services were conducted)—had been completed, and on the Feast of Pentecost of that year (May 19) the altar was dedicated. It may well have been on that day that the first new polyphonic music for Paris was heard.

It is difficult for us to realize what an impressive sight this magnificent new building must have been. Even today the visitor to the Cathedral of Notre Dame is startled by its elevation and the grandeur of its interior space. In 1182 no building even approached its awesome height. The choir of Notre Dame soars to over one hundred feet from the pavement to the crown of its vaults.

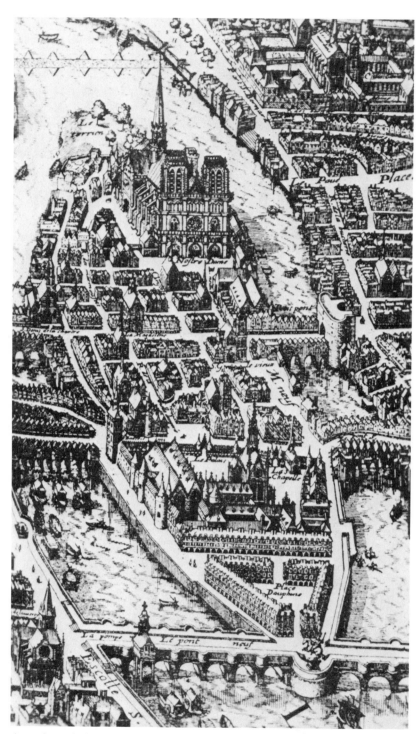

An early rendering of the center of Paris, showing the river Seine and the Ile de la Cité, with the Cathedral of Notre Dame at the east end (top) of the island. Melchior Tavernier, *Plan de Paris,* c. 1630.

Cathedral of Notre Dame in Paris—interior view from the east end, showing the facing choir stalls.

LEONINUS

The rising splendor of this remarkable cathedral, a jewel of the new Gothic style, inspired the creation of a similarly splendid body of music to fill its vaults. The polyphony written for Notre Dame brought together some of the previous experiments in combining the sacred chant with a new musical line, and at the same time went far beyond them in the scope and comprehensiveness of its achievement. It also immortalized a single individual, whose name has survived as the creator of the first cycle of Notre Dame polyphony. His name was Master Leo, though he is better known by the more familiar, diminutive form of his name: Leoninus.

Leoninus, like many of the great composers of the Middle Ages, was a poet as well as a composer.[1] He was born around 1135 and educated at the cathedral school of Notre Dame in Paris. He obtained the degree of Magister (Master) at the university and in the 1180s was appointed one of the administrators of the cathedral. He was actively involved in cathedral affairs until his death in the early 1200s. During the latter part of his life, he became important enough to have written letters to the popes Hadrian IV and Alexander III, and to Cardinal Henry of Albano. He also received a magnificent gift from the King of France, Louis VII.

The poetic work of Leoninus that survives comprises some short poems in the form of letters (for example, to the dignitaries mentioned above) and some on general moral topics. He was also the author of a much larger work, the *Historiae Sacrae,* a lengthy version in Latin verse (over 14,000 lines) of the first eight books of the Bible.

But it is as the composer of the first comprehensive body of polyphony in the history of Western music that Leoninus is known to us today. A music treatise—written in England, but obviously based on first-hand knowledge of Paris—records:

> And note that Master Leoninus, according to what was said, was the best composer of organum [polyphony]. And he made a great book of organum from the Mass and Office chants to elaborate the divine service.

This "great book" (known in Latin as the *Magnus Liber*) was copied into several different music manuscripts. Some of them originated in Paris, but others were compiled in other cities (which shows how the new music must have spread throughout Europe). All of them date from the thirteenth century, many years after the original date of composition of the Magnus Liber; however, by analyzing their contents it is possible to arrive at a fairly accurate picture of the form the original Magnus Liber may have taken.

---

[1]The biography of Leoninus has been established by Craig Wright, "Leoninus, Poet and Musician," *Journal of the American Musicological Society* XXXIX (1986): 1–35.

The music is compiled in two cycles, one for the Mass and one for the Office. Both are arranged in the order of the liturgical calendar. For example, the Office cycle begins with a setting of *Iudea et Ierusalem,* a responsory for Christmas Vespers, and continues with polyphonic settings of chants for Epiphany, Easter, Ascension, Pentecost, and so on. The Mass cycle begins with settings of the Gradual and Alleluia for Christmas and similarly continues in the order of the liturgical year. All these settings are of responsorial items and of only the *solo* portions of these items. Leoninus left the *choral* portions to be sung in plainchant. Without the plainchant, the polyphonic sections are fragments, making neither musical nor liturgical sense. In the same way, the entire pieces are only parts of complete services—since Leoninus embellished with polyphony only two or three items out of the many chants to be sung in the Mass and Office.

The Mass for Pentecost, for example, which we examined in detail in Chapter 4, would have been celebrated in Paris in plainchant except for

Bishop Maurice de Sully is memorialized in stone on the south portal of the cathedral he dreamed of and founded but never saw completed.

The technological marvel and intricate design of the cathedral are displayed in the overlapping arches of the ambulatory of Notre Dame.

the responsorial chants—the two Alleluyas, which are given polyphonic settings in the Notre Dame manuscripts.[2] The polyphonic settings for the Pentecost Mass, therefore, embellish those chants that are already highly melismatic in style and that involve the singing of solo performers.

Which services did Leoninus choose to elaborate in this way? The compositions in the Magnus Liber are designed for some of the most important feasts in the Church calendar, feasts such as Christmas and Easter, of course, which were important at every church, but also feasts that were highly ranked at the Cathedral of Notre Dame in Paris, such as Purification and Pentecost.

---

[2]The manuscripts also preserve another polyphonic piece for the Pentecost Mass—a Processional, which precedes the Introit and would have been sung to accompany a procession through the church prior to the celebration of the Mass itself. The Processional is also a responsorial chant.

THE MUSICAL STYLE OF THE MAGNUS LIBER

With his assiduous application of polyphony to the solo portions of some of the chants for important feasts, Leoninus transformed the musical quality of liturgical observance. Those portions which had previously stood out subtly in performance for their soloistic rendering and melismatic music were now elaborated to a remarkable degree. A brief intonation which might previously have taken ten seconds to sing in plainchant now took ten or twenty times that long to sing in its polyphonic setting. That this changed the balance of the music in the service goes without saying. It is equally clear that this new and complex music must have provided an opportunity (and created a challenge) for the most accomplished of solo singers.

But the change in the balance of the service, and the conspicuous alternation between polyphony and plainchant, were by no means the only elements of this new music. Within the polyphonic sections themselves, Leoninus built a subtle interplay of three different styles that depended both upon the relationship of one musical line to the other and the relative rhythm of both.

The names for these styles come from the musical theorists of the thirteenth century. Johannes de Garlandia, who was the first important theorist to discuss the music of Notre Dame, and was probably a teacher at the University of Paris, writes:

> And it should be known therefore that or organum in its generic sense polyphony] there are three species, that is to say discant, copula, and organum. . . .

Two of these names—discant and organum—(as well as the ambiguity of the word organum) are familiar to us from our consideration of earlier polyphony. We shall see how these styles have evolved from the earlier repertories and how the third style—copula—fits in to the musical composition as a whole.

The new discant (see Ex. 9-1) is a development out of the old note-against-note method of composition which we have already seen evolve from early parallel organum to the more flexible groupings in music of the Aquitainian manuscripts and in the Codex Calixtinus. It is a highly sophisticated and intricate interweaving of two musical lines according to a carefully organized system of rhythmic patterns. What had been missing from the previous polyphonic repertories was a system by means of which the neumes in neume-against-neume settings could be rhythmically arranged. From the music treatises of Garlandia and other theorists we learn how this problem was solved. A completely new rhythmic system was invented, which was the foundation of the new polyphony. It was the means by which the discant sections could be rationally composed and performed and by which the two separate musical lines could be made to conform with each other. It was a system which became the basis of musical composition for the next century. Its creation may rightly be called a breakthrough.

EXAMPLE 9-1 Discant.

The system was based on repeated rhythmic patterns called *rhythmic modes*. There were six of these, making use of three different note lengths. Example 9-2 shows the six modal patterns.

EXAMPLE 9-2 The rhythmic modes.

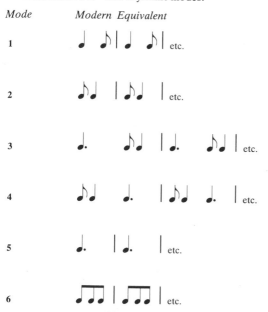

The development of the full system of rhythmic modes probably took place over some time. First- and second-mode rhythms are closely related, obviously, and fifth mode is a straightforward basis for underpinning either of these. (If the upper voice is in first or second mode, the lower voice can easily use the fifth mode.) Sixth mode is a more active version of Mode 1 or Mode 2, with the long notes divided into two short notes. Third and fourth modes, however, involve some conceptual novelties: the combination of three different note lengths, and a unit of repetition ("foot") that is twice as long as that of Modes 1 and 2. Third and fourth modes are related variants of each other and must have evolved at about the same time, but probably somewhat later than the other modes.

The rational rhythmic organization of the separate musical lines in the new polyphony also allowed stricter control of the intervals formed between them. These were carefully classified in a gradated series of perfect consonances, imperfect consonances, and dissonances. The perfect consonances were the unison, octave, fifth, and fourth; thirds were considered imperfect consonances; dissonances were the second, seventh, and sixth. Inclusion of the sixth among the dissonances is the most unexpected feature of this series, although a century later the sixth seems to have become accepted as an imperfect consonance like the third.

The interval structure of discant depended upon a progression of perfect and imperfect consonances, with a scattering of dissonances, moving to cadences upon perfect consonances. This structure was regarded as the basis for polyphonic composition for at least two hundred years.

At the opposite pole from discant among the styles of Notre Dame polyphony is organum. It does not have the two moving lines of discant, nor is it governed by the rhythmic modes. One of the lines (the chant line) contains extended notes, while the other (the one that is newly composed) moves above and around these long notes in a free and flexible manner (see Ex. 9-3). Clearly organum has not changed very much from its earlier incarnations in twelfth-century polyphony, except that it is now more clearly distinguished from its surroundings, whereas before, as we have seen, the distinction between organum and discant was often not clear-cut.

EXAMPLE 9-3 Organum.

The nature of the rhythm of the upper voice in organum has long been controversial among scholars, but it appears to be based upon the intervals created between the two voices. If the interval is dissonant, the note is short; if it is consonant, it is long. Depending upon the degree of consonance and dissonance (a minor second is more dissonant than a major seventh; an octave is more consonant than a fourth), a note is either longer or shorter. (In performance this seemingly complicated procedure is enormously facilitated by the fact that the chant line is holding long pitches.) The treatises of the time tell us that there are certain exceptions to these principles. Opening notes may sometimes be long even if they are dissonant (these opening gestures can be seen graphically represented in the manuscripts); penultimate notes are long whether they are dissonant or not; sometimes a long chain of descending notes appears, all of which are short. But in general the rhythm of the newly composed upper voice in organum style is dependent upon its degree of consonance and dissonance with the notes of the chant. This creates a highly flexible effect of one line moving freely above and around the other, which serves as a fixed point of reference. But it is a freedom with a logical and highly rational basis.

The third musical style in the polyphony of Notre Dame is known as copula ("connection"). This is a style that is midway between discant and organum. It occurs in the middle of polyphonic sections and contains features of both other styles: it has the sustained chant tones in the lower voice that form the basis of organum and, in the other voice, the modal rhythmic patterns that characterize discant (see Ex. 9-4). Copula also has another feature that differentiates it from the other two styles. It is built from patterned phrases of melodic sequence in the newly composed voice. These phrases, sung according to the rhythmic modes, stand out clearly over the long notes in the chant.

EXAMPLE 9-4 Copula.

All of these styles consist of a lower voice containing the original notes of the chant, while the upper voice is newly composed. (However, voice crossing still occurs fairly frequently.) In discant the chant melody in the lower voice is arranged in a regular rhythm according to one of the rhythmic modes, and the newly composed upper voice is also in modal rhythm. In organum the notes of the chant melody are sustained, and the new voice weaves a flexible line above and around these notes in a rhythm derived from the intervals that are formed as it moves. In copula the chant notes are sustained, while the new voice has melodic sequences in modal rhythm.

In order to understand how these three styles are utilized within a single composition, let us look at the polyphonic setting of the first Alleluya from the Pentecost Mass (Ex. 9-5), a piece we have examined already in its plainchant version (see pp. 103–5).

The opening intonation, for soloists, is set in organum style, with the original pitches of the chant in long notes. The upper voice weaves a musical tracery above these notes (occasionally dipping below them), coming to cadences on unisons, fourths, or fifths. In the middle of this intonation, two brief copulas stand out, with their regular rhythm and melodic sequence. The intonation is followed by the repetition of "Alleluya" with the jubilus, sung by the choir, just as in the plainchant original.

The soloists then sing the polyphony composed for most of the verse "Spiritus sanctus . . . "—that portion of it that was sung by soloists in the plainchant. Again, the original notes of the chant are in the lower voice. The composer makes use of all three polyphonic styles in this part of the setting: the verse begins with organum, moves to copula on the fourth and fifth notes of the chant, and then has two long discant sections (with a few brief organum passages interspersed to articulate the flow of the music); between the two discant sections, at the word "[in]visibili," there is another copula passage.

The modal rhythms are quite flexibly applied, though within each of the discant sections a prevailing mode can be recognized. In the section beginning "procedens . . . " the pattern is mostly rhythmic Mode 3 in the upper voice and Mode 5 in the lower voice. In the second discant section ("hodie perlustravit") the pattern is mostly rhythmic Mode 2 in both of the voices. This second discant section is mainly a setting of the long melisma on the "a" of "perlustravit" from the original chant.

The last word of the verse ("potentia") is sung by the choir, as it was in the original chant. The setting of the final "Alleluya" is brief, partly in organum, partly in discant style, and the polyphonic portion is again followed by the conclusion sung in chant by the choir.

The application of polyphony to the solo portions of this chant—the opening intonation, the solo verse, and the repetition of the Alleluya— creates a composition of great power and scope. The fluid interpenetration of the three styles—discant, copula, and organum—combined with the additional contrast of the surrounding plainchant, make for a constant variety of texture, an elaboration of the liturgy suitable for the architectural monument whose vaults it was designed to fill.

EXAMPLE 9-5 Polyphonic setting of *Alleluya, Spiritus Sanctus,* Florence, Biblioteca Medicea-Laurenziana, Pluteus 29.1.

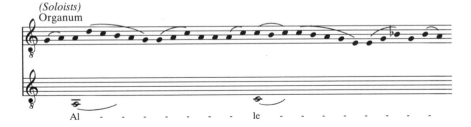

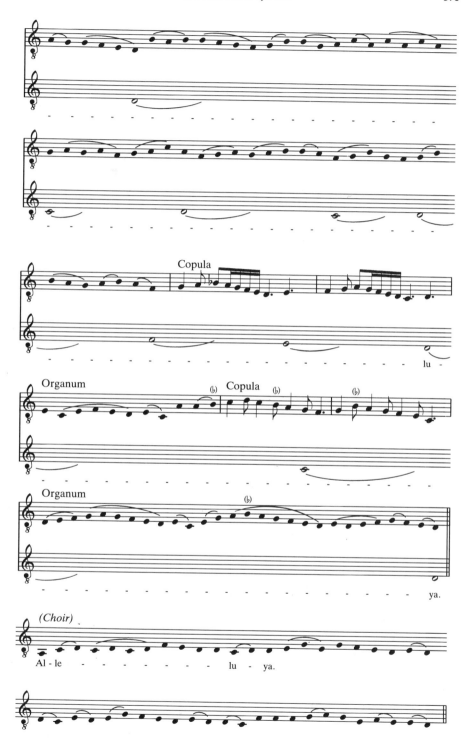

Alleluya.   Alleluya.
Alleluya.   Alleluya.

℣. Spiritus sanctus procedens a throno   ℣. The Holy Spirit proceeding from its .
apostolorum pectora invisibili hodie   throne has today purified the hearts of
perlustravit potentia.   the apostles with invisible power.

Alleluya.   Alleluya.

CONDUCTUS

Apart from the two large cycles of polyphonic settings of liturgical chants, the Notre Dame manuscripts contain a considerable number of separate compositions that are settings of Latin poems. These are usually known by the catch-all term "conductus." We have encountered the term previously as meaning Latin processional songs, but it quickly became a far more general term, referring to any newly composed song with a Latin text.

The texts of the Notre Dame conductus range widely in subject matter. Some are sacred, but many are reflections on contemporary political events or homages to persons living or recently deceased. Still others reflect outrage at the corruption of the clergy or are satires on modern society. The lively contemporaneity of many of the texts marks the popularity of the genre. Among the authors of the texts were well-known contemporary figures such as Philip the Chancellor and Walter of Châtillon. Philip was a high-ranking member of the administrative clergy of the Cathedral of Notre Dame, and Walter was an internationally known writer and poet (see p. 237).

From the musical point of view what is important about the conductus is the fact that they are written in verse. The regularly recurring rhythms of the Latin texts encouraged strophic musical settings of these texts and the use of the patterned rhythms of the rhythmic modes to declaim the words.

Many of these conductus are monophonic, testifying to the lively tradition and the still predominant role of monophonic music in the twelfth and thirteenth century. There are also, however, more than one hundred two-part conductus, about sixty three-part conductus, and three conductus written in four parts.

The musical style of the conductus could not be further from that of the polyphonic chant settings of the Magnus Liber. In place of the sharply differentiated rhythms of the separate voices in liturgical polyphony, the voices of the conductus move in very similar rhythms. And whereas the musical phrases in the polyphonic settings of the liturgy are fairly irregular, the phrases in conductus are regular and repetitive, reflecting the verse structure of their texts. Except for some of their elaborate ornamental caudas (see the following discussion), the syllables in conductus change frequently, according to the natural rhythm of the verse, which allows for a clear and understandable rendition of the words. As these were new poems, rather than time-honored and familiar chants, this was a desirable aim.

The two-part conductus in Example 9-6 is a celebration for Christmas. It is an excellent example of the style, with the voices moving in very similar rhythms (based on the first rhythmic mode), and with mostly consonant intervals. The meaning, sound, and meter of the text are thus made patently clear, while occasional rhythmic shifts and passing dissonances en-

Original notation of the beginning of the conductus *Flos Ut Rosa Floruit* (see Example 9-6), British Library, London.

liven the texture of the music. Each of the four stanzas of the text uses the same metrical pattern and has similar music. The words "nova genitura," which appear at the end of the first and second stanzas and in the middle of the fourth, act as a kind of refrain. The brief melismatic passage at the end of the piece is known as a *cauda,* or "tail," (from which the later musical term *coda* is derived). Sometimes these caudas were considerably extended and created long melismatic sections at the end of a piece. As in many other types of music designed to carry verse, it was usually the penultimate syllable that was ornamented in this way. Despite the name, caudas are sometimes also found at the beginning of a conductus, thus extending the first syllable of the verse as well.

EXAMPLE 9-6 Conductus, *Flos Ut Rosa Floruit,* London, British Library, Add. 27630.

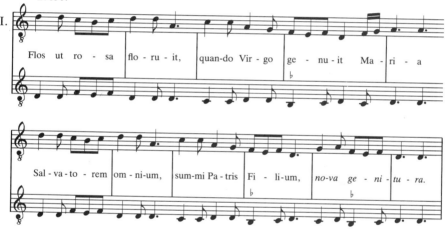

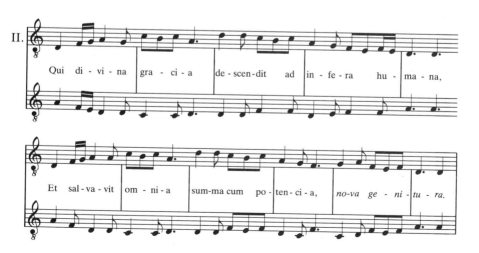

III. Can - te - mus hym - num glo - ri - e, can - ti - co le - ti - ci - e lau - dan - do,

Sol - lem - pni - zan - tes ho - di - e re - gi re - gum iu - sti - ci - e gra - ci - as a - gen - do.

IV. Qui na - tus est de vir - gi - ne mi - sti - co spi - ra - mi - ne, *no - va ge - ni - tu - ra.*

Er - go no - stra con - ci - o psal - lat cum tri - pu - di - o

be - ne - di - cat Do - - - - - - - - - mi - no.

I. Flos ut rosa floruit, quando Virgo	I. A flower bloomed like a rose, when
genuit Maria	the Virgin Mary gave birth
Salvatorem omnium, summi Patris	To the Savior of all people, the Son
Filium, *nova genitura.*	of the highest Father, *in a birth of*
	utter newness.

II. Qui divina gracia descendit ad infera humana,
Et salvavit omnia summa cum potencia, *nova genitura.*

II. In divine grace he came down to humanity below
And saved us all with his immense power, *in a birth of utter newness.*

III. Cantemus hymnum glorie, cantico leticie laudando,
Sollempnizantes hodie regi regum iusticie gracias agendo.

III. Let us sing a hymn of glory, praising him with a song of joy,
And celebrate today by giving thanks to the justice of the king of kings.

IV. Qui natus est de virgine mistico spiramine, *nova genitura.*
Ergo nostra concio psallat cum tripudio benedicat Domino.

IV. He was born of a virgin by a mystical spirit, *in a birth of utter newness.*
Therefore let this group dance and sing praises and bless the Lord.

Polyphonic conductus represent a significant break from the liturgical anchor of most earlier music, for they were among the first polyphonic compositions that had no connection to plainchant and that were newly composed throughout. (A few conductus deliberately borrow material from chants, but these are deviations from the norm.)

PEROTINUS AND FURTHER DEVELOPMENTS IN THE THIRTEENTH CENTURY

Not long after the creation of the original Magnus Liber, with its two-part settings of the solo portions of responsorial chants for the Mass and Office, composers began to evolve new applications for this exciting new approach to the music of the liturgy, and to expand upon the achievement of Leoninus. These developments took two forms: the composition of alternative polyphonic fragments to insert as substitutes into existent settings, and the composition of entirely new settings in more than two parts. We do not know to what extent Leoninus himself took part in these modifications and extensions of his original work, although since he lived until after 1200 it is quite possible that he was actively involved in them himself.

Another name, however, has come down to us as the principal author of these developments. The thirteenth-century English music treatise that is the source for our information about Leoninus and the Magnus Liber continues its discussion as follows:

And the Magnus Liber was in use up to the time of Perotinus the Great, who edited it and made a large number of better *clausulae* or sections, since he was the best composer of discant and better than Leoninus. But this is not to say anything about the subtlety of his [Leoninus's] organum.

The treatise also names several specific compositions of Perotinus the Great, including some three- and four-part pieces, and states that his music was in use in the Cathedral of Notre Dame and elsewhere for a very long time.

Unfortunately there is no other biographical information about this important figure, but from the few scanty references to him and his compositions in the treatises we can deduce several things about Perotinus: (1) He was active after the work of Leoninus; (2) he wrote a great deal of music (the English treatise refers to his "book or books"); (3) he revised the Magnus Liber; (4) he wrote very many *clausulae*; (5) he was an expert at writing discant; (6) he wrote music in three and four parts (we even know the names of several of his compositions); and (7) he was famous both during and after his lifetime.

CLAUSULAE

What are these *clausulae* that Perotinus wrote? The word *clausula*, like many terms in medieval music theory, is taken from Latin grammar, where it means a "clause" or part of a sentence. In the same way, the musical clausula is a part or section of a complete composition.

The Notre Dame manuscripts that survive contain many hundreds of clausulae, gathered together separately and following the same liturgical order as the Magnus Liber itself. They range from short snippets of settings to quite long passages, and are mostly in two parts, sometimes in three or four. Evidently they were one of the ways in which the Magnus Liber was revised, for they can be inserted into the earlier settings, at appropriate locations, as substitutes for sections of the original compositions. Let us look at an example.

In the polyphonic setting of the Alleluya from the Pentecost Mass given as Example 9-5, there is a section of discant at the words "a throno apostolorum." Example 9-7 is a clausula for that section. The same words of the chant are used, and the same portion of the chant melody is in the lower voice, but the notes are written in different rhythmic values, and a new upper voice has been composed. This clausula could therefore replace the earlier section of polyphony, making a new composition, without damaging the integrity of the words or the chant melody.

This seemingly straightforward idea had a number of important consequences, for clausulae began to develop into independent compositions in their own right and formed the basis for the motet—one of the most fertile and long-lived musical forms of the Middle Ages. We shall examine this development later. For the time being, however, we should note that the clausula constituted the most modern form of composition and that composers invested it with their most concentrated experimental efforts. Some of the new compositional techniques found in clausulae include: systematic organization of phrase structure; voice exchange, in which musical phrases are exchanged between voices; and, perhaps most significant from the

repetition

EXAMPLE 9-7 Clausula, Florence, biblioteca Medicea-Laurenziana, Pluteus 29.1.

... a throno apostolorum   ... from the throne of the apostles

point of view of later music, repetition or other manipulation of the musical phrases of the chant.

About this time the lower voice of a polyphonic chant setting—the voice based on a chant melody—began to be known as the "tenor," from the Latin *tenere* ("to hold"). Composers of clausulae started to develop new techniques involving deliberate manipulation of the tenor, usually by repeating a section of the melody, sometimes even by stating the melody backwards. In Example 9-8 we may see the evolution of this technique. Example 9-8a is the word "Domino" as chanted in the Gradual of the Mass for Easter. Example 9-8b is the two-part polyphonic setting of that word in discant style from the Magnus Liber: the chant melody has been arranged into the rhythmic patterns of Mode 5, and a new voice has been added. Finally, Example 9-8c shows a clausula that was designed to replace the original discant section. It can be seen that the chant melody is stated twice (measures 1–13 and 14–26), providing for a new and extended upper part.

EXAMPLE 9-8   (a) Portion of Easter Gradual in plainchant; (b) discant section from
Magnus Liber, Florence, Biblioteca Medicea-Laurenziana, Pluteus 29.1; (c) clausula,
Florence, Biblioteca Medicea-Laurenziana, Pluteus 29.1.

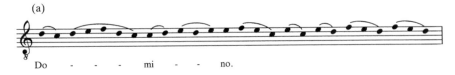

(a)

Do - - - mi - - no.

Domino.   To the Lord.

(b)

Do - - - - - - - - - - - - - - - - mi -

- - - - - - - - no.

Domino.   To the Lord.

(c)

Do - - - - - - - - - - - - - - - - - - - mi -

Domino.   To the Lord.

This technique of repeating a musical phrase in the tenor line has extremely important connotations. It signifies the acceptance by medieval composers of the concept that the notes of a sacred chant may be considered independently from their liturgical context. We have seen how, up to this point in the history of Western music, the words and notes of a chant were considered inviolable. Even when a chant was troped, the original words and music almost always remained intact. Even when a newly composed line was added to a chant, as in early polyphony, the original words and music remained intact. The manipulation of the tenor of a clausula (which has at least a portion of the original notes and words of a sacred chant in the proper context and in the correct order), by repetition or any other technique, marks the moment at which composers began to regard sacred music as musical *material,* subject to intellectual arrangement for artistic, and not purely for liturgical, aims.

TRIPLA AND QUADRUPLA

The three- and four-part compositions of Perotinus, known as *tripla* and *quadrupla,* are musical landmarks of a different sort. They seem to be the first compositions ever to have been written for more than two voices. (The three- and four-part conductus mentioned above were probably written somewhat later.)

The three-part compositions that we know to have been written by Perotinus are *Alleluya Nativitas* for the Nativity of the Virgin Mary and *Alleluya Posui Adiutorium* for the Feast of St. Nicholas. Perotinus is also known to be the composer of the four-part settings of *Viderunt Omnes,* the Gradual for Christmas and Circumcision, and *Sederunt Principes,* the Gradual for St. Stephen's Day.

The musical style of these pieces differs in some important ways from the two-part chant settings of Leoninus. In the first place, and most immediately noticeable, the fluid organum style has disappeared. With the addition of a third (or third and fourth) part to the texture, the subtle and flexible wandering of organum, based as it was upon single intervals, became impossible. It was necessary for the voices above the chant to be properly coordinated, and a device for this lay at hand—that of modal rhythm. Both upper parts were controlled throughout by a regular rhythmic structure, under the sway of the modal system. The tenor still alternated between modal-rhythmic sections and sustained-note sections, but there was no differentiation in the upper voices. Copula could still be composed, as this style had always used modal rhythm in the upper voice. But now there were two (or three) voices employing melodic sequence instead of only one.

Partly as a result of the loss of organum style, and partly as a result of the trend toward clearer and more systematic organization, the phrases in the tripla and quadrupla are shorter and more regular than in the two-voice settings. Shifts between different modal rhythms are less frequent, and the first mode is favored. Voice exchange appears commonly, and standardization of structure and design sets in. The music appears more self-assured, less rhapsodic and experimental.

Example 9-9 shows the beginning of the three-voice setting of the Alleluya for the Feast of St. Nicholas composed by Perotinus. The richness and grandeur of this music are remarkable. In the polyphonic sections the tenor shifts between long notes (sometimes held for great lengths) and the regular rhythmic patterns of the modes. Above this foundation, the two upper voices intertwine, cross, and interlock with hypnotic intensity, moving from phrase to phrase with some startling dissonances as well as points of purest consonance. The dynamic rhythms and shifting textures of this piece are bound together into a unified whole by the authoritative words of the liturgy.

EXAMPLE 9-9 Perotinus, *Alleluya, Posui Adiutorium,* beginning only. After Yvonne Rokseth, *Polyphonies du XIIIe siècle: le manuscrit H196 de la Faculté de Médecine de Montpellier* (Paris: L'Oiseau-lyre, 1935–39).

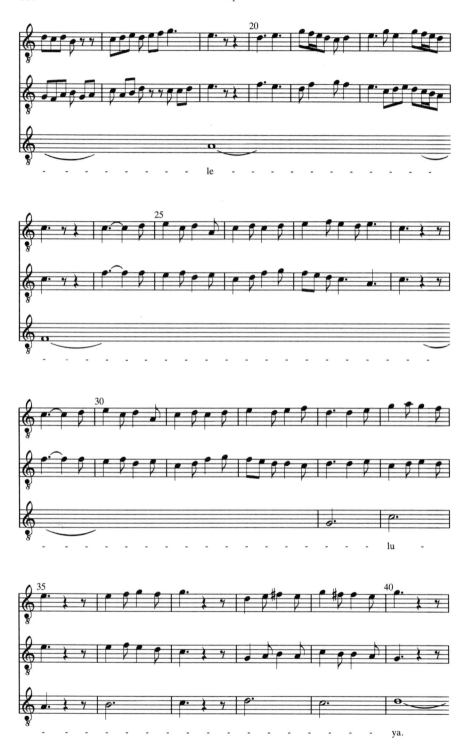

[a], al - le - lu - - - ya.

℣. Po - - - - - - - - - - - - - - - - -

- - - - - - - - - - - - - -

| Alleluya. | Alleluya. |
| Alleluya. | Alleluya. |

℣. Posui auditorium super potentem et exaltavi electum de plebe mea.

℣. I have provided assistance to the powerful one and I have raised up the chosen one from my people.

Alleluya.

Alleluya.

FROM CLAUSULA TO MOTET

As mentioned earlier, the creation of clausulae to be inserted into complete, previously made compositions was a significant step in the evolution of a new musical form—the motet. Let us now consider the development that led from one to the other.

At first, clausulae had no independent existence. They were exactly what they were called: "clauses"—parts of a whole. But the very fact that they were separately composed, albeit on fragments of a chant tenor, and were separately notated—being collected into groups in separate portions of the manuscripts—clearly led composers to begin thinking of them as separate compositions. Thus clausulae gradually evolved from fragmentary, incomplete sections of a piece to entirely independent compositions in their own right. This process, which did not take place overnight, of course, may be clearly traced by examining the following examples.

In the two-part version of *Alleluya, Spiritus Sanctus,* given as Example 9-5, one of the main discant sections is composed on the text "hodie perlustravit." This discant section (like others in the composition) was provided with clausulae; one of them is shown here in part (Ex. 9-10a). The chant notes are arranged in groups based on the fifth rhythmic mode, and a new upper voice has been written above them.

EXAMPLE 9-10a   Clausula, Florence, Biblioteca Medicea-Laurenziana, Pluteus 29.1.

Hodie perlustra[vit].   Today it has purified.

The first stage in the transition from clausula to motet was taken when composers began to add words to the upper voice of a clausula. This was a process exactly like the troping of chant melismas by adding text to them. It should not be surprising that such a technique was applied to the clausula, for, as we have seen, throughout the Middle Ages full advantage was usually taken of any opportunity for elaboration, especially elaboration of the liturgy. In the polyphonic chant settings of Notre Dame and the earlier repertories it seems probable that the text sung in the upper voice was the same as that in the tenor; but in clausulae, which contained only a portion of the original chant, the text did not make sense entirely by itself. (In the clausula in Example 9-10a, for example, the text means "today it has purified.") Furthermore, as we have seen, the tenor of a clausula came to be regarded as a musical structure, the foundation of a composition, rather than as the inviolable representation of a sacred part of the liturgy.

So composers began to add words to the upper voices of clausulae, troping the original text by commenting on the meaning of the chant or the feast to which it belonged, or on some other topic. Initially, these words were in Latin and had clearly a liturgical relevance. This type of composition came to be called a *motet*. Example 9-10b is such a Latin motet, with words added to the upper voice of the clausula of which Example 9-10a shows the beginning. The words added are a call to repentance, and they take their impetus from the original sense of the tenor's chant fragment, "it has purified." Not only does the new text contain the word "perlustra" ("purify") in its sixth line, but it also ends with the same words as the chant fragment upon which it is built: "hodie [pie] perlustravit." Moreover, syllables in the newly written text are designed to rhyme with those of the chant. Over the syllable "Ho-" of "Hodie" the upper voice sings "O"; over "-di-" the upper voice sings "[Cali-]di," and over "-e" "[Con-] ver-te-re." The word "perlustra" appears (measures 15–16) when the chant has "[per-] lustra," and the final word is "perlustravit," as the chant line has the final syllable of the same word. Such relationships between the new text and the tenor's chant fragment, as well as the idea of troping or commenting upon the sense of the chant, were common features of the early Latin motet.

EXAMPLE 9-10b Latin motet, *O Natio/Hodie Perlustravit,* Wolfenbüttel, Herzog-August-Bibliothek, Helmstedt 1099.

O natio, que vitiis	O nation, you who are overthrown
Que studio serpentis	By the vices and energy
Callidi perverteris	Of the clever serpent,
Convertere; consiliis	Repent! With true
Veris	Wisdom
Cor perlustra,	Purify your heart,
Ne vixeris	Lest you live
Frustra.	In vain.
Te pervertentem	Abandon
Desere;	The one who perverts you;
Sequere	Follow
Te convertentem,	The one who converts you,
Et eum amplectere	And embrace him
Qui tibi sitiens,	Who thirsts for you,
Moriens,	And who, dying,
Brachia	Stretches out
Propria	His arms
Porrigit.	To you.
Erigit	He lifts you up
Languidam,	When you are weak,
Te sordidam	Cleanses you
Mundat,	When you are dirty,
Mundam fecundat,	Nurtures you when you are clean,
Tibi dimittens	Forgives you
Debitum,	Your sins,
Spiritum emittens,	And sends forth his spirit,
Qui radios glorie	Which the pious rays of
Pios hodie	Glory today
Pie perlustravit.	Piously has purified.

Tenor:
    Hodie perlustravit.

Tenor:
    Today it has purified.

Very soon, however, the added texts began to be written in the vernacular, in French, and to take on a decidedly secular slant. Poems were used which had the same theme as contemporary vernacular songs: love—in all its humorous, conventional, self-pitying, serious, blatant, and gentle aspects. And from the French word *mot,* which means "word," came the name for the new genre. In Example 9-10c, the Latin text of the previous example has been replaced by a French text: a poem spoken by a pining lover. The music is the same.

Finally, composers began to write completely new upper parts for motets, no longer relying on the existing clausulae. What was always retained, however, was the tenor part, the fragment of chant which formed the foundation of the composition. The rhythm could be changed, and repetition might be used, but the original pitches were always there. The final manifestation of the piece whose evolution we have been tracing is as a three-part motet (Ex. 9-10d), with two new upper parts—new both in their words and in their music. The tenor is still the melody of "Hodie perlustravit," but its pitches have been arranged into a completely new rhythmic pattern.

EXAMPLE 9-10c French motet, *Dame Que J'aim/Hodie Perlustravit,* beginning only, Wolfenbüttel, Herzog-August-Bibliothek, Helmstedt 1099.

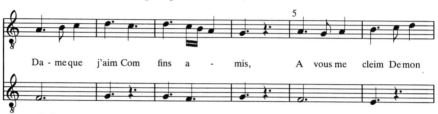

Dame que j'aim	Lady, whom I love
Com fins amis,	As a courtly mistress,
A vous me cleim	To you I lament
De mon cuer, qui m'a mis . . .	From my heart, which has put me . . .

Tenor: *Tenor:*

Hodie perlustravit.   Today it has purified.

EXAMPLE 9-10d Three-voice French motet, *Quant Voi/Au Douz Tans/Hodie Perlustravit,* beginning only. From Yvonne Rokseth, *Polyphonies du XIIIe siècle: le manuscrit H 196 de la Faculté de Médecine de Montpellier* (Paris: L'Oiseau-lyre, 1935–39).

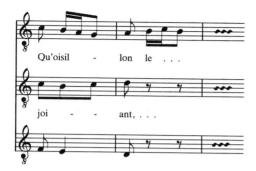

Qu'oisil - lon le . . .

joi - - ant, . . .

I. Quant voi yver repairier
   Et la froidour,
   Qu'oisillon le . . .

II. Au douz tans pleisant,
    Qu'oisiau sunt joiant . . .

Tenor:
   Hodie perlustravit.

I. When I see winter return
   And also the cold,
   Which birds . . .

II. In sweet, pleasant weather,
    When birds are happy . . .

Tenor:
   Today it has purified.

THE MOTET TO 1275

The motet quickly became the most popular form of new music in the thirteenth century. Paris remained the center of its production, but soon it caught on in other countries, and manuscripts from Germany, Spain, and England show how composers throughout Europe quickly imitated the new Paris fashion. The three-voice motet became the standard type, with both of the upper voices having different poetic texts, each with its own rhyme scheme and phrase structure. This *polytextuality* is a characteristic feature of the motet. The upper voices may even be in two different languages, one in Latin, and the other in French.

The simultaneous singing of two different texts may appear to be a strange phenomenon. Certainly it obscures the clarity of the words. But it is not untypical of the medieval approach to art. Simplicity and clarity were not necessarily the most desirable aims. If a composer wanted to express a text clearly he could always write a conductus. The motet had other features which appealed to the medieval mind; indeed its very complexity was one of these. The motet was a highly intellectual genre, and the circles in which it was cultivated—court, cathedral, and university—were inhabited by educated and sophisticated people. The liturgical basis of its tenor, the irregularity of its phrase structure, the counterpoint of its upper voices, the interplay of its textual meanings—these were the elements that made the motet one of the most enduring artistic inventions of its time.

Many of the motets that have survived from this period appear in several different versions. Sometimes a motet seems to have gone through a variety of incarnations, mixing Latin and French texts, adapting one language to the other, or abandoning one set of texts for another, different set. But the trend was increasingly away from the liturgical and towards the secular. By the middle of the century, the tenor seems to have been performed instrumentally, thus cutting all but its melodic tie to the original chant; and the motet with two secular French upper voices became the standard form.

HOCKET

One technique that came to be used as a textural device in the upper voices of motets was known as *hocket.* This involved the breaking-up of the melodic lines of both voices by the insertion of short rests. Notes in one voice would sound during the rests in the other voice (as in the brief excerpt of Example 9-11). The word hocket means "hiccup" in Latin and Old French. The technique and the resulting musical texture are very distinctive.

EXAMPLE 9-11   Hocket technique, London, British Library, Add. 24198.

As with many musical terms which denote both a device and a genre, hocket also came to mean a composition that used this technique throughout. There are several pieces in the motet manuscripts which are hockets and have no text in the upper voices. In structure they are motets without words. The tenor is a section of chant, and the upper voices are in more or less the same range, characterized by hocket texture throughout. We know from clues in the manuscripts and from contemporary theorists that these are instrumental pieces, and that they were often played on recorders or flutes.

Example 9-12 is one of several hockets based on the same tenor, a chant fragment on the words "In seculum," whose melody is repeated (across the rhythmic groupings) starting in measure 23. The upper voices indulge in the kind of snappy interchange that led contemporary writers to associate the genre with "wantonness" and youth. Apart from one spectacular example in the fourteenth century, the hocket as a genre died out very quickly, but the technique of hocketing came to play an important role as a textural and articulating device in later music.

EXAMPLE 9-12 *In Seculum* hocket. From Gordon Anderson, *Compositions of the Bamberg Manuscript: Bamberg, Staatsbibliothek, Lit. 115 (olim Ed. IV. 6.),* Corpus Mensurabilis Musicae, vol. 75 ([Rome]: American Institute of Musicology, 1977).

In seculum

THE CONDUCTUS-MOTET

Brief mention also should be made of a hybrid form of composition which enjoyed a brief existence in the first half of the thirteenth century. This was the conductus-motet, which combined features of both types of music. It had a tenor part written in short rhythmic patterns like a motet, but the upper voices both carried the same text in the same rhythm, like a conductus. This form seems to have fallen into disfavor by the middle of the century; indeed both the conductus-motet and the conductus itself were soon abandoned as a result of the growing popularity of the motet and its later manifestations.

Original notation of the beginning of the motet *Mout Me Fu Grief/Robins M'aime/ Portare* (from one of the largest motet manuscripts of the thirteenth century (see Example 9-14), Faculté de Médecine, Montpellier.

THE MOTET ENTÉ

The connection between the new French motet and French secular song has already been mentioned. When motet texts were written in the vernacular, they were more or less indistinguishable from the texts of trouvère songs, although they were often less regular in their metrical and poetic design. One place where this connection was overtly acknowledged was in motets which deliberately quoted from contemporary popular songs of the trouvères. In these pieces the quotation from a song (usually its refrain) is grafted onto the text of the motet in such a way that it forms a natural part of its new context. It was from this grafting technique that this kind of motet took its name: it was known as the *motet enté* ("grafted motet"). The quotation may occur in either of the upper voices, it may appear at any point in the text, and it may or may not be accompanied by its original music. Clearly the sly incorporation of quotations from trouvère songs was another one of the intellectual challenges that appealed to the motet's thirteenth-century audiences.

The easiest quotations for us to identify today are those which use refrains from trouvère compositions that have become well-known in their own right. In Chapter 7 (pp. 288–95) we saw how the refrain of a song by Adam de la Halle was quoted in one of his own motets. Example 9-13 is another song by Adam de la Halle which became popular from its appearance at the beginning of *The Play of Robin and Marion* (see p. 328). The song is sung by the shepherdess Marion to express her love for Robin. It contains a single stanza framed by a two-line refrain of charming simplicity. The refrain of this song is quoted intact, with both its words and music (transposed), at the beginning and end of the middle voice part of the motet in Example 9-14 (which was not written by Adam but by some other composer, who remains anonymous). Indeed, the entire text of this voice is written in the same format and meter as the original song, though with new words and new music apart from the refrain. This is set off from the remainder of the poem by rests in the voice part. The upper voice carries a completely different text, written from a man's point of view and lamenting the absence of his beloved.

EXAMPLE 9-13   Adam de la Halle, *Robins M'aime, Robins M'a*. After Friedrich Gennrich, *Adam de la Halle: Le Jeu de Robin et de Marion, Li Rondel Adam*, Musik-wissenschaftliche Studienbibliothek, vol. 20 (Langen: [Author], 1962).

Ro - bins   m'a   de - man - de - e,   si m'a - ra.

Ro - bins   m'a - ca - ta co - te - le

D'es - car - la - te   bonn' et   be - le,

Sous-ka - ni'   et   chain-tu - re - l'A - leu - ri - ra!

Ro - bins   m'ai - me,   Ro - bins   m'a.

Ro - bins   m'a   de - man - de - e,   si m'a - ra.

Robins m'aime, Robins m'a.
Robins m'a demandee, si m'ara.

Robins m'acata cotele
D'escarlate bonn' et bele,
Souskani' et chainturel' Aleuriva!

Robins m'aime, Robins m'a.
Robins m'a demandee, si m'ara.

Robin loves me, Robin has my love.
Robin has asked for me, he may have me.

Robin bought me a cloak
Of beautiful bright scarlet,
A gown and a sash. Hurrah!

Robin loves me, Robin has my love.
Robin has asked for me, he may have me.

EXAMPLE 9-14   Motet, *Mout Me Fu Grief/Robins M'aime/Portare*. From Yvonne Rokseth, *Polyphonies du XIIIe siècle: le manuscrit H196 de la Faculté de Médecine de Montpellier* (Paris: L'Oiseau-lyre, 1935–39).

lis, Quant vous ver - rai? Da - me de va - lour, Ver - mel -

m'ai - me, Ro - bins m'a. Ro - bins

le com-me rose en mai, Pour vous sui en grant do - lour.

m'a de - man - de - e, si m'a - ra.

I. Mout me fu grief li departir
   De m'amiete,
   La jolie au cler vis,
   Qui est blanche et vermellete
   Comme rose par desus lis,
   Ce m'est avis;
   Son tres douz ris mi fait fremir

   Et si oell vair riant languir.

   Ha, Dieus! com mar la lessai!
   Blanchete comme flour de lis,
   Quant vous verrai?
   Dame de valour,
   Vermelle comme rose en mai,
   Pour vous sui en grant dolour.

I. It grieved me greatly, the parting
   Of my loved one,
   The pretty one with the shining face,
   As pale and pink
   As rose against lily,
   It seems to me;
   Her sweet lovely laughter makes me
       tremble,
   Her smiling gray eyes make me
       faint.
   Oh God, how painful to leave her!
   Little white lily,
   When shall I see you?
   Worthy lady,
   Red as a rose in May,
   Because of you am I in great pain.

II. *Robins m'aime, Robins m'a.*
   Robins m'a demandee, si m'ara.

Robins m'achata corroie
Et aumonniere de soie;
Pour quoi donc ne l'ameroie?
   Aleuriva!

Robins m'aime, Robins m'a.
Robins m'a demandee, si m'ara.

Tenor:
   Portare.

II. *Robin loves me, Robin has my love.*
   Robin has asked for me, he may
      have me.

Robin bought me a satchel
And a silk purse;
Why shouldn't I love him? Hurrah!

Robin loves me, Robin has my love.
Robin has asked for me, he may
   have me.

Tenor:
   To carry.

In its general style (and apart from its use of quotation), the motet in Example 9-14 is a good example of the motet at about the middle of the thirteenth century. The tenor is based upon a segment of plainchant (identified by the Latin "Portare" at the beginning), the melody of which occurs completely in measures 1–10. A partial restatement of it appears in measures 11–14, and further complete and partial statements (measures 15–24, 25–27, 28–34) form the basis for the remainder. The tenor is the slowest-moving part. The middle voice has slightly faster note values and lies in the middle of the sonority. The upper voice has the longest text and therefore the fastest note values. Although the two texted voices cross occasionally, the upper voice stays mostly in a higher range than the middle voice. When one of the texted voices rests, the motion is always continued by the other. Perfect consonances occur at cadences (mm. 6, 9, 15, etc.), which are approached by contrary or parallel motion, including parallel fifths and octaves; passing dissonances are fairly frequent.

Between 1250 and 1275 the motet displayed an increasing tendency to break away from the rigid patterns of the rhythmic modes. Even before this time, theorists and composers had recognized that the rhythmic modes were theoretical constructs which did not completely describe the variety of actual music, in which non-modal combinations of rhythms and notes shorter than those theoretically allowed had already appeared. Now, after the middle of the century, motets increasingly included even more complex rhythmic combinations and a higher proportion of short notes. In the modal system only three note values had been projected: the long (either ♩. or ♩), and the short (♪). The long note was called in Latin a *longa,* the short note a *brevis* (English: breve). A new, even shorter value came to be used after the middle of the century: the fraction of a breve called *semibrevis,* or semibreve. The motets of this period include a large number of semibreves, and therefore the upper voices can carry many syllables of text. The result is an almost patter-like declamation, requiring superb control and clarity of diction from the singers.

The following motet is a composition from this period, in which the tenor is constructed from the first phrase of the plainchant Sequence from the Mass for Easter Sunday. The chant phrase is shown in Example 9-15a; the motet based on it in Example 9-15b. In the modern transcription of the motet, longs appear as quarter notes, breves as eighth notes; the new semibreve values are rendered as sixteenth notes.

EXAMPLE 9-15a   Chant, *Victimae Paschali Laudes,* first phrase only.

Vic - ti - mae pas - cha - li   lau - des   im - mo - lent   Chri - ti - a - ni.

Victimae paschali laudes immolent   Let Christians offer up praises to the pas-
   Christiani.   chal victim.

EXAMPLE 9-15b   Motet, *C'il S'entremet/Nus Hom/Victimae Paschali Laudes.* From W. Thomas Marrocco and Nicholas Sandon, *Medieval Music: The Oxford Anthology of Music* (London: Oxford University Press, 1977).

mor bla-mer,   Mes loi-au-ment sans boi-di - e   La doit cil gar - der,   Qui joi'-

Qui n'en puet a - voir   So - las   ne se-cors: Fors maus et do - lours   Ce co-

III

en vieut re - co - vrer,   Et gar - de Qu'il ne mes-di-e   De s'a - mi - e,   Qui doit

vient il   re - ce - voir.   Dont si   me sem-ble por - voir   Que c'est   grant fo - lors

IV

ho - no - rer;   Quar s'il en dit   vi - le - ni - e,   Nul con-fort n'i   doit tro-ver.

D'a - mer l'ou on   n'a po - oir   D'a - ve - nir,   car c'est la - bours   Sans preu a - voir.

V

I. Cil s'entremet de folie
    Qui contr'amors veut parler,
    Car honor et cortoisie
    Aprent en d'amer.
    Et pour ce ne doit on mie
    Bon'amor blamer,
    Mes loiaument sans boidie
    La doit cil garder,

I. He is foolish
    Who wishes to speak against love,
    For honor and courtesy
    Are learned from loving.
    For this reason one should not
    Criticize true love,
    But preserve it
    Loyally and without deceit,

Qui joi'en vieut recovrer,   If one wishes to gain joy from it,
Et garde   And keep
Qu'il ne mesdie   From speaking evil
De s'amie,   Of one's lady,
Qui doit honorer;   Who must be honored;
Quar s'il en dit vilenie,   For if she is slandered,
Nul confort n'i doit trover.   No joy can come of it.

II. Nus hom ne porroit savoir   II. No one can know
     Que c'est d'amer par amours,   What it is to love truly,
     Car teus se pain'en espoir   For a man like that hopes in vain
     Qu'avoir en puet les douçors,   To get sweet reward from it,
     Et sert loiaument toz jours   And serves loyally every day,
     Qui n'en puet avoir   But never has
     Solas ne secors: Comfort or joy from it:
     Fors maus et dolours,   What he gets are pain and suffering,
     Ce covient il recevoir.   And quite rightly.
     Dont si me semble porvoir   Therefore it seems clear to me
     Que c'est grant folors   That it is sheer folly
     D'amer l'ou on n'a pooir   To love where one has no control
     D'avenir, car c'est labours   Over the future, for it is labor
     Sans preu avoir.   Without any recompense.

Tenor: *Tenor:*
     Victimae paschali laudes.   Praises to the paschal victim.

The tenor of the motet arranges the chant fragment into five repetitive patterns based on the first rhythmic mode, making a five-measure phrase in the transcription (there are no barlines in the original). This five-measure phrase is repeated throughout the motet, requiring five statements (indicated by Roman numerals) to complete the composition. This five-by-five arrangement is the kind of deliberately intellectual approach to the construction of the tenor that grew out of the repetitions and other simple manipulations of the tenors of clausulae and early motets, and became one of the main features of the later repertory.

The beginnings of poetic lines in the upper voices are indicated in the score by upper-case letters in the text. As can be seen, the musical phrases of the upper voices usually correspond to the poetic lines and are marked off by rests. This is invariably the case in the middle voice (except for the very last line), but less so in the upper voice, which sometimes runs phrases together to create musical continuity. Further variety is created by the overlapping or coincidence of phrases in the upper voices with each other or with the tenor. Examples of the constant variety of texture and phrasing which the composer has managed to achieve within this short piece may be seen in the following places.

In measure 4 all three voices have a rest at the same time, and both of the upper voices reach the end of a poetic line. This suggests a regularity of phrase structure which is immediately contradicted, for the tenor does not actually complete its melody until the next measure, and simultaneous rests in all three parts do not occur again in the piece. The tenor and the middle voice have simultaneous rests at several places (mm. 6, 8, 10, 13, 20, and 22), but of these places it is only in measures 10 and 20 that the end of a phrase in the middle voice coincides with the end of a complete five-measure melodic statement in the tenor. And note that at both of these points the composer has deliberately placed the beginning of a new line in the upper voice to cover the gap and carry forward the motion of the music.

The voices inhabit fairly distinct ranges, although the middle voice crosses below the tenor quite frequently. The intervals formed by the beginnings and ends of phrases are mostly fifths and octaves, although there are also some thirds between the tenor and the middle voice (beginning of mm. 3, 8, 11, and 18). Passing dissonances are frequent, and there are several instances of dissonances on what today we would call the "beat" (middle of mm. 8, 13, and 24; beginning of m. 10).

By this time, as we have noted, it is probable that the tenor would have been performed instrumentally, although it could have been sung to a neutral syllable. It is unlikely that the original words of the chant would have been sung. The fragmentary chant text given below the tenors of motets at this time acts more as an identifying label than as a vocal text. In the motet of Example 9-15b there is no obvious connection between the words of the chant and the texts of the upper voices; sometimes, however, there is a deliberate play on words between the chant label and the new poetry. For example, below the texts of two love poems in a French motet, the chant may have as its label the Latin words "And your heart shall rejoice," or "Listen, daughter." The real meanings of these words were of course entirely different in their liturgical contexts, but taken out of context they could resonate significantly with the love poetry being declaimed above them. Part of the delight of the audience must have lain in trying to recognize the melodies of the tenors and associate them with the implied words of the chant.

The upper voices of motets also were designed to project an interplay of meanings. In the motet that we have been discussing, the upper voice states "He is foolish/Who wishes to speak against love." And the middle voice, although it starts out with a conventional phrase in favor of love, actually ends up by doing precisely what the upper voice has called foolish—speaking against love. In another motet one of the voices launches a savage attack on members of the priesthood: "They are hypocrites, drinkers, and liars. They spend their time counting money in secret hiding-places. They are steeped in crime and lust." The other voice of the same motet lavishes upon the same priests paeans of praise: "They are fountains of virtue, ornaments of grace. They lead their flocks to the sweet pastures of glory."

THE LATE THIRTEENTH-CENTURY MOTET

In the last quarter of the thirteenth century, the motet continued to evolve along the lines previously established. The tenor, constructed on an organizational and intellectual basis, formed the foundation for the work. The names *motetus* and *triplum* became standardized for the middle and upper voices respectively, and these became more and more differentiated in range and rhythm. The motetus stayed mostly in the range between the tenor and the triplum but could cross occasionally both below the tenor and above the triplum. Its motion was somewhat faster than that of the tenor. The triplum was the highest voice and had the fastest notes.

In this period a new notational system was developed which allowed more freedom than ever in the application of semibreves. Previously each breve could be divided only into two or three semibreves; now, in the new motet, any number of semibreves, from two or three up to eight or nine, could equal a breve. This allowed for an even faster rhythmic rate for the triplum and an even more rapid delivery of the text than had previously been possible. The new notational system was the invention of a certain Petrus de Cruce, about whom almost nothing is known; even his theoretical precepts have survived only in reports by other theorists. The motets with the new multiple division of the breve are known as Petronian motets after him.

The clear differentiation between tenor, motetus, and triplum in Petronian motets is shown in Example 9-16. Here the tenor is confined exclusively to long notes in patterns of the fifth mode separated by rests. The chant is labelled "annuntiantes," which means "announcing," and the melody is a portion of a chant which speaks of "announcing praise to the Lord." Both upper voices are singing the praises of a lady.

In measure 37 the melody of the chant in the tenor is begun again, but this time the long notes are continuous and are not interrupted by the rests. The first statement of the melody thus takes up thirty-six measures— nine phrases of four measures—while the second statement of the melody takes up twenty-seven measures. The ratio of the first part of the tenor to the second is therefore 36:27 or 4:3. This mathematical underpinning of the composition may not appear significant to the modern listener, but it was certainly considered important by medieval composers and listeners alike. Not only does it give the work a feeling of compression and intensity towards the end (which in fact may be sensed by the listener), but it also provides a rational basis for the composition, one which is founded upon balance, order, and proportion.

The motetus part is less regularly arranged but also has been carefully composed to act as a counterbalance to the tenor. It starts out in five-measure phrases separated by rests. Thus the end of the first phrase coincides with the beginning of the second phrase of the tenor (measure 5), while the end of the second phrase coincides with the end of the third phrase of the tenor (measure 11). Motetus and tenor continue to overlap in different ways throughout the piece. In the second portion of the piece, where the tenor is without rests, the motetus adds to the intensity and continuity of the music by having far longer phrases than before; indeed, the motetus only has one rest in the whole of this last portion. The restatement of the tenor melody (beginning at measure 37) is also marked by the simultaneous entry of the motetus.

The triplum is characterized from the outset by the fast notes and rapid declamation of the Petronian style. Semibreves (sixteenth notes in the transcription) appear in groups of from two to seven. The phrases of the triplum indulge in the same kind of variety of coincidence and overlap with the tenor as do the phrases of the motetus. However, the musical line of the triplum is far more continuous than that of either of the other voices, for although there are some short rests, there is no single measure in which the triplum is not sounding.

The texts of the upper parts are thematically related to each other in this motet, for they are both written from the point of view of the poet in love. The many fast notes of the triplum carry a text that is more than twice as long as the text for the motetus. Both poems are restricted to very few rhymes (the triplum uses three: *-age, -on, -ir*; the motetus only two: *-er, -ie*), but they are different in each poem, which further distinguishes the two parts. Although ten-syllable lines are common, both poems are marked by considerable irregularity of line length.

Interval arrangement and dissonance control are much the same as before, with fifths and octaves at cadences and brief dissonances mostly as passing notes. Note also the careful application of the F♯ in the triplum whenever there is a B♮ in the tenor.

EXAMPLE 9-16   Motet, *Aucun Ont Trouve/Lonc Tans/Annuntiantes,* Montpellier, Faculté de Médecine, H196.

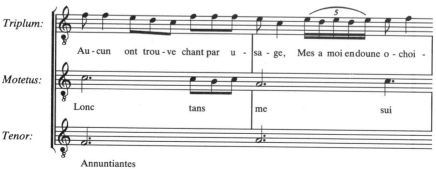

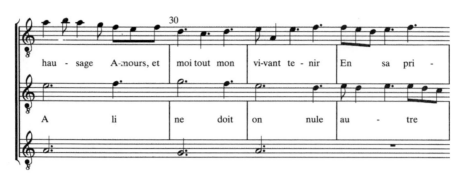

hau - sage A - mours, et | moi tout mon | vi-vant te - nir | En   sa   pri -

A   li | ne   doit   on | nule   au   -   tre

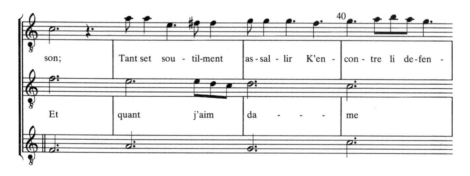

- son. | Ne ja pour ce | ne   pen - se - rai | vers li mes - pri -

com   -   pa - - - rer.

son; | Tant set sou - til-ment | as - sal - lir | K'en - con - tre li de-fen -

Et | quant   j'aim | da - - - - me

dre ne s'en puet | on: | For - ce   de | cors   ne   plen -

si | proi - si - e, | Que   grant   de -

van - ta - ge N'ai   je, ne   pour   moi   nule au-tre rai - son.

die,   En   bien   a - - - mer.

Triplum:

Aucun ont trouve chant par usage,

Mes a moi en doune ochoison
Amours, qui resboudist mon courage
Si que m'estuet faire chançon.
Car amer me fait dame bele et sage

Et de bon renon.
Et je, qui li ai fait houmage,
Pour li servir tout mon aage
De loial cuer sans penser trahison,

Chanterai, car de li tieng un si douz heri-
    tage,
Que joie n'ai se de ce non.
C'est la pensee que mon douz mal m'a-
    souage
Et fait esperer garison.
Ne pour quant seur moi puet clamer
    hausage
Amours, et moi tout mon vivant tenir en
    sa prison.
Ne ja pour ce ne penserai vers li mespri-
    son;
Tant set soutilment assallir,
K'encontre li defendre ne s'en puet on:
Force de cors ne plente de lignage

Ne vaut un bouton;
Et si li plaist de raençon
Rendre a son gre, sui pries et l'en fais
    gage
Mon cuer, que je met du tout en aban-
    don.
Si proi merci, car autre avantage

N'ai je, ne pour moi nule autre raison.

Triplum:

Some people have composed their songs
    by habit,
But Love gives me a reason,
For he boosts my courage so much
That I have to write a song.
For he makes me love a wise and beauti-
    ful lady
Of fine reputation.
And I, who have given her my pledge
To serve her all my life
With a loyal heart and without betraying
    her,
I will sing, for from her do I have such
    sweet promises,
That I have joy from nothing else.
And it is this thought that softens my
    sweet pain
And makes me hope for a cure.
Yet Love can claim lordship over me

And keep me in his prison all my life.

Nor shall I disdain him for that;

For he knows how to attack so subtly
That there is no defense against him.
Neither physical strength nor highest-
    ranking lineage
Are worth a button;
And if it pleases him to offer ransom
Willingly, I am ready and offer as hostage

My heart, which I put at every risk.

So do I ask for mercy, for I have no other
    advantage
Nor any other power on my side.

Motetus:

Lonc tans me sui tenu de chanter,	For a long time I have refrained from singing,
Mes or ai raison de joie mener,	But now I have a reason to be joyful,
Car boune amour me fait desirer	For true love makes me desire
La mieus ensegnie, k'on puist en tout le mont trouver;	The finest lady one could find in the whole world;
A li ne doit on nule autre comparer.	She can not be compared to any other.
Et quant j'aim dame si proisie,	And when I love a lady so worthy,
Que grant deduit ai du penser,	That I have the greatest pleasure from thinking of her,
Je puis bien prouver	I can certainly prove
Que mout a savoureuse vie,	That he has a full and happy life,
Quoi que nus die,	Whatever anyone says,
En bien amer.	Who is truly in love.

Tenor:

Annuntiantes.

Tenor:

Announcing.

ENGLISH MOTETS

The motet seems to have been widely cultivated in England. However, although there was obviously a great deal of musical activity in England in the thirteenth century (and throughout the fourteenth century), many of the manuscripts have not survived. Nevertheless, a large number of fragments, pieces of parchment used for binding, and scattered single pages have been discovered in recent years, and some of this music has therefore been able to be reconstructed.

The largest group of pieces seems to have originated in the cathedral of Worcester, a town in the western part of central England: the pages containing this group (a total of forty or fifty pages in more or less integral condition) have been called the Worcester Fragments. These and other partial manuscripts and single pages in London, Oxford, and other English libraries provide evidence of a lively and sophisticated English musical tradition which gradually came more and more under the influence of the French style.

In the late thirteenth century, English motets were distinguished from their French counterparts by two factors. First, they were all settings of sacred Latin texts, most of which are Marian in inspiration; there seems to have been no interest in writing vernacular, secular poems for motets as there was in France. Second, many of the English motets are not based on a fragment of plainchant but on a newly-composed melodic phrase known as a *pes* (see Ex. 9-17). The word means "foot" or "foundation." Usually the pes is repeated several times throughout the composition, producing the type of constant melodic and rhythmic support known in later music as an *ostinato*. Over this repeated tenor, which was probably played instrumentally, the upper voices carry the two Latin texts and often indulge in voice exchange.

EXAMPLE 9-17   Pes. From Luther Dittmer, *The Worcester Fragments: A Catalogue Raisonné and Transcription,* Musicological Studies and Documents, vol. 2 ([Rome]: American Institute of Musicology, 1957).

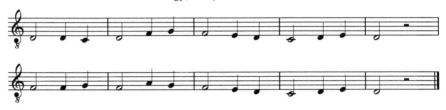

As mentioned above, voice exchange is a technique in which two (or occasionally more than two) voices exchange musical phrases. One voice will sing a phrase (A) while the other voice is singing a different phrase (B). Then each voice will simply repeat the other voice's music.

$$\begin{cases} \text{AB} \\ \text{BA} \end{cases}$$

Sometimes this technique is used pervasively throughout a piece as a structural device. The resulting composition is known as a *rondellus.* A rondellus may be written over a pes, or the tenor voice can also take part in the voice exchange, thus making a three-part rondellus. A round (*rota*) was also occasionally composed with a pes; a famous example from the thirteenth century is the song *Sumer is icumen in,* sometimes also known as the Summer Canon.

Example 9-18 is a three-part rondellus in honor of St. Peter. Its lilting first-mode rhythms and rich combination of voices in the same range help to disguise the careful, indeed rigid, construction of the piece. Apart from the first fifteen and the last six measures, which act as introductory and concluding passages, all three voices take part in the rondellus technique. The rondellus itself falls into two sections (mm. 16–48 and 49–87). In the first section the voices exchange phrases of eleven measures (A, B, and C); in the second section they exchange phrases of thirteen measures (D, E, and F). The second section is distinguished from the first by its higher range and chromatic inflections. The combination of the phrases in all three voices may be represented thus:

$$\begin{cases} \text{A B C} \quad \text{D E F} \\ \text{C A B} \quad \text{F D E} \\ \text{B C A} \quad \text{E F D} \end{cases}$$

Since all three voices are in the same range, and since each phrase is always accompanied by the two other phrases, within each section of the rondellus the same music is repeated three times, although the voices carrying each phrase are different. The introductory passage (mm. 1–15) sets the two top voices in close imitation over the support of the third voice. The concluding passage (measures 87–93) is a fragmentary and varied restatement of the beginning of the rondellus itself.

All three texts praise St. Peter and indulge in a considerable amount of exchange of their own. This textual exchange, however, is often in counterpoint with the exchange of phrases in the music. (The musical phrases taking part in the exchange are marked with upper-case letters in the score; the textual phrases are indicated by lower-case letters in the fully printed-out texts after the music.) The tension between textual and musical structure and the irregularity of phrase lengths throughout the piece contribute to its remarkable life and energy, which is manifest despite the high degree of rigor in its architecture.

EXAMPLE 9-18 Rondellus, *Fulget Caelestis Curia*. After Denis Stevens (ed.), *The Treasury of English Church Music, Vol. I: 1100–1545* (London: Blandford Press, 1965).

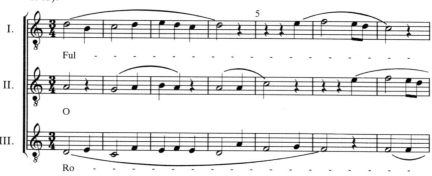

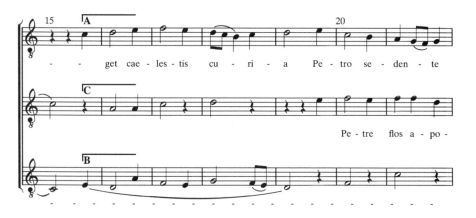

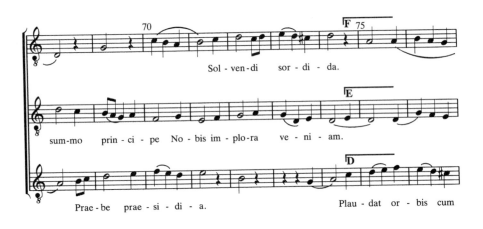

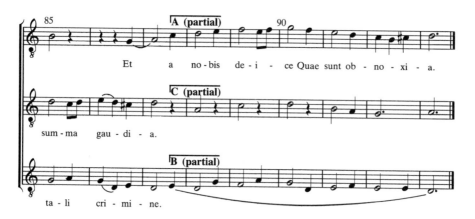

Et a no-bis de-i-ce Quae sunt ob-no-xi-a.

sum-ma gau-di-a.

ta-li cri-mi-ne.

I.
a { Fulget *caelestis curia* [x]
Petro sedente praeside
Sub poli principe.
b { Roma gaudet de tali praesule
Dato divino munere.

c { Plaudat orbis cum gloria
Petro privilegia
Portante cuncta a mortali crimine
Solvendi sordida. [y]
Petre tu nobis respice
Et a nobis deice
Quae sunt obnoxia.

II. O Petre flos apostolorum
O Pastor *caelestis curiae* [x']
Oves pasce melliflue
Ducens ad gaudia.
Nostra corda fove laetitia

Praebe praesidia. [z]
Nostrorum scelerum tolle malitiam
A summo principe
Nobis implora veniam.
Nos duc ad summa gaudia.

III. b { Roma gaudet de tali praesule
Dato divino munere.
a { Fulget caelestis curia
Petro sedente praeside
Sub poli principe.

Solvendi crimina [y']
Praebe praesidio. [z]
c { Plaudat orbis cum gloria
Petro privilegia
Portante cuncta a mortali crimine.

I.
a { *The heavenly court* [x] gleams,
Where Peter sits as protector
Beneath the prince of the world.
b { Rome rejoices in such a patron,
Given by the favor of God.

c { The world applauds with glory
As Peter bears all the burdens
Of mortal sin,
Removing all stain. [y]
O Peter, look down on us
And take away from us
Everything that is unworthy.

II. O Peter, flower of the apostles,
O shepherd of *the heavenly court,* [x']
Feed your flock sweetly
And lead them to joy.
Favor our hearts with happiness,

Give us your protection. [z]
Remove the evil of our misdeeds;
Beg for pardon for us
From the highest prince.
Lead us to the highest joys.

III. b { Rome rejoices in such a patron,
Given by the favor of God.
a { The heavenly court gleams,
Where Peter sits as protector
Beneath the prince of the world.

Of removing all sins [y']
Give us your protection. [z]
c { The world applauds with glory
As Peter bears all the burdens
Of mortal sin.

SUMMARY

At the end of the twelfth century and the beginning of the thirteenth, Paris became the main center for innovations in polyphonic music, as it did for intellectual activity, architectural achievements, and financial and political affairs throughout Europe. The Magnus Liber, designed for the Cathedral of Notre Dame, with its intense, florid polyphonic elaborations of the liturgy, and its interweaving of three separate polyphonic styles within the framework of the sacred chant, established a foundation in rhythm, counterpoint, and structure that was to influence music for two hundred years.

During the thirteenth century two important musical changes took place. These were (1) a shift from a concentration upon liturgical music to a new concern with secular themes, and (2) a change in the length of compositions from large constructions of architectural scope and magnificence to short, intimate pieces of a highly concentrated density. Both of these changes were a result of the movement of music from church to court or chamber. Interestingly enough, the composers and the audience were not different. The new, sophisticated, secular music was cultivated by the educated clerics who made up the administrative bureaucracies of the cathedrals and churches of the large towns—notably Paris, but in other European centers too. The new musical genre *par excellence* was the motet, which displays vividly in its evolution both the shift from sacred to secular and the striking compression of musical and poetic elements. The conductus, totally different in its construction and sonority, was briefly popular. But the motet, with its increasingly differentiated voice parts, its theoretical as well as actual foundation in the liturgy, and its simultaneous rendering of different poems, represented the most fertile genre of the century.

COMMENTS ON NOTATION AND PERFORMANCE

The important conceptual breakthrough that resulted in the system of the rhythmic modes was partially dependent upon a notational breakthrough. As we have seen, in ninth-century chant notation small letters were written over the notes to indicate performance details, including those of rhythm. By the twelfth century, however, the rhythm of chant seems to have become evened out, and the complex details of performance seem to have fallen into disuse. The notators and composers of Notre Dame polyphony invented a new method of indicating the several different values of the rhythmic modes, but their new method depended upon an old technique. It will be remembered that in the old chant notation, groups of notes were drawn together as neumes, which showed the notes that belonged together over a syllable. In a melisma several neumes were drawn one after the other. The new method designated the *pattern* of the neumes, which previously had (as far as we know) little or no rhythmic significance, as being the indicator of rhythmic values.

In the first mode, for example, which contains a regular alternation of long and short notes, the rhythm was indicated by a three-note neume followed by a succession of two-note neumes (Ex. 9-19). (At this time neumes were called *ligatures*—notes "bound" together.) In the second mode, the pattern was a succession of two-note ligatures (Ex. 9-20). Each of the modes had its own distinct pattern of ligatures, which indicated its rhythmic values. Thus an old system was given new meaning for the music of the late twelfth and early thirteenth centuries.

EXAMPLE 9-19   Notation of first rhythmic mode.

EXAMPLE 9-20   Notation of second rhythmic mode.

The square shape of the notes in these examples is a reflection of the new Gothic style of writing. Its neat and logical appearance caused this notation to become fixed as the standard notation for chant from the thirteenth century up to the present day.

In transcriptions of compositions from this period, all passages in modal rhythm (that is, discant passages and the upper parts in copulas) may be easily indicated in modern notation. The lower parts of copula and organum passages, with their long drawn-out notes, have to be notated rather differently (we have used whole notes with slurs). And the upper parts in organum passages, which do not make use of the system of rhythmic modes and are dependent upon a subtle and highly flexible rhythm derived from the level of consonance with the lower part, cannot be notated in modern values at all, for modern notation is too rigid and proportional to express the graceful flow of this style. For organum, therefore, we have to resort to the neutral note heads used for chant.

To coordinate the parts, many of the later examples have been transcribed with bar lines, even though these were not a feature of the original notation. In the less regular, more wayward phraseology of the earlier pieces, a system of lines to join staves has been adopted, or bar lines in the separate parts only.

A brief look backwards: In the polyphonic repertory before Notre Dame and before the development of the system of rhythmic modes (in

Late medieval manuscript showing the square, tidy appearance of both words and music that was typical of the Gothic style, Bibliothek der Benediktinerabtei, Metten.

other words, in Aquitainian polyphony and that of Codex Calixtinus), we have no clues about how the parts were coordinated. In note-against-note passages this is obviously not difficult, although, as in most medieval music, we still have no evidence regarding tempo, articulation, or voice quality. The real difficulty lies in coordinating the neume-against-neume passages, for often there are a different number of notes in each neume. A three-note neume in one part may be written against a five-note neume in another. The intervals formed between the parts may be some indication as to how they are to be aligned, but no definitive solution has been found.

A brief look forwards: In the second half of the thirteenth century a modification of the modal-rhythmic system enabled individual note shapes to indicate values by means of their own graphic representation. No longer was the organum style in fashion. The motet was the principal genre, and the three voices of the motet, with their individual texts and different note lengths, could be kept distinct and precisely coordinated. A notation giving all necessary rhythmic information was now at hand. It was the beginning of a time when the notation of compositions was not just a memory aid or an act of compilation and preservation, but the presentation of sufficient information so that musicians who had never heard a piece before could perform it. In that sense it was the beginning of the modern era.

DISCOGRAPHY

Example 9-5   Polyphonic setting of *Alleluya, Spiritus Sanctus.*
Tape One, Side Two.

Example 9-6   Conductus, *Flos Ut Rosa Floruit.*
Capella Antiqua München, *Ars Antiqua: Organum, Motette, Conductus,* Telefunken SAWT 9530/31-B (Side IV).

Example 9-9   Perotinus, *Alleluya, Posui Adiutorium.*
Tape Two, Side One. Studio der frühen Musik, *Vox Humana: Vokalmusik aus dem Mittelalter,* EMI Reflexe 1C 069-46 401; also on Purcell Consort of Voices/Praetorius Consort, *Medieval Paris: Music of the City,* Candide CE 31095.

Example 9-10b   Latin motet, *O Natio/Hodie Perlustravit.*
Tape Two, Side One. Early Music Quartet, *Secular Music circa 1300,* Telefunken SAWT 9504-A Ex.

Example 9-12   *In Seculum* hocket.
Tape Two, Side One. Purcell Consort of Voices/Praetorius Consort, *Medieval Paris: Music of the City,* Candide CE 31095; also on The Early Music Consort of London, *Music of the Gothic Era,* Archiv 2723 045 (Side III) or Archiv 415 292-2.

Example 9-13   Adam de la Halle, *Robins M'aime, Robins M'a.*
TAPE TWO, SIDE ONE. Early Music Quartet, *Secular Music circa 1300,* Telefunken SAWT 9504-A Ex; Musica Reservata, *Medieval Music & Songs of the Troubadours,* Everest 3270; Cambridge Consort, *Jeu de Robin et Marion,* Turnabout 34439.

Example 9-14   Motet, *Mout Me Fu Grief/Robins M'aime/Portare.*
TAPE TWO, SIDE ONE. Early Music Quartet, *Secular Music circa 1300,* Telefunken SAWT 9504-A Ex; also on Musica Reservata, *Medieval Music & Songs of the Troubadours,* Everest 3270.

Example 9-15a   Chant, *Victimae Paschali Laudes.*
TAPE TWO, SIDE ONE. Choeur des Moines de l'Abbaye Saint Pierre de Solesmes, *Chant Gregorian,* London A4501; also on Choir of the Monks of the Benedictine Abbey of St. Martin, Beuron, *Liturgia Paschalis,* Archiv 3088/90 (Side V).

Example 9-15b   Motet, *C'il S'entremet/Nus Hom/Victimae Paschali Laudes.*
Pro Cantione Antiqua, *Medieval Music: Ars Antiqua Polyphony,* Peters International PLE 115 (Oxford University Press OUP 164).

Example 9-16   Motet, *Aucun Ont Trouve/Lonc Tans/Annuntiantes.*
TAPE TWO, SIDE ONE. Studio der frühen Musik, *Vox Humana: Vokalmusik aus dem Mittelalter,* EMI Reflexe 1C 069-46 401; The Early Music Consort of London, *Music of the Gothic Era,* Archiv 2723 045 (Side IV) or Archiv 415 292-2; Schola Cantorum de Londres, *Adam de la Halle et le 13ème siècle,* Harmonia Mundi 443.

Example 9-18   Rondellus, *Fulget Caelestis Curia.*
Soloists & Chorus of the Accademia Monteverdiana, *The Worcester Fragments,* Nonesuch H-71308.

BIBLIOGRAPHICAL NOTES

An accessible introduction to the intellectual life of the Middle Ages and the growth and significance of the universities is Anders Piltz, *The World of Medieval Learning,* trans. David Jones (Totowa: Barnes and Noble Books, 1981). Aspects of medieval university life are presented in Lynn Thorndike, *University Records and Life in the Middle Ages* (New York: Columbia University Press, 1944) and David Knowles, *The Evolution of Medieval Thought* (New York: Vintage Books, 1962). Students' letters are discussed in Charles Haskins, "The Life of Mediaeval Students as Illustrated by Their Letters," in *Studies in Mediaeval Culture* (Oxford: The Clarendon Press, 1929).

The remarkable story of the construction of the Cathedral of Notre Dame may be read in Allan Temko, *Notre Dame of Paris* (New York: The Viking Press, 1955).

For the biography of Leoninus see Craig Wright, "Leoninus, Poet and Musician," *Journal of the American Musicological Society* XXXIX (1986): 1–35.

Craig Wright has also traced the entire medieval history of the liturgy and its music at the Cathedral of Notre Dame in *Music and Ceremony at Notre Dame of Paris: 500–1500* (Cambridge: Cambridge University Press, forthcoming).

Modern editions of the polyphony of Notre Dame will be published in *Magnus Liber Organi: Parisian Liturgical Polyphony from the Twelfth and Thirteenth Centuries,* 7 vols. (Monaco: L'Oiseau-lyre, forthcoming).

Two of the largest motet collections are given in transcription in Yvonne Rokseth, *Polyphonies du XIIIe siècle,* 4 vols. (Paris: L'Oiseau-lyre, 1935–39) and Gordon Anderson, *Compositions of the Bamberg Manuscript: Bamberg, Staatsbibliothek, Lit. 115 (olim Ed. IV. 6.),* Corpus Mensurabilis Musicae, vol. 75 ([Rome]: American Institute of Musicology, 1977). Ernest Sanders, "Motet," in *The New Grove,* provides a revealing sketch of the history of the medieval motet.

Gordon A. Anderson, *Notre-Dame and Related Conductus,* Gesamtausgaben, vol. 10 (Henryville, Pennsylvania: Institute of Mediaeval Music, 1979–) and Janet Knapp, *Thirty-five Conductus for Two and Three Voices,* Collegium Musicum, no. 6 ([New Haven]: Yale University Department of Music, 1965) present a large number of thirteenth-century conductus in transcription.

English music of this period, including motets and other genres, may be studied in the series Polyphonic Music of the Fourteenth Century, vols. 14–17: *English Music of the Thirteenth and Early Fourteenth Centuries,* ed. Ernest Sanders (Monaco: L'Oiseau-lyre, 1979); *Motets of English Provenance,* ed. Frank Harrison (Monaco: L'Oiseau-lyre, 1980); *English Music for Mass and Offices (I),* ed. Frank Harrison, Ernest Sanders, and Peter Lefferts (Monaco: L'Oiseau-lyre, 1983); and *English Music for Mass and Offices (II) and Music for Other Ceremonies,* ed. Frank Harrison, Ernest Sanders, and Peter Lefferts (Monaco: L'Oiseau-lyre, 1986).

TEN
INSTRUMENTAL MUSIC TO 1300

Very little instrumental music from the Middle Ages has survived in written form. However, there is an abundance of evidence that suggests that it was widespread, popular, and frequently performed throughout the period. Manuscript miniatures, sculptures, descriptions of banquets, festivities, and courtly entertainments, letters, and poems all give a rich and lively impression of the amount of music that must have been performed exclusively on instruments.

No doubt a great deal of popular vocal music was not written down either, for the music that was thought to be worth preserving by means of the time-consuming and costly practice of transcribing it onto parchment was, at least until the late eleventh century, exclusively liturgical. Surely people sang songs in fields and in the streets, as they have from time immemorial. It is only very recently, in the nineteenth and twentieth centuries, that popular and folk music of this kind, both vocal and instrumental, has been thought worthy of preservation.

We know not only that instruments played a vigorous role in the music of the Middle Ages, but also that they were more diverse in size and sound than can possibly be imagined from the standardized instruments of today. It would be a great mistake to imagine that instruments were primitive in quality or unsophisticated, or that instrumentalists were limited in technique, just because they existed so long ago. Indeed, as far as we can determine, the diversity of instruments was far greater then than it is now, and professional musicians were highly skilled.

The attitude towards instrumental players was an ambivalent one. The best of them were much in demand, and yet as a group they were considered decadent—classed with actors and other public performers as being of suspicious character. Their music was too attractive to be of high moral worth. In part, this attitude harks back to Augustine and before him to Plato (see pp. 30 and 23) and the fear that the sheer sensual pleasure of music militated against concentration upon the proper values of this world and the next. Partly, too, it reflected the fact that minstrels (joglars, jongleurs) occupied a low position in the highly stratified medieval society. Their job was entertainment, and this involved—besides playing music— the exhibition of strange animals, tumbling, juggling (hence the Occitan and Old French names), and telling jokes.

Occasionally in the later Middle Ages minstrels are found on the regular payrolls at the courts of noblemen and kings. They seem to have been paid at about the same level as other servants, such as doorkeepers and attendants. One class of instrumentalist was singled out for higher renumeration: the trumpet player, who had special ceremonial duties. Often, however, minstrels seem to have been itinerant, wandering from place to place to find work.

The music that was played instrumentally during this period must be reconstructed partly by hypothesis and partly by extrapolation from the few instrumental pieces that do survive from the time. It falls into three groups: improvised music, instrumental performance of vocal pieces, and dance music.

IMPROVISED MUSIC

Performers have always improvised on their instruments. It is only when the vast majority of music is written down that improvisation falls into disuse. At a time when written music was scarce, performers depended upon improvisation for most of their playing. Indeed, it is very likely that during the greater part of the Middle Ages musicians were not trained in reading music. Their ability lay in hearing and remembering—and of course in their skill.

From the first part of the fourteenth century one manuscript, known as the Robertsbridge Codex, gives some idea of the coloristic and decorative way in which instrumentalists (in this case keyboard players) improvised. A simple tenor line in the left hand is overlaid with florid running passages in the right.

Each instrument of course dictates the range, style, and manner of improvisation. A plucked instrument suggests different possibilities than a blown instrument. The player improvises according to the special qualities his instrument possesses.

We even have evidence that performers improvised together. Perhaps they played simultaneously more or less ornamented versions of the same melody, or they may have imitated, supported, and "played off" each other. A German writer describes two musicians improvising in such a way that "neither of them let any note that the other played go unnoticed in his own playing." Skilled musicians will play their instruments on any appropriate occasion, formal or informal, and the less they are inhibited by written notation, the more they will rely on their own creative ability.

INSTRUMENTAL PERFORMANCE OF VOCAL PIECES

We have seen (pp. 331–32) how instrumentalists often devised an accompaniment for songs from the structure and content of the song itself. There must have been many cases in which the melody also served for performance without a singer. Well-known melodies passed easily from place to place, and instrumentalists acted as the bearers and transmitters of these tunes. We know that vocal compositions provided the basis for instrumental performance from the earliest written examples in the fourteenth century, and they must have done so for centuries beforehand. Motets, vernacular and Latin songs, and chant melodies such as hymns and sequences were compositions that instrumentalists adapted and performed in their own way. A late twelfth-century poem speaks of fiddlers playing such vocal pieces as lais and chansons de geste.

DANCE MUSIC

By far the largest repertory of instrumental music from the Middle Ages is in the form of dance music. In this category there is some overlap with the previous ones, for some of the dances were also sung, and certainly many dance pieces were improvised.

Johannes de Grocheio, a theorist writing about 1300, mentions several types of dance, both vocal and instrumental. These differ mainly in the length and regularity of their sections and in the appearance or absence of a refrain. The *ductia* ("leading dance"?) was a group dance. It was quick and light and was sung by groups of young men and women. It has a small number of sections of equal length. The *stantipes* ("foot-placing dance"?) has a larger number of sections, which vary in length. It may have been a couples dance. Both the ductia and the stantipes have refrains, and both of them, Grocheio tells us, are difficult enough to dance that they force young people to concentrate and thus avoid erotic thoughts.

These two types, the stantipes and the ductia, have vocal as well as

Three instrumentalists accompany a couple dancing, Österreichische National-bibliothek, Vienna.

instrumental forms. A purely instrumental form mentioned by Grocheio is the *nota*. This has sections of irregular length and phrasing, without refrains, and may therefore have been specifically choreographed rather than being a generic dance form as the others were.

A handful of all three of these dance types is found in various English and French manuscripts. In one French manuscript a group of ductias and stantipes are written down together. The ductias are just labelled "dances," but the stantipes are called by the French name *estampie*.

An example of the ductia, the simplest of the three forms, from this manuscript is given in Example 10–1. This piece has only three sections—known as *puncta*—and the first and second endings are the same for all three. (If this dance were sung as well as played, these endings would serve as the refrain.) The dance is absolutely regular in its structure. Each of the three sections or puncta is eight measures long in the modern transcription (without the endings), and each is divided into two four-measure phrases with a rest between them. The first and second endings for each punctum are also four measures long. The rhythmic and melodic affinity between the puncta is clear, yet each one is subtly different.

EXAMPLE 10-1   Ductia, Paris, Bibliothèque Nationale, fonds français 844.

The estampies from this same collection are lively and elegant dances, many of which are called "royal" dances. We do not know why. They have from four to seven puncta which vary in length within each dance, and the endings or refrains may also vary, both in melodic content and in length. Often the puncta of estampies share melodic material and are differentiated only by their opening few notes. In Example 10-2, *La Quinte Estampie Real* ("The Fifth Royal Estampie"), there are four puncta of different length—four, eight, seven, and six measures respectively. There is a close rhythmic and melodic relationship between the puncta, although no material is directly shared between them. But all share the same endings, and each ending occurs both in an open form (cadencing on C) and in a closed form (cadencing on A).

The most complex of the medieval dances seems to have been the *nota,* which had no vocal equivalent, and was characterized by irregularity of phrasing and repetition scheme. The nota in Example 10-3 is preserved in a manuscript in the Bodleian Library at Oxford. It is the longest of the medieval dances that have survived in written form, consisting of twelve puncta. Some of the puncta have repeats indicated; some do not. A delightful pattern of expectation, fulfillment, and surprise is established by the

EXAMPLE 10-2 Estampie, *La Quinte Estampie Real,* Paris, Bibliothéque Nationale, fonds français 844.

close similarity among some of the puncta and the newness of others. The first three, for example, are identical except for their first three notes, which reach ever higher in pitch. This similarity is reinforced by the square eight-measure phrases and the quirky additional measure in the second ending. Extension and compression, irregularity of phrase length (including three- and five-measure phrases), and a careful contrast of range and melodic contour are utilized in the succeeding puncta to make for an instrumental dance of constant fascination. The rhythmic and melodic irregularity, however, is balanced by a constant pitch-goal focus, for all the puncta end on F. The final punctum is unusual in that its brief five measures are notated polyphonically. It is not difficult to read from this passage a hint as to the ways in which these seemingly simple, single-line melodies might have been elaborated in actual performance.

EXAMPLE 10-3   Nota, Oxford, Bodleian Library, Douce 139.

INSTRUMENTS

Medieval instruments may be divided into categories according to the way their sound is produced. Nomenclature, however, was very variable and imprecise in the Middle Ages. The same instrument could have several different names, and the same name could cover quite different instruments. Musical instruments are depicted in a large number of medieval paintings, carvings, sculptures, and manuscript miniatures, but the precision of their representation is very variable. Instruments are often included for their symbolic power, and scientific exactitude cannot be expected, any more than it can in much modern painting.

Very few actual instruments have survived from the Middle Ages; their revival has had to be based mostly on written and pictorial evidence,

Vielle played between the knees, Fitzwilliam Museum, Cambridge.

Vielle played at the shoulder, Angel Choir, Lincoln Cathedral.

as well as deductions drawn from the music itself. The following descriptions therefore cannot be definitive, although recent research and craftsmanship have made great strides in the reconstruction of medieval instruments. The instruments cited here are only the most common ones out of the enormous number that we know to have been in use.

Bowed Instruments

The commonest and most versatile of the bowed instruments seems to have been the *vielle* (otherwise known as *fiedel, viuola,* and other names). It was played either at the shoulder or, held downwards, on the lap. It could be either oval or waisted and had a flat back and a neck with an unfretted fingerboard. The number of strings, usually of gut or silk, ranged from two to five or more, and occasionally one string acted as a drone. The flat bridge allowed the performer to play more than one string at a time. Although the tone of the vielle is relatively soft, chords strongly bowed can be heard in a sizeable ensemble.

This instrument was widely used throughout the Middle Ages, and because of its variety of available stringings and tunings it had great versatility. Johannes de Grocheio indicates that the vielle was particularly suitable "at feasts." Often vielle players played in groups. When King Edward I knighted his son in England, twelve vielle players took part in the ceremonies. And a mid-thirteenth-century romance describes an occasion on which "two hundred good fiddlers, well in tune, sat apart on benches in pairs and fiddled the dance."

Another bowed instrument in wide use was the *rebec*. This was much smaller than the vielle and had a rounded back and a pear-shaped body. It also was played either held downwards or on the shoulder. The rebec usually had two or three strings, of which one was sometimes a drone. The sound is small but very intense, having a characteristic plangent quality. The instrument plays in the high register, and was considered suitable both for informal country gatherings and dances and in sophisticated urban settings.

Other bowed instruments included the *crwth* (pronounced "crooth"), a bowed lyre with a variable number of strings, and the *lira,* a low instrument with heavy strings.

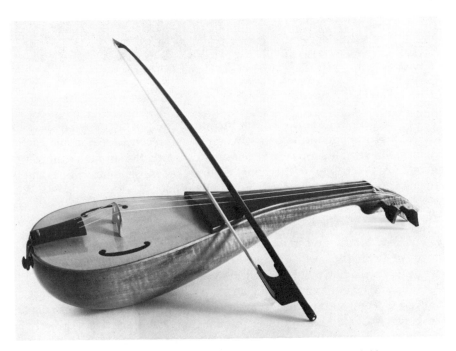

Rebec, modern reconstruction. Photograph courtesy of Mr. Thomas Binkley.

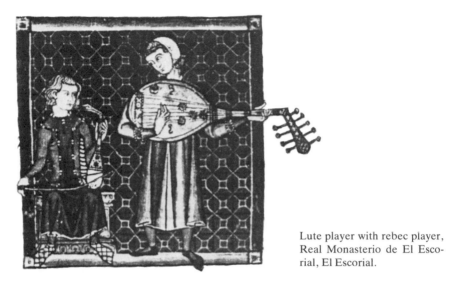

Lute player with rebec player, Real Monasterio de El Escorial, El Escorial.

Plucked Instruments

Members of the *lute* family appear to have a very long history that stretches back to prehistoric times. In the Middle Ages several different types and sizes of lute were known. Common to all of them was a rounded back, delicate construction, and flat fingerboard, usually fretted. The thin strings produce a light, clear sound. Medieval lutes seem often to have been played with a plectrum, at least two types of which (stiff and flexible) were in use.

A special kind of lute was the *chitarra Saracenica* ("Saracen guitar"), which had an extremely long neck and a small body. Wire strings produce a clangorous, metallic sound. The instrument is particularly suitable for accompanying rather than for playing melody lines.

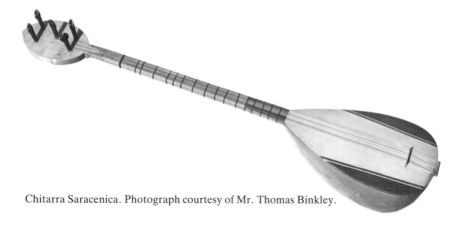

Chitarra Saracenica. Photograph courtesy of Mr. Thomas Binkley.

Small plucked instruments were of many kinds, and belonged to the *cittern* family. They differ according to whether the back is rounded or flat, and the shape of the sides. All, however, were wire-strung and played with a plectrum.

The *psaltery* was an instrument popular in biblical, ancient, and classical times. Possibly because of its biblical associations, it was frequently depicted in medieval paintings and manuscript miniatures. As with all instruments in the Middle Ages, the name covers a multiplicity of types. Common to them all was a wooden soundbox with strings of graduated length stretched from one side to the other and attached at both ends. Shapes ranged from triangular to rectangular to trapezoidal. It may be played held in front of the chest or resting on the lap.

The medieval *harp* was small, with fewer strings than the psaltery, and was plucked by the fingers and thumb. It sounds in the middle and high registers. From its connection with King David in the Bible, the harp held a position of prominence both in the poetry and in the instrumental music of the Middle Ages.

Blown Instruments

The modern division into "woodwind" and "brass" for this group is not applicable or useful, since many instruments sounded by lip vibration were not made of brass. They may be better divided into categories of loud and soft, a division which was current at the time, although there were

Angels playing psaltery (right) and harp, Archivo Histórico Nacional, Madrid.

King David with harp, British Library, London.

some species that cut across even these broad definitions. Among "loud" instruments were those which were specifically used for outdoor activities—ceremonies, fanfares, and the like—such as trumpets, horns, oliphant, and shawm.

Trumpet players were the elite of medieval instrumentalists. Their skill was required in battles, at tournaments, and for splendid outdoor ceremonies. The technique of bending brass had not yet been applied to the

Trumpets, Real Monasterio de El Escorial, El Escorial.

trumpet and so the middle-register instruments were very long—perhaps as long as six feet. The long instrument was known as the *buisine* or *trompe.* There were also shorter, higher-pitched trumpets, for which the name *trompette,* the diminutive of trompe, was often used. In the later Middle Ages the *slide-trumpet* was developed, an instrument with a single loop and a joint to allow one part of the tubing to slide over the other, thus changing the length of the tube and the pitch. This overcame the limitations of the harmonic series to which all fixed-length trumpets are subject. (The valve as a means of altering the sounding length of a brass instrument was an invention of the nineteenth century.)

Medieval horns were made out of animal horn, often from simple cowhorn. They were sometimes provided with fingerholes, and a range of a fourth or fifth could be sounded. The most precious type of animal horn was the *oliphant,* made from an ivory tusk, but these were more often status symbols than practical musical instruments.

Horn player with an instrument made of animal horn, British Library, London.

One double-reed instrument was classified among the "loud" instruments—the *shawm,* or *bombarde* as it was sometimes called. This was made of wood and had a conical bore, a flared bell, and six to eight fingerholes. Several representations of various sizes of this instrument are extant, as are descriptions of their use. They must have been very loud, for they are often grouped with trumpets and drums in outdoor processions and ceremonies. Modern counterparts of the shawm may be heard in the public squares of the Middle East today. Both in medieval depictions and in modern use, shawm players seem often to make use of circular breathing, by puffing out their cheeks and relying on the air pressure to keep the reed vibrating while a quick breath is taken through the nose. This makes possible the playing of continuous streams of melody without a break.

The "soft" blown instruments include several other reed instruments as well as different varieties of flutes. Reed instruments in which the reed is enclosed include the *bagpipe* and the *douçaine.* Medieval bagpipes were far quieter than the modern large Scottish counterpart—perhaps nearer to the traditional small Uillean pipes of Ireland. They are often depicted without drones.

The *douçaine* is one of a number of terms for a type of instrument which had a cylindrical wooden body with finger holes, and a reed enclosed by a wooden cap. The sound is described by medieval writers as soft and low.

The word *flute* covered an enormous variety of instruments, including cross-blown flutes, panpipes, whistles, and end-blown flutes like recorders and the *nai* or notched flute found today in the Middle East and Asia. The panpipes were particularly prevalent in the eleventh and twelfth centuries. They seem to have come in many different sizes and with a varying number of pipes.

One combination of single pipe and drum was particularly popular during this period—the *pipe and tabor.* The pipe was a long, thin, cylindrical recorder with only three holes: two in the front and one in the back. The tabor was a drum slung over the shoulder and played with one hand, while the other hand held and fingered the pipe. Overblowing on the pipe (the same technique used on the modern "penny whistle") enabled the player to achieve a wide range, and the pipe-and-tabor combination allowed a single person to accompany dancing or processions with both melody and percussion.

Keyboard Instruments

The main medieval keyboard instrument of church and chamber was the *organ.* It was built in many different sizes, which may be generalized into three types: the "great" organ, the "positif," and the "portatif." Great organs were built into churches, and medieval writings resonate with ac-

Pipe and tabor, Angel choir, Lincoln Cathedral.

counts of their huge sound and the efforts taken to play them. The bellows were operated by manpower (documents list from two to as many as seventy men), and the wind pressure must have required a considerable counteractive force at the keyboard, perhaps even blows from the fists.

Two pipe and tabor play-
ers, Real Monasterio de
El Escorial, El Escorial.

The positif organ was a chamber-sized instrument whose bellows
could be operated by one person while another sat at the keyboard. The
name derives from the fact that it could be "placed" ("positioned") on a
bench or table.

By contrast the smallest organ was known as the portatif. It could
easily be held and played by one person. Many pictures show players with
the instrument on their lap: one hand reaches behind the instrument and
operates the bellows, while the other hand plays on the keyboard. Its range
was about an octave and a half.

A curious combination of keyboard and stringed instrument was the
hurdy-gurdy. This came in both small and large varieties, requiring either
one or two players. The principle on which the instrument was built involved the sounding of strings by means of a wheel, which rubbed against
them and was turned by a crank. The strings were enclosed in a box, and
their length was altered (and different pitches obtained) by means of keys
which could be pressed against them from the outside of the box. There
were usually one or more drone strings which sounded continuously.
Hurdy-gurdys are still found in use for traditional music in several European countries.

Positif organ in a domestic scene, Staatliche Kunstsammlungen, Dresden.

Percussion

More complexity exists in the names of percussion instruments than with any other group. Since most of the names seem to be onomatopoeic *(tambour, trommel, timbrel)*, it is difficult to determine precisely what is meant by each name. The two main types of drum seem to have been the

Two monks at a posi-
tif organ. The nearer
one is operating the
bellows. Bibliothèque
Royale, Brussels.

Portatif organ held on the knee, Zentral-
bibliothek der Deutschen Klassik, Weimar.

Large hurdy-gurdy operated by two players, Cathedral of Santiago de Compostela.

tabor, a medium-sized drum mentioned above in the pipe-and-tabor combination, and the *nakers,* a pair of quite small drums. Skin tension was probably not very great on either of these types, and playing technique seems to have involved single strokes (though these may well have incorporated complex patterns) rather than rolls. A single, fairly heavy stick was used for the tabor, and a pair of small sticks for the nakers.

The *tambourine* was small and light and could produce intricate rhythmic patterns. It was probably not shaken but struck lightly with the fingers.

Melodic percussion instruments included the *bells,* usually a small set suspended from a wooden frame, and the *dulcimer,* a psaltery which was played by striking the strings rather than by plucking them.

SUMMARY

The structural principle which characterizes dance music of the Middle Ages is that of short repeated sections, called *puncta,* each of which has its own first and second ending. Some dances use the same two endings for each of the puncta, thus giving a rounded form to the whole dance. Others repeat puncta within the dance or use closely related music from one punctum to another. Three types of dance music existed, depending upon the number of puncta and their regularity of phrasing.

The range and variety of instruments suggests that the liveliness, breadth, and color (as well as the amount) of medieval instrumental music was far greater than the surviving written music would suggest. Despite the constant strictures against instruments in church, there is evidence that the liturgy was sometimes accompanied by instruments. The great tenth-century organ at Winchester, and the vielles and psalteries seen in French churches must have played something. We just do not know exactly what it was. On the other hand, surviving dances that have been notated, as well as a wealth of pictorial and written evidence, present a picture of a vivid and compelling tradition of music that must have filled the courts and chambers, the streets and marketplaces of the medieval world with resounding, rhythmic vitality.

One of the oldest surviving instruments from the Middle Ages: a fourteenth-century recorder, Gemeentemuseum, The Hague.

Rebec player accompanies psalm singing, Biblioteca Nazionale Marciana, Venice.

DISCOGRAPHY

Example 10-1 Ductia.
Schola Cantorum de Londres, *Adam de la Halle et le 13ème siècle,* Harmonia Mundi 443 (Side II, Band 7); also on Musica Reservata, *Medieval Music & Songs of the Troubadours,* Everest 3270 (Side II, Band 2).

Example 10-2 Estampie, *La Quinte Estampie Real.*
TAPE TWO, SIDE ONE. Studio der frühen Musik, *Musik der Spielleute,* Telefunken 6.41928 AW (Side I, Band 4); also on Studio der frühen Musik, *Minnesänger & Spielleute,* Telefunken 6.35618 (Side III, Band 4); Studio der frü-

hen Musik, *Musik des Mittelalters,* Telefunken 6.35412 EX (Side VII, Band 4); The Early Music Consort of London, *Music of the Crusades,* Argo ZRG 673; and Musica Reservata, *Medieval Music & Songs of the Troubadours,* Everest 3270 (Side I, Band 5).

Example 10-3   Nota.
TAPE TWO, SIDE ONE. Studio der frühen Musik, *Musik der Spielleute,* Telefunken 6.41928 AW (Side II, Band 5); also on Studio der frühen Musik, *Minnesänger & Spielleute,* Telefunken 6.35618 (Side IV, Band 5); and Studio der frühen Musik, *Musik des Mittelalters,* Telefunken 6.35412 EX (Side VIII, Band 5).

Other records containing instrumental music of the Middle Ages include: Studio der frühen Musik, *Estampie: Instrumentalmusik des Mittelalters,* EMI Reflexe 1C 063-30 122; and Sequentia, *Spielmann und Kleriker (um 1200),* Harmonia Mundi 1C 067-99 921 T.

In addition to the items listed above, medieval instruments may be heard on many of the recordings listed in the discography for Chapter 7; also on David Munrow and the Early Music Consort of London, *Instruments of the Middle Ages and Renaissance,* EMI SLS 988; Musica Reservata of London, *Instruments of the Middle Ages & Renaissance,* Vanguard 71219/20; and David Munrow, *The Mediaeval Sound,* Musical Heritage Society MHS 1454.

BIBLIOGRAPHICAL NOTES

Articles on various aspects of medieval instrumental music include Hendrik van der Werf, "Estampie," and "Ductia," in *The New Grove;* and Timothy McGee, "Medieval Dances: Matching the Repertory with Grocheio's Descriptions," *Journal of Musicology,* forthcoming.

Some of the pieces are available in *Music in Medieval and Renaissance Life: Anthology of Vocal and Instrumental Music, 1200–1614,* ed. Andrew Minor (Columbia: University of Missouri Press, 1964) and in P. Aubry, *Estampies et danses royales: Les plus anciens textes de musique instrumentale au moyen âge* (Paris: Librairie Fischbacher, 1907; reprint, Geneva: Minkoff, 1975). A compete edition of all known dances from before the fifteenth century is Timothy McGee, *Medieval Instrumental Dances* (Bloomington: Indiana University Press, forthcoming).

The treatise of Johannes de Grocheio may be read in translation in Albert Seay (trans.), *Johannes de Grocheo Concerning Music* (Colorado Springs: [Colorado College Music Press], 1973).

The clearest and most entertaining introduction to medieval instruments, fully illustrated, is David Munrow, *Instruments of the Middle Ages and Renaissance* (London: Oxford University Press, 1976); a two-record set demonstrating the instruments and including Munrow's book in paperback was produced by EMI Records Ltd. (SLS 988). Other surveys include Anthony Baines, *European and American Musical Instruments* (London: Chancellor

Press, 1983); Mary Remnant, *Musical Instruments of the West* (New York: St. Martin's Press, 1978); Jeremy Montagu, *The World of Medieval and Renaissance Musical Instruments* (Woodstock: Overlook Press, 1976); Anthony Baines, *Musical Instruments through the Ages,* (2nd edition, [Harmondsworth]: Penguin Books, 1966); and Curt Sachs, *The History of Musical Instruments* (New York: W. W. Norton and Co., 1940).

The history of individual instruments and their families may be pursued through the bibliography in Munrow (see above) and in the separate articles in *The New Grove Dictionary of Musical Instruments* (ed. Stanley Sadie), 3 vols. (London: Macmillan Publishers Ltd., 1984; reprint, 1985).

Frederick Crane, *Extant Medieval Musical Instruments* (Iowa City: University of Iowa Press, 1972) discusses those instruments that have actually survived from the Middle Ages.

Medieval representations of musical instruments may be seen in Emanuel Winternitz, *Musical Instruments and their Symbolism in Western Art* (London: Faber and Faber, 1967); Heinrich Besseler and Max Schneider (eds.), *Musikgeschichte in Bildern* (Leipzig: Deutscher Verlag für Musik, 1961–); and Karl Michael Komma, *Musikgeschichte in Bildern* (Stuttgart: A. Kröner, 1961).

ELEVEN

THE FOURTEENTH CENTURY
IN FRANCE

After the musical achievements of the thirteenth century, there was in France at the beginning of the fourteenth century a sense of adventure, a newly felt freedom in composition and performance. This self-conscious exuberance, combined with a feeling of new directions taken, of past restrictions abandoned, has appeared at other times in Western musical history since the period around 1300. (The late sixteenth century and the early twentieth century have been other such occasions.) But the early fourteenth century was the first in which the sense of newness was so often referred to in contemporary writings, both approvingly and disapprovingly.

Around 1320 several treatises appeared, echoing in their titles or in their content the contrast between the "old" music and the "new." One of them, the *Ars Nova* ("New Art") of Philippe de Vitry, has even given its name to the age, which is often known as the Ars Nova period in music. Another music theorist, Johannes de Muris, wrote a book which is called *Ars Novae Musicae* ("The Art of New Music"). A third writer complained about the new style and the abandonment of the civilized traditions of the past; this was Jacques de Liège, whose treatise *Speculum Musicae* ("Mirror of Music") is an immense and encyclopedic work in seven long books.

All of these men spent much of their careers in Paris, which testifies to the continuing importance of the French capital and its university in the dissemination and performance of music and in the production of theoretical writings about its nature, composition, and style. All of them appear to have been both students and teachers at Paris, although their later activities may have taken them further afield. Johannes de Muris, for example, was also a mathematician and an astronomer, who traveled extensively in the course of his career. (We know that he was in Normandy in 1321 to study the eclipse of the sun.)

The most prominent of these writers was Philippe de Vitry, who was a poet and composer himself in addition to being a music theorist. He studied at the University of Paris where he later became a teacher. He held administrative positions as secretary and adviser to three French kings, and was often sent on diplomatic missions to other courts, including that of the pope. Ultimately he became a bishop, a post he held for the last ten years of his life.

From Philippe de Vitry's treatise, from the comments, both positive and negative, of other writers about the new trends of the fourteenth century, and from the music of the time, it is possible to determine what it is that makes the compositions of this period so new and different. Of course, as with all innovations, the new structures and ideas were built firmly upon the foundation of the past.

For some reason, not very many musical manuscripts have survived from the first part of the fourteenth century. We therefore have to base our knowledge of the repertory on only a few sources, which probably give us an unrepresentative view. However, we can reconstruct in general the types of music that were popular in this period, partly from documentary evidence and partly from retrospective analysis.

The composition of monophonic songs continued, and some genres of song became traditionally associated with monophonic performance. Some composers, however, had already begun to set their songs to polyphony, as we saw briefly in Chapter 7 (see pp. 286–88). Adam de la Halle had written several polyphonic rondeaux; and there are others by a certain Jehan de Lescurel, a French cleric who was ultimately hanged for debauchery, and by other, anonymous composers. The style of these settings is fairly simple note-against-note-polyphony, usually with the main melody in the middle voice, like the rondeau by Adam de la Halle in Example 7-9.

Another genre derived from a single-line melody was the *chace*. The word means "chase" or "hunt," and the pieces play on the double meaning of the word, for they are three-part canons in which the voices "chase" each other, and they also have texts which describe lively outdoor hunting scenes. Despite their simple method of construction, these pieces can be quite complex, with the three canonic voices interlocking in fascinating and colorful ways.

THE "ROMAN DE FAUVEL"

One of the most famous compositions from the early fourteenth century is a satirical play containing music. This is the *Roman de Fauvel* ("The Story of Fauvel"), and it was written jointly by several members of the French court, including Gervais du Bus, the king's notary; Chaillou de Pesstain, an administrative official; and the king's secretary, royal emissary, and music theorist, Philippe de Vitry.

The play is a satire on the French court and on the evils that flourished there. It is written in the tradition of the animal fables which were popular in French literature in the twelfth and thirteenth centuries. The central character is the donkey Fauvel, the letters of whose name represent the six vices: Flattery, Avarice, Untruthfulness, Variability, Envy, and Laziness. Fauvel has turned the world upside down. The Church is corrupt, knights sworn to do good are practising sin, the country is in slavery. Even the king and the pope fawn on the donkey. Fortune raises Fauvel to the heights of power, and he marries the lady Pride in a magnificent scene of revelry and jousting. Their progeny rule the world.

The play must have been immensely popular in the French court and other intellectual circles, for it was copied into several manuscripts, one of which contains all the music as well as several detailed miniatures depicting various scenes from the play, with costumes, masks, props, and musical instruments.

The poetry of the Roman de Fauvel is rich and lively, and the music is enormously varied. There are over one hundred and fifty compositions in the play, which range from plainchants to secular songs to conductus to motets. There are pieces in Latin and in French, monophonic and polyphonic pieces, and pieces that range from the oldest and most traditional styles to the newest and most modern. They give us a fascinating picture of the diversity of musical practice at the opening of the fourteenth century. We shall concentrate here upon the latest styles, the most up-to-date compositions, but not before commenting briefly upon the longevity and continued applicability of the earlier genres which also appear in this work.

Of the monophonic pieces, a large number are liturgical items carefully selected to fit—ironically—into the context of the play. Others are sequences, or conductus from the Notre Dame repertoire. All of these are in Latin, but there are also many monophonic French songs, including lais and rondeaux. The polyphonic pieces are all motets, but here too there is a wide historical range. There are two- and three-voice compositions (and even one for four voices). Some of the motets are from the early Notre Dame repertoire, some are later pieces with French texts, while others represent the very newest motet style of the early fourteenth century. From this last group we see that the motet had continued to hold its place as the genre in which all structural and stylistic innovation took place.

A miniature from the manuscript of the *Roman de Fauvel,* showing the donkey Fauvel in the top frame and several assorted actors, dancers, and instrumentalists (some with masks) in the two lower frames, Bibliothèque Nationale, Paris.

THE ISORHYTHMIC MOTET

Some of the newest motets in the Roman de Fauvel appear to be by Philippe de Vitry himself, and a few others of his motets are preserved in scattered manuscript sources, although it seems overall that only a very small part of his compositional work has survived. From these pieces, however, it is possible to gain a clear picture of the style of the motet as it had evolved by the first quarter of the fourteenth century.

The fourteenth-century motet is a far grander piece than its thirteenth-century forebear. It is longer and more substantial. There is often a reversion to the use of Latin for the upper voices, and the label of the tenor text continues to represent a comment upon the meaning of the motet as a whole. Sometimes the tenor melody is newly composed. Whether the poems are in Latin or French, the subject matter is often political or satirical rather than conventionally amorous as in the thirteenth century. A tendency developed to write "occasional" motets—motets designed to mark a specific occasion, such as a change of monarch, the downfall of a traitor, the forging of a new alliance. The distinction between the rhythm of the upper voices has become less marked, although the poem for the triplum is still usually longer than that for the motetus, and its declamation is therefore faster. There is an expansion of the range of available note lengths in the direction both of longer and of shorter values. The division of a note into either three or two smaller notes is now possible at every rhythmic level. No longer is triple rhythm primary, but duple and triple rhythms are constantly juxtaposed.

The main feature of the fourteenth-century motet, however, is its structure. We have seen how the arrangement and proportions of the tenor were of concern in the thirteenth-century motet, from simple tenor repetitions in clausulae to more complex patterns in later pieces. Now such structural devices were raised to a new level of interest and rationality, and motet composition brought the architecture of the piece into central focus.

The arrangement of the tenor part in the fourteenth-century motet is based upon the manipulation of rhythm and melody as separate elements. This feature has come to be known as *isorhythm,* which means "equal rhythm." It is not a good name. First, it implies that only rhythm is affected. Second, the application of the term to fourteenth-century motets and not to earlier ones suggests that it was a completely new technique, which, as we have seen, was not the case. Nonetheless, the term has become so widely used that we shall continue to refer to motets exhibiting this feature as "isorhythmic" motets, as long as it remains clear that it is not a revolutionary technique that is involved, but the codification and refining of an old one.

In order to see how the isorhythmic principle works, and to set its development in the proper historical context, let us examine briefly again the tenors of two motets given as Examples 9-15b and 9-16 (see pp. 408–9 and 413–18). In both of these, the elements of pitch pattern and rhythmic pattern are separately treated. In Example 9-15b the pitch pattern is five measures long. The rhythmic pattern is one measure long. Therefore it takes five rhythmic patterns to complete one pitch pattern. In Example 9-16 the pitches unfold over thirty-six measures, while the rhythmic pattern is four measures long. Thus there are nine rhythmic patterns to one statement of the pitch pattern.

These examples demonstrate the techniques which laid the foundation for the construction of isorhythmic motets by composers of the fourteenth century. The rhythmic pattern and the pitch pattern were considered as separate elements which could be separately manipulated. The names for these elements were *talea* ("segment") for the rhythmic pattern and *color* ("color") for the pitch pattern. The main differences between thirteenth-century motets and those of the Ars Nova were that in the later motets (1) the rhythmic pattern or talea was longer and more complex, (2) there could be more than one kind of talea employed in a piece, and (3) the end of the talea and the end of the color did not necessarily coincide: there could be overlap between them.

Example 11-1 gives the tenor of a fourteenth-century isorhythmic motet. The statements of the pitch pattern are labelled COLOR I and II, those of the rhythmic pattern Talea A1, A2, etc. for the repetitions of the first rhythmic pattern; B1, B2, etc. for the repetitions of the second rhythmic pattern. It can be seen that there are two statements of a single color and several statements each of two different taleas (Talea A and B); the first talea (Talea A) occurs three times and part of a fourth, the second (Talea B) also three times and part of a fourth. Particularly noteworthy is the fact that the second statement of the color begins in the middle of a talea; there is a deliberate overlap between the two elements.

EXAMPLE 11-1   Isorhythmic tenor.

Composers found many different ways to manipulate these structural elements in isorhythmic motets. Sometimes there is an exact relationship between the number of occurrences of a given talea and those of the color (3:2, for example, or 5:3); sometimes the talea is designed to read the same backwards and forwards. Rhythmic diminution is often found towards the end of an isorhythmic motet: the pattern of the talea stays the same, but all the values are diminished by a half or a third. Isorhythm is also occasionally used in brief passages in the upper voices as well as in the tenor.

All these techniques were ways that composers of the fourteenth century found to rationalize and make coherent large-scale compositions. It was natural that they should use numerical and proportional systems to do so, for not only were numbers regarded symbolically in the Middle Ages (three represented the Trinity, four signified the Gospels, seven stood for the Gifts of the Holy Spirit, etc.), but composers depended upon a sense of scale and proportion to make structural sense out of their work. It has often been said that the structure of an isorhythmic motet cannot be heard, that it is hidden and complex and mystical. Certainly the number symbolism of medieval motets has a mystical quality, but repeated hearings of a piece can make quite clear its underlying structure, including the interplay between color and talea, the repetitions of each element, and the intensifying nature of diminution.

Example 11-2 is an isorhythmic motet by Philippe de Vitry. It seems to have been composed about 1320, at the middle of his career. The tenor melody is in Mode 5, Lydian, and is labelled "Neuma quinti toni" ("Neuma of the fifth mode"). A *neuma* was a formulaic melody, designed to demonstrate and fix in the ear the characteristic pitches of a particular mode. In the motet this melody is laid out so that the first statement of the pitch pattern (COLOR I) takes up four statements of the first rhythmic pattern (Talea A1, A2, A3, and A4). In the last part of the motet (mm. 97–130), the

EXAMPLE 11-2 Philippe de Vitry, motet, *Douce Playsence/Garison Selon Nature/ Neuma Quinti Toni,* Ivrea, Biblioteca Capitolare.

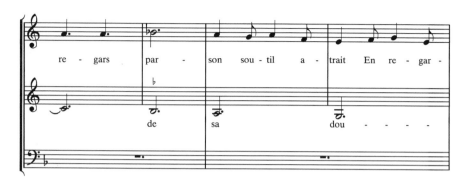

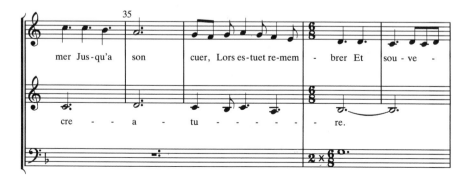

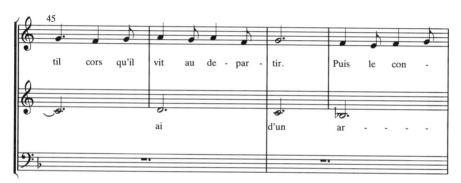

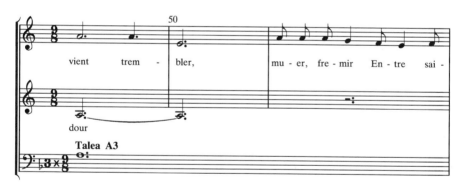

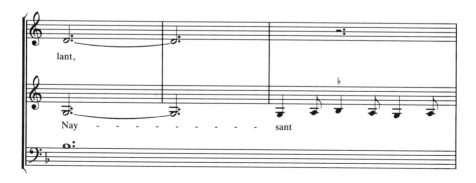

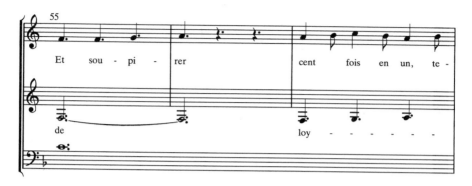

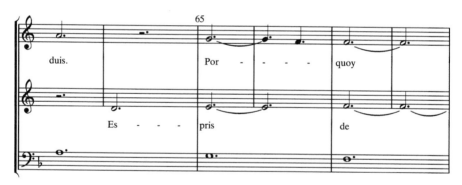

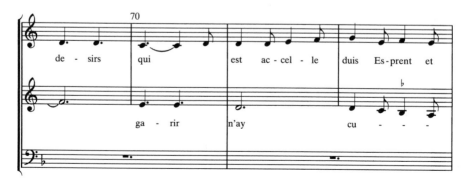

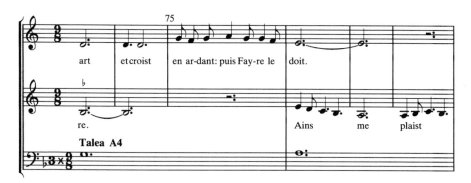

art   et croist   en ar-dant: puis Fay-re le   doit.

re.   Ains   me   plaist

Talea A4

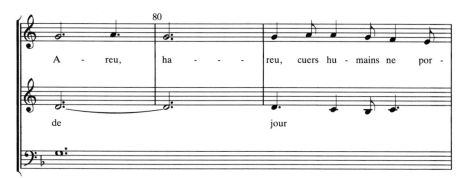

A - reu,   ha - - -   reu, cuers hu - mains ne   por -

de   jour

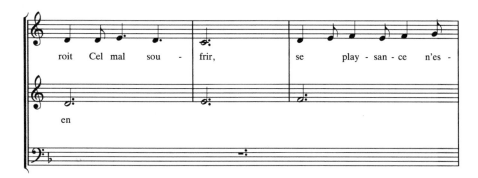

roit Cel mal sou - frir,   se   play - san - ce n'es -

en

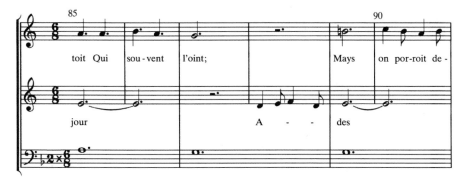

toit Qui sou - vent l'oint;   Mays   on por-roit de -

jour   A - - des

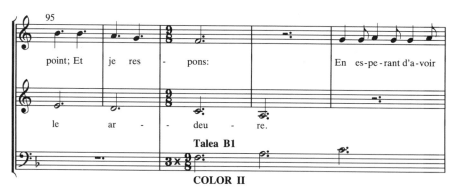

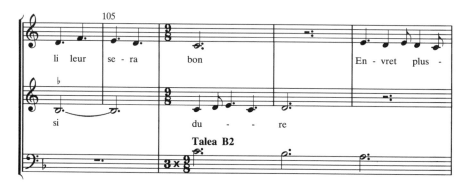

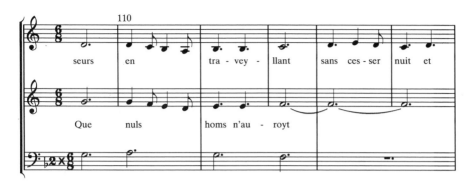

seurs en tra - vey - llant sans ces - ser nuit et

Que nuls homs n'au - royt

jour, Don-ques doit bien l'a-mo - reu - se do - lour Ve -

vi - gour Du sof -

Talea B3

nir a gre, En a - ten - dant la tre - sau - te plan -

frir sans la dou - - - - - - - -

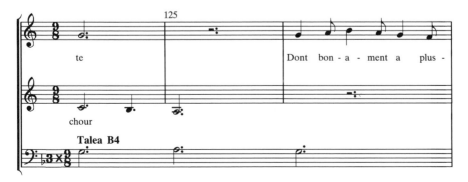

te Dont bon - a - ment a plus -

chour

Talea B4

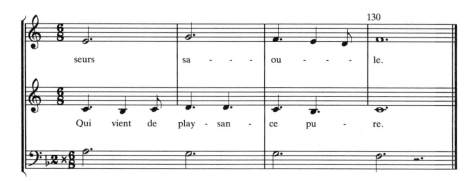

Triplum:

Douce playsence est d'amer loyalment,
Qar autrement ne porroit bonement
Amans suffrir celle dolour ardant
Qui d'amors naist.
Quant ces regars par son soutil atrait
En regardant parmi soy mesmes, trait
Sans soy navrer,
L'impression de qu'il veut amer
Jusqu'a son cuer;
Lors estuet remembrer
Et souvenir
Du gentil cors qu'il vit au departir.
Puis le convient trembler, muer, fremir
Entre sailant,
Et soupirer cent fois en un, tenant
Le dous soupirs qui livrent au cuer non
Par les conduis.
Porquoy desirs qui est accelle duis
Esprent et art et croist en ardant: puis
Fayre le doit.
Areu, hareu, cuers humains ne porroit
Cel mal soufrir, se playsance n'estoit
Qui souvent l'oint;
Mays on porroit demander biau apoint
Comment lo mal puet plaire qui si
    point;
Et je respons:
En esperant d'avoir bon gueredon
Por en saisir, quant li leur sera bon
Envret plusseurs en traveyllant sans
    cesser nuit et jour,
Donques doit bien l'amoreuse dolour
Venir a gre,
En atendant la tresaute plante
Dont bonament a plusseurs saoule.

Motetus:

Garison selon nature
Desiree de sa doulor

Triplum:

It is sweet delight to love and be loyal,
For otherwise no lover could truly
Bear this burning anguish
That is born from love.
When the eyes, with a gentle glance,
Look around them and draw,
Without harm to themselves,
The image of her whom they wish to love
Down to the very heart;
Then must he recall
And remember
The noble person he had to leave.
Then must he tremble and go pale, shake
And shiver,
And sigh a hundred times, uttering
The sweet sighs which the heart releases
Without permission.
For desire, which is drawn to her,
Is lit and flames higher as it burns: then
Must he faint.
Alas, alas, no human heart could
Bear this suffering, if delight did not
Soothe its pain;
But one could rightly ask,
How suffering so harsh could give such
    pleasure;
And I answer:
Hoping to have a good reward
To enjoy at his leisure,
The lover will labor ceaselessly night and
    day;
Then will his loving anguish
Be recompensed,
While he awaits the hidden treasure
Which gives full release to lovers.

Motetus:

The cure of nature
Is the desire of every

Toute humaine creature.
Mais je qui ai d'un ardour
Naysant de loyal amour
Espris de garir n'ay cure.
Ains me plaist de jour en jour
Ades plus telle ardeure.
Ne pourquant elle est si dure
Que nuls homs n'auroyt vigour
Du soffrir sans la douchour
Qui vient de playsance pure.

Tenor:
Neuma quinti toni.

Human creature for his anguish.
But I, who burn with a fire
Born from loyal love,
Have no hope for healing.
And from day to day
These flames please me more.
And yet they are so harsh
That no man could have the strength
To bear them without the sweetness
That comes from pure delight.

Tenor:
Tune of the fifth mode.

pitch pattern is stated once more (COLOR II), but there is diminution and intensification on several levels. The tenor notes are now all dotted half-notes; thus the earlier $3 \times \frac{9}{8}$ values (o:) have been diminished by two-thirds, and the $2 \times \frac{6}{8}$ values (o·) diminished by a half. Also, the long rests in the middle of each earlier talea have been eliminated, and the rests at the end of each earlier talea have been diminished by a half. Again, however, there are four occurrences of the new talea (Talea B1, B2, B3, and B4). And again, four taleas make up one color.

There are other important aspects of the style of this motet which should also be briefly mentioned. The range of note values has increased, allowing a strong contrast between the upper parts and the slow-moving tenor. The tenor voice has now become more than ever the foundation of the motet, not only in terms of its structure, but also in terms of its sonority. The upper voices move in much faster note values, but the triplum has more of the smaller notes and carries more text.

One vital feature that pervades this piece, as it does most music of the fourteenth century, is the constant interplay between triple and duple meters. The original notation is able to convey this aspect of the music far more clearly than the modern transcription, but certain aspects of this interplay may still be perceived. The first talea is made up of twelve $\frac{9}{8}$ measures followed by twelve $\frac{6}{8}$ measures. $\frac{9}{8}$ is of course a triple meter, whereas $\frac{6}{8}$ is a duple meter. Each talea is therefore built in the proportion 3:2. All of the taleas in the first section of the piece follow this same pattern, so that there is a constant alternation between triple and duple meter. The final section (where the tenor is diminished) continues this alternation, although here the relationships have changed. Because of the different levels of diminution and the suppression of some of the rests, each talea is made up of three $\frac{9}{8}$ measures plus six $\frac{6}{8}$ measures. There is thus in these taleas a proportion between triple and duple meter of 3:4, increasing the amount of duple meter by exactly two times. Also, because of the diminution, in this section the alternation between triple and duple meters is far more easily perceptible.

A certain amount of isorhythm has pervaded the upper parts of this motet also, but it is subject to some slight variation: see, for example, the triplum in the eight measures preceding each new talea in the tenor (mm. 17–24, 41–48, 65–72, and 89–96). As can be seen, isorhythmic construction in the upper voices tends to be used to articulate the main divisions of the overall structure. This articulation is also aided by the deliberate coincidence of phrase endings with cadences at these structural points (mm. 25, 49, 73, and 97). The cadences reinforce the Lydian mode of the tenor, being on F, A, G, and F. Of these cadences only the one on G contains the third— an imperfect interval—thus creating a sense of greater continuity before the final section of the piece.

The texts of *Douce Playsence/Garison Selon Nature* are traditional in nature—poems that speak of the pains and pleasures of love. Although the poems are very different from each other (and that for the triplum is nearly three times as long as that for the motetus), there are many deliberate echoes between them. Both make use of the image of burning, and the motetus ends with the words "playsance pure" ("pure delight"), reminiscent of the triplum's opening: "Douce playsence" ("Sweet delight"). In this piece, of course, there is no sense of reflection or commentary from the text of the tenor, since the tenor melody is not taken from a chant and has no text.

GUILLAUME DE MACHAUT

The central part of the fourteenth century in France was dominated by one composer to such an extent that his work is taken as representative of the entire period. He is one of the first composers of the Middle Ages about whom we know many biographical details and to whom we are able to ascribe an entire corpus of music. This is partly because he was famous in his own lifetime, partly because a complete retrospective collection of his works survives, and partly because administrative records and documents from the fourteenth century are more numerous and better preserved than those from earlier centuries.

Like many people in medieval times, Guillaume de Machaut took his name from his place of origin. His name means "William from Machaut"—Machaut, also spelled Machault, being a small town in the northern part of France. This system of naming is true of many of the other people mentioned in this book, people such as Johannes de Garlandia and Phillipe de Vitry.[1] Guillaume de Machaut, therefore, should be given his full name, or he should simply be called Guillaume. However he is mostly known today (improperly but irrevocably) as Machaut.

---

[1] Johannes took his name from a street in Paris near the university, and Phillipe was named after a small town south of Paris now known as Vitry-on-the-Seine.

Machaut was born about 1300 and died in 1377, and was therefore most active in the middle fifty years of the fourteenth century. He was educated at Rheims, an important town in northeastern France, one of the main centers of the trading fairs and the site of an impressive thirteenth-century cathedral (heavily damaged by bombing during the First World War). This cathedral was the seat of an archbishop and the place where the kings of France were traditionally crowned. In 1323 Machaut became secretary to John of Luxembourg, King of Bohemia, and remained in that position until 1346 when the king was killed at the Battle of Crécy. During this time he was also appointed as one of the canons of the cathedral at Rheims—an administrative post which carried some additional income. After the death of King John, Machaut served successively in the courts of some of the most important members of the French nobility, including Charles, King of Navarre; John, Duke of Berry; and Charles, Duke of Normandy, who later became King Charles V of France. From a long autobiographical poem we also learn of Machaut's passionate liaison in his later years with a nineteen-year-old girl named Péronne. Machaut died at the considerable age (in medieval terms) of seventy-seven, having spent the last few years of his life coordinating and copying (or having copied) all of the works he had produced during a prolific career.

To literary historians Machaut is known primarily as a poet. His many poetic works are considered important representatives of the French literary style of the fourteenth century. This style is known as the "second rhetoric"—a term which implies a renewal of the great rhetorical art of Classical Antiquity. In French fourteenth-century poetry it involved clever word play, puns, elaborate imagery, and intricate patterns of meter and rhyme. Guillaume de Machaut was a master of the style and was almost certainly the author of all the poetry for his musical settings. One should keep this aspect of Machaut's work in mind, for much of his music is written with the style and structure of the verse in the forefront of the overall design.

Machaut was a prolific composer who wrote in the main musical forms of the time, including motets and secular songs. He seems to have been the first to have consistently applied polyphony to the traditional song forms, and within his own lifetime he brought the polyphonic song from its simple origins to the height of perfection and subtle craftsmanship. He also wrote one complete hocket and a polyphonic setting of the entire Ordinary of the Mass.

Machaut's musical style is finely honed, delicate, and intense. It depends upon the rhythmic innovations of fourteenth-century theory, especially the interplay of duple and triple meters. Machaut also favored the subtle use of syncopation to enliven the polyphonic texture. His music is crafted with great economy of means, using small melodic motifs to unify and make cohesive each composition. There are both conservative and innovative aspects to Machaut's work, for although he broke new ground in his establishment of the polyphonic song and the linking of the items of the Mass Ordinary by polyphony, he also continued or revived older musical forms and practices, such as hocket, monophonic song, and a preference for French texts in motets.

The Motets

Machaut wrote over twenty motets, the style of which is indebted to that of Philippe de Vitry, although there are some important differences between the overall emphases of the two composers. Whereas most of Philippe's surviving motets use Latin texts, most of Machaut's have French texts in both upper voices. (There are two which mix French and Latin.) The French texts are traditional love poems or philosophical musings, whilst the Latin motets are political or occasional pieces. Machaut uses isorhythmic structure in his motets, like Philippe de Vitry, but the taleas in the tenor are longer, and isorhythm appears more frequently in the upper voices. Machaut often clarifies the structure of his motets by having the beginnings of poetic stanzas in the upper voices coincide with a change of talea in the tenor, by creating clear cadences at structural points, and by using isorhythm (sometimes including syncopated or hocket passages) in the upper voices to precede and signal each one of these cadences.

In his choice of tenors Machaut was guided particularly by the affective quality of the labeling words. A brief selection of the Latin tenor labels for his motets includes the following: "Very bitter," "I sigh," "I shall die for you," "Release me," and "More beautiful than all." These tenors (still segments of chant) all occur with French poems in the upper voices.

As mentioned above, Machaut's Latin motets were mostly written with political content or for particular occasions. An early one was composed for the election of the Archbishop of Rheims. Towards the end of his life Machaut turned to the Latin motet once more. His last three motets are pleas for peace during the ravages of the Hundred Years War—the long drawn-out (1337–1453) conflict between England and France for control of territory in Normandy, Flanders, and Aquitaine. These last three motets display another feature in common: they are all written for four voices, instead of the usual three. One four-voice motet had made an appearance in the Roman de Fauvel, but the genre was still a rarity. In Machaut's four-voice motets, the additional voice is called a *contratenor*, which means a voice written "against the tenor," and is in the same range and uses the same long note values as the tenor. The contratenor also carries no text, and moves in counterpoint with the tenor, often crossing above or below it, creating a fuller sonority for the composition and a richer, heavier foundation for the text-carrying motetus and triplum above.

Example 11-3 is the opening of one of these last motets of Machaut. It was probably written during the winter of 1359–1360, when the English, under Edward III, laid siege to Rheims. Edward hoped to be crowned at the traditional coronation site of the French kings, but the town did not sur-

EXAMPLE 11-3   Guillaume de Machaut, motet, *Christe, Qui Lux Ex/Veni, Creator Spiritus/Tribulatio Proxima,* beginning only. After *Polyphonic Music of the Fourteenth Century,* vol. 3, ed. Leo Schrade (Monaco: L'Oiseau-lyre, 1956).

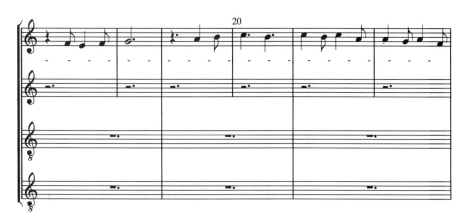

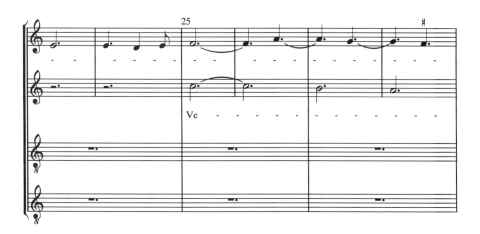

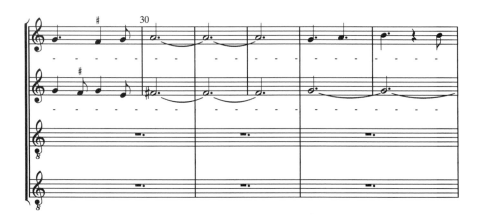

Talea A1

COLOR I

Talea A1

COLOR I

Tribulatio proxima est et non est qui adjuvet.

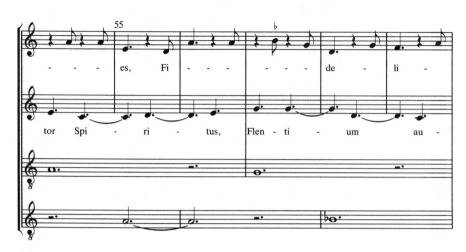

Triplum:
　Christe, qui lux es et dies,
　Fideliumque requies,
　Nos visita.
　Tu fu- . . .

Motetus:
　Veni, Creator Spiritus,
　Flentium audi gemitus,

　Quos nequi- . . .

Tenor:
　Tribulatio proxima est es non est qui ad-
　　juvet.

Triplum:
　Christ, you are both light and day,
　Respite for the faithful,
　Come to us.
　You . . .

Motetus:
　Come Spirit and Creator,
　Hear the laments of those who are weep-
　　ing,
　Whom . . .

Tenor:
　There is present tribulation, but there is
　　nobody to help.

render, and Edward and his huge army ultimately set off for Paris, where a treaty was signed with the French.

The texts of the two upper voices and the chant from which the tenor melody is taken contain a highly concentrated web of allusions, as was by now typical of this intellectually demanding genre. The two upper voices begin with the first lines of hymns. The triplum quotes the first line of the hymn *Christe, Qui Lux Es Et Dies* ("O Christ, you who are both light and day,"), which was sung at the service of Compline during Lent. As the Office service held before retiring for the night, Compline stresses protection and comfort, and this hymn contains specific requests and petitions for protection, including the lines "Defend us this night," "Let the enemy not surprise us," and "Look down on us, our Defender." These lines are not given in the motet, which goes on to make other petitions, but they would have been known by the audience and brought to mind simply by the quotation of the first line of the hymn.

The motetus also starts with words from a well-known hymn. *Veni, Creator Spiritus* is the first line of a hymn which was sung at Vespers on the Feast of Pentecost, but it was also widely used in other ceremonial and liturgical contexts. It has connections with Rheims, for it is known to have been sung at the Council of Rheims in 1049, and may have been particularly popular in the town. Later lines in the hymn, again not used in the motet but brought to mind by association, include "May you repel the enemy far from us and grant us peace," and "May we avoid all harm." This hymn also has connections with the sequence *Veni, Sancte Spiritus,* a sequence which asks for consolation and addresses the Holy Spirit as a "sweet refuge" and "comforter of the soul."

These allusions to the siege of Rheims may seem distant and far-fetched today, but they would certainly not have been considered so in the fourteenth century. A motet was inherently a demanding and complex composition, as its polytextuality and isorhythmic structure make clear, and quotations, cross-references, and allusions were a part of its historical tradition.

There are many other such allusions in the two texts of the upper parts which cannot be examined here; they include deliberate echoes of other chants, both by means of the meter of the texts and by their contents, and references to biblical stories. The most striking allusion to the circumstances under which the motet was composed is made by the tenor. The portion of chant that is used for this voice is the setting of the words "Tribulatio proxima est et non est qui adiuvet" ("There is present tribulation, but there is nobody to help"), the verse of a responsory sung at Matins in Easter week. The words of the opening antiphon of this chant (not given in the motet) are "Circumdederunt me" ("They have surrounded me"), and the full text of the antiphon is: "They have surrounded me—lying men, without a reason. But you, O Lord, my Defender, take my side." Finally, it is not by accident that the three texts of the motet, the tenor chant and the first lines of the triplum and motetus respectively, refer to the three manifestations of God—the Father ("Domine"), the Son ("Christe"), and the Holy Spirit ("Creator Spiritus").

The newly written continuing texts of the upper parts tie all these allusions together, for they contain appeals for protection and laments over the disarray of the people, and both conclude with the Latin word for "peace." Taken together, the spoken and unspoken resonances of this motet contain a dramatic reflection of human responses to desperate circumstances. But the cruel reality of the historical situation is transmuted into a work of art of great density and depth.

The motet is in four voices, with two texted upper parts and a tenor and contratenor. As with many of Machaut's Latin motets, an introductory section precedes the commencement of the isorhythmic structure. In this introductory section the triplum begins alone, is then joined by the motetus, and finally, for the first strong cadence, by the tenor and contratenor. The main (isorhythmic) part of the motet contains four taleas in the tenor part for the first statement of the pitch pattern and four taleas in diminution (by half) for the second statement. The contratenor is also fully isorhythmic and follows this same pattern exactly, though it has its own melody and its own taleas. The upper parts are partly isorhythmic, especially in the passages which precede the ends of taleas in the lower parts. The text of the triplum is written as six metrical and rhyming stanzas, the text of the motetus as four. Stanza divisions in the triplum coincide exactly with the changes of talea in the lower parts until just before the diminished final section, when they start to overlap. On the other hand, stanza divisions in the shorter text of the motetus consistently overlap with these structural divisions. There is a certain amount of simple syncopation in the motetus, and this coincides with hocketing in the triplum (see, for example, mm. 54–59). Main cadences are on C, G, C, and F (these are repeated in the diminished section). At the first three of these cadences, the contratenor is below the tenor; at the final cadence, the tenor sounds the lowest pitch.[2]

The Mass

During the fourteenth century plainchant manuscripts began to group together the chants of the Ordinary of the Mass—Kyrie, Gloria, Credo, Sanctus, and Agnus Dei. (Sometimes the Credo was omitted, since its old melody was considered standard, and sometimes the final item of the Mass, the Ite Missa Est, was included.) This grouping of the chants had important musical consequences. Since these items were invariable, they could be considered and treated as a group, even though they are separated in the liturgy. Composers could therefore write settings of these items which could be sung at Mass on many different occasions and would not be restricted to only one day of the year.

Although there are other polyphonic settings of individual items of

---

[2]The length of this composition prevents our printing it in full. It is, however, easily available in modern editions. Recordings are listed in the discography at the end of the chapter.

the Ordinary of the Mass from the fourteenth century (these are discussed at the end of this chapter), Machaut is the first composer whom we know to have written a complete group of these settings. Machaut's Mass was probably written sometime between 1350 and 1360; in one manuscript it is entitled *Messe de Notre Dame* ("Mass of Our Lady"). It includes all five items of the Ordinary and also the Ite Missa Est. The music is for four voices throughout and employs the most modern rhythmic devices of duple and triple meters and syncopation. There is a clear distinction in style between the Gloria and Credo and the other items of the Mass. The Gloria and the Credo, those items of the Ordinary which have the longest texts, are written in conductus style with short, clear phrases, primarily syllabic text setting, and large sectional divisions marked by very strong cadences. Example 11-4, from the beginning of the Gloria, exemplifies the musical style of these two movements. (The priest's intonation was traditionally left in plainchant.)

The initial cadence of this example, to the word "pax" in measure 4, may also stand as an instance of two important aspects of fourteenth-century music. First, this type of cadence is often known as a "double leading-tone" cadence, since there is a half-step movement both to the main note (D) and to the fifth (A). The main note is approached from a C♯ (this progression appears in this case in parallel octaves) and the fifth from a

EXAMPLE 11-4 Guillaume de Machaut, Mass, beginning of Gloria. After *Polyphonic Music of the Fourteenth Century,* vol. 3, ed. Leo Schrade (Monaco: L'Oiseaulyre, 1956).

bus   bo - nae vo - lun - ta - tis.

bus   bo - nae vo - lun - ta - tis.

bus   bo - nae vo - lun - ta - tis.

bus   bo - nae vo - lun - ta - tis.

Gloria in excelsis Deo.	Glory to God in the highest.
Et in terra pax hominibus bonae	And on earth peace to men of
voluntatis.	good will.

G♯. The double leading-tone cadence is common in fourteenth-century polyphonic music and particularly so in Machaut. It is an attractive sound, creating a sense of great expectation and satisfactory arrival. In later music this parallel movement would be avoided and even censured under the opprobrious label of "parallel fifths." The second important aspect of this cadence is the necessary application of the sharp accidental to the lower C and the upper G, added editorially above these notes in the score and necessitated by the appearance of the upper C♯ in the original manuscript. Further such modifications are necessary in measure 5. The application of accidentals in performance to notes that are not thus inflected by the composer is a technique commonly discussed by music theorists from the thirteenth century onwards. It results in what was known as *musica ficta* ("feigned music"). The exact nature of musica ficta and the full extent of the situations in which it might occur in medieval and later music continue to be controversial among scholars.

The other items of Machaut's Mass—the Kyrie, Sanctus, Agnus Dei, and Ite Missa Est—are written in the style of the isorhythmic motet. With the exception of the Ite Missa Est, their tenor parts are based on melodies taken from the relevant liturgical plainchants: a Kyrie melody for the Kyrie movement, a Sanctus melody for the Sanctus, and so on. One vital difference, however, separates these settings from the normal isorhythmic motet: all of the four voices (triplum, motetus, contratenor, and tenor) sing the same text. This makes for a very different texture and effect, and obscures the isorhythmic structure far more than when the function of each voice is clearly distinguished by its text (or, in the case of the tenor and contratenor, lack of text).

An excerpt from the Kyrie of the Mass (Ex. 11-5b) can represent the style of these movements. The excerpt is the very beginning of the Mass; all four voices sing the relevant liturgical text: "Kyrie eleison." The triplum has a modest amount of syncopation (mm. 8, 11, 20, and 23) and hocketing (mm. 10 and 22), while the motetus is more straightforward rhythmically and is written in a slightly lower range. The tenor melody uses the pitches of a Kyrie plainchant (Ex. 11-5a) that we have studied in several of its manifestations in this book (see Examples 4-2, 6-5, and 8-10.) In this section of the Mass the chant is arranged in patterns of the third rhythmic mode. Both the tenor and contratenor are isorhythmic. Each tenor talea is made up of three measures plus one measure rest and there are seven taleas (the last one omitting the final rest). The melody is stated once through, therefore there is only one color. The contratenor sounds both below and above the tenor. Its color is also only stated once, but there are two complete statements of its rhythmic pattern (talea 2 of the contratenor begins in measure 13) and one partial statement to round out the section.

The mode of the tenor melody is Mode 1, Dorian. At the outset the tenor begins on A, and the contratenor sounds the D below; at the final

EXAMPLE 11-5a   Kyrie plainchant melody.

Ky - ri - e,   e - - - - - le - i - son.

Kyrie, eleison.   Lord, have mercy.

EXAMPLE 11-5b   Guillaume de Machaut, Mass, first section of Kyrie. After *Polyphonic Music of the Fourteenth Century,* vol. 3, ed. Leo Schrade (Monaco: L'Oiseau-lyre, 1956).

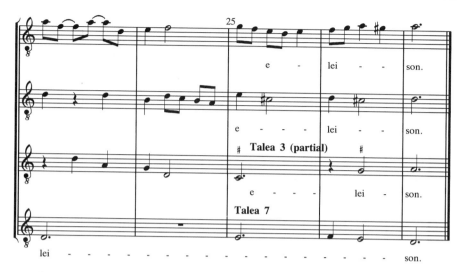

Kyrie, eleison.   Lord, have mercy.

cadence the roles are reversed, and since the tenor descends to the D, the contratenor can fill in the A above. This final cadence is a double leading-tone cadence, as are other cadences in this section (mm. 4–5, 6–7, 16–17), and some involve the use of musica ficta. Even in this short section, the composer supplies constant variety by making some of these cadences coincide with new taleas in the tenor, by suggesting other cadences in the counterpoint which are then undermined or sounded only very briefly, and by avoiding cadences in places which would otherwise call for them. Throughout the Kyrie, and throughout the whole Mass, Machaut manipulates a series of cadential articulations, like punctuation in written speech, to provide flow and trajectory for his music.

Other features create unity in the Mass as a whole. The first three movements end on D, while the last three end on F. Short linking passages, all of similar configuration, are used to join sections or phrases throughout the Mass. Occasional words are stressed by being set to long, static notes. And the Gloria and Credo, which stand out from the other items and are related to each other by their conductus style, are further linked by their final Amens, which have similar music, isorhythmic in structure and enlivened by syncopation and hocket.

The Secular Songs

By far the majority of Machaut's works are secular songs. The traditional genre of love poetry set to music gained new life in his hands; it was to remain one of the most important genres for the next two centuries. It was not only that Machaut wove subtle polyphonic textures for these songs, which had been restricted almost exclusively to monophonic settings up to his time. He also revived some older forms, himself writing several monophonic songs as a considerable part of his output.

Among the most important of Machaut's monophonic secular songs are the lais. Brief mention has already been made (see pp. 274–75) of a type of poetry and song known as the lai, which grew up in northern France and whose main exponent in the twelfth century was Marie de France. The lai differed from other medieval secular songs in its length and the irregularity of its verse. Each of its stanzas was in a different poetic form and thus required new music, in contrast to the strophic construction of most other types of song. In the thirteenth century both lyric and narrative lais had continued to be composed, their main characteristics being the freedom and irregularity of the verse, the different verse scheme for each stanza, and the new music for each stanza.

By Machaut's time the lai had crystallized into a rather more regular form. Each stanza still had its own rhyme scheme, length, and number of lines; but the number of stanzas was fixed at twelve. A sense of balance and closure was achieved by having the last stanza in the same form as the first. This is echoed in the musical form: each stanza has its own music, but the music of the first stanza is repeated (often transposed) for the last. Machaut gave further symmetry and cohesion to his lais by dividing each of the stanzas into parallel halves; the second half, with new words but repeated line lengths and rhyme scheme, repeats the music for the first half. He also employs a wealth of ingenuity in the repetition, expansion, and recombination of short melodic motifs throughout a piece to provide a subtle sense of unity.

The first stanza of one of Machaut's lais (Ex. 11-6) demonstrates the style and simple beauty of the form. This lai is *Le Lay de la Fonteinne* ("The Lai of the Fountain"), and the text is highly allegorical, since the lady addressed in the poem turns out to be the Virgin Mary.

EXAMPLE 11-6   Guillaume de Machaut, *Le Lay de la Fonteinne,* stanza 1. After *Polyphonic Music of the Fourteenth Century,* vol. 2, ed. Leo Schrade (Monaco: L'Oiseau-lyre, 1956).

Que mes maus weille a - li - gier.
M'o - tri - - e - ra de li - gier.

Mais si se tient chie - re
Et a bon - - - ne chie - re,

Et tant la truis dure et fie - re
Sans fin, sans a - mour le - gie - re,

Sans a - mo - li - ier,
Sans a - me - nui - sier,

Qu'a - dou - cir de ma pri - e - re Ne puis son dan - gier.
Ne joy - e qu'a li s'af - fie - re Ne puet homs tri - er.

I. Je ne cesse de prier A ma dame chiere Que mes maus weille aligier. Mais si se tient chiere Et tant la truis dure et fiere Sans amoliier, Qu'adoucir de ma priere Ne puis son dangier.	I. I never cease to pray To my dear lady That she might relieve my pain. But she is so unapproachable And I find her so hard and aloof And without compliance, That I cannot soften her heart With my prayer.
S'en weil une autre acointier Qui joie pleniere M'otriera de ligier. Et a bonne chiere, Sans fin, sans amour legiere, Sans amenuisier, Ne joye qu'a li s'affiere Ne puet homs trier.	So I shall take up with another one, Who will willingly grant me The fullest of joy. And she will do it with a good will, Without limits or a flighty love, And without diminishment, So that no one could find A comparable joy.

The stanza is of sixteen lines; the same music serves for the first eight lines and again for the next eight. The form of the verse is clarified by ending each line either on a long note or with a rest, except for the last two lines of each half stanza, which are run together. The setting is primarily syllabic, and a subtle sense of departure and return is created by the control of beginning and ending pitches of each phrase, by choice of vocal range, and by placement of rhythmic activity. Cohesion and unity are provided by the pervasive use of similar melodic motifs, three of which are labeled in the score. The first incorporates either a rise from or a descent to G (x and x′). The second (y) involves the descending third E–D–C. And the third is both a rhythmic and a melodic motif (labeled z). Other, less obvious motifs, as well as a gentle use of syncopation, unify the careful and artistic music of this lai.

Some of Machaut's lais have been shown to contain disguised polyphonic sections. The single written-out voice part may prove to be only one voice in a canon, or the music of different stanzas may combine to create polyphony. In the Lai of the Fountain the manuscript unequivocally designates every even-numbered stanza as a *chace*. And indeed each of these stanzas, although provided with only one line of music, can be performed as a three-voice canon. Throughout the lai, therefore, there is an alternation between monophonic and polyphonic performance. Since Machaut always used the poetic form and music of his first stanza for the last stanza of his lais, it turns out that the music of Stanza 1, transposed up a fifth, becomes a three-voice canon for Stanza 12. Example 11-7 gives the beginning of Stanza 12 of the Lai of the Fountain, with the canon written out as it would have been sung.

EXAMPLE 11-7 Guillaume de Machaut, *Le Lay de la Fonteinne*, stanza 12, beginning. After *Polyphonic Music of the Fourteenth Century*, vol. 2, ed. Leo Schrade (Monaco: L'Oiseau-lyre, 1956).

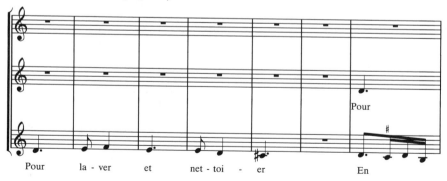

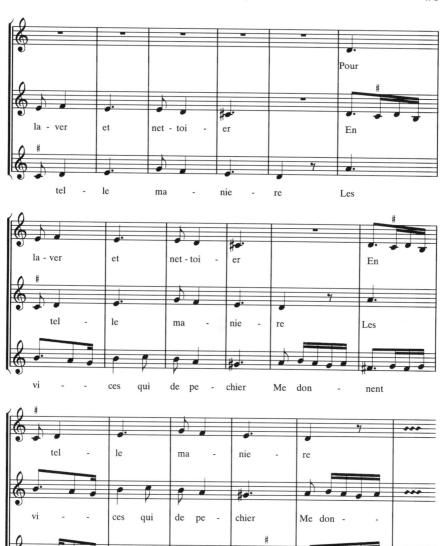

XII. Pour laver et nettoier
   En telle maniere
   Les vices qui de pechier
   Me donnent matiere,
   Vierge, que ta grace ac- . . .

XII. To cleanse and wash away
   Like this
   The faults which
   Provide access to sin,
   O Virgin, may you grant grace . . .

The existence of polyphonic sections for some of Machaut's lais should not prevent us from appreciating the subtlety and interest of the monophonic music from which most of them are constructed. Machaut's concern with this "old-fashioned" genre is demonstrated by the fact that he wrote no fewer than nineteen lais, each one of which is exquisitely crafted and displays its own individual and perfect balance between music and text.

The rest of Machaut's considerable legacy of secular songs were all written in one of three forms known as the *formes fixes* ("fixed forms")—the *virelai,* the *rondeau,* and the *ballade.* The fixed forms were poetic types, all of which dealt with the theme of courtly love, but each of which had different qualities and affects and ranged from the unpretentious to the sophisticated to the complex. All three of the forms have only two sections of music; what distinguishes them is the distribution of the text between these sections and the patterns of repetition of both text and music. We shall discuss them in progressive order of complexity.

The simplest of the fixed forms to which Machaut devoted his attention was the virelai. Like the lai, the virelai was a traditional genre, its roots reaching back to the twelfth and thirteenth centuries. Reflecting this tradition, only eight of Machaut's more than thirty virelais are polyphonic, most of these having relatively simple two-part settings. The remainder are monophonic songs in the style of previous repertories but invested with Machaut's sensitive text setting and subtle craftsmanship and employing the new rhythmic procedures of the fourteenth century.

The name of the virelai suggests that its origins may have been in a dance form, for the word *virer* in Old French means to "turn" or "twist." Like an enormous number of the most successful musical forms throughout the history of music, the form soon lost its direct, practical function as an accompaniment to dancing but retained its vitality as a vehicle for some of the most accomplished of purely musical creations.

The structure of the virelai is one that we have encountered before in the ballata and lauda in Italy and the cantiga in the Iberian peninsula (see pp. 297 and 305). There are two sections of music, which are sung in the following pattern: AbbaA. (The upper-case letters indicate the refrain, which is sung between each of the stanzas.) Usually a virelai had three stanzas of poetry, in which case the entire pattern can be represented as follows: AbbaAbbaAbbaA. This is a form whose repetition scheme, symmetrical but constantly renewed development, and rounded refrain pattern seems to have appealed to composers in many different places and historical eras. Whether there was a line of influence from a single prototype, or whether the different repertories employing the form evolved independently is still a matter for debate.

The form is a particularly satisfying one, for it allows a shifting contrast between the first section and the second. There is a constant balance between the new and the familiar. As the song progresses, the refrain, both in its words and music, becomes better known and stands in greater contrast to the new lines of poetry. The length and number of lines in the refrain and the stanzas can vary, as can the rhyme scheme, but the musical structure to which the poem is set remains the same.

As a result of their traditional dance heritage, many of Machaut's virelais are in the lilting meter which is best transcribed in modern notation as $\frac{6}{8}$. Some of the polyphonic virelais, which may be of later date, use different meters, and employ the contrast between duple and triple groupings that is so characteristic of Machaut's rhythmic style. Text setting is usually syllabic, and the structure of the verse is clear.

Example 11-8 is representative of the style. This is probably one of Machaut's later virelais, but it still retains its light and delicate affect. The refrain (A) consists of six text lines, the b section of three. This disparity is reflected in the length of the musical sections: the first section has twenty-five measures, the second only thirteen. The two-part texture is light and transparent, with the tenor part—textless, hence instrumental—providing a simple foundation and support for the voice as well as occasional touches of rhythmic interest. The voice part is involved in a constant and delicate fluctuation between duple and triple groupings. Although the prevailing meter is $\frac{2}{4}$ in the modern transcription, the music slips constantly in and out of $\frac{6}{8}$ meter (these passages are indicated by small notes above or below the staff). Each part is separately written without barlines in the original manuscript, thus facilitating this subtle fluctuation of meter. Obviously some passages may be read either in $\frac{6}{8}$ or $\frac{2}{4}$, and sometimes a grouping will begin in one meter and turn into the other, or there may be elision between one grouping and the next. Only the clearest passages have been indicated in the score.

EXAMPLE 11-8 Guillaume de Machaut, virelai, *Moult Sui.* From *Polyphonic Music of the Fourteenth Century,* vol. 3, ed. Leo Schrade (Monaco: L'Oiseau-lyre, 1956).

bien a - - me - e   De mon doulz a - mi
tous lo - e - e   Plus que je ne di,

Qu'il ha toute a - mour guer - pi   Et son cuer a
Qui mon cuer ha si ra - vi   Qu'on-ques mais en -

tou - tes   ve - - - - - - - - - - - -
a - mou - re - - - - - - - - - - - -

- - e   Pour l'a - - mour de mi.
- - e   Fa - me - ne fu - sy.

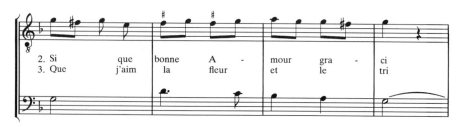

2. Si   que bonne A -   mour gra -   ci
3. Que j'aim la   fleur et   le   tri

I. *Moult sui de bonne heure nee,*
   Quant je sui si bien amee
   De mon doulz ami
   Qu'il ha toute amour guerpi
   Et son cuer a toutes vee
   Pour l'amour de mi.

   Si que bonne Amour graci
   Cent mille fois, qui
   M'a si tres bien assenee

   Que j'aim la fleur et le tri
   De ce monde cy,
   Sans part et sans decevree.

   Pour sa bonne renommee
   Qu'est cent fois de tous loee
   Plus que je ne di,
   Qui mon cuer ha si ravi
   Qu'onques mais enamouree
   Fame ne fusy.

   Moult sui de bonne heure nee, . . .

I. *I was born at a very good time,*
   Since I am so well loved
   By my sweet friend
   That he has renounced all other loves
   And denied his heart to all others
   For the love of me.

   So I thank kind Love
   A hundred thousand times,
   For he has equipped me so well

   That I love the flowers and blossoms
   Of the present world,
   Without prejudice and without deceit.

   I thank him for his good reputation,
   Which is praised a hundred times by all,
   More than I can say,
   For he has captured my heart so much
   That there never was a woman
   More in love than me.

   I was born at a very good time, . . .

II. Nos cuers en joye norry
    Sont, si que soussi
    Ne riens qui nous desagree
	II. Our hearts are so full of joy,
	    That we have no worries
	    And nothing troubles us,

N'avons, pour ce que assevi Sommes de mercy, Qu'est souffisance appellee,	For we have been granted Such favor, Which we call contentment,
Un desir, une pensee, Un cuer, une ame est entee En nous, et aussi De voloir sommes uni. Onques plus douce assamblee, Par ma foy, ne vy.	That one single desire, thought, Heart, and soul are grafted In us, and we share Every single wish. In truth, never was seen A happier couple.
Moult sui de bonne heure nee, . . .	*I was born at a very good time*, . . .

III. Nompourquant je me defri
    Seulette et gemi
    Souvent a face esplouree,
	III. And yet I grieve
	    Alone and lament often,
	    My face full of tears,

Quant lonteinne sui de li; Qu'ay tant enchiery Que sans li riens ne m'agree.	When I am far from him; For I am so in love That without him nothing pleases me.
Mais d'espoir sui confortee Et tres bien asseuree Que mettre en oubly Ne me porroit par nul sy, Dont ma joie est si doublee Que tous maus oubly.	But hope comforts me And gives me full assurance That he could in no way Forget me, And so my joy redoubles And I forget all my sadness.
Moult sui de bonne heure nee, . . .	*I was born at a very good time*, . . .

The music stresses the line endings in some cases, and runs lines together in others. For example in the first section, there are cadences, sometimes followed by rests, in measures 5–6, 12, 21–22, and 25. These coincide with the endings of lines 1, 3, 5, and 6 in the refrain. Lines 2 and 3, and 4 and 5, are made to run together, which reflects their meaning as connected clauses. Three levels of completion are distinguished in the cadences throughout the piece. The most final-sounding cadence is that on a unison G, the cadence with which both sections of the music end. Less complete is the cadence on G with a fifth or octave above it, used at intermediate points in both sections (mm. 12 and 29). The most incomplete sonority is that of a third, on F♯ and A. This occurs in measure 21 and for the first ending of the b section (m. 37).

Unity is imparted to the piece by the use of several of the same measures of music in both sections. Measures 17–22 from the a section reappear to conclude the b section (first ending), and measures 23–25 (the last three measures of the a section) are also used for the second ending of the b section. Even more integrally, a four note eighth-note motif appears in different contours throughout the piece, tying the fabric of the whole composition together. Against this unity is set the contrast of the prevailingly higher range of the second section, which serves to delineate the form—a technique we have seen used to good effect in the earlier, monophonic, song repertoire. The delicately evocative nature of the poetry, with its simple use of only two rhymes throughout all three stanzas, its short text lines, and its contented outlook (thrown into relief by the passing regret expressed in the third stanza), is matched by a musical setting of an extraordinarily elusive beauty and charm.

Machaut wrote about twenty songs in the form of the rondeau. This is a form we encountered previously in the work of Adam de la Halle and Jehan de Lescurel. Like the virelai, the rondeau probably had origins in the dance, for its name suggests a circle or a "round-dance." It also employs a refrain, but the repetition pattern of the music is rather more complicated than that of the virelai. This pattern may be represented as follows: ABaAabAB.

In the fourteenth century the poetic form of the rondeau often had only one stanza of eight lines, so that, in contrast to the virelai, each one of the musical sections in the eight-part repetition scheme contained only a single line of verse. The main difference from the virelai lies in the more involved repetition pattern and in the fact that the refrain takes up both sections of the music (A and B). In the middle of the stanza the first line of the refrain occurs by itself (A), usually with a subtle shift of poetic meaning. This contributes to the literary as well as the musical subtlety of the form and led to the popularity of the rondeau in educated courtly circles in the fourteenth and fifteenth centuries.

The form of the rondeau is the most difficult of the three fixed forms to remember. Medieval treatises on the second rhetoric, realizing this, sometimes gave miniature examples to help readers learn the form. Each of the eight lines in a stanza can be represented by a single word, and the rhyme scheme and refrain pattern can thus be demonstrated in the simplest possible way. The following miniature rondeau is from one of these treatises:

Je	I
Bois.	*Drink.*
Se	If
Je	I
Ne	Don't
Vois.	See (her).
Je	I
Bois.	*Drink.*

This of course is only a clever example designed to help in memorizing the form. No real rondeau has only one word per line. But it can serve to fix the rondeau pattern quickly in the mind.

The more sophisticated nature of the rondeau, compared to the virelai, is reflected in the fact that all of Machaut's musical settings are polyphonic. About a third are for two voices, most are for three voices, and two are
four-voice settings. In all of them only one part carries the text (usually it is
called the *cantus*), and the remaining parts are instrumental. In the two-voice
settings there is an instrumental tenor, and in the three-voice settings a tenor
and a contratenor. The motivic and rhythmic structure are often quite intricate, and metric interplay and syncopation are common.

In *Doulz Viaire Gracieus* (Ex. 11-9), the arrangement of the voices is
unusual. Instead of a cantus part supported by a tenor and contratenor, the
cantus is the middle voice and there are instrumental triplum and tenor parts.
This was the arrangement usually adopted by Adam de la Halle in his three-
voice settings, and it may indicate that the piece is an early one in Machaut's
output. The setting is delicate and of great beauty, with the sung text appearing in the middle of the musical texture. Both tenor and triplum briefly echo

EXAMPLE 11-9 Guillaume de Machaut, rondeau, *Doulz Viaire Gracieus*. From
Polyphonic Music of the Fourteenth century, vol. 3, ed. Leo Schrade (Monaco:
L'Oiseau-lyre, 1956).

Doulz viaire gracieus,	Sweet, gracious countenance,
De fin cuer vous ay servy.	I have served you with a faithful heart.
Weillies moy estre piteus,	Take pity on me,
Doulz viaire gracieus;	Sweet, gracious countenance;
Se je sui un po honteus,	If I am a little shy,
Ne me mettes en oubli.	Do not forget me.
Doulz viaire gracieus,	Sweet, gracious countenance,
De fin cuer vous ay servy.	I have served you with a faithful heart.

the voice part once (in mm. 7 and 8 respectively). Otherwise the tenor is mostly in long notes, stressing the G focus of the first section and the B♭ focus of the second section. (The shift in pitch focus creates a hint of incompletion at the ending.) The finely-spun triplum creates a counterpoint with the cantus, moving in parallel and contrary motion with it and adding the continued motion necessary to link together the two sections (m. 5).

There are some subtle shifts of meter in the piece which can be seen only if one ignores the rigidity implied by the meter and barlines of the modern transcription. In measure 4, for example, the triplum really shifts momentarily into ⁶/₈ meter. In measures 2 and 3 the tenor moves in half and quarter notes and is actually briefly in ²/₄ (or ³/₂) meter. In measure 11 cantus and triplum have ⁶/₈ measures against the ³/₄ of the tenor. These kinds of metrical shifts are typical of Machaut's fluid rhythmic style, as we have seen, and anticipate the even more intricate rhythmic interplay which occurs in his complex pieces.

The poem of this rondeau is in the standard one-stanza eight-line form, with the rhyme scheme reflected in the musical sections. The first rhyme (-*eus*) occurs only in the first section of the music, the second (-*i*) only in the second. The address to the beloved's face, which forms the first line of the refrain, aptly recurs as the fourth line of the poem (as it must in the rondeau form). Each line has seven syllables, and the text setting is mostly syllabic, although brief melismas ornament it. The motion in the cantus is primarily conjunct, but the brief phrase in measure 6 which serves as an impetus for the echoes in the other parts stands out by its higher pitch. The downward leap of a fifth in the cantus in measures 10–11 elegantly prepares the ending.

Another rondeau by Machaut demonstrates the variety possible within the genre. This piece (Ex. 11-10) is written for a disposition of parts that became more or less standard in fourteenth-century French song. Below a text-bearing cantus voice lie two instrumental parts: a tenor and a contratenor. These are written in the same range and frequently cross, though at opening and closing sonorities the tenor is the lowest voice.

The repetition scheme is the same as for the previous example, and again there is only one stanza; however, the relationship between text and music is slightly different, for two poetic lines are accommodated at each appearance of the first section of the music. These lines have two rhymes, *-ire* and *-our,* and the single lines in the second musical section pick up the *-our* rhyme again. The poem contrasts a dignified lady with a nervous lover, and the shortening of the refrain in the middle increases the pace of the poetry and adds to the impression of nervousness and trepidation. There are melismas in the cantus part on the first syllable of each text line and on the penultimate syllable of the lines in the b section. The melisma from measure 8 to measure 15 is particularly striking, with its descending, almost hypnotic, varied sequential pattern. There are constant metrical fluctuations in all of the parts, as well as passages of syncopation. Each of the parts seems to have its own rhythmic identity, although tenor and contratenor often share rhythmic outlines. Again, a motif of four eighth notes unifies the piece (it is announced at the outset in descending form in the contratenor) and again the b section is set into relief by its higher range. Structural cadences are all on D (mm. 7, 19, and 31), and parallel motion is common. The cadence at the end of the a section is made incomplete by the inclusion of a third, while that at the end of the b section has the octave and the fifth.

EXAMPLE 11-10   Guillaume de Machaut, rondeau, *Comment Puet On.* From *Polyphonic Music of the Fourteenth Century,* vol. 3, ed. Leo Schrade (Monaco: L'Oiseaulyre, 1956).

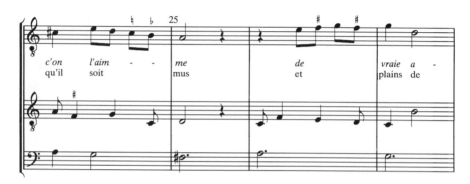

Comment puet on mieus ses maus dire	*How can someone best express his pain*
A dame qui congnoist honnour	*To a lady who knows honor*
Et c'on l'aimme de vraie amour,	*And whom he truly loves,*
Quant amans ressoingne escondire	When as a lover he fears rejection
Et s'a de son courrous paour?	And dreads her anger?
Comment puet on mieus ses maus dire	*How can someone best express his pain*
A dame qui congnoist honnour,	*To a lady who knows honor,*
S'elle voit qu'il tramble et souspire	If she sees that he trembles and sighs,
Et mue maniere et coulour,	And his behavior and his color change,
Et qu'il soit mus et plains de plour?	And he is tearful and cannot speak?

Comment puet on mieus ses maus dire	*How can someone best express his pain*
A dame qui congnoist honnour	*To a lady who knows honor*
Et c'on l'aimme de vraie amour?	*And whom he truly loves?*

Machaut reserved for the third of the fixed forms, the ballade, his most complex and intricately organized music. He also wrote more poems in this form than in any other—more than forty ballades with music and nearly two hundred without music.

The overall form of the music for a ballade is deceptively simple. There are two sections of music, the first of which is sung twice and the second of which is sung once, to set each stanza. This would give the form aab for each stanza (and indeed it is often indicated that way). However, this obscures an important aspect of the relationship between the music and the text. Ballades usually have three stanzas of seven or eight lines, and the last line of each stanza is the same; it is a refrain. Thus a better scheme to demonstrate the form is aa(b + C). A fairly common variant of this form has the second section of the music repeated as well as the first. The refrain text then comes only at the end of the second statement of the b section: aab(b + C).

The ballade seems to have represented for Machaut the most experimental of his forms, for there are many variants in his choice of the number of voices and in the nature of the text settings. There are a large number of two- and three-voice ballades, two four-voice ballades, and even, unexpectedly, one for only one voice. He also experimented by incorporating in some ballades a feature which we usually associate only with the motet: polytextuality. One ballade has two different simultaneous texts, and two have three texts. Machaut even wrote one ballade which makes extensive use of isorhythm. Having noted this variety of approach to the form, it is nevertheless true that the significant majority of the ballades are for either two or three parts, with a single text, for a cantus and tenor, or cantus, tenor, and contratenor.

The ballade is far more melismatic than the virelai or rondeau. Most often the melismas occur on the penultimate syllables of text lines, as had become standard in musical settings of vernacular poetry, and thus usually towards the end of each musical section. Metrical complexities are common, as are syncopation and other rhythmic devices, shifts of pitch focus, and freedom of dissonance. Careful structure is a feature of the form, with unity provided by the subtle repetition of short melodic and rhythmic motifs and by a common use of musical rhyme (the repetition of music at the same or at a different pitch level) between the endings of the first and second sections. The music of Machaut's ballades is always constructed with great finesse, brilliant and delicate control of texture and rhythmic life, and a careful and sensitive handling of the modal color, the departure from and return to pitch goals, and the timing of approaches to cadences.

     A single example must suffice to represent this wealth of exquisite mu-
sic. The ballade *Honte, Paour, Doubtance* (Ex. 11-11) is written for three
voices—a cantus, which carries the text, and an instrumental tenor and contratenor. The music begins founded on G, and there is a marked double
leading-tone cadence from measure 3 to 4, in which the leap of an octave from
the anticipated note of resolution in the cantus is a particularly striking feature. Shifts of pitch focus continue through the first section to the first ending
and its unexpected cadence on F. The second ending of the first section, however, turns this to B♭. The second section begins on F, but has a cadence to
long notes on C (m. 24). This cadence is anticipated by the long notes on C in
measure 22, whose consonance is made incomplete by the presence of the
third (E♭) in the cantus. Other chromatic inflections throughout the piece and
a high level of dissonance add to the sense of wavering stability in the music—
a sense implied by the *doubtance* ("hesitation") in the first line of the text. A
musical rhyme (from the second ending of the first section) ends the second
section of the piece.

EXAMPLE 11-11   Guillaume de Machaut, ballade, *Honte, Paour, Doubtance*. After
Polyphonic Music of the Fourteenth Century, vol. 3, ed. Leo Schrade (Monaco:
L'Oiseau-lyre, 1956).

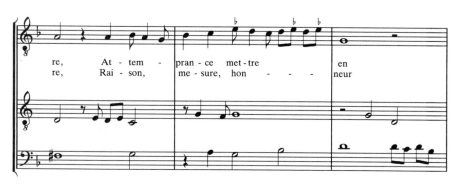

re,   At - tem - pran - ce met - tre   en
re,   Rai - son,   me - sure, hon - - - neur

sa   vo - len - te;
et   hon - ne -

ste:

Doit en son cuer fi - gu - rer, Et mes - di - sans   seur

tou-tes riens doub-ter,   Et   en   tous   fais   estre a-mou-reus cou - ar -

de,   Qui   de   s'on - neur   wet fai-re bon-ne

gar - - - - - - - - - - - - - - - - - - - de.

I. Honte, paour, doubtance de mef-
     faire,
   Attemprance mettre en sa volente;
   Large en refus et lente d'octroy
     faire,
   Raison, mesure, honneur et hon-
     neste:
   Doit en son cuer figurer,

   Et mesdisans seur toutes riens
     doubter,

I. Shame, fear, hesitation to do
     wrong,
   Temperance in desire;
   Generosity in refusals and slowness
     to grant requests,
   Reason, moderation, honor, and in-
     tegrity:
   All these things must she carry in
     her heart,
   Hesitating to speak ill of anything,

Et en tous fais estre amoureus couarde,
Qui de s'onneur wet faire bonne garde.

And all the time being a timorous lover—
The lady who wishes to protect her honor.

II. Sage en maintieng, au bien penre exemplaire,
Celer a point s'amour et son secre,

Simple d'atour et non vouloir attraire
Pluseurs a li par samblant d'amitie,

Car c'est pour amans tuer;
Foy, pais, amour et loyaute garder:

Ce sont les poins que dame en son cuer garde,
Qui de s'onneur wet faire bonne garde.

II. Wise in her bearing, taking goodness as an example,
Hiding completely her love and her secrets,

Simple in her dress and not wanting to attract
Many people to her by a pretence of friendship,

For that would kill her lover,
Guarding her faith, country, love, and loyalty:

These are the points that the lady keeps in her heart—
The lady who wishes to protect her honor.

III. Quar quant amour maint en cuer debonnaire,
Jone, gentil, de franchise pare,

Plain de cuidier et de joieus afaire

Et de desir par plaisence engenre,
C'est trop fort a contrester,
Qu'il font souvent senz et mesure outrer;
Pour ce ades pense a ces poins et resgarde,

Qui de s'onneur wet faire bonne garde.

III. For when love takes over a good-natured heart
That is young, well-bred, endowed with openness,

Full of pleasant thoughts and joyful deeds

And desire born of pleasure,
It is too strong to resist,
So that people often exceed common sense and moderation;
For this reason she always contemplates and pays attention to these points—

The lady who wishes to protect her honor.

The transcription given here attempts to reflect in modern notation some of the metrical shifts of the original; but even this cannot capture, for example, the five-note groups of the tenor and contratenor in measures 5 and 6, the fluctuation between $\frac{2}{4}$ and $\frac{6}{8}$ in the cantus in measures 7, 8, 16, and 26, and the large duple groupings ($\frac{6}{4}$) in the tenor in measures 16, 23, and 28. Here, more than ever, each one of the parts has an independent life, informed by its own rhythmic structure and direction.

Each of the three stanzas of the poetry is brilliantly constructed to form a lengthy grammatical unit whose sense is completed only by the climactic last line—the refrain line, which finally gives the *subject* of the stanza: "The lady who wishes to protect her honor." The text is distributed spaciously over the music, and syllabic passages alternate with ornamental melismas. The refrain line in each stanza is clearly silhouetted by the long cadence immediately preceding it in measure 24. Its penultimate syllable receives an elegant melisma whose curving flow is grouped and phrased by rests.

Inner unity is provided by a melodic motif of four eighth notes, which recurs throughout the piece in different contours and combinations. Motion and stasis are carefully balanced in the whole composition. Text and music combine to create a work whose inner beauties reveal themselves only upon extended acquaintance—just like the lady in the poem.

It is appropriate that the work of Guillaume de Machaut is taken as representative of the fourteenth century in France, for he was the most accomplished of French composers in the period after Philippe de Vitry. He wrote in a wide range of musical forms from the most conservative to the most modern, and he was by far the most prolific composer of his time. The generation of composers that was active in the last quarter of the fourteenth century depended heavily upon the achievements of this man, who came from the small town of Machaut in the north of France to become poet and composer to dukes, princes, and kings, and who left a literary and musical legacy of tremendous depth and scope.

LITURGICAL POLYPHONY

Apart from Machaut's complete setting of the Ordinary of the Mass there was a considerable amount of other activity in fourteenth-century France in the composition of liturgical polyphony. We have mentioned above that plainchants for the Mass (as well as for the Office) continued to be composed throughout the period during which polyphony grew and flourished; indeed, chant still represented the most widely performed music of the Middle Ages. We also observed new trends in the fourteenth century in the way these chants were grouped in the manuscripts.

These trends continue in several aspects of liturgical music. First, there are a considerable number of polyphonic settings of the items from the Ordinary of the Mass. Second, these tend to be written into the manuscripts in collections: all the Kyrie settings together, all the Credo settings together, and so on. And third, there begin to be some manuscripts which group together one setting each of all the items from the Ordinary—a single mass Ordinary "cycle."

Apart from Machaut, the composers of these settings are not known. However the origins of the manuscripts suggest that they were active at several of the major cities and courts of France, including Paris, Toulouse, Avignon, and Tournai.

The musical styles of these settings are quite disparate, although almost all of them are written in three-part polyphony (as opposed to the four-part Mass of Machaut). In general, the musical styles fall into three overall categories, although there are variants and combinations of these.

The first may be called conductus style. Here all three voices carry the text (the same text) and move in more or less the same rhythm throughout. Brief passages of short notes in one or other of the voices may enliven the texture in places. The second style may be called the tenor-based style. This is sometimes known as motet style, but there are so many differences between this music and the contemporary motet that the classification does not seem very useful. This style has an instrumental tenor as a foundation. It is usually not isorhythmic and is newly written for the piece in long note values. Both upper voices are in faster notes and both carry the same text (the text of the Ordinary item). The item is usually divided into large sections by the use of cadences in all voices. The third style is influenced by the music written for secular songs. We may call it song style. Here a single text-carrying voice is supported by a tenor and a contratenor in longer notes.

The appearance of polyphonic settings of the Ordinary items of the Mass in the fourteenth century suggests both a new attitude towards liturgical polyphony and a new approach to performance. The interest of composers had shifted away from Proper items—the main focus of attention in the polyphony of Notre Dame—to items that could be performed more often. Polyphony in the liturgy was gradually becoming more usual. There was a move away from solo chants like the Gradual and Alleluia of the Mass and the Responsories of the Office to choral chants. Polyphony was no longer the exclusive preserve of trained soloists but could be sung by the choir (certainly also trained singers, but not virtuosos), and the music—more restrained, less vivid than the liturgical polyphony of Notre Dame—reflects this change in performing personnel.

The fact that the music was designed for the choir is known partly from the traditional allocation of the Ordinary to choral singing, but partly also from the omission of the solo intonations from the polyphonic settings of the Gloria and the Credo. It will be remembered that the Gloria begins with the words "Gloria in excelsis Deo," sung by the priest who is celebrating the Mass. The choir then continues with the remainder of the text, beginning "Et in terra pax." Similarly in the Credo the priest sings the intonation "Credo in unum Deum," and the choir continues "Patrem omnipotentem." The polyphonic settings of these two items in the fourteenth century therefore omit the opening phrases and begin with the words for the choir—a tradition that was maintained in many of the Mass settings in the later history of Western music.

One final observation should be made about fourteenth-century liturgical polyphony: whereas in the past composers had concentrated upon the writing of new music for the shorter texts of the Mass Ordinary—the Kyrie, Sanctus, and Agnus Dei—now there was a new emphasis upon those texts which, because of their length (and, in the case of the Credo, because of the traditional predominance of one or two plainchant melodies), had remained in the background of activity: the Gloria and the Credo.

The Tournai Mass

Let us look briefly at one of the polyphonic Mass cycles that have survived from the fourteenth century. It is preserved in a manuscript in the library of the Cathedral of Tournai and is therefore known as the Tournai Mass. (Tournai is in the southwestern part of present-day Belgium; from the twelfth to the sixteenth centuries it belonged to the kingdom of France.)

The Tournai Mass consists of the five main items of the Ordinary of the Mass and also a setting of the Ite Missa Est. All of the movements are composed for three voices and all five items of the Ordinary are set in conductus style. (The Ite Missa Est is written as a short motet with a Latin motetus and French triplum.) However, there is considerable variety of approach to the use of the conductus style, and it is possible that the various items of the Mass may have been composed at different periods and put together as a cycle by a later scribe.

The opening measures of each of the movements are given in Example 11-12. As can be seen, the Kyrie, Sanctus, and Agnus Dei are in a conductus style that is reminiscent of the parallel musical writing of the thirteenth century, with modal rhythms and similar rhythm in all the voices. The Gloria and the Credo, however, appear to be much more modern. As has been mentioned above, it was these items that received the focus of attention of composers in the fourteenth century. The Gloria and the Credo of the Tournai Mass have the simultaneous declamation of the text in all three voices that is one of the primary characteristics of conductus style, but they also display the new rhythmic groupings and contrasts and the double leading-tone cadences of the most up-to-date compositions of the fourteenth century. (The priest's intonations remain in plainchant.) The final

EXAMPLE 11-12 Mass of Tournai: (a) Kyrie, beginning only; (b) Gloria, beginning only; (c) Credo, beginning only; (d) Sanctus, beginning only; (e) Agnus Dei, beginning only; (f) Ite Missa Est, beginning only. After Charles Van den Borren, *Missa Tornacensis,* Corpus Mensurabilis Musicae, vol. 13 ([Rome]: American Institute of Musicology, 1957).

(a)

Kyrie, . . .   Lord, . . .

(b)

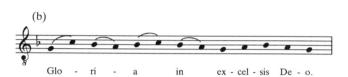

Glo - ri - a in ex - cel - sis De - o.

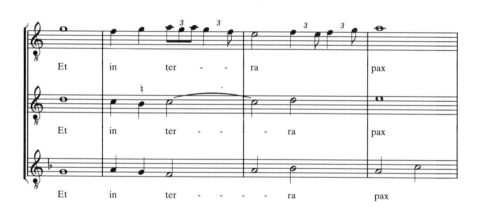

Et in ter - - ra pax

Et in ter - - - ra pax

Et in ter - - - - ra pax

ho - - mi - ni - bus

ho - - mi - - - ni - - - - bus

ho - - mi - - ni - bus

Gloria in excelsis Deo.   Glory to God in the highest.
Et in terra pax hominibus . . .   And on earth peace to men . . .

(c)

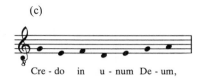

Cre - do   in   u - num De - um,

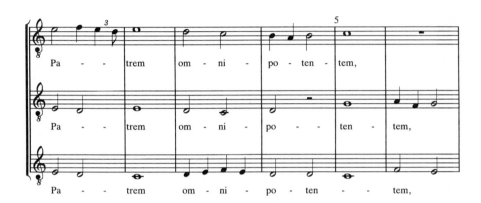

Pa - - trem   om - ni - po - ten - tem,

Pa - - trem   om - ni - po - - ten - tem,

Pa - - trem   om - ni - po - ten - - tem,

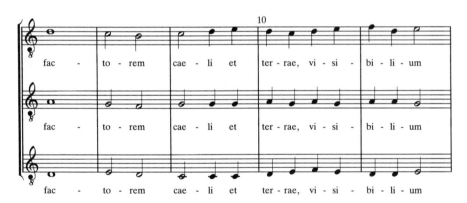

fac - to - rem cae - li et ter - rae, vi - si - bi - li - um

fac - to - rem cae - li et ter - rae, vi - si - bi - li - um

fac - to - rem cae - li et ter - rae, vi - si - bi - li - um

om - ni - um   et in - vi - si - bi - li - um.

om - ni - um   et in - vi - si - bi - li - um.

om - ni - um   et in - vi - si - bi - li - um.

Credo in unum Deum,
Patrem omnipotentem, factorem caeli et
  terrae, visibilium omnium et invisibi-
  lium.

I believe in one God,
The omnipotent Father, creator of the
  heaven and earth, of everything visible
  and invisible.

(d)

Sanctus, . . .

Holy, . . .

(e)

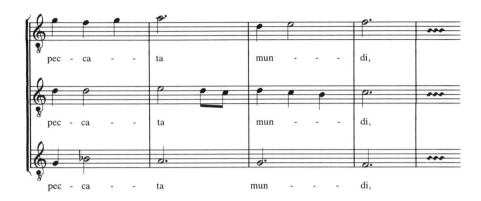

Agnus Dei, qui tollis peccata mundi, . . .   Lamb of God, you who remove the sins of
                                              the world, . . .

(f)

Triplum:	*Triplum:*
Se grasse n'est a mon maintien contraire,	If her grace is not opposed to my well-being,
Et vraie amours garnie de desir . . .	And true love is accompanied by desire . . .

Motetus:	*Motetus:*
Cum venerint miseri degentes ad os- . . .	When the poor and needy come to your house . . .

Tenor:	*Tenor:*
Ite, missa . . .	Go, you [are] dismissed.

item, the Ite Missa Est, closes the Mass with the further contrast of a movement written in the true style of a motet. The Mass text is in the tenor, which is isorhythmic, while above it the Latin motetus and French triplum declaim different texts. The motetus moralizes on the subject of charity, while the triplum is a secular poem.

There are three other Mass cycles from fourteenth-century France, two of which are incomplete but all of which have more or less sustained qualities of uniformity. One has movements that are linked by their having been composed in song style. The Agnus Dei setting of another contains musical quotations from earlier movements. The third seems to be unified by its very disparateness—all of the movements are composed with different arrangements of the text and in different styles; the final movement even expands to four parts, only two of which are texted. The Mass cycles of fourteenth-century France are therefore mostly compilations rather than compositions; other, similar compilations could be made up from the many separate Mass movements that survive from this time. Nevertheless, the fact that items from the Ordinary of the Mass were being set to polyphonic music, and that contemporary scribes and archivists were beginning to consider them as cycles, reflects a new approach to the music of the liturgy—one that had important consequences in later centuries.

SUMMARY

Music in fourteenth-century France was characterized by a sense of innovation. Important developments were made in the realms of rhythm, the architecture of the motet, and the application of polyphony to secular songs. The satirical play, the Roman de Fauvel, contains a large retrospective collection of musical items, ranging from those of a century earlier to those in the most modern style. In almost every genre, new and old, the composer Guillaume de Machaut was the preeminent composer of the age. In his Mass and motets, as well as in the lais and the three fixed forms of secular song, he displayed his control of rhythmic flexibility, of overall structure, of pitch focus, and of poetry, of which he was also a master. In the field of liturgical polyphony, composers wrote in a variety of styles, concentrating upon the invariable texts of the Ordinary of the Mass. Many independent settings of these texts have survived, a few of which were grouped into cycles to form complete compositions for insertion into the liturgy at the appropriate points.

COMMENTS ON NOTATION AND PERFORMANCE

The notational system of the fourteenth century was far better able to reflect the flexible flow of the music than our modern notation. It was without barlines and therefore unconfined to the regular recurrence of rhythmic groupings. The interplay of duple and triple meters was indicated by signs which were devised at the beginning of the century. A circle with a dot in it [⊙] meant triple groups at both levels: three groups of threes [$\frac{9}{8}$]. A circle without a dot in it [○] meant a triple group at the higher level and duple groups at the lower level: three groups of twos [$\frac{3}{4}$]. A half circle with a dot [☉] meant two groups of threes [$\frac{6}{8}$]; and a half circle without a dot [⊂] meant two groups of twos [$\frac{2}{4}$]. These signs could be changed in the course of a piece and could be different in the different parts. Syncopation was easily rendered by single notes; it did not require the complicated system of barlines and ties that we need today.

In the fourteenth century the different parts of a composition were written separately, not in score format. The independence of each part was thus graphically shown in the manuscripts. Most of the manuscripts were designed for preserving the music, not for performance. Almost certainly the musicians of the time learned their parts by heart and played them from memory—a skill that later became rare.

The following plate shows a ballade of Machaut in its original notation. The cantus part is unlabeled but has text written out underneath it (the remainder of the text is written above). In the middle of the third line the tenor part begins (labeled "Tenor"). Careful examination of the tenor part will show that, mixed in with the notes, several small circles and half circles are drawn to indicate the metrical shifts of the music. The contratenor part is written out starting in the middle of the next line.

It seems fairly certain that the tenors of fourteenth-century motets were performed instrumentally. In secular songs both the tenor and the contratenor seem to be instrumental, and performance with a sustaining instrument such as a vielle on the tenor line and a plucked instrument such as a lute on the contratenor line yields a firm yet transparent texture over which the voice may be clearly heard, as well as exploiting the melodic architecture of the individual parts to their fullest.

The question of whether instruments doubled the voice lines in liturgical polyphony has not yet been settled. A fuller sound is produced when instruments are included, but it is usually at some loss of clarity and purity of tuning.

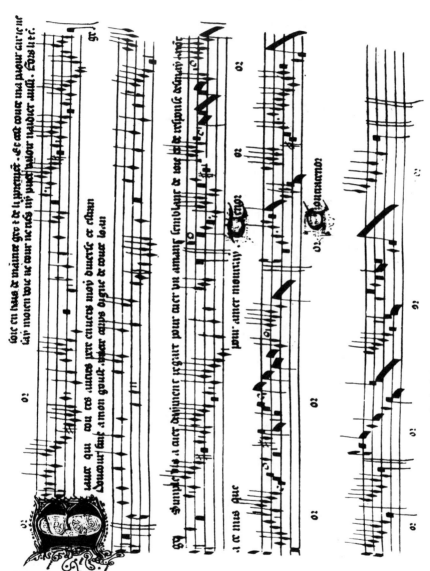

Paris, Bibliothèque Nationale, fonds français 9221.

517

DISCOGRAPHY

Example 11-2   Philippe de Vitry, motet, *Douce Playsence/Garison Selon Nature/Neuma Quinti Toni.*
TAPE TWO, SIDE ONE. Capella Cordina, *The Ars Nova,* Music of the Middle Ages, vol. IX, Expériences Anonymes EAS 83 (Musical Heritage Society MHS 899).

Example 11-3   Guillaume de Machaut, motet, *Christe, Qui Lux Es/Veni, Creator Spiritus/Tribulatio Proxima.*
Capella Antiqua München, *Guillaume de Machault: Messe de Nostre Dame und Motetten,* Telefunken SAWT 9566-B; also on The Early Music Consort of London, *Music of the Gothic Era,* Archiv 2723 045 (Side VI) or Archiv 415 292-2.

Example 11-4, Example 11-5b   Guillaume de Machaut, Mass.
The Boston Camerata, *Guillaume de Machaut: Messe de Nostre-Dame, Chansons,* Harmonia Mundi HMC 5122; also on Capella Antiqua München, *Guillaume de Machault: Messe de Nostre Dame und Motetten,* Telefunken SAWT 9566-B; Taverner Consort, *Messe de Nostre Dame (Guillaume de Machaut),* EMI CDC 7 47949 2; and The Purcell Choir, *Machaut: Mass, Secular Works,* L'Oiseau-lyre SOL 310. (The Kyrie alone is on *Opus Musicum: The Mass,* Arno Volk Verlag OM 201/03 [Side I, Band 4].)

Example 11-6, Example 11-7   Guillaume de Machaut, *Le Lay de la Fonteinne.*
TAPE TWO, SIDE ONE. Studio der frühen Musik, *Guillaume de Machaut: Chansons 1,* EMI Reflexe 1C 063-30 106.

Example 11-8   Guillaume de Machaut, virelai, *Moult Sui.*
TAPE TWO, SIDE ONE. Studio der frühen Musik, *Guillaume de Machaut: Chansons 2,* EMI Reflexe 1C 063-30 109.

Example 11-9   Guillaume de Machaut, rondeau, *Doulz Viaire Gracieus.*
TAPE TWO, SIDE ONE. Studio der frühen Musik, *Guillaume de Machaut: Chansons 2,* EMI Reflexe 1C 063-30 109.

Example 11-10   Guillaume de Machaut, rondeau, *Comment Puet On.*
TAPE TWO, SIDE ONE. Studio der frühen Musik, *Guillaume de Machaut: Chansons 2,* EMI Reflexe 1C 063-30 109.

Example 11-11   Guillaume de Machaut, ballade, *Honte, Paour, Doubtance.*
TAPE TWO, SIDE TWO. Studio der frühen Musik, *Guillaume de Machaut: Chansons 2,* EMI Reflexe 1C 063-30 109.

Example 11-12   Mass of Tournai.
Pro Cantione Antiqua, London, *Missa Tournai, Missa Barcelona,* Harmonia Mundi 1C 065-99 870; also on Capella Antiqua München, *Missa Tournai, um 1330 (Anonymus), Motetten, um 1320,* Telefunken SAWT 9517-A.

Some of the *Roman de Fauvel,* including spoken narrative, may be heard on Studio der frühen Musik, *Roman de Fauvel,* EMI Reflexe 1C 063-30 103; also on Clemencic Consort, *Le Roman de Fauvel,* Harmonia Mundi HMC 90994.

BIBLIOGRAPHICAL NOTES

A brief summary of the significance of the term Ars Nova is given in David Fallows, "Ars Nova," in *The New Grove.*

Philippe de Vitry's works may studied in *Polyphonic Music of the Fourteenth Century,* vol. 1 (Monaco: L'Oiseau-lyre, 1956). His treatise is available in translation in Leon Plantinga, "Philippe de Vitry's Ars Nova: A Translation," *Journal of Music Theory* 5 (1961): 204–223.

A facsimile edition of the Roman de Fauvel may be seen in P. Aubry, *Le Roman de Fauvel* (Paris: P. Geuthner, 1907). A new edition of the whole manuscript in which the Roman de Fauvel is contained is *Le Roman de Fauvel in the Edition of Chaillou de Pesstain: A Facsimile Reproduction of the Manuscript Paris, Bibliothèque nationale, f.fr. 146,* introduction by François Avril, Nancy Freeman Regelado, and Edward Roesner, edited by Edward Roesner (New York: Broude Brothers, forthcoming).

A short introduction to the life and work of Guillaume de Machaut is Gilbert Reaney, *Guillaume de Machaut,* Oxford Studies of Composers, vol. 9 (London: Oxford University Press, 1971). Machaut's musical works are available in two principal editions: *Guillaume de Machaut: musikalische Werke,* ed. Friedrich Ludwig and Heinrich Besseler, 4 vols. (Leipzig: Breitkopf & Härtel, 1926–54); and *Polyphonic Music of the Fourteenth Century,* vols. 2–3, ed. Leo Schrade (Monaco: L'Oiseau-lyre, 1956).

Fourteenth-century liturgical polyphony is discussed in more detail in Richard H. Hoppin, *Medieval Music* (New York: W. W. Norton and Co., Inc., 1978), and edited in Hanna Stäblein-Harder, *Fourteenth-Century Mass Music in France,* Corpus Mensurabilis Musicae, vol. 29 ([Rome]: American Institute of Musicology, 1962).

TWELVE

THE FOURTEENTH CENTURY
IN ITALY

While the developments described in the previous chapter were occurring in France, on the other side of the Alps in the republics and city-
states of Italy, important musical activities were also taking place. Until the
last part of the century, these two repertories seem to have developed independently, and theorists often contrasted the French and Italian musical
styles, stressing their different rhythmic and melodic qualities. In fact, if
one can characterize broadly two such large and accomplished musical repertories, it could be said that the interest of French composers lay in rhythmic structure, both on the large scale, as in the technique of isorhythm, and
on the small scale, in the interaction and juxtaposition of duple and triple
groupings, while Italian music focused on melodic flow and virtuoso display
of the voice.

In contrast to the growing centralization of French political power,
Italy in the fourteenth century (*trecento*) was divided into a collection of
city-states and republics, each of which had independent sovereignty.
Commerce between East and West had made Italy into a land of merchants, traders, shipbuilders, and bankers, but the old noble families,
which had been supported by popes and emperors vying for power, continued to control great wealth. The cities they represented constantly clashed
over territorial claims, but this did not prevent growing prosperity and the
rise of a great culture. In art and architecture, in painting and literature and

music, trecento Italy was the site of a flowering of artistic endeavor that produced some of the great masterpieces of the age.

In literature, the century had opened with the magnificent *Divine Comedy* of Dante. Born into a noble family in the independent city of Florence—a city wealthy and famous from its trade in silk, tapestries, and jewels—Dante forged in his epic poem a new synthesis of the medieval views on the relationship between man and God, and made his own dialect, that of Tuscany, the new, flexible, expressive literary language for all of Italy. In this he was followed by the two great poets and writers of the fourteenth century, Petrarch and Boccaccio, in whose works, together with those of many other poets, Italian literature established a lyric style and a rhythmic and melodious flow that was perfectly suited to music.

In architecture, as well as in literature and music, Italy in the fourteenth century stood apart from the rest of Europe, with achievements that were no less impressive. In a country where the tradition of the ancient Roman basilica was still strong, where the Franciscan movement stressed simplicity, and where the color of the countryside and the quality of light are so much features of the landscape, the churches of Italy had a grace and harmony that evoked an atmosphere different from the awesome splendor of the French or English Gothic. Three of the greatest buildings from this time are in Florence: the church of Santa Croce, with its magnificent wooden ceiling and delicately bright interior; the Cathedral, which was built in the fourteenth century, though its towering dome was added later; and the city hall, known as the Palazzo Vecchio, whose fortress-like exterior is surmounted by a watch tower of forbidding grace.

In painting, fourteenth-century Italy nurtured several of the greatest masters, whose work was influential for centuries. Giotto, a Florentine, and a group of painters in the nearby city of Siena, which included Duccio and his pupil Simone Martini, invested their works with a dignity and naturalism that still shine from their frescoes and altar panels. On the walls inside the city hall of Siena—the Palazzo Pubblico—a series of frescoes by the Sienese painter Lorenzetti depicts life in the city and in the countryside under a well-ordered government. In these paintings the streets and the fields teem with activity, and both the city and the hills of Tuscany display the colors and proportions which they still bear today.

In the 1340s both Florence and Siena underwent a series of disasters that affected both cities for decades. There were economic and governmental upheavals and several crop failures, and the plague, a constant threat during the Middle Ages, swept through the area, killing half the local inhabitants and eventually an estimated two-thirds of the entire population of Europe. The outbreak of 1348, the worst ever recorded, became known as the Black Death.

Reactions to these disasters were two-fold. Partly there was widespread pessimism and a renewed emphasis upon the cult of death and the apocalypse (the end of the world). Others took the view that if life was

Fresco by Ambroglio Lorenzetti, *Good Government in the City*, Palazzo Pubblico, Siena.

short and unpredictable it should be enjoyed to the full. The storytellers of Boccaccio's wonderful book *The Decameron* are in the latter category. Educated young people from wealthy families, they take refuge during the plague in a villa outside Florence, and there entertain each other with stories and songs and dancing. No better insight into late medieval life can be given than by this fascinating, bawdy, serious, noble, comic, moving book.

The Decameron also provides an insight into one of the early forms of secular song that became popular in Italy during the fourteenth century. This was the ballata.

THE EARLY BALLATA

We have encountered the ballata in our discussion of Italian vernacular song during the thirteenth century (see p. 297). Its form is a common one, for it appears as the framework for the lauda, the cantiga, and the virelai. Two sections of music, the first used as a vehicle both for the refrain and part of the stanza, are repeated in the following pattern: AbbaA. If there are several stanzas, the form continues: AbbaAbbaAbbaA. As mentioned earlier, the name ballata indicates its origin as a dance song, for the Italian word *ballare* means to dance. Throughout *The Decameron* the young people sing ballatas and dance, often accompanied by instruments. The following description occurs at the end of the first day in the book.

> . . . they all wandered off towards a stream of crystal-clear water, which descended down the side of a hill and flowed through the shade of a thickly wooded valley, its banks lined with smooth round stones and green grasses. When they reached the stream, they stepped with bare arms and legs into the water and played several games together. When it was nearly time for supper, they made their way back to the house and there they dined together merrily.
>
> After supper, the instruments were sent for, and the leader of the group for the day commanded that a dance should begin, which Lauretta should lead, while Emilia was to sing a song accompanied by Dioneo on the lute. Immediately Lauretta began to lead the others in the dance, while Emilia sang the following ballata in amorous tones. . . .

Unfortunately, no music survives for the ballatas in Boccaccio's book. But these poems and others from the time often share a particular quality of expression—delicate, evocative, and graceful—usually on the topic of love.

The earliest examples of ballatas with music are preserved in a manuscript from the first half of the fourteenth century. They are all monophonic, and a further group of monophonic ballatas occurs in a later manuscript. In all of these, the words are clearly expressed through long flowing lines and delicately shaped melodic contours. The first and penultimate syl-

lables of each line are given florid melismas, while the intervening syllables
are set in a more syllabic style. Even the early monophonic ballatas have
fairly elaborate music, and it is probable that a stage in the development of
the ballata—from a simple tune for dancing to the earliest examples preserved in the manuscripts—is missing from our records.

Example 12-1 is a monophonic ballata from the earliest group. The
text is unusually strong, with its bitter denunciation of love, though the last
stanza turns from cynicism to personal lamentation. The voice presents the
text clearly in a flowing style with clear articulation of the words and transparency of verse structure. Each section of the music sets single lines of the
text, and in both sections the first and penultimate syllables receive the
longest melismas. The cadences are clearly defined, with a closed cadence
on G and an open cadence on A, and the two sections are subtly distinguished by slightly different ranges. This ballata has three stanzas; the refrain would be sung between each one of them. It is likely that in the kind of
performance described by Boccaccio the refrain would have been sung by
the group, while a soloist sang the stanzas.

EXAMPLE 12-1 Monophonic ballata, *Per Tropo Fede.* From *Polyphonic Music of
the Fourteenth Century,* vol. 11, ed. W. Thomas Marrocco (Monaco: L'Oiseau-lyre,
1978).

I. *Per tropo fede talor se perigola.*
   Non e dolor ne piu mortale spasemo
   Come, sença falir, cader en
     biasemo:

   El ben se taci e lo mal pur se cigola.
   Per tropo fede talor se perigola.

I. *Too much trust puts man into danger.*
   It is not pain or mortal anguish
   That is surely to be blamed:

   Good keeps quiet, while evil flourishes.
   Too much trust puts man into danger.

II. Lasso colui che mai se fido in fe-
mena,
Che l'amor so veneno amaro se-
mena,
Onde la morte speso se ne spigola.
Per tropo fede talor se perigola.

II. Pity him who ever puts his trust in
women,
For Love sows its bitter poison,

Which is often reaped as Death.
Too much trust puts man into danger.

III. Oime, ch'amor m'a posto in cotal
arçere,
Onde convienne ognor lagreme
sparçere,
Si che de doglia lo mio cor formi-
gola.
Per tropo fede talor se perigola.

III. Alas; for love has put me into such a
state,
That I must weep endless tears,

And my heart is shaken by grief.

Too much trust puts man into danger.

The ballata was soon superseded by two other song forms which became very popular in the middle of the century. Later in the century, however, it returned in polyphonic settings, and it became the favorite form of
one of the masters of Italian music.

THE MADRIGAL

The most common form of mid-fourteenth-century Italian music
was the *madrigal*. The etymology of the name is unclear, and even medieval
commentators disagreed as to its origins. The name was revived during the
Renaissance for musical settings of vernacular poetry, but these were quite
distinct from the medieval form of the madrigal. The madrigal poem had
many variants in its early stages but by the middle of the century had crystallized into a fairly standard poetic form. This had two or three stanzas of
three lines each, followed by a final two-line stanza known as a ritornello.
The opening stanzas were all sung to the same music, the final ritornello to
new music.

The form of the poetry is usually made very clear by the music. Each
line is set off by cadences within each section, and the ritornello is distinguished from the opening stanzas by a change of meter in the music. The
subject matter of madrigals was usually pastoral or amatory, although later
they also became ceremonial, moralistic, or autobiographical.

Most madrigals of the fourteenth century are for two voices, although some were written for three voices. All parts are usually texted, and
the upper voice is florid, with rapid melismas on the first and penultimate
syllables and more syllabic text setting between them. The lower voice
moves in longer note values, though occasional short imitative passages are
shared between the voices. Parallel consonances, especially parallel fifths
and octaves, are common (though they are often disguised by the rapid passage work of the upper voice), and both parts often come to a cadence on a
unison.

The composers of the mid-century mostly came from the towns and city-states of northern Italy, including Padua, Verona, Bologna, Milan, and especially Florence—places where they were supported by noble families. The composer of the madrigal in Example 12-2 obviously came from Bologna, as he was called Jacopo da Bologna. Little else is known about his life except that he was active around the middle of the century and worked at princely courts in Milan and Verona.

The text of *Fenice Fu'* is an allegorical reference to Jacopo's return to the Milanese court after an absence of some years. The madrigal is in two stanzas and is set for two voices, both of which carry the text. Most of the text is sung at the same time by both voices, which makes for a clearly audible presentation of the words. Exceptions are the beginnings of new poetic lines, where each voice enters in turn. In measures 12–13 and 45–46 the new lines are articulated by imitation between the voices. As is common in madrigals, the ritornello (sung following the two stanzas) introduces a change of meter. Cadences at the ends of sections are on unisons (an open cadence on A at the end of the first section, final cadence on D at the end of the ritornello). Intermediate cadences are on a sixth (m. 12), a tenth (m. 20), and one unison on A (m. 44), which has already been established as an incomplete sonority in the context of the piece. Parallel fifths and octaves are common. Melismas are on the antepenultimate syllables of each line (which are accented in twelve-syllable lines). A delightful moment of "word-painting" occurs in measures 16 and 17 on the first syllable of the word *tortora* ("turtle-dove"), when the voices exchange notes in a hocket-like passage that resembles the cooing of the dove.

EXAMPLE 12-2 Jacopo da Bologna, madrigal, *Fenice Fu'*. From *Polyphonic Music of the Fourteenth Century,* vol. 6, ed. W. Thomas Marrocco (Monaco: L'Oiseau-lyre, 1967).

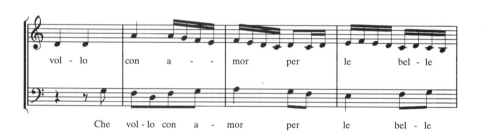

I. Fenice fu' e vissi pura e morbida,

   Et or sun trasmutat' in una tortora,

   Che volo con amor per le belle or-
   tora.

I. I used to be a phoenix and lived pure
   and gentle;

   Now I am transformed into a turtle-
   dove,

   And I fly, filled with love, over the
   beautiful meadows.

II. Arbore seco mai 'n acqua torbida,	II. I am a dry tree which is never in muddy waters.
No' me deleta may per questo dubito,	I have no pleasure on account of this doubt,
Va ne l'estate l'inverno viene subito.	For it goes in the summer and comes as soon as winter returns.
Ritornello:	*Ritornello:*
Tal vissi e tal vivo, e posso scrivere	Thus did I live, and thus do I live; and I can write
Ch' a donna non e piu che honesta vivere.	That a woman has no greater calling than to live virtuously.

THE CACCIA

The third main musical form of fourteenth-century Italian secular song was the *caccia*. Like its French counterpart, the *chace,* the caccia played on the double meaning of the word: "hunt" and "canon." The Italian caccia is a three-part piece, but only the two upper voices are canonic; the lowest part is an accompanying instrumental part in longer note values.

There are far fewer caccias than either of the other main song forms, but they are so lively and appealing that they must have been popular with their courtly audiences, one of whose main pastimes was hunting. Not all caccia texts deal exclusively with the hunt, however. Some describe a fishing expedition, or a fire, or street scenes. Common to them all is an outdoor atmosphere and the dramatic effect of cries or shouts set into the text in realistic manner. The verse is freely written in one long stanza of irregular length. Occasionally the poem is rounded off, as in the madrigal, by a two-line ritornello.

The music is florid and rapidly articulated in the two upper parts. A characteristic feature of the caccia is the long space between the canonic entries of the voices. The realistic shouts of the text are usually set in a high range so that they stand out dramatically from the surrounding texture. If there is a ritornello, the space between entries is usually reduced, the cries in the text have usually quieted down, and there is a change of meter.

The caccia in Example 12-3 is by Gherardello da Firenze (Gherardello from Florence). He was born in about 1320 and died in 1362. He was a member of the clergy at the Florence cathedral and became a priest there. Besides some liturgical music he also composed a considerable number of secular songs, including monophonic ballatas, madrigals for two voices, and the three-voice caccia of our example. A magnificently produced manuscript from the early fifteenth century (known as the Squarcialupi Codex after one of its early owners) contains a miniature of Gherardello and a copy of this piece in its original notation.

The text is a description of a hunt, written as an irregular succession of lines of different lengths and incorporating dialogue, shouts, and realistic conversation. The tenor serves as an instrumental foundation for the two upper voices, which are canonic throughout. There is a space of ten measures in the modern transcription between the entries of the upper voices, and the dialogue stands out dramatically with its high notes. The

EXAMPLE 12-3 Gherardello da Firenze, caccia, *Tosto Che L'Alba.* After *Polyphonic Music of the Fourteenth Century,* vol. 7, ed. W. Thomas Marrocco (Monaco: L'Oiseau-lyre, 1971).

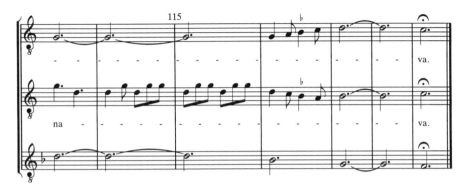

Tosto che l'alba del bel giorn'appare,	As soon as the dawn of the beautiful day appeared,
Disveglia i cacciatori, "Su, su, su, su, ch'egli e tempo!"	It woke the hunters. "Wake up! Wake up! It's time!"
"Allecta gli can, te, te, te, te, Viuola. Te, Primera, te!"	"Call the dogs. Here, here, Viola!" Here, Primera, here!"
Su alto al monte con buon cani a mano	They were up on the hill, with the good dogs in hand
E gli bracchet'al piano	And the setters on level ground,
Et nella piaggia ordine ciascuno.	And everyone in place on the slope.
"I' veggio sentire	"I can see
Uno d'i nostri miglior bracchi. Sta avisato!"	One of our best dogs starting off! Get ready!"
"Bussate d'ogni lato	"Beat the bushes from each side,
Ciascun le macchie, che Quaglina	Everyone. Quaglina's barking."
"Aio, aio, a te la cerbia vene!	"Watch out! Watch out! The deer's coming towards you!
Carbon l'a prese ed in boccha la tene.	Carbona has taken it and is holding it in her mouth."
Ritornello:	*Ritornello:*
Del monte que' che v'era su gridava, "All'altra, all'altra", e suo corno sonava.	Someone who was up on the hill shouted: "Get the other one! Get the other one!" And he blew his horn.

ritornello continues the cries and even imitates the sound of the hunting horn with its reiterated motif in measures 108–109 and 114–115. The ritornello is set off from the remainder of the piece by the cadence that precedes it, the slight change of modality brought about by the B♭ in the tenor, the fast notes, and the closer entries of the canonic voices. Fifths, octaves, and unisons are predominant sonorities throughout the piece, and principal cadences contain only the doubled fifth.

The Canonic Madrigal

One hybrid form should be mentioned here. It is known as the *canonic madrigal*. The canonic madrigal differs from the caccia in the following ways: its text is in madrigal form instead of in the free form of the caccia, and it does not involve the realistic shouts and cries that are characteristic of the caccia. It differs from the regular madrigal, however, in its pervasive use of canon.

Original notation of the caccia *Tosto Che L'Alba,* headed by a miniature of its composer, Gherardello da Firenze (see Example 12-3), Biblioteca Medicea-Laurenziana, Florence.

A fresco shows Florence in the fourteenth century, Galleria degli Uffizi, Florence.

FRANCESCO LANDINI

The most renowned composer of the second half of the century was Francesco Landini (1325–1397). His father was a painter and a member of Giotto's circle in Florence. Landini contracted smallpox as a child and lost his sight; he might otherwise also have been a painter. He turned, however, to music and made a career as an organist, designer and builder of organs, music director, instrumentalist, singer, and poet. He held positions in sev-

Francesco Landini with portatif organ. Squarcialupi Codex, Biblioteca Medicea-Laurenziana, Florence.

eral of the churches in Florence, and was involved in designing the organ for the new cathedral. He must also have been a considerable intellectual, for he took an active role in contemporary learning, and in philosophical, religious, and political debates.

On his tombstone and in the Squarcialupi Codex Landini is portrayed with a portatif, the small organ which became his trademark. Contemporary accounts describe Landini's playing as so sweet that the birds stopped their singing to listen to him. Another chronicler writes:

> When he came of age, and understood the sweetness of melody, his first art was the voice, and then he began to play stringed instruments and the organ. He was wondrously proficient in music and played instruments which he had never seen, to the amazement of all. It was as though he had the use of his eyes, for his hands were so fast when he began to play the organ, and he played so correctly and with such musicality and such sweetness, that he was incomparably superior to all other organists within memory.

It is the word "sweetness" (*dolcezza* in Italian) that is constantly mentioned in connection with Landini's playing and his music. The new literary style of the age was also called "sweet," and it is this lyricism that is at the heart of Landini's melody and sonority. Landini wrote only secular songs, and he concentrated almost exclusively upon the ballata, which, in its new polyphonic form, underwent a great resurgence in the second half of the century. Landini, by far the most prolific composer of the time, wrote one canonic madrigal, one caccia, nine madrigals, and one hundred and forty ballatas.

Landini's ballatas fall into two main groups: about two-thirds of them are written for two voices, the rest for three voices. The dating of most of Landini's ballatas is uncertain, but recent research has suggested that the two-voice pieces come from the earlier part of his career, while the three-voice pieces are probably later. Through an examination of these compositions it is possible to trace the development of Landini's music and of the music of fourteenth-century Italy as a whole.

The flourishing of Italian music as a separate indigenous art was glorious, but it was brief. During the second half of the fourteenth century Italian music gradually came more and more under the influence of French practices. It will be remembered that, insofar as generalizations of this type are possible, French music concentrated upon short melodic motifs and rhythmic intricacy, while Italian music in its heyday emphasized long flowing lines and vocal display. Variations were common in the arrangement of text too, but the "standard" disposition in French three-part songs had a single texted upper voice supported by an instrumental tenor and contratenor. Italian songs usually had two texted upper parts.

Most of Landini's two-voice ballatas have text in both voices, in the Italian tradition. Of the three-voice ballatas, some have text in all three voices, the largest number adopt the French arrangement of having text only in the cantus, while some display an arrangement that seems to be an amalgam of the two styles—text in the cantus and tenor, bound together by an instrumental contratenor. From this pattern it has been suggested that

Landini was increasingly influenced by the French style, but that he ultimately forged a new international style of his own. The late ballatas particularly display an expressiveness and flexibility of form that mark the sum-
mit of musical *dolcezza*.

Two of Landini's ballatas are given as Examples 12-4 and 12-5. The
first (Ex. 12-4) is a two-voice piece, perhaps from the composer's early
years, with text in both voices. The poem is cast as a single stanza, express-
ing the traditional topics of love, loyalty unto death, the pain of separation,
and the hard-hearted lady. The music carries three lines of poetry in each
section, and cadences set off each of them (mm. 6, 11, and 18; 24, 28, and
34). The upper voice is florid and rapidly articulated, but both voices sing
the same syllables more or less simultaneously throughout. The second section has a change of pitch focus with its opening B♭ in the tenor and last
cadence on C. The first section both begins and ends on G. All the cadences
in the piece are on unisons or octaves; parallel perfect consonances are less
frequent than in the earlier repertory. (The C cadence of the second section
is approached, however, by parallel octaves.) Melismas are on the first and
penultimate syllables of each line. A certain amount of French influence
may be seen in the occasional shifts of meter (m. 10 in the tenor, m. 26 in
both voices), but the clarity of the declamation, the vocal display, and the
move from rapid articulation to consonant areas of repose (even by means
of occasional dissonance, such as the diminished fourth C♯-F in m. 12) are
purely Italian traits.

EXAMPLE 12-4 Francesco Landini, ballata, *Donna, S'i' T'o Fallito*. After *Polyphonic Music of the Fourteenth Century*, vol. 4, ed. Leo Schrade (Monaco: L'Oiseau-
lyre, 1958).

mio, co - me tu   sa - - - - - - - - - - - - -   y.
bel che   tol - to m'a - - - - - - - - - - - - -   y?

mio,   co-me tu   sa - - - - - - - - - - - - - -   y.
bel   che tol - to m'a - - - - - - - - - - - - -   y?

Donna s'i' t'o fallito,	*Lady, if I deceived you,*
O d'altr'amor che'l tuo seguir consento,	*Or ever followed another love but you,*
Son di morir per le tuo man contento.	*I would willingly die at your own hands.*
Ma s'io ti porto et o portato fede	But I have been and still am faithful to you,
E sempre'l tuo volere	And have always followed
Seguito piu ch'el mio, come tu say.	Your will more than my own, as you know.
Perch'a diletto ognor mi fai dolere,	Why, then, do you always delight in making me suffer,
Vegendo tuo merçede	For I see no mercy
Mancar nel viso bel che tolto m'ay?	In your beautiful face, which you have taken away from me?
Vuo' tu, perch'io t'amai	Do you enjoy—since I loved you,
E tanto t'amo, c'altro ben non sento,	And still love you so much that I have no other happiness—
Tener la vita mia in tal tormento?	Holding my life in such torment?
Donna s'i' t'o fallito,	*Lady, if I deceived you,*
O d'altr'amor che'l tuo seguir consento,	*Or ever followed another love but you,*
Son di morir per le tuo man contento.	*I would willingly die at your own hands.*

The second example, the exquisite *Gram Piant' Agli Ochi* (Ex. 12-5), may, on the stylistic evidence summarized above, be assigned to the later part of Landini's career. Again, a single stanza laments the pain of love, but the poignant images of the refrain make more concrete the passion of the poet and set in vivid contrast the metaphorical death of his soul with his reluctance to live. The musical setting has text in the cantus and tenor voices, while an instrumental contratenor lies mostly between the two in range, binding the two together, enriching the sonority, and adding rhythmic interest. The melodic curves of the cantus are beautifully shaped, from the opening slow rise of a fifth to the reiterated sixteenth-note motifs which occur throughout the piece. Cadences are carefully controlled, for a perfect balance between expectation and fulfillment: the first section opens and closes on F with an intermediate cadence on G, while the second section opens on A and has its middle cadence also on A before closing back on

F. The last few measures of each section are rhymed, which adds a great sense of unity and repose. In these measures the long, slow, decelerating descent of the tenor contributes markedly to the effect.

Each section of the music is used to set two lines of text. Melismas are placed on the first and penultimate syllable of each line in keeping with the accentuation of the poetry. The text of each line is declaimed with perfect clarity, and in both sections the ends of the lines are marked by clear cadences, long notes, and (at the intermediate cadences) rests. The sonority is overwhelmingly consonant, with only a few very brief dissonances in the form of passing notes (sixteenths in the modern transcription). The cadence from measure 8 to measure 9, with its move by the cantus down from the seventh degree (F♯) to the sixth (E) before reaching the octave (G), became a hallmark of Landini's style. It is often called a "Landini cadence," though it appears in the music of many other composers also. It may be used to ornament a cadence with or without the double leading-tone.

EXAMPLE 12-5 Francesco Landini, ballata, *Gram Piant' Agli Ochi*. From *Polyphonic Music of the Fourteenth Century,* vol. 4, ed. Leo Schrade (Monaco: L'Oiseau-lyre, 1958).

Gram piant'agli ochi, greve dogli'al core,	The eyes full of tears, the heart full of grievous pain,
Abonda senpre l'anima, si more.	The soul is filled to overflowing, and dies.

Gram piant'agli ochi, greve dogli'al core,
Abonda senpre l'anima, si more.

The eyes full of tears, the heart full of
    grievous pain,
The soul is filled to overflowing, and dies.

Per quest'amar' ed aspra dipartita
Chiamo la mort'e non mi vol udire.

For this cruel and bitter departure
I call on Death, but he will not hear me.

Chontra mia voglia dura questa vita,
Che mille morti mi convien sentire,

Against my will this life endures,
Which would rather undergo a thousand
    deaths.

Ma bench'i' viva, ma' non vo' seguire,
Se non vo', chiara stella et dolçe amore.

But although I live, I would never follow,
If I did not wish it, this brightest star and
    sweetest love.

Gram piant'agli ochi, greve dogli'al core,
Abonda senpre l'anima, si more.

The eyes full of tears, the heart full of
    grievous pain,
The soul is filled to overflowing, and dies.

Contemporaries of Landini regarded him as the greatest composer
of the age. More than one quarter of all the music preserved from Italy in

the fourteenth century is by him, and the Squarcialupi Codex, designed to present an overall picture of Italian music of its time, is almost half filled with music by "Master Francesco the Blind."

INSTRUMENTAL MUSIC

The works of Landini and Machaut appear together for the first time in another manuscript from the early fifteenth century which contains keyboard arrangements of a large amount of fourteenth-century music, both French and Italian. This manuscript is called the Faenza Codex after the town in northern Italy where it is kept. By and large the keyboard versions in the Faenza Codex take the tenor from the original secular songs and add a highly embellished upper line above it. When the original is in two parts, the upper line is based on the cantus; when the original is in three parts, the upper line often draws on both the cantus and contratenor. From theoretical descriptions and from surviving instruments we know that by the fourteenth century organs were being built with at least a two-octave range with all the half steps. It is tempting to imagine Landini himself playing some of these arrangements. The music is fast and ornate, with erratic, florid passagework, requiring a fluent and polished technique on the part of the performer. The facsimile page from the manuscript (p. 549) shows at a glance the running passages in the right hand over the long notes in the left. In the original, the staves are drawn in red ink, notes in black.

Example 12-6a gives the first few measures of the instrumental arrangement from this manuscript of Machaut's *Honte, Paour, Doubtance,* the ballade given as Example 11-11 (see p. 504). The music has been transposed up a fifth, and the meter has been changed, but the tenor line is otherwise almost exactly the same, and the upper line is a highly ornamented version of the original cantus.

EXAMPLE 12-6a Instrumental arrangement of *Honte, Paour, Doubtance,* beginning only. After Dragan Plamenac, *Keyboard Music of the Late Middle Ages in Codex Faenza 117,* Corpus Mensurabilis Musicae, vol. 57 ([Rome]: American Institute of Musicology, 1973).

Example 12-6b shows the beginning of the keyboard version in the Faenza Codex of a Landini ballata entitled *Non Avra*. (The opening of the original song is also given.) Here the instrumental arrangement incorporates both the cantus and the contratenor of the original in its passagework, including not just the rhythmic motion of both parts but also many of the original pitches.

EXAMPLE 12-6b Instrumental arrangement of *Non Avra,* beginning only, with portion of original song. From Dragan Plamenac, *Keyboard Music of the Late Middle Ages in Codex Faenza 117,* Corpus Mensurabilis Musicae, vol. 57 ([Rome]: American Institute of Musicology, 1973).

Finally, in addition to arrangements of secular songs there are also some arrangements of plainchants. Example 12-6c is an ornamented instrumental version of the Kyrie melody that we have already studied in several different manifestations (see Examples 4-2, 6-5, 8-10, and 11-5b). The chant (slightly altered) is in the tenor, and above it a newly written upper part contains running passages and rhythmic motifs. This upper part obviously had no previous model upon which it had to draw, and it seems more coherent and less erratic than those of Examples 12-6a and 12-6b. The composer had the freedom to create virtually a new composition with its own phrase structure, which he does by forming cadences (mm. 5, 9, 12, 14, 18, 21, 23) of greater or lesser articulating power throughout the piece, which either coincide with or ignore phrasing points in the original chant.

EXAMPLE 12-6c   Instrumental arrangement of Kyrie, with original plainchant melody. From Dragan Plamenac, *Keyboard Music of the Late Middle Ages in Codex Faenza 117,* Corpus Mensurabilis Musicae, vol. 57 ([Rome]: American Institute of Musicology, 1973).

Instrumental arrangement of Kyrie chant, beginning only, from the Faenza Codex (see Example 12-6c). Faenza, Biblioteca Communale.

Although the compositions in the Faenza Codex were probably intended for keyboard performance, there is nothing to suggest that some of them, especially the song arrangements, might not have been played on two instruments, with one performer playing the tenor line and another playing the upper, ornamented part. The chant arrangements, however, were probably performed upon the organ in a liturgical setting. The practice of having the phrases of a chant alternately sung by the choir and played upon the organ became widespread in later centuries and was known as *alternatim* performance.

These examples, together with the other keyboard pieces preserved from the fourteenth century, suggest that instrumental music of this time depended for a large part of its repertory upon vocal originals (mostly secular songs, but also chants and motets), like instrumental music from before 1300.

The remainder of the instrumental pieces from the fourteenth century are dances. Some polyphonic examples appear in the keyboard manuscripts, but a large group, included in a collection of Italian vocal music of the time, has only a single melody line, much like the dances from earlier centuries. The survival of this collection is fortunate indeed, for it contains, in what is actually a rather quickly and informally produced manuscript, no fewer than fifteen dances from fourteenth-century Italy. Most of them are designated *istampitta,* the Italian equivalent of estampie. Four are labeled *salterello,* which means "little jumping dance." One is called *trotto* ("the trotting dance"). The two last dances of the group are double dances, with a main dance followed by an after-dance that presents the same melody in varied form. These last two have intriguing names: "The Lament of Tristan" and "The Manfredina." Some of the istampittas also have titles, which may refer to cities, songs, places, or young ladies' names.

The dances in this collection are fascinating, extended compositions, many of them far longer than the estampies of the previous century. Their wayward melodies and bright chromatic coloring have led some commentators to suggest an influence from the Middle East. The salterellos and the paired dances are fairly regular in form and may have been general dances with repetitive patterns of steps. Many of the istampittas, however, involve changes of meter, irregular sections, and asymmetrical phrasing. These could have been independently choreographed, or their composers may simply have used the dance form as the basis for extended instrumental compositions, to be played as entertainment in the gardens or courtyards of noble families.

The form of all these dances is derived from the dance forms of the thirteenth century. All have repeated sections (puncta), which are given first and second endings and often share melodic material. The intense and vivid nature of these pieces is exemplified by the istampitta called *Ghaetta* (Ex. 12-7), which may take its name from the seaport on the western coast of Italy between Naples and Rome. The four puncta or sections all share the same first and second endings, which are preceded by seventeen measures that are also the same in each section. Other correspondences between sections serve to unify the composition (compare, for example, measures 23–35 and 276–288, 80–112 and 157–189), which is otherwise given great drive and momentum by its irregularity of phrasing, its shifts between triple and duple groupings, and its surprising and colorful chromaticisms.

EXAMPLE 12-7   Istampitta, *Ghaetta,* London, British Library, Add. 29987.

LITURGICAL POLYPHONY

The interest in polyphonic settings of liturgical items seems not to have been as marked in Italy in the fourteenth century as it was in France. However, there are a considerable number of surviving examples. Most of these are motets, with hymn or antiphon texts, or settings of texts from the Ordinary of the Mass. There are also several compositions on the Benedicamus Domino text, which, it will be remembered, may serve as the final item either for the Office or, on some occasions, for the Mass. The musical style of all of these pieces is very varied and ranges from the quite old-fashioned to the most modern.

Several of the Mass movements are in two-part note-against-note settings in an old-fashioned style that became known as *cantus binatim* ("doubled chant"). In cantus binatim, two parts move either in different ranges in both contrary and parallel motion or in the same range with frequent voice-crossing. It seems likely that these represent a style of performance that was widespread, and they may reflect a practice of improvisation going all the way back to the early theoretical descriptions of polyphony in the tenth and eleventh century. After all, it should not be forgotten that Guido of Arezzo, who described some of the early polyphonic practices (see p. 341), was an Italian who lived and worked in some of the main centers of Italy. The simple but effective style of these settings is illustrated in Example 12-8, which is part of the opening of a Credo from the Mass. Here the voices move primarily in different ranges and come to cadences on octaves, fifths, or unisons.

EXAMPLE 12-8   Beginning of Credo in *cantus binatim* style. After *Polyphonic Music of the Fourteenth Century,* vol. 12, ed. Kurt von Fischer and F. Alberto Gallo (Monaco: L'Oiseau-lyre, 1976).

Credo in unum Deum,	I believe in one God,
Patrem omnipotentem, factorem caeli et terrae, visibilium omnium, et invisibilium. . . .	The omnipotent Father, creator of the heaven and earth, of everything visible and invisible. . . .

An intermediate style appears in several of the motets. These are
constructed in the thirteenth-century manner, with modal rhythms and po-
lytextual upper voices. All the texts, however, are liturgical in nature.
Some Benedicamus Domino settings are also written in this fashion, but in
these all the voices carry the same text.

Finally, several Mass Ordinary movements and some of the Benedicamus Domino settings have music that is influenced by the style of contemporary secular songs, especially the madrigal and ballata. One interesting
manuscript contains the so-called "Florence Mass," which is a collection of
polyphonic settings of items from the Ordinary, each written by a different
composer. The Mass must have been composed about the middle of the
century, since the composers were all members of the Florentine circle at
about that time. The Kyrie is missing from the collection and may have
been performed in plainchant. The other movements are mostly for two
voices and are strongly influenced by the style of the madrigal, with florid
melismas in the upper voice and lucid declamation of the text. The Gloria,
Credo, and Sanctus also show elements of cantus binatim style, for the
voices are often in similar rhythms or in the same range with frequent crossing. The Sanctus even contains passages in which decorated and plain versions of the same melody are sung simultaneously, leading to much parallelism and a high degree of dissonance. The opening measures of the four
main movements of the Florence Mass cycle are given in Example 12-9.
(The Benedicamus Domino, in three voices, is not illustrated.)

EXAMPLE 12-9 The "Florence Mass": (a) Gloria, beginning only; (b) Credo, beginning only; (c) Sanctus, beginning only; (d) Agnus Dei, beginning only. After *Polyphonic Music of the Fourteenth Century*, vol. 12, ed. Kurt von Fischer and F. Alberto
Gallo (Monaco: L'Oiseau-lyre, 1976).

(a)

Glo - ri - a   in   ex - cel - sis De - o.

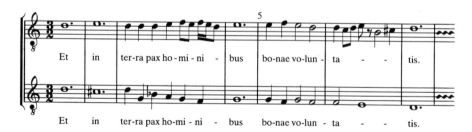

Et   in   ter-ra pax ho-mi-ni - bus   bo-nae vo-lun - ta - - tis.

Et   in   ter-ra pax ho-mi-ni - bus   bo-nae vo-lun - ta - - tis.

Gloria in excelsis Deo.   Glory to God in the highest.
Et in terra pax hominibus bonae volun-   And on earth peace to men of good
  tatis. . . .   will. . . .

(b)

Cre - do in u - num De - um,

Pa - - - - - - - - - trem

Pa - - - - - - - - - - - - - trem

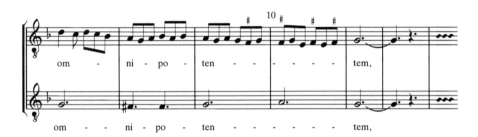

om - ni - po - ten - - - - - tem,

om - - ni - po - ten - - - - - tem,

Credo in unum Deum,   I believe in one God,
Patrem omnipotentem, . . .   The omnipotent Father, . . .

(c)

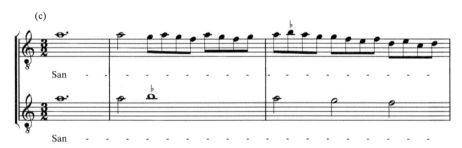

San - - - - - - - - - - - -

San - - - - - - - - - - - -

- - - - - - - - - - - ctus,

- - - - - - - - - - - ctus,

Sanctus, . . .   Holy, . . .

Agnus Dei, qui tollis peccata mundi, . . .   Lamb of God, you who remove the sins of
                                                          the world, . . .

All these liturgical pieces—about fifty or so in all—suggest that liturgical polyphony in Italy was more widespread than was once thought, but that its performance depended to some extent upon older improvisational and compositional techniques. It was not until the early fifteenth century that Italian composers began to concentrate extensively upon Mass composition, and it is in features of these later settings as well as in other pieces from the time that we find the beginnings of a new musical era. Before examining these prophetic trends, however, we need to see how the French and Italian styles began to influence each other in a setting of considerable importance in the history of the late Middle Ages—the palace of the popes in Avignon.

SUMMARY

The sudden appearance of a fully-fledged Italian musical art about 1325 suggests that a link in the chain of musical development from the thirteenth-century laudas to the secular songs of the fourteenth century may be missing. However, the flowering of a new literary style and language is reflected in the earliest songs, which are the monophonic ballatas. By the middle of the century, composers from the towns of northern Italy such as Bologna, Padua, and especially Florence were favoring other genres: the madrigal, with its set poetic form and florid vocal style; and the caccia, with its lively, naturalistic depiction of outdoor events and strict canonic structure.

The composer who dominated the second half of the century was Francesco Landini, who concentrated almost exclusively upon the new polyphonic ballata. In his works, and in those of other Italian composers of the later fourteenth century, evidence of French influence appears, but the Italian qualities of elegant melodic contour, lyricism, consonance, and vocal beauty reach new heights of perfection.

Instrumental performance seems to have been widespread, and written exemplars are based upon vocal models or are dance melodies. These may be quite elaborate and extended compositions. Liturgical polyphony took the form of motets on sacred texts or of settings for the Ordinary of the Mass and the Benedicamus Domino. Styles ranged from simple two-part polyphony, to three-part motet style in modal rhythms, to the style of contemporary vernacular song.

DISCOGRAPHY

Example 12-1   Monophonic ballata, *Per Tropo Fede.*
Esther Lamandier, *Domna,* Alienor Al 19 (Harmonia Mundi HM 69); also on Esther Lamandier, *Decameron: Ballate monodiques de l'Ars Nova florentine,* Astrée AS 56.

Example 12-2   Jacopo da Bologna, madrigal, *Fenice Fu'.*
Pro Musica Antiqua, *The Early Renaissance: Madrigali e Caccie from the Codex of Antonio Squarcialupi,* Archiv ARC 3003; also on The Early Music Consort, *Ecco la primavera: Florentine Music of the 14th Century,* Argo ZRG 642.

Example 12-3   Gherardello da Firenze, caccia, *Tosto Che L'Alba.*
Musica Reservata, *Music from the Time of Boccaccio's "Decameron,"* Philips 802 904 LY (SAL 3781); also on Pro Musica Antiqua, *The Early Renaissance: Madrigali e Caccie from the Codex of Antonio Squarcialupi,* Archiv ARC 3003; and *History of European Music, Part Two: Music of the Middle Ages and Renaissance,* vol. IV, Musical Heritage Society OR 437.

Example 12-4   Francesco Landini, ballata, *Donna, S'I' T'O Fallito.*
TAPE TWO, SIDE TWO. Studio der frühen Musik, *Francesco Landini,* EMI Reflexe 1C 063-30 113 C.

Example 12-5   Francesco Landini, ballata, *Gram Piant' Agli Ochi.*
TAPE TWO, SIDE TWO. Studio der frühen Musik, *Francesco Landini,* EMI Reflexe 1C 063-30 113 C; also on Pro Musica Antiqua, *The Early Renaissance: Madrigali e Caccie from the Codex of Antonio Squarcialupi,* Archiv ARC 3003; Studio der frühen Musik, *Frühe Musik in Italien, Frankreich, und Burgund,* Telefunken SAWT 9466-B; and Musica Reservata, *Music from the Time of Boccaccio's "Decameron,"* Philips 802 904 LY (SAL 3781).

Example 12-6a   Instrumental arrangement of *Honte, Paour, Doubtance.*
TAPE TWO, SIDE TWO. Studio der frühen Musik, *Guillaume de Machaut: Chansons 2,* EMI Reflexe 1C 063-30 109 C.

Example 12-6b   Instrumental arrangement of *Non Avra.*
TAPE TWO, SIDE TWO. Studio der frühen Musik, *Francesco Landini,* EMI Reflexe 1C 063-30 113 C.

Example 12-6c   Instrumental arrangement of Kyrie.
TAPE TWO, SIDE TWO.

Example 12-7   Istampitta *Ghaetta.*
TAPE TWO, SIDE TWO. Studio der frühen Musik, *Estampie: Instrumentalmusik des Mittelalters,* EMI Reflexe 1C 063-30 122 C; also on Musica Reservata, *Music from the Time of Boccaccio's "Decameron,"* Philips 802 904 LY (SAL 3781).

BIBLIOGRAPHICAL NOTES

Fourteenth-century Italian music, including the works of Landini and items of liturgical polyphony, is available in two main editions: *Polyphonic Music of the Fourteenth Century* (Monaco: L'Oiseau-lyre, 1956–), each volume of which is preceded by an introductory essay, and *The Music of Fourteenth-Century Italy,* Corpus Mensurabilis Musicae, vol. 8 (Amsterdam [and Rome]: American Institute of Musicology, 1954–64).

The best study of the music is not in English: Kurt von Fischer, *Studien zur italienischen Musik des Trecento und frühen Quattrocento* (Bern: P. Haupt, [1956]), but a guide to further literature is Viola L. Hagopian, *Italian Ars Nova Music: A Bibliographic Guide to Modern Editions and Related Literature,* 2nd edition (Berkeley: University of California Press, 1973).

A brief but useful survey of the period is given in F. Alberto Gallo, *Music of the Middle Ages II* (Cambridge: Cambridge University Press, 1985).

The keyboard elaborations of Italian and French secular songs are considered in Gerald Bedbrook, *Keyboard Music from the Middle Ages to the Beginnings of the Baroque* (London: Macmillan Publishers Ltd., 1949). Dance music is discussed in Timothy McGee, "Eastern Influences in Medieval European Dances," in *Cross-cultural Perspectives on Music,* ed. Robert Falck and Timothy Rice (Toronto: University of Toronto Press, 1982).

THIRTEEN
"PERFECT BEAUTY"

In the late Middle Ages the city of Avignon in the south of France became for over one hundred years the city of the popes. Constant battles in Rome had made the traditional residence unsafe, and when a Frenchman was elected pope at the beginning of the fourteenth century, he chose to establish his court in Avignon instead of in Rome. The papal palace, which may still be seen today, is a stout and secure fortress, with small windows and gaunt battlements. Avignon itself, still one of the most beautiful of medieval French cities, is surrounded by thick walls. In 1348 the whole city was bought from the countess of Provence by Pope Clement VI. Succeeding popes continued to make Avignon their home until 1417, when conflicting claims to the papacy were settled, and Rome became again the papal city. During the last part of this era, from 1378 to 1417 (a period known as the Great Schism), an extraordinary situation arose when there was simultaneously a French pope in Avignon and a rival Italian pope in Rome—and even, briefly, a third claimant in Pisa. According to a retrospective decision as to the correct line of succession, those popes considered improperly elected were named "antipopes."

The papal court at Avignon was renowned both for its corruption and for its extravagance. The palace housed large numbers of cardinals and other high church officials, as well as secretaries, clerics, painters, poets, and musicians. The payroll of the court listed at one time about a thousand employees. Petrarch lived in Avignon during the reign of Clement VI and wrote of the beauty of the place (and the shamelessness of its inhabitants). Simone Martini, the Sienese painter, adorned the interior walls of the palace with exquisite murals. The rooms were ornately furnished and hung with rich tapestries. Wealth from fees, property income, donations, and bribes accumulated in fabulous amounts.

Musicians from both France and Italy were attracted to Avignon, but the music that flourished there was, at least until the end of the fourteenth century, primarily French in style. In the first part of the century elaborate liturgical services were conducted, although little of the music has survived. There were two chapels, each with its own choir—the main one with as many as forty singers, and the pope's private chapel with ten or twelve. Some Latin motets and several of the polyphonic Mass settings mentioned earlier (see p. 508) seem to have originated in Avignon, and polyphonic hymn compositions with the plainchant melody embellished in the upper voice were also popular. Fashion seems to have fluctuated, however, for the Avignon pope John XXII issued an edict in 1325 condemning elaborate settings of the liturgy. For some time after this edict, plainchant and parallel organum must have been the rule at Avignon.

From the last part of the fourteenth century, the majority of compositions that survive from Avignon are secular songs with French texts, written in the fixed forms made popular by Machaut but with a self-conscious stylistic quality of their own. The musical heyday of the court, indeed, seems to have begun after the death of Machaut in 1377 and may be considered to be roughly contemporaneous with the Great Schism.

The special musical style of Avignon seems to have spread to some of the other noble courts in the area, even to those as far away as Aragon in the Iberian peninsula and Cyprus, an important French cultural outpost, in the eastern Mediterranean. Its center, however, remained the papal court, where the main source of patronage lay.

THE AVIGNON STYLE

The Avignon style, which has received many different names (all of which stress its subtlety and intricacy of manner, but none of which are entirely satisfactory), took the sonorities, rhythms, and textures of Machaut's secular songs, as well as their forms, as its starting point, and developed all these aspects to their ultimate point. If Machaut had written the cantus of his songs with low passages to illustrate despair, then there was no reason why a song could not be written with *all* the parts very low for a special obscure effect. If Machaut had applied chromatic coloring to a song to express hesitation and doubt, then extreme chromaticism and dissonance might be used *throughout* a composition. Most particularly, Machaut had shown how the new rhythmic freedoms of the fourteenth century—the interplay of duple and triple rhythms, syncopation, and irregular groupings—might be used to create subtle effects within a secular song. And one of the most characteristic features of the late fourteenth-century style is its rhythmic complexity, a complexity not found again in Western music until the twentieth century and one which involves at times complete independence between the voices in the polyphonic texture.

During the approximately forty-year span of this style, its development and modification may be divided into three stages. In the first stage, composers began to enlarge upon the flexibility of rhythm and texture inherent in the achievements of Machaut. In the second stage, the style reached its most extreme point of freedom and intricacy. In the third stage, a reaction to such complexity set in, and composers deliberately adopted a simplicity and accessibility of manner that was to become the hallmark of much fifteenth-century music.

At the Avignon court, French and Italian composers had the opportunity to rub shoulders and learn from each other's music; many of the names of musicians active at Avignon are Italian, though the forms and language of their songs are French. Rhythmic interest had always been a French musical characteristic, and in the second stage of the Avignon style manipulation of rhythm at every level of a composition is one of the main features. But by the third stage we can see Italian *dolcezza* exerting its seductive power on the songs; lyricism begins to be sought again, rhythms are clearer and more fluent, and interdependency of the voices has returned.

A shift in the relative frequency of the fixed forms also became evident during this time. The virelai and ballade began to give way to the rondeau. Although composers continued to cultivate all three forms to some extent, by the mid-fifteenth century the rondeau was by far the predominant form for secular songs. However, in the late fourteenth century a special type of virelai appeared: to its tradition of popular origins this added ideas from the French chace and Italian caccia and concentrated upon realistic shouts and cries, depicting, either directly or symbolically, outdoor scenes of great activity. A subspecies of this type focused on bird calls; several virelais evoke the sounds of nightingales, larks, and cuckoos.

The virelai in Example 13-1 uses fanfares and battle cries to symbol-

EXAMPLE 13-1 Grimace, virelai, *A L'Arme, A L'Arme.* After Willi Apel, *French Secular Compositions of the Fourteenth Century,* Corpus Mensurabilis Musicae, vol. 53 ([Rome]: American Institute of Musicology, 1970–72).

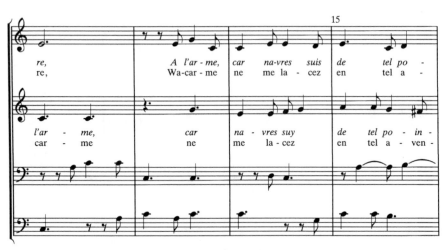

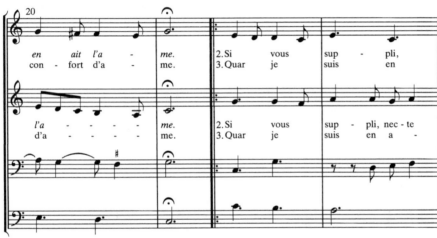

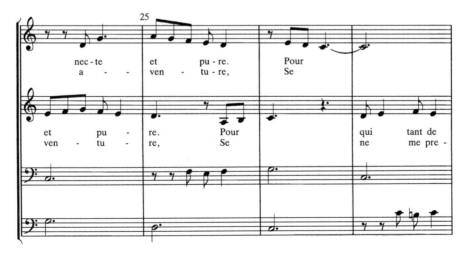

*A l'arme, a l'arme, sans sejour et sans
    demour.
Car mon las cuer si est en plour.
A l'arme, tost, doulce figure,
A l'arme, car navres suis de telle
    pointure
Que mors suy sans nul retour:
Diex en ait l'ame.*

A l'arme, a l'arme, sans sejour et sans...

To arms! To arms! Without any
    delay,
For my weary heart is grieving.
To arms! Quickly, sweet love,
To arms! For I have been struck by such
    an arrow
That I shall surely die without reprieve.
May God receive my soul.

Si vous suppli, necte et pure,
Pour qui tant de mal endure,
Qu'armer vous voeillies pour moy,

Thus I beg you, pure and lovely one,
For whom I suffer so much,
To take up arms on my behalf.

Quar je suis en aventure,
Se ne me prenes en cure,
Dont souvent ploure en requoy.

For I am at great risk
If you do not take my side.
Therefore do I weep.

Wacarm', wacarme, quel dolour et quel langour	To battle! To battle! What pain and anguish
Suefre, dame, pour vostre amour.	Do I suffer for your love, my lady.
Wacarme, douce creature,	To battle! Sweet creature,
Wacarme, ne me lacez en tel aventure	To battle! Do not leave me at such risk
Sans confort d'ame.	Without a friend.
A l'arme, a l'arme, sans sejour et sans demour,	*To arms! To arms! Without any delay,*
Car mon las cuer si est en plour.	*For my weary heart is grieving.*
A l'arme, tost, doulce figure,	*To arms! Quickly, sweet love,*
A l'arme, car navres suis de telle pointure	*To arms! For I have been struck by such an arrow*
Que mors suy sans nul retour:	*That I shall surely die without reprieve.*
Diex en ait l'ame.	*May God receive my soul.*

ize the warfare of love and capitalizes upon the age-old image of the mortal wounds inflicted by love's arrows. Battle imagery was of course of real immediacy in fourteenth-century France. About the composer, Grimace, little is known. He seems to have been active in the first stage mentioned above, for his style in other pieces is still closely tied to that of Machaut. The present virelai is written in four parts, with the same text in both upper voices. The instrumental parts join in the close imitative entries between the voices at the outset, and there is a considerable amount of rhythmic play and syncopation between the tenor and the contratenor throughout the piece. The second section of the music is distinguished by moving initially in more chordal texture, and its first ending is made incomplete by the sounding of the third (G♯) in the top voice. The text plays upon the double meaning of the opening cries ("Alarm!" and "To arms!").

In the second stage of the Avignon style, intricacy reached its height. Writers revelled in word games and elaborate manipulations of the poetry, and subtlety and sophistication affected every aspect of the music. Deliberate irony was often established between poem and music: a song written in very low range, with remote sonorities and obscure texture, is entitled *Toute clarte* ("All clarity"). On the other hand, the music may deliberately reflect the meaning of the text. A poem whose first line reads "Music can keep its secret no longer" is given a three-part setting whose cantus, though written in $\frac{2}{4}$, is finally revealed as being in $\frac{6}{8}$ meter. The double meaning of a poem whose title is *Contre le temps* is only established by the music: the phrase means "According to the weather" and also "Against the time," and the poem revels in love and joy and freedom in accordance with the fine weather, while the music sets two parts in $\frac{6}{8}$ against one in $\frac{3}{4}$.

The text of one song from this period, in discussing music (as many of them do), mentions that music should be "played, heard, and seen." This latter aspect, the "seeing" of music, also presented an opportunity for particular delight. Many of the compositions are notated in the manuscripts with unusual devices such as colored ink or special note shapes. To some

Original notation of a rondeau in the shape of a heart. The composer's name, Baude
Cordier, is written at the top. Musée Condé, Chantilly.

extent these are a necessary facet of the intricate meters and rhythms in the
music itself. But in some cases they supply an additional level of artistic
sophistication for the pleasure of the composers and their audience. The
piece mentioned above which discusses music is called *The Harp of Melody*. It is notated in the shape of a harp, with the notes written on staff lines
formed by the strings. There is also a piece written as a three-part canon,
whose first line reads "I am composed completely by a compass," and it is
notated in completely concentric circles, drawn as though by a compass.

And one rondeau, which tells of the composer's gift to his lady of his heart, is written in the shape of a heart in the manuscript; a small heart also takes the place of the French word for "heart" in the text underlay (see the illustration opposite).

A composition from this middle stage of the late fourteenth-century style is *Beaute Parfaite* ("Perfect Beauty"). It was written by Anthonello de Caserta, an Italian composer of the Avignon circle, who came from the small town of Caserta near Naples and wrote songs in both French and Italian, using the three French fixed forms and the Italian forms of madrigal and ballata.

"Perfect Beauty" (Ex. 13-2b) is a French ballade and displays some of the rhythmic practices of the time as well as the close interrelationships among the members of the Avignon circle and the self-referential nature of some of their music. The song is a setting of a beautifully written, melancholy poem by Machaut, as a tribute to that composer. The opening phrase is also a modified quotation of the beginning of the melody line of *The Harp of Melody* (Ex. 13-2a), a quotation that would have been immediately recognized by the other musicians and audiences of the court.

EXAMPLE 13-2a   Opening melody of Jacob Senleches' *The Harp of Melody*.

EXAMPLE 13-2b   Anthonello de Caserta, ballade, *Beaute Parfaite*. After Willi Apel, *French Secular Compositions of the Fourteenth Century*. Corpus Mensurabilis Musicae, vol. 53 ([Rome]: American Institute of Musicology, 1970–72).

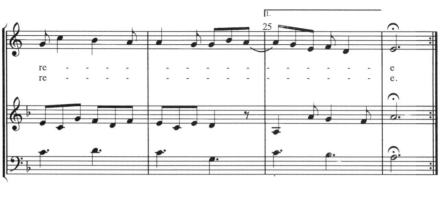

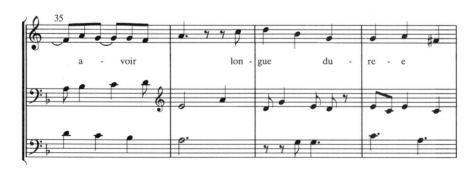

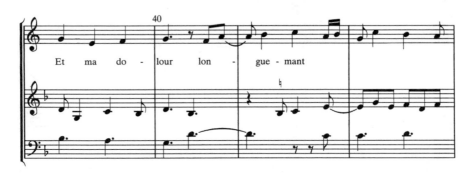

Et   ma   do - lour   lon - gue - mant

en - - - du - rer,   *Puis*

que

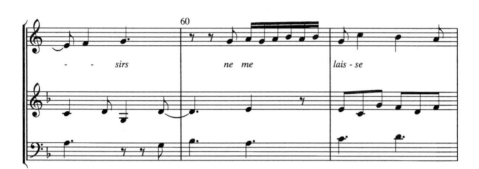

I. Beaute parfaite, bonte sovrayne,
    Grace sans per, douçour esmeree
    Me fait languir en contree lontayne

    En desirant ma dame desiree.
    Si ne puis pas avoir longue duree
    Et ma dolour longuemant endurer,
    Puis que desirs ne me laisse durer.

II. Car j'ay desir qui se travaille et
        peinne
    De moy deffaire, et ma dame hon-
        nouree

I. Perfect beauty, regal goodness,
    Grace without equal, sweet purity:
    These make me languish in a far-off
        land,
    Yearning for love of my lovely lady.
    I cannot survive for long
    Or continually bear this pain,
    Since desire never leaves me alone.

II. For I have such desire, which strives
        utterly
    To destroy me, and my honored
        lady

Ne scet mie que j'aie si grief peinne	Does not know that I have such grievous pain
Pour li que j'aim plus que nulle riens nee;	For her whom I love more than anyone alive.
Si que pour ce ma joie est si finee	That is why my joy is so completely ended
Que riens ne puet mon cuer reconforter,	That nothing can offer comfort to my heart,
Puis que desirs ne me laisse durer.	*Since desire never leaves me alone.*

III. Mais se celle qui de long m'est procheinne	III. But if she, who, though far away, is near to me
Par souvenir et par douce pensee	In my memory and sweet thoughts,
Sceust pour voir qu'en loiaute certeinne	Could see that my heart serves her
La sert mes cuers en estrange contree,	With absolute loyalty in a strange land,
Ma joie en fust toute renouvelee.	My joy would be quite revived.
Mais je voy bien qu'il me convient finer,	But I see clearly that it is better for me to make an end.
Puis que desirs ne me laisse durer.	*Since desire never leaves me alone.*

The exquisitely crafted poetry calls upon alliteration, assonance, delicate rhythmic patterns, and subtle word play for its haunting effect. In the first stanza, for instance, the slow, dispirited sounds of "languir," "lontayne," "longue," "[do]lour," and "longuemant" are reinforced by their sharing of the consonant "l." And the alliteration upon "d" in this stanza ("douçour," "desirant," "dame," "desiree," "duree," "dolour," "desirs," "durer") comes to a climax in the fourth line:

En desirant ma dame desiree.

The intricate and expressive word play of the poem is exemplified by the three different meanings of the words with the same sound that end the last three lines of the first stanza: "duree," "[en]durer," and "durer," and by the line before the refrain in the last stanza: "finer" here means both "end my life" and "end the poem."

Anthonello has composed a setting for this poem of fluidity and grace, in which all three of the parts seem to take their own direction, with clear pitch goals and rhythmic contours, but with independent motion. This hazy outline and transparency of texture is carefully controlled, however, for the underlying cadence structure is completely regular and provides points of stability and repose for the shifting and flexible flow of the music.

The first five measures exemplify in miniature the technique used throughout. All three parts follow their own rhythmic and melodic directions. The tenor has long notes in $\frac{6}{8}$ and makes a gradual descent to G at the beginning of measure 5. The G is not heard before this point, and the cadence is given focus by the increase in motion and shift of meter in measure

4. The contratenor is in $\frac{3}{4}$ meter throughout this opening passage, moving both in contrary and parallel motion with the tenor. Its aim is D, which it reaches, in contrary motion to the tenor, also at measure 5. The cantus is the most active voice, but it alternates between eighth-note motion and sustained notes in such a way that its underlying rhythm is completely obscured. The long-range syncopation may be rationalized, as is demonstrated by the small notes added above the staff, but the overall effect is of an improvisatory rhapsodizing. The sense of the passage is revealed, and an overall impression of order restored, when the cantus reaches G at the beginning of measure 5 and all three voices join in a perfectly regular cadence.

The remainder of the piece continues this subtle balance between ambiguity and clarity. The text lines end on standard cadences, the refrain is clearly articulated, the melismas are in normal places, but the flow of the music is released from its conventional bonds by constant rhythmic transformation.

This technique of obscuring definitive outlines by metric juxtaposition and long-range syncopation is the motivating force of the music. But its aim is not rhythmic complexity alone, for that is far too limited a goal. Its aim is a poetic and musical style of tremendous sophistication and subtlety, in which the music floats freely like the diaphanous fabric of a dress in a soft breeze, held by stitches at only the most essential points. Its aim is perfect beauty.

The final stage in the development of the Avignon style saw a return to simplicity of texture and a more directly dependent relationship between the voices, including passages of free imitation—that is, imitation not involving strict procedures such as canon. Italian influence on French songs became noticeable, as composers began to adopt Italian ideas of lyricism and consonance. Some of the older Italian genres were revived with slightly different content. Madrigals, for example, began to have texts of a philosophical or ceremonial nature. Italian composers continued to write in the French fixed forms, and the rondeau became more popular, both in terms of its accessibility and in terms of its proportional representation in the overall literature.

The result of these trends was a gradual fusing of the French and Italian styles, which had for many years been quite distinct, and the creation of an international style, which combined the qualities of both and lasted for much of the fifteenth century. The music of this stage is more consonant, less self-conscious and stylized than the music which preceded it. It uses imitation to point up a direct relationship between the voices; it avoids complexity or ambiguity of rhythm; and it aims at clarity and fullness of texture. This international style is paralleled in the painting and sculpture of the period around 1400, which displays a soft, naturalistic quality, with fluid lines and fuller modelling than the art of the previous century. Detailed scenes and outdoor landscapes, rounded figures, and contrast of light and shade mark the new period.

Politically there was no respite from the constant series of battles and truces known as the Hundred Years' War. In Italy, rivalry and bloodshed continued between the powerful noble families of the cities and small states. The French king Charles VI was insane for the last thirty years of his reign, and in the power vacuum different dukes fought for control. In 1415 the English army made a new assault and conquered the French at the battle of Agincourt, after which the English held most of the northern part of France, including Paris. An English ally, the duke of Burgundy in the west, became increasingly powerful, and after the return of the popes to Rome the Burgundian court was the main source of patronage for artists and musicians for the remainder of the fifteenth century.

The new simpler style of the early fifteenth century may be represented by the song *Je Demande* (Ex. 13-3) by Jean Haucourt (also known as Acourt). The text is direct and plain, with a deliberately colloquial flavor; the musical setting is short, and apart from the brief final melisma the words are mostly set syllabically. Rhythms are square, and the melody moves either in conjunct motion or with leaps of fourths and fifths. Some rhythmic subtleties of the intricate style remain (for example, the shift between duple and triple meter throughout), but these have been standardized and simplified almost to the point of mere convention. Vigor and vitality are given to the piece by the slight irregularity of phrasing: the first section falls into two five-measure phrases; the second section is in two four-measure phrases followed by a six-measure phrase. But on the whole the song is accessible and straightforward and composed in a popular style that recalls, in both its text and music, the simple songs of Adam de la Halle.

EXAMPLE 13-3   Jean Haucourt, rondeau, *Je Demande*. After Gilbert Reaney, *Early Fifteenth-Century Music,* Corpus Mensurabilis Musicae, vol. 11 ([Rome]: American Institute of Musicology, 1955–   ).

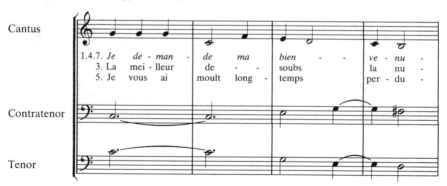

e: Il   a   long -   temps que   ne   vous
e   Est - es,   se   l'a - ves   fait   ain - -
e.   Dont j'ay   es -   te   en   grant   sou - -

vi.   2.8. Di - tes,   sui   je   plus   vo - stre a - mi?
si.   6. Mais de   tous   mes   maulx   sui ga - ri,
si.

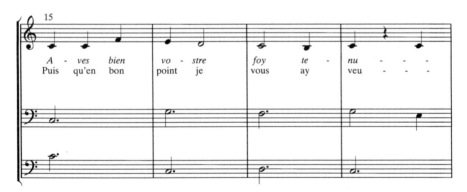

A - ves   bien   vo - stre   foy   te -   nu - - -
Puis qu'en   bon   point   je   vous   ay   veu - - -

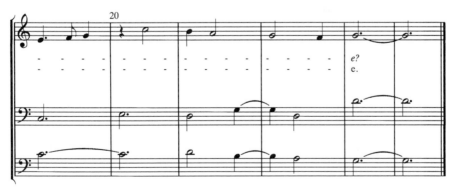

- - - - - - - - - - - e?
- - - - - - - - - - - e.

Je demande ma bienvenue:	*I want my welcome home:*
Il a longtemps que ne vous vi.	*It's a long time since I've seen you.*
Dites, sui je plus vostre ami?	*Tell me, am I still your friend?*
Aves bien vostre foy tenue?	*Have you been faithful to me?*
La meilleur desoubs la nue	You are the best girl
Estes, se l'aves fait ainsi.	In the world if you have.
Je demande ma bienvenue:	*I want my welcome home:*
Il a longtemps que ne vous vi.	*It's a long time since I've seen you.*
Je vous ai moult longtemps perdue.	I'd lost you for a very long time,
Dont j'ay este en grant sousi.	Which worried me a lot.
Mais de tous mes maulx sui gari,	But now I'm cured of all my woes,
Puis qu'en bon point je vous ay veue.	Since I've seen you looking so good.
Je demande ma bienvenue:	*I want my welcome home:*
Il a longtemps que ne vous vi.	*It's a long time since I've seen you.*
Dites, sui je plus vostre ami?	*Tell me, am I still your friend?*
Aves bien vostre foy tenue?	*Have you been faithful to me?*

ENGLISH MUSIC

During the fourteenth century music in England continued partly to parallel developments on the continent and partly to represent special local interests. As we have seen, most manuscripts of English music up to this time are incomplete or fragmentary. Nonetheless, reconstruction of these has provided a picture of a lively and flourishing musical culture, especially in the genre of the motet. By the late fourteenth century and early fifteenth century, the emphasis seems to have changed. One large manuscript known as the Old Hall manuscript, which was copied in about 1415 and has come down to us more or less complete, contains a representative sample of compositions from this time. Most of them are polyphonic settings of Mass movements, grouped together in the manuscript by text, with all the Glorias together, all the Credos together, and so on. Some of these appear to belong together in pairs, but there is no evidence that an entire unified Mass Ordinary could be constructed from the collection. One curious feature is the complete lack of any Kyrie settings. Perhaps it was common in England to keep the Kyrie in plainchant, even when the other items in the Ordinary were set polyphonically. A far more mundane explanation is also possible, however. Since the Kyrie settings would have appeared at the beginning of the manuscript, that section may have become detached at an early stage and lost. Other pieces in the Old Hall manuscript include polyphonic settings of sequences and antiphons, and some motets with liturgical texts.

Most of the pieces in this collection are attributed to composers by name, and there is a wide diversity of background and origin among them. A Gloria setting and a Sanctus setting are by a "King Henry," who may have been either Henry IV or Henry V of England. Some of the other composers seem to have had connections with the continent and probably trav-

eled there often. The English political and military presence in Fr:
the alliance between England and the dukes of Burgundy must have
great deal of commerce between England and the continent dui
time. The two best-known composers whose names appear in the (
manuscript are Leonel Power and John Dunstable. Power is also represented in several continental manuscripts and thus may have been active
there as well as in England; Dunstable was in the service of the Duke of
Bedford, who lived in France for more than ten years early in the fifteenth
century.

Stylistically, the music in the collection displays both continental
and English practices. Some of the pieces are written in the complex meters
and rhythms typical of late fourteenth-century French music. Other French
characteristics that appear are isorhythm and polytextuality, both in the
motets and in some of the Mass movements. Canon, which is used as a
structural technique in several of the Mass movements, may have been inspired by the Italian caccia. But many of the compositions in the collection
are written in a special type of conductus style that seems to have been a
specifically English invention. In these compositions, all the voices (usually
three) carry the same text in more or less the same rhythm, and there is
a constant succession of both perfect and imperfect intervals. If there is a
plainchant melody, it usually appears in the middle voice. This style, often
known as "English discant," differs from the continental conductus style in
its clear delineation of voice range. Each of the voices stays within its own
relatively narrow range, and the voices hardly ever cross. Another distinction lies in the existence of a previously composed chant melody as a frequent part of the texture, a feature that did not occur in conductus. Many
English treatises from the fourteenth and fifteenth century describe the
practice of improvising this kind of note-against-note polyphony to a chant,
and the written versions in the Old Hall manuscript must represent only a
small portion of the music that was sung in this manner.

One interesting feature of several of the Mass movements in the Old
Hall manuscript is their use of textural variety as a structural device. Passages for two voices, probably sung by a soloist on each part, alternate with
full choral sections in three or four parts.

In the long texts of the Gloria and Credo movements, an element of
polytextuality is created by dividing the text among the voices. This gives
the impression of a motet, with different words being sung simultaneously,
though the texts are of course not from different sources but from the same
liturgical item of the Ordinary. This technique allows all of the text to be
sung without making the Gloria and Credo much longer than the other
movements of the Mass.

The Old Hall manuscript presents a synopsis of the musical genres
and styles that were being cultivated in England at the turn of the century.
Local practices are very much in evidence, but interaction with Italian and
especially French music and musicians resulted in many fertile cross-

influences and a rich variety of stylistic trends, as well as new solutions to liturgical and musical problems.

JOHANNES CICONIA

On the continent, the most distinguished composer of the late fourteenth and early fifteenth centuries was Johannes Ciconia (c. 1370–1412). He was also the most prolific, and in his music may be seen a variety of the styles that were being cultivated during this vigorous period, including some elements that foreshadow the music of the Renaissance. Ciconia was a northern composer, born in Liège (in what is now Belgium), who seems to have spent time at the papal court at Avignon and the final ten years of his life in Italy as a teacher at the University of Padua and a member of the administrative staff of Padua Cathedral. He had connections with important Italian noble families in other cities in the north of Italy, including Lucca, Milan, and Venice.

Ciconia was the author of a theoretical treatise which discusses the relationship of meters and tempos in music and attempts to reconcile the differences between French and Italian practices. This aspect of his work is significant, for Ciconia's own music stands as a synthesis of French and Italian (and possibly even English) styles at the opening of the fifteenth century—a synthesis that represents the end of one era in the history of Western music and the beginning of another.

Ciconia was accomplished in a variety of musical genres. He wrote secular songs, both in French (virelais) and in Italian (ballatas and madrigals). He essayed the most advanced styles of rhythmic complexity and he revived older forms. He wrote polyphonic Mass movements, including both some linked pairs of items from the Ordinary and some separate pieces. And he composed a considerable number of motets, which prefigure the resurgence of the genre for special occasions or celebrations, an important element of the motet tradition of the Renaissance.

Both in his motets and in his secular songs and Mass movements, Ciconia's music displays a sense of equality among the voices—a tendency towards homogeneity rather than contrast—which is one of the essential distinctions between music of the Renaissance and music of the Middle Ages. Rhythmic and melodic sequence, as well as imitation, are features which tend to link the voices of a composition together and set them on an equal footing in the musical texture. These are characteristic features of Ciconia's style as well as of music of the later fifteenth century. Other such features by which Ciconia's music stands on the cusp of change include the use of long chords to halt momentarily the flow of the music; shifts of texture from sections for full choir to brief duet passages; an attempt to reflect in the musical setting the meaning of the words of the text; and a melding of

French rhythmic practices with Italian qualities of melodic projection and sonorous sweetness.

All of these characteristics may be heard in the Ciconia composition *Una Panthera* (Ex. 13-4). The form of the text and the music proclaim it at once as a madrigal. There are two stanzas of three lines each, followed by a two-line ritornello. The madrigal text is written in honor of the city of Lucca, whose coat of arms depicts a panther and which was supposed to have been founded by Mars, the Roman god of war. Juppiter, Mars, and the panther join forces to protect the city, which is praised for sharing its advantages equally among all its citizens.

The music retains traditional characteristics of the fourteenth-century madrigal: it has two voices carrying the text, supported by an instrumental part, and there is new music for the ritornello section. The florid upper voice is also typical of the genre. Several features, however, are taken over from other genres. The arrangement of voices is that of the ballata, in which the text is assigned not to two upper voices but to the cantus and tenor, while the contratenor is instrumental. The constant metrical changes, syncopations within the meter, juxtapositions of duple and triple groupings (at several different levels), and phrases across the main groupings all reveal French compositional influence. Finally, there are some aspects of the music that point to the style of the future; these include repetition (mm. 2–4 and 32–34), imitation (mm. 2–3, 28–31, 36–37, 44–47), sequence (mm. 12–13, 25–26, 51–54), duet texture (mm. 28–29, 44–45), long chords (mm. 7–8, 21–22, 62–64, 65–67), and depiction in the music of the meaning of the text (notice the fanfare-like chords and rhythmic movement on the words "Triumpho" and "gloria" in measures 84–85). All these

EXAMPLE 13-4   Johannes Ciconia, madrigal, *Una Panthera.* From *Polyphonic Music of the Fourteenth Century,* vol. 24, ed. Margaret Bent and Anne Hallmark (Monaco: L'Oiseau-lyre, 1985).

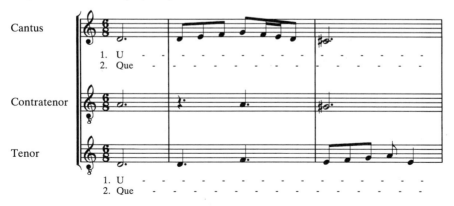

na, U - na pan - the - ra in con - pa - gnia de Mar - - - -
sta, Que - sta gu - ber - na la ci - ta Lu - ca - - - -

U - - na pan - the - ra in con - pa - gnia de Mar - - - -
Que - - sta gu - ber - na la ci - ta Lu - ca - - - -

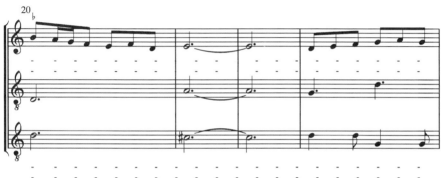

te,
na

te,
na

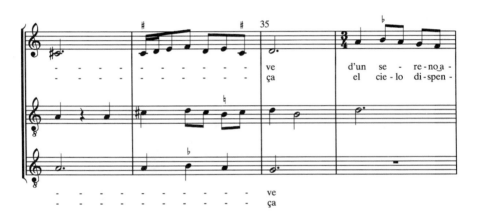

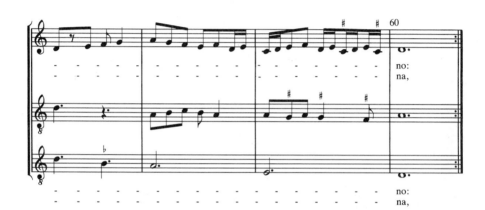

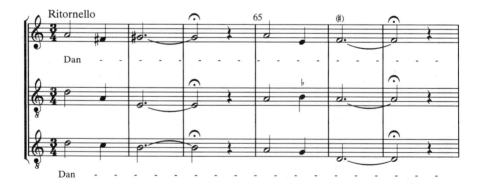

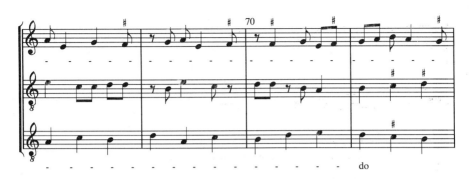

I.	Una panthera in conpagnia de Marte,	I.	A panther in the company of Mars,
	Candido Jove d'un sereno adorno,		Shining Juppiter with a peaceful aspect,
	Constante e l'arme chi la guarda intorno:		Constant are the arms which guard this group:
II.	Questa guberna la cita Lucana	II.	It governs the city of Lucca
	Con soa dolceça el cielo dispensa e dona,		With sweetness, and heaven bestows its gifts
	Secondo el meritar, iusta corona,		According to merit—a just crown,

Ritornello:

Dando a ciascun mortal, che ne sia
   degno,
Triumpho, gloria e parte in questo
   regno.

Ritornello:

Giving to every mortal what is
   deserved:
Triumph, glory, and a share in this
   kingdom.

features are found in music of the following era, but of them all perhaps the most important is imitation. As we have seen, imitation had appeared in two different guises in fourteenth-century music. In strict form, as canon, it was the foundation of both the French chace and the Italian caccia. Otherwise, it had appeared only sporadically—most notably as free imitation in the Italian madrigal. Its appearance in Ciconia's music is of a different kind, for it is prominently used to highlight structural points in the music and text (the beginnings of new lines), and it is a compositional device of central importance not only in creating overall textural variety but also in erasing the clear-cut distinctions of voice function that were typical of medieval polyphonic song.

All of these aspects of Ciconia's madrigal *Una Panthera*—its link to tradition, its borrowing from other genres and national styles, its modern techniques of text and voice relationship—create a piece of considerable individuality and presence. It may be representative of a crucial and transitional historical era, but it is also a superbly crafted composition in its own right.

In addition to secular songs in both Italian and French, Ciconia composed a number of motets, most of which were written to celebrate public occasions such as the installation of a new bishop or an alliance between cities. These motets show a move away from the formal procedures of the past and towards a new homogeneity and simplicity of style. The majority are not isorhythmic, and those that are use only the simplest devices, such as single repetition. The tenors are not taken from chant but are newly written. Often the upper voices share the same text instead of singing different texts simultaneously, and they also maintain the same range and melodic importance, which again is underlined by imitation.

The panther from the coat of arms of the
city of Lucca, Palazzo Cenami, Lucca.

Ciconia also composed music for the Ordinary of the Mass. Curiously, only Gloria and Credo settings have survived. This may be the result of chance, or it may reflect the particular absorption of composers with these items at this time. Although Ciconia wrote some independent settings of these texts, some related pairs of movements have been identified, though there is still some disagreement as to how many of these settings really belong together. It will be remembered that similar such paired movements are found in the Old Hall manuscript, and it seems as though both English and continental composers were becoming interested in the challenge of unifying by musical means the separate items of the Ordinary.

The following Gloria-Credo pair by Ciconia (Ex. 13-5a and 13-5b) contains sufficient unifying features that its composition as a unit is not in doubt. The tenor parts of both movements are in the same mode; both movements are written in the same vocal range and have the same arrangement of voices; and there is a sharing of musical material and a similarity in overall form between the movements.

The clarity and simplicity of the text setting in these compositions is the most notable element of their style. Each sentence of the text is distinctly declaimed and marked off by cadences. Contrasting imitative passages mark the beginnings of sentences, and the texture is constantly varied between counterpoint and chordal style, between rhythmic fragmentation and conductus-like parallelism. The scoring is high and light, with two voices in the cantus range over a texted tenor. The second cantus crosses frequently above the first. Passages for only one or two voices increase the overall transparency of the setting.

Some moments of the Gloria recall the textual mirroring of *Una Panthera*; the hocket-like repetitions of the word *pax* ("peace") at the opening are particularly striking. Parallelism in the text is brought out by musical parallelism, and note the increasing intensity (brought about by a rise in pitch) of the "Domine . . ." statements in measures 30–32 and 41–43.

EXAMPLE 13-5a Johannes Ciconia, Gloria, beginning only. From *Polyphonic Music of the Fourteenth Century,* vol. 24, ed. Margaret Bent and Anne Hallmark (Monaco: L'Oiseau-lyre, 1985).

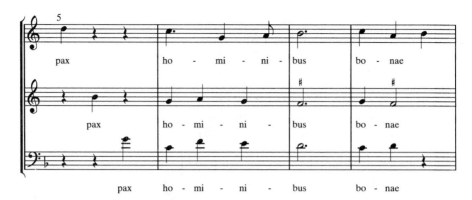

pax   ho - mi - ni - bus   bo - nae

pax   ho - mi - ni - bus   bo - nae

pax   ho - mi - ni - bus   bo - nae

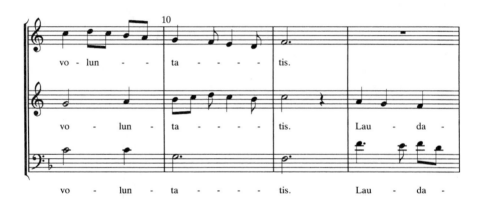

vo - lun - - ta - - - tis.

vo - lun - ta - - - tis.   Lau - da -

vo - lun - ta - - - tis.   Lau - da -

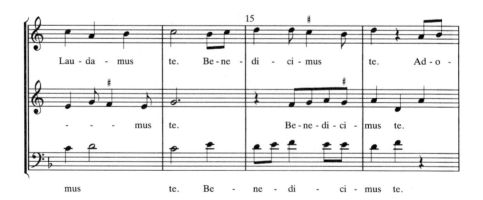

Lau - da - mus   te.   Be - ne - di - ci - mus   te.   Ad - o -

- - - mus   te.   Be - ne - di - ci - mus   te.

mus   te.   Be - ne - di - ci - mus   te.

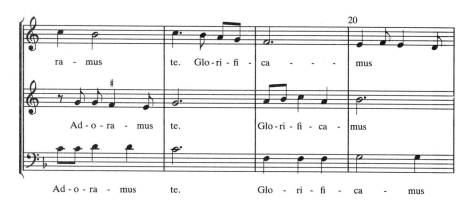

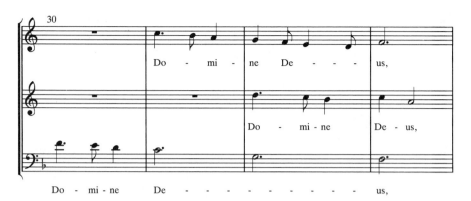

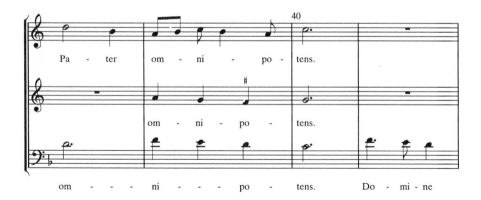

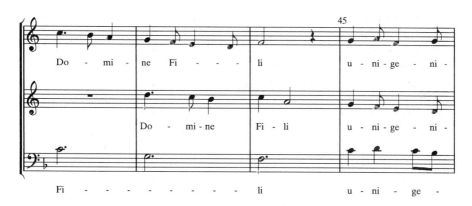

Gloria in excelsis Deo.	Glory to God in the highest.
Et in terra pax homnibus bonae voluntatis.	And on earth peace to men of good will.
Laudamus te.	We praise you.
Benedicimus te.	We bless you.
Adoramus te.	We adore you.
Glorificamus te.	We glorify you.
Gratias agimus tibi propter magnam gloriam tuam.	We thanks to you on account of your great glory.
Domine Deus, Rex caelestis, Deus Pater omnipotens.	O Lord God, heavenly King, God the omnipotent Father.
Domine Fili unigenite Jesu Christe. . . .	O Lord the Son, only-begotten Jesus Christ. . . .

In the Credo an even greater variety of imitative possibilities is exploited (compare, for example, mm. 6–8 and 15–16), and syncopation is added to the rhythmic palette. Many motifs and whole passages are borrowed from the Gloria, including the use of long chords on the words "Jesum Christum" ("Jesu Christe" in the Gloria). A greater density of texture is utilized, sometimes for textual reasons (see mm. 29–34, where the repetitions of the text are given emphasis by stretto—closer imitative entries) and sometimes seemingly for purely musical ones (note the heightened activity in mm. 49–55). Both movements have long melismatic Amens, which share rhythmic and melodic motifs, and in which the characteristic rhythmic sequence of Ciconia's style is particularly in evidence.

EXAMPLE 13-5b Johannes Ciconia, Credo, beginning only. From *Polyphonic Music of the Fourteenth Century,* vol. 24, ed. Margaret Bent and Anne Hallmark (Monaco: L'Oiseau-lyre, 1985).

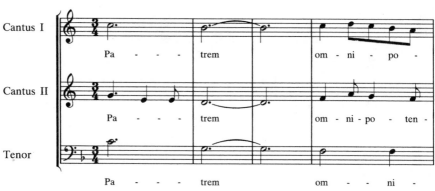

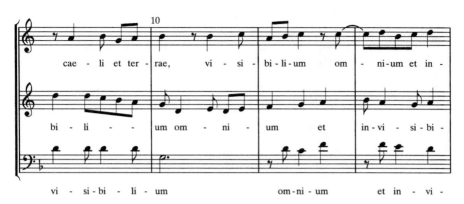

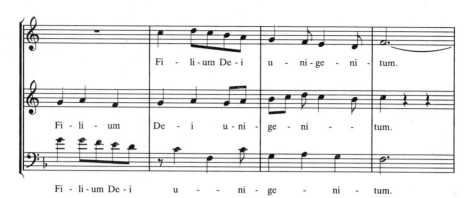

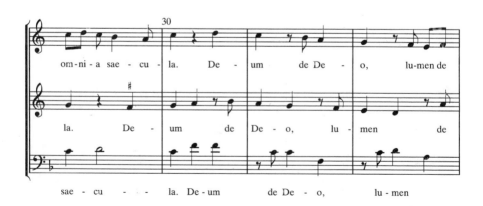

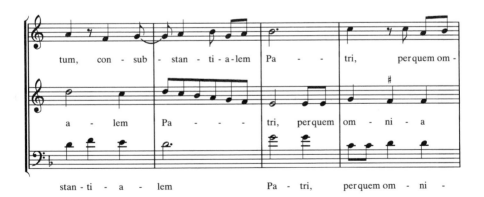

Credo in unum Deum,
Patrem omnipotentem, factorem caeli et
    terrae, visibilium omnium et invisibi-
    lium.
Et in unum Dominum Jesum Christum,
    Filium Dei unigenitum.
Et ex Patre natum ante omnia saecula.

I believe in one God,
The omnipotent Father, creator of the
    heaven and earth, of everything visi-
    ble and invisible.
And in one Lord Jesus Christ, the only-
    begotten Son of God.
And born from the Father before all
    time.

Deum de Deo, lumen de lumine, Deum verum de Deo vero.	God of God, light of light, a true God of a true God.
Genitum, non factum, consubstantialem Patri, per quem omnia facta sunt.	Born, not made, of one substance with the Father, by whom all things are created.
Qui propter nos homines, et propter nostram salutem descendit de caelis. . . .	Who descended from heaven on behalf of us men and our salvation. . . .

Ciconia wrote Mass movements in both three and four voices, and his settings of these texts represent a new attitude towards Mass composition—one that became the norm in the fifteenth century. Architectural concerns such as isorhythm or the adoption of secular song styles are no longer paramount. The music is shaped by the text, whose content and structure are made very clear by changes of texture and by cadences. Duet passages, like those found in the music of Old Hall, are clearly designated and are set off from the prevailing sections for the full choir. Cadences mark the ends of sentences, and imitation is used as a structural device at the beginning of text phrases.

Thus, in his secular songs, motets, and Mass movements, Johannes Ciconia shows the influence of a vivid musical past combined with the new techniques and approaches of an innovative present. Ciconia stood at the boundary between two major periods in the history of musical style. Like other great composers who lived at a time of change, his artistic achievements both transcended and were partially responsible for that change.

CONCLUSION

Musically speaking, with the death of Ciconia in 1412 the Middle Ages were over. But a thousand years of history, a thousand years of literary and musical composition, did not disappear overnight. All the music of the next generation, of the next century, was firmly based upon a medieval foundation. Plainchant composition continued actively, and the liturgy was continually enriched by new pieces. The literary themes, the polyphonic procedures of secular song, were moved alive and vivid into the courts of the fifteenth century. Instrumental music continued to be based upon improvisation, vocal models, and the dance. Even the complex rhythmic devices of the Avignon style continued to intrigue for a while. In the fifteenth century, composers made musical cycles out of the items of the Mass Ordinary, and brought the melodies of secular songs into those cycles as unifying devices, just as thirteenth- and fourteenth-century composers had combined French love poems with liturgical tenors in the motet. In all genres the melodic modes continued to form the basis of compositional procedure.

There were changes, of course. Accessibility and homogeneity became the rule, as opposed to the intellectualism, the striking contrasts, of the past. Motets lost their isorhythmic foundation, and polytextuality disappeared. In both Mass and motet, parts were made equal in significance by pervasive melodic imitation, and long passages were written in chordal style. Consonance prevailed, and fuller chords, containing the third as well as the fifth, made the texture thicker and less transparent. All three of the fixed forms continued to serve as frames for secular songs, but the rondeau outstripped the other forms. As in the motet and Mass, imitation was used to integrate the texture, and rhythms became simple and clear.

The color and diversity, the visual and aural challenges, the intellectual delights, the intriguing contrasts of medieval music were gone. But the procedures, concepts, techniques, and genres that evolved during the Middle Ages continued to exert their influence upon music for a long time. Plainchant acted as a fundamental reference as well as a melodic stimulus for Monteverdi and Mozart and Benjamin Britten. In the seventeenth and eighteenth centuries commentators noticed the same disparity between French and Italian music as they had in the fourteenth. Composers continued to write polyphonic Masses. Much of the work of Palestrina or Bach or Penderecki or Bernstein cannot be fully understood without knowledge of the Church liturgy. The whole history of the love song up to the nineteenth and twentieth centuries is rooted in the soil of the Occitan-speaking lands of southern France. Even opera has direct links to the Latin and vernacular dramas of the Middle Ages.

The Middle Ages witnessed the establishment of the Christian liturgy, the bonding of music and text, functional analysis of melody, the growth of polyphony, the evolution of musical instruments, the rationalization of rhythm and musical notation, the establishment of strophic song, the flowering of individual national languages, the invention of sophisticated formal structures for the setting of poetry, the development of music drama, the fullest exploration of musical style.

For all these historical reasons medieval music is of prime importance in the history of Western culture and is therefore worthy of prolonged investigation and intimate acquaintance. But there are far more compelling reasons than these, for medieval music represents a repertoire of unparalleled diversity and scope and contains a wealth of beauty and an abundance of spiritual, intellectual, and emotional satisfaction, while at the same time posing tremendous challenges and offering tremendous rewards to performers and audiences alike.

Medieval music stimulates the intellect as well as satisfying the emotions. It offers a range of artistic achievement from monumental compositional structures to the most delicate miniatures. It represents the richest and the most diverse legacy of our musical heritage.

DISCOGRAPHY

Example 13-1   Grimace, virelai, *A L'Arme, A L'Arme.*
The Early Music Consort of London, *The Art of Courtly Love,* EMI SLS 863 (OC 191 05410-2).

Example 13-2a   Opening melody of Jacob Senleches' *The Harp of Melody.*
Ensemble Organum, *Codex Chantilly: Airs de Cour,* Harmonia Mundi HMC 1252.

Example 13-2b   Anthonello de Caserta, ballade, *Beauté Parfaite.*
TAPE TWO, SIDE TWO.

Example 13-3   Jean Haucourt (Acourt), rondeau, *Je Demande.*
Musica Reservata, *Music of the Hundred Years' War,* Philips SAL 3722 (839 753 L).

Example 13-4   Johannes Ciconia, madrigal, *Una Panthera.*
TAPE TWO, SIDE TWO. Studio der frühen Musik, *Johannes Ciconia,* EMI Reflexe 1C 063-30 102; also on Clemencic Consort, *Johannes Ciconia: Madrigaux & Ballades,* Harmonia Mundi HM 10068.

Example 13-5a   Johannes Ciconia, Gloria.
TAPE TWO, SIDE TWO. Studio der frühen Musik, *Johannes Ciconia,* EMI Reflexe 1C 063-30 102.

Example 13-5b   Johannes Ciconia, Credo.
Studio der frühen Musik, *Johannes Ciconia,* EMI Reflexe 1C 063–30 102.

Other late fourteenth-century pieces, including some of those mentioned in the text but not given as examples, may be found on Ensemble Organum, *Codex Chantilly: Airs de Cour,* Harmonia Mundi HMC 1252. More songs from the early fifteenth century are recorded on Gothic Voices, *The Garden of Zephirus: Courtly Songs of the Early Fifteenth Century,* Hyperion CDA 66144.

BIBLIOGRAPHICAL NOTES

The significance of Avignon in the fourteenth century is sketched in Joseph R. Strayer, "Avignon," in *Dictionary of the Middle Ages* (New York: Charles Scribner's Sons, 1983) and covered in more detail in Elliott Binns, *The History of the Decline and Fall of the Medieval Papacy* (Hamden, Connecticut: Archon Books, 1967). Music at the papal chapel is discussed in Andrew Tomasello, *Music and Ritual at Papal Avignon, 1309–1403,* Studies in Musicology, vol. 75 (Ann Arbor: UMI Research Press, 1983). The Avignon style is analyzed in Jehoash Hirshberg, "The Music of the Late Fourteenth

Century: A Study in Musical Style," (Ph.D. dissertation, University of Pennsylvania, 1971). One of the most extreme examples of rhythmic complexity is transcribed and analyzed in Nors Josephson, "Rodericus, *Angelorum psalat,*" *Musica Disciplina* 25 (1971): 113–126.

A study of the text forms with examples and a musical appendix is contained in Nigel Wilkins, *One Hundred Ballades, Rondeaux and Virelais from the Late Middle Ages* (Cambridge: Cambridge University Press, 1969).

The stylistic shift discussed in the preceding chapter may be seen by comparing the contents of Willi Apel, *French Secular Music of the Late Fourteenth Century* (Cambridge, Massachusetts: Mediaeval Academy of America, 1950), which also contains a useful introductory essay, and Willi Apel, *French Secular Compositions of the Fourteenth Century,* Corpus Mensurabilis Musicae, vol. 53 (Rome: American Institute of Musicology, 1970–72) with the music in Gilbert Reaney, *Early Fifteenth-Century Music,* Corpus Mensurabilis Musicae, vol. 11 (Rome: American Institute of Musicology, 1955–83).

The music of Johannes Ciconia is available in *Polyphonic Music of the Fourteenth Century,* vol. 24, ed. Margaret Bent and Anne Hallmark (Monaco: L'Oiseau-lyre, 1985), and Suzanne Clercx, *Johannes Ciconia: Un musicien liégois et son temps (vers 1335–1411),* 2 vols. (Brussels: Académie Royale de Belgique, 1960).

The insufficiently known repertory of the English motet in the fourteenth century is discussed in Peter Lefferts, *The Motet in England in the Fourteenth Century* (Ann Arbor: UMI Research Press, 1986).

The works of Leonel Power and John Dunstable and the contents of the Old Hall manuscript, as well as the musical style of the fifteenth and sixteenth centuries, are discussed in more detail in the next volume in this series: Howard Brown, *Music in the Renaissance* (Englewood Cliffs: Prentice Hall, Inc., 1976).

INDEX

CONTENTS
OF THE ACCOMPANYING
CASSETTES

TAPE TWO, SIDE ONE

Examples:

9–9   Perotinus, *Alleluya, Posui Adiutorium*
9–10b   Anonymous, Latin motet, *O Natio/Hodie Perlustravit*
9–12   Anonymous, hocket, *In Seculum*
9–13   Adam de la Halle, *Robins M'Aime, Robins M'A*
9–14   Anonymous, motet, *Mout Me Fu Grief/Robins M'Aime/Portare*
9–16   Anonymous, motet, *Aucun Ont Trouve/Lonc Tans/Annuntiantes*
10–2   Anonymous, estampie, *La Quinte Estampie Real*
10–3   Anonymous, nota
11–2   Philippe de Vitry, motet, *Douce Playsence/Garison Selon Nature/Neuma Quinti Toni*
11–6   Guillaume de Machaut, *Le Lay de la Fonteinne,* stanza 1
11–7   Guillaume de Machaut, *Le Lay de la Fonteinne,* stanza 12
11–8   Guillaume de Machaut, virelai, *Moult Sui*
11–9   Guillaume de Machaut, rondeau, *Doulz Viaire Gracieus*
11–10   Guillaume de Machaut, rondeau, *Comment Puet On*

TAPE TWO, SIDE TWO

Examples:

11-11   Guillaume de Machaut, ballade, *Honte, Paour, Doubtance*
12–4   Francesco Landini, ballata *Donna, S'I' T'O' Fallito*
12–5   Francesco Landini, ballata, *Gram Piant' Agli Ochi*
12–6a   Anonymous, instrumental arrangement of *Honte, Paour*
12–6b   Anonymous, instrumental arrangement of *Non Avra*
12–6c   Anonymous, instrumental arrangement of Kyrie
12–7   Anonymous, *Istampitta Ghaetta*
13–2b   Anthonello de Caserta, ballade, *Beaute Parfaite*
13–4   Johannes Ciconia, madrigal, *Una Panthera*
13–5a   Johannes Ciconia, Gloria

To order the two 90-minute cassettes for *Music in Medieval Europe* (ISBN 0-13-608621-7), contact your local college bookstore, or write to Prentice Hall, Order Department, 200 Old Tappan Road, Old Tappan, NJ 07675, or call 201-767-5937, weekdays, 8:45–4:30 ET.